Colonialism
Past and Present

SUNY series in
Latin American
and
Iberian Thought and Culture

Jorge J.E. Gracia and Rosemary Geisdorfer Feal, Editors

Colonialism Past and Present

Reading and Writing about Colonial Latin America Today

Edited by

Alvaro Félix Bolaños
and
Gustavo Verdesio

State University of New York Press

Published by
State University of New York Press, Albany

For information, address State University of New York Press,
90 State Street, Suite 700, Albany, N.Y. 12207

Production by Michael Haggett
Marketing by Anne M. Valentine

Library of Congress Cataloging-in-Publication Data

Colonialism past and present : reading and writing about colonial Latin America
today / edited by Alvaro F. Bolaños and Gustavo Verdesio.
    p. cm.— (SUNY series in Latin American and Iberian thought and culture)
Includes bibliographical references and index.
ISBN 0-7914-5145-3 (alk. paper)—ISBN 0-7914-5146-1 (pbk. : alk. paper)
1. Latin America—Civilization. 2. Latin America—History—To 1830—
Historiography. 3. Latin America—Social conditions. 4. Latin America—In
literature. 5. Spanish American literature—Social aspects. 6. Spanish American
literature—History and criticism. I. Bolaños, Alvaro Félix, 1955- II. Verdesio,
Gustavo. III. Series.

F1412 .C643 2001
980—dc21   2001042008

10 9 8 7 6 5 4 3 2 1

To Lisa M. Schuhmacher and Pamela K. Gilbert

Contents

Colonialism Now and Then

Colonial Latin American Studies in the Light of the Predicament of Latin Americanism

Gustavo Verdesio

The need for a study of colonial Latin America may not require, in this day and age, a whole lot of justification. However, it may still be important to emphasize the connections between the colonial past (that is, the object of Latin American colonial studies) and the present. The idea behind this project is, then, to present the reader with studies of colonial topics and issues that, at the same time, pay attention to the consequences the colonial situation being analyzed has for the different Latin American peoples and ethnic groups of present-day independent republics.[1] In other words, what this volume is proposing is, following the ideas advanced by José Rabasa in the article included here, to establish a nexus between the "antiquities" we study and the current situation of the descendants of the human contingents who shared the colonial experience, between the colonial situations of the past and the colonial legacies of the present.[2]

In this book, then, the concept "colonial legacies" plays an important role. However, in a recent article, Ricardo Kaliman has questioned the utility of the notion of colonial legacies for an understanding of the present. In his opinion, that concept, "though it is used in the desire to reveal and condemn, is in fact limited to emphasizing the analogy that can be established between cultural elements in the past and in the present, and generally ignoring the specific form that these elements assume in practical contemporary consciousness" (1998, 263). In other words, what Kaliman sees as a flaw in the notion is that it suggests that "the colonial structures were passed on to subsequent society in a compact and stable block" (263). I am persuaded that Kaliman misinterprets the meaning the expression "colonial legacies" has in Walter Mignolo's work, for whom the relationship between past and present is not a self-evident one: scholars need to dig in the past in order to see the connection between it and

1

our present (1989b, 52). In this way, historical processes can be reconstructed and traces of our shared past recovered, with the purpose of understanding the colonial legacies that continue to inform our present. The strategy of studying colonial legacies is not, in my opinion, another way of justifying mere analogies, but a tool for understanding the genesis of current situations of social injustice. By genesis I mean, in this context, the beginning of a process that led, throughout the centuries, to these social situations. This means that the expression "colonial legacies" does not simply describe an analogy between colonial and present-day social situations—something like a stable structural homology between past and present—but rather entails a notion of change and historical process, contrary to Kaliman's belief that it ignores the workings of the mechanisms of social reproduction (1998, 263). In Mignolo's words, the "legacies of the Spanish empire in the Americas are what connect the fifteenth and sixteenth centuries with the present" (1995 viii). That is why it is convenient, in Rabasa's opinion, if one is embarked in the task of constructing a decolonizing agenda for the present, to elaborate, first, "an inventory of the colonial legacy of modernity, before even beginning to conceptualize 'elsewheres' to dominant Western rationalities ("Of Zapatismo," 420). The way in which colonial legacies are understood in this book has, then, much more to do with the relations between the beginning and the current stage of a historical process than with mere structural analogies between past and present.

This project can be better understood if one views the research being produced in the field of Latin American colonial studies from a broader perspective: that of its position in the framework of Latin American literary and cultural studies. That is why it is convenient, first, to establish what kind of assumptions we, the practitioners of the discipline, bring to bear on the colonial texts and situations that are the object of our studies. Second, it is also necessary to trace a map of the academic and theoretical contexts within which we carry on those practices.

As regards the first issue, it is obvious that the overwhelming majority of those of us who study colonial texts come from social strata and ethnic groups that have nothing (or very little) to do with some of the historical agents of the colonial period. What I mean is that the victims of colonialism, the wretched of the earth, are not well represented in the ranks of those who study the past from an academic perspective. On the contrary, their numbers are very low. Almost nonexistent. As a consequence, the vast majority of those of us who write about the colonial period are either of *criollo* origin or *mestizos* totally integrated into the occidentalized society that predominates in most Latin American republics, or scholars from Europe or the United States. The representation of historical subjects and agents such as the Amerindians or the African slaves, then, is in the hands, most of the time, of subjects who do not belong to those ethnic groups. This situation, which could seem trivial for many a scholar, is a crucial factor with regard to the issue of representation of colonial situations.

The question asked by Gayatri Chakravorty Spivak a while ago—"Can the Subaltern Speak?"—is very difficult to answer. However, it is clear in the current academic situation that the present-day subaltern has not been able, yet, to write colonial historiography. The present-day subaltern has not been able, either, to have access to a discursive practice in the area of colonial literary studies. Those of us who produce knowledge in the field must assume the responsibility with which we are faced: to make sense of the universe of discourse of an era. However, this is not the only responsibility we have. There is another one, albeit a less evident one, that consists in studying the literary texts as a product of a situation of injustice that is the historical foundation of the social injustices suffered by many inhabitants of the continent in the present.

The majority of the articles included in this volume study, precisely, social situations of the past understood as the origin, or the antecedent, of present social situations. The rest focuses on some of the readings of those colonial situations produced by present-day scholars and writers. These investigations are motivated by the need to offer academic alternatives to predominant disciplinary practices. The hegemonic disciplinary practices consist of, as Alvaro Félix Bolaños points out in his contribution to this book, studying the colonial texts from a literary perspective that, in the best cases, forgets the injustice that characterizes the colonial situations that produced the aforementioned texts; in the worst cases, modern scholars end up celebrating the ethnocentric gaze of the *criollo* and European subjects—who were, more often than not, the authors of the canonical texts.

Although Walter Mignolo (1986) and Rolena Adorno (1988) stated, a few years ago, that the area of colonial studies was undergoing a paradigm shift (an expression that deserves to be discussed), it is my opinion that this is not true from a statistical perspective.[3] It is true that the majority of the important theoretical contributions to the field in the last years have tended to privilege the study of texts and perspectives previously repressed by the rigid criteria of colonial canon formation, yet, it is not true that the majority of the works published in the field follow the theoretical paths opened by the aforementioned theoretical contributions, as a careful examination of most of the volumes on that subject suggests. For example, among the works published in *Conquista y contraconquista* (a volume that collected the papers read at the conference on the Quincentennial of the "discovery" organized by the Instituto Internacional de Literatura Iberoamericana), only three or four could qualify as investigations produced in the framework of the so-called new paradigm, that consists of—among other things—expanding the colonial canon through the incorporation of texts produced by subaltern subjects such as Guaman Poma and in proposing reading practices capable of accounting for the discursive plurality and diversity of the colonial period. The rest of the works published in that collection continue a critical tradition that privileges Western (or Occidental) axiologies, at the same time that it limits the research agenda to a literary or, in the best of cases, a discursive study of the texts. The same coexistence of these two modes of understanding the discipline can be found in other collective publications in the area of Latin American colonial studies (see the volumes edited by Jara and Spadaccini, Cevallos et al., and Williams and Lewis). In a significant number of the articles they contain, the colonial situations that originated the texts celebrated as cultural monuments belonging to the national patrimony of the modern Latin American nation-states are absent from the analysis.

On the other hand, scholars who could qualify as practitioners in the framework of the new paradigm, have such different research agendas that it is very difficult, sometimes, to imagine them as being part of the same group. For example, Mabel Moraña's work on the Latin American Baroque entails a revision of the previous scholarship on the topic, especially in the articles where she concludes that the Baroque esthetic trend served, depending on the authors, either the cause of the consolidation of the colonial status quo or the resistance to it (1988; 1989). Although this way of viewing a historical period is still strongly anchored in what Angel Rama called *la ciudad letrada* (the lettered city), it does incorporate a new sociological perspective when it focuses on the *criollo* elites' uses of certain esthetic means for political ends. Sara Castro-Klarén, for her part, like Rolena Adorno (1986), has dedicated some of her works to the study of noncanonical authors of *mestizo* or Amerindian descent, as examples of resistance-writing by subaltern subjects (1994; 1996), while Regina Harrison has studied, instead, some Andean oral traditions (1989). As a final example, we can see Mignolo's work, who has studied multiple aspects of what he calls "colonial semiosis" (that is, the totality of signic or semiotic interactions that take place in colonial situations), in a wide range that includes both the indigenous (mostly Andean and Meso-American) territorial representations and their "scriptural" practices (see, for instance, his *Writing Without Words*). This brief list of authors may give the reader an idea of the diversity that exists among the scholars who could be considered as part of the new paradigm.

I make reference to this methodological and theoretical diversity in order to present the reader with a portrait of the discipline as one where little consensus exists with regard to intellectual production. If to the diversity found in the ranks of those who are producing within the framework of the new paradigm we add the high number of scholars who still produce in a disciplinary framework dominated both by the notion of the Belles Lettres and *criollo* ideology, the situation in the field of colonial studies can scarcely be considered as one where "a paradigm shift" has occurred. What I mean is that, in order to be able to talk about paradigm shifts, it is necessary that a consensus (about the principles that regulate the discipline, about how knowledge is validated, etc.) exists among all the practitioners of a discipline. For a paradigm is the dominant framework within which knowledge is produced at a specific time and in a certain discipline. The state of affairs of colonial studies, as we have seen, does not allow us to talk about such thing as a new paradigm. I propose, instead, to understand the practices Mignolo considers as symptoms of a paradigm shift, as academic practices that propose a new mode of intellectual production in the area. In this way, we can view that group of academic works as representative of an emergent mode of production, but not as the (statistically) dominant one in the discipline. The articles in this book can be viewed, if not as a part of that new mode of production, at least as ones that follow the paths opened by it. They represent a good sample, I believe, of the state of affairs of this field of studies, exhibiting both the most significant advances in the discipline as well as some of the theoretical and disciplinary problems we still encounter in our practice. Although there are still many needed improvements in the practice of Latin American colonial studies, the articles included in this book are important steps towards a decolonization of the production in that field.

The endorsement of this kind of disciplinary (and ethical) mode of production is necessary because, in general, what we—the majority of the scholars in the area, regardless of cultural or ethnic background—, bring to the study of the texts are centuries of Occidental education, an education that taught us to forget the oppressed ethnic groups of the continent when the task at stake is to produce a national narrative. That is why, in most of the studies produced in the traditional disciplinary framework (and, more often than not, even in the ones that inscribe themselves in the new mode of production), the critic positions him/herself in a way that resembles, suspiciously, the one held by the European and *criollo* authors of the texts under study.

Regardless of nationality, most of the critics who do not embrace the new mode of production in the field exalt the following values: the prose that prefigures the "novela del lenguaje" (or the New Hispanic American Novel, in Carlos Fuentes' lingo) and the exotic peculiarity that would confer some value (maybe "difference") to the studied text. Our perspective, then (even in the case of the best intentioned among us), is still a European one—a perspective that, far from showing any signs of change, seems to become more and more alien to the interests and views of the socially marginalized groups in Latin America. One of the reasons the distance between the critic and the subaltern subject is increasing can be found in the academic context of knowledge production.

As is well known, postcolonial theory is one of the most prestigious theoretical frameworks in the American academic milieu. As a consequence, its propagation to the Third World has been fast and efficient. It is not unusual to see some Latin American critics resorting to Homi K. Bhabha's or Gayatri Spivak's theoretical contributions to study Latin American texts. It is understandable. After all, postcolonial critics have proposed a series of readings and critical practices that put into question the traditional readings of the cultural products of countries that suffered British colonialism. The importance and value of this theoretical paradigm are undeniable and a dialogue with it should find a place in the agenda of scholars in the field of Latin American studies.

However, as Jorge Klor de Alva (1992, and 1995), Hugo Achugar (1997), and Mabel Moraña (1997) have rightly pointed out, the social realities on which postcolonial theory is based are very different from the ones we, in Latin American colonial studies, work with. To begin with, postcolonial theory deals with situations that arose from capitalist nineteenth-century colonial situations. Experts on Latin American Colonial Studies, for their part, have to study social situations wherein the economic and political organizational principles were closer to mercantilism than to the kind of capitalism developed by the British Empire in the nineteenth century (Klor de Alva 1992, 17). Besides, the subaltern subjects defined as colonial subjects in India differ dramatically from the ones we, Latin Americanists, understand as such. The colonial subject of India is an Indian who had to tolerate not only the presence of an invader but also one who dominated the territory and the politico-economical system. In Latin America, the definition of the colonial subject is quite different. In Klor de Alva's opinion, it cannot be said that in colonial Latin America the *mestizo*'s status was similar to the Amerindian's and the African's. Many of the former were able to successfully participate in the rules that organized social life in the continent, whereas the latter remained in an abject oppression that continues in the present. It is in the ranks of the latter that we can find the Latin American colonial subject, then (Klor de Alva 1995, 246–47, 255).

Among the many differences that could be found between the situations described by postcolonial theory and the ones studied by experts on colonial Latin American studies, perhaps the most interesting one is the language in which they are usually written. Although it is true that scholarly work on colonial studies is written in several languages, among them English, it is also true that, in the case of postcolonial theory, the vast majority of the fundamental texts are produced in English by Third World diasporic intellectuals. This is not a trivial datum, as Antonio Cornejo Polar warned us in his last work, because in the hierarchies of languages in the global world, English is the privileged one.

Latin America, like any other dependent culture, reads with much attention the intellectual production originated in the First World. As a consequence, the theoretical ideas produced in English by migrant Third World intellectuals working in American universities have an impact on the academic work produced from, and by, Latin America. The privileged status of the works written in English, the better circulation they enjoy and the Europeanized education of most Latin Americanists (both from Latin America and the rest of the world), makes possible that the theoretical corpus produced to explain social realities very different from Latin American ones inform a significant percentage of the critical production on the colonial period. The consequence of the linguistic hierarchy that dominates the circulation of ideas in this globalized world is the erasure of a series of critical traditions of Latin American origin that already proposed, before the heyday of postcolonial theory, a decolonizing agenda. This situation was denounced by Mignolo several years ago (in 1993) when he responded to a 1991 article by Patricia Seed that celebrated the adoption of postcolonial ideas and concepts by some scholars specializing in the colonial period. Seed praised, among others, the seminal book by Beatriz Pastor (which, by the way, had been published in Spanish almost ten years earlier). Mignolo, for his part, pointed out that in Latin America there was already a significant corpus of criticism of colonial legacies before the irruption of postcolonial theory. He quoted authors as influential as Edmundo O'Gorman and Angel Rama, who inaugurated critical agendas that should be considered as decolonizing ones.[4] In his response, Mignolo goes as far as to suggest that the omission of these Latin American scholars could be interpreted as a symptom of a certain academic imperialism.

Antonio Cornejo Polar, in the above quoted article, calls attention to one of the forms that academic imperialism takes; I am referring to the absence of English translations of Latinamericanism's fundamental texts produced in Latin America. A good example of this is the unforgivable delay in the publication of an English version of *La ciudad letrada,* by Angel Rama (a book published in the early-eighties whose long overdue translation appeared in the mid-nineties). This lack of reciprocity, this lack of equality in the intellectual exchange at a global scale, is another element that characterizes the context in which we, scholars on the colonial Latin American period, produce knowledge nowadays.

I would also like to call attention to the lack of academic prestige of Spanish nowadays. For this reason, and in spite of the fact that most of the colonial legacies that are colonial studies scholars' object of study are inscribed in that language (and in Quechua, Aymara, Quiché and Nahuatl, among many other indigenous languages), one finds the following problem: if one wants to participate in a global theoretical dialogue, one has to write in English, because Spanish does not have much intellectual currency today. As Mignolo has pointed out in his monumental *The Darker Side of the Renaissance*:

> Writing in Spanish means, at this time, to remain at the margin of contemporary theoretical discussions. . . . To write in Spanish a book that attempts to inscribe Spanish/Latin American and Amerindian legacies into current debates . . . and into colonial legacies and postcolonial theories means marginalizing the book before giving it the possibility of participating in an intellectual conversation . . . dominated by English. (viii)

Another consequence of the marginal position of Spanish and the Spanish-speaking intellectual tradition is the need to import theories produced in English about colonial legacies inscribed in that language. Some of the few colonial studies produced in the framework provided by the new mode of production proposed and defended by Mignolo and Adorno, among others, find their theoretical inspiration in another critical branch of postcolonial descent: Subaltern studies. This is a very attractive theoretical endeavor, because it attempts to develop new relations between scholars in the field of Latin American studies and those human beings posited as their object of study (Rabasa and Sanjinés 1994, viii). As the founding statement of the Latin American Subaltern Studies group explains, this is a theoretical practice that emerges at a moment when progressive intellectuals are disappointed in Marxism, a disappointment caused by the failure of the experiences in the countries of so-called *socialismo real*—real socialism (1994, 1). It emerges, too, amidst the globalization period. In a historical moment when everything is marketable and tends to the homogeneization of differences, we should be cautious as regards our own intellectual practices. In this context, in Moraña's opinion, the subaltern enters the international market as a commodity as well as a category that levels and homogenizes regional differences (1997, 48). Whether one subscribes to her assessment of subaltern studies or not, it is reasonable to say that those who have Latin America as its object of study, should refrain from using such theoretical frameworks without subjecting them, first, to a careful scrutiny. One of the main problems with resorting to these theories originated in the center—that is, in the United States or Europe—is that such an operation may very well lead the critic—if she/he is not careful enough—to a construction of Latin America as an object of study partially shaped by a First World perspective. A good example of that kind of construction of the object of study is Román de la Campa's most recent book, where the author produces a representation of Latin Americanism that is totally dependent on First World theories. In his opinion, the corpus of criticism produced by Latin Americanists—primarily in the United States, but also in the rest of the world—is mostly based on a branch of poststructuralism: deconstruction (1999, vii). This representation of the Latin American critical tradition in the area of literary studies does not seem to be able to find room in its model for trends represented by Marxist critics such as Hernán Vidal and Neil Larsen—who find their predecessors in authors like José Carlos Mariátegui and Roberto Fernández Retamar, among others—as well as by those critics with strong ties to the social sciences—represented, for example, by Agustín Cueva. Moreover, such a representation fails to account for the influential work of more recent critics like the recently deceased Antonio Cornejo Polar—who could hardly qualify as a practitioner of deconstruction. Román de la Campa's representation of Latin Americanism is, then, an incomplete one because it is blind to any Latin Americanist theoretical enterprise that is not based on some

First World theories. Moreover, it is my contention that it is so because of the preconceived ideas he brings to the analysis. The object of study, in this way, takes shape as a consequence of the excessive importance de la Campa assigns to certain First World theories. That is why, as scholars of Latin American colonial studies, we should focus (without denying the possible usefulness of theoretical frameworks produced in the First World) on the study of the specific social situations that are the foundation and beginnings of our present. And we should do it with the tools that best serve that goal—be they postcolonial theory, subaltern studies, or any other theoretical tradition—, yet without forgetting the specificity of the colonial situations we are trying to make sense of.[5]

Having said that, I want to clarify that some of the Latin American Subaltern Studies group's objectives coincide with the goals pursued by the editors of this volume. The founding statement clearly calls for a theoretical practice that requires from the critic a stronger sense of social and political responsibility as well as a solidarity with subaltern subjects. In this respect, this book should be viewed as a critical endeavor that continues a tradition whose most recent avatar is Subaltern Studies, but whose antecedents include a number of scholars—such as José C. Mariátegui, Angel Rama and Antonio Cornejo Polar, to mention only three of the most influential ones—who attempted to understand Latin America and its culture from an independent, decolonizing perspective. This means that although it is true that scholars in the field of colonial studies can choose to be the bearers of a Latin American critical tradition, this choice does not rule out the possibility of entering a critical dialogue with postcolonial theory and subaltern studies—a dialogue that requires some caution, though, because of the risks one runs while resorting to theoretical constructs originating in social and cultural formations that are alien to one's object of study.

I hope the reader understands that to have some reservations with regard to subaltern studies does not entail a denial of the need to concede an epistemological privilege to certain social agents; it does not mean, either, a return to certain *criollista* conceptions that John Beverley calls, in his new book, "neo-Arielism" (1999, 18–19).[6] In order to respond to such suspicions, let us point out that any form of *criollismo* would, precisely, rule out those analyses of colonial situations—like the ones included in this book—that criticize its national project. Besides, *criollismo* is the type of intellectual and social movement more prone to embrace, acritically, the theoretical contributions generated in the "civilized" First World. For a thorough portrayal of *criollismo*'s modus operandi, it should suffice to remember Domingo F. Sarmiento's (or any other leader of a Latin American independent republic's) project, based on a narrative that attempted to erase from the face of the earth the local knowledges of marginal ethnic groups and, in some cases, the human groups themselves. What this book does is, precisely, the opposite of *criollismo*: an in-depth study of the peculiarities of Latin American colonial situations that take into account its consequences for the situations of social injustice of the present; a

study that holds the historical agents that created that social injustice responsible and that does not forget the memories of the colonial subjects demonized
or repressed by hegemonic power. In other words, what this book offers is a
study of Latin American roots that lays bare the domination strategies used by
the *criollo* national project.

Finally, the reader should not get the impression that I am advocating a
Latin Americanism produced by Latin American subjects who live in Latin
America. A passport does not give one privileged access to the right tools to
account for a given object of study. On the contrary, some of the theoretical
frameworks produced today in Latin America by Latin American scholars can
also be subject to criticism from the disciplinary perspective of the new mode
of intellectual production in the field of Latin American colonial studies. Two
examples will suffice to illustrate the point. One of the most popular theoretical tools today in Latin Americanism is the notion of hybridity as developed
by Néstor García Canclini. Reading both his *Culturas híbridas* (1990) and
Consumidores y ciudadanos (1995) one gets the impression that there is something missing from the analysis. For example, the way in which he seems to
marvel at—and, often, celebrate—the hybrid practices of the subaltern, seems
to leave in the shadows—as Neil Larsen has pointed out—the constitutive violence that lies at the origin of the social situation that serves as the framework
for the aforementioned hybrid practices. That violence started, as is well
known, with the cultural clash that some call, euphemistically, the colonial encounter.[7] The colonial violence that is the origin of Latin American hybrid
cultures is, then, absent from García Canclini's analysis.

The most recent work by another critic from the periphery, the Argentinean Beatriz Sarlo, is perhaps the most perfect incarnation of the "neo-
Arielism" (or neo-*criollismo*) mentioned by John Beverley (and by other
colleagues at the aforementioned LASA conference in Chicago) in his new
book: she proposes a critical agenda that should focus on a return to the study
of the cultural production typical of the lettered city—that is, an agenda that
proposes to privilege the study of literature and other elite cultural manifestations promoted by the narratives of nationhood (1997, 36, 38). Such a critical
project (which entails an utter rejection of cultural studies—a theoretical endeavor that Sarlo now considers as very detrimental to Latin American studies), is definitely unacceptable to those of us in the area of colonial studies who
adhere to a project like this book, because—among other reasons—it proposes
to limit our research *only* to, precisely, the cultural production that erased the
subaltern or oppressed subjects from the universe of meaning created by official national narratives. However, it should be pointed out that there are, in
Latin America, other kinds of research projects that are closer to this book's
than to Sarlo's. I am referring to, for example, Zulma Palermo's (1997) and
Gladys Lopreto's (1996) work, which focuses on the retrieval of marginal nar-

ratives of the colonial period. The idea behind their respective agendas is to understand the present through the study of the stories that have been erased by the official Argentinean national narrative.

As can be seen, the location in which theory is produced neither guarantees nor precludes its explanatory value. I am stating this truism because of a certain fictional dialogue authored by Alberto Moreiras in one of his most recent interventions:

> Take your average non-Latin American Latinamericanist: he (sic) must hear, as a constant background murmuring, that his (sic) efforts to think Latin America from his (sic) location in the cosmopolitan university have, as a damning condition of possibility, his (sic) all too comfortable installation in the methodological trends and fashions of world-hegemonic university discourse. (1997, iv)
> ... the Latin American Latinamericanist finds his (*sic*) dubious legitimation in the positing of location as final redemption. But then location was precisely what always already delegitimized his (*sic*) outsiding other. How can location function simultaneously as a source of legitimation and as its opposite? The apparent answer is: "proper" location works, improper location does not. (1997, iv)

Although Moreiras describes this fictional dialogue as "a staged fight, a wrestling match between jokers" (1997, v), it could be better described as a counterpoint between a non-Latin American Latinamericanist (like himself) and a Latin American Latinamericanist who sounds like Hugo Achugar (1998, where he grants epistemological privilege to those critical discourses that come from the periphery—) [97][8] or, to some extent, Nelly Richard (when she gives locality an important role in the elaboration of theory—) [1997, 346]. This staged dialogue is the platform from which Moreiras advances his very well-founded argument against locational thinking. However, I think his argument leaves the ground on which some critical strategies stand— those that put emphasis on the issue of the situation of enunciation—untouched. In other words, his argument does not invalidate the claims of those who, like Mignolo, believe that what matters is "who is talking, about what, where and why" (Mignolo 1993, 122). According to him, although one must pay attention to locality because local circumstances have an impact on the politics developed by a given subject, this does not mean one should give it an ontological status that determines the production of knowledge (1993, 122). If scholars are not totally determined by their circumstances, then, their positioning does not depend so much on geographic location (although it should be taken into account), but rather on the ideological interests they choose to defend or embrace. Alberto Moreiras is right when, echoing Walter Mignolo, he points out that "no thinking exhausts itself in its conditions of enunciation"

(1997, vi). However, it is also true that no thinking comes from a vacuum. In this light, the strategy he proposes to replace critical practices focused on the situation of enunciation (vi), a strategy which he calls "dirty" (in the sense that no thinking proceeds from disembodiment) atopianism, looks more atopian (that is, anti-locational) than dirty (an embodied thinking). In the case of the field of colonial studies, there is no room for non-positional thinking. The ideological position one assumes is crucial for the outcome of one's research, for there are no third spaces or third ways in the study of the colonial past: one either embraces the winners' (the European's or *criollo*'s) world view or sides with the subjects who still live in subalternity. One can do this from any location. What cannot be done, at the risk of being complicit with hegemony, is to pretend one does not speak from a certain position.

As we have seen throughout this preface, we are, in the present, far from being free of colonialism in a broad sense. First, we saw the existence of a neocolonialism in the production of the modern scholars that adhere to the world views promoted by the *criollo* or European authors of the colonial period. Later, we saw that there is an academic colonialism exerted upon those who write about a culture whose language, Spanish, is far from being considered hegemonic in the present. The fact that the author of this preface, a Spanish-speaking Uruguayan, is writing this introduction in English is—as we saw in Mignolo's quote on the lack of intellectual currency of the Spanish language today—a confirmation of the predicament of Spanish-speaking intellectuals from the periphery trying to make themselves heard in the framework of an English-dominated academic world. Moreover, that colonialism imposed on non-English speakers manifests itself, also, in the origin of the tools—which come, more often than not, like postcolonial theory and subaltern studies, from the capitalist center—we use to account for our object of study.

There is still another kind of colonialism that needs to be avoided. I am referring to the uses of indigenous pasts in order to create discourses of Latin American identity. Amaryll Chanady, in her study on authors such as José Martí, Mariátegui, and Fernández Retamar, has already warned against the perils of those discourses in which the Amerindian tradition is appropriated in order to differentiate between a national or supranational (that is, regional) identity and an external hegemonic power (1990, 36, and passim). Those discourses represent the Indian as a pretext for a discursive practice of resistance, but deny him/her "the status of subject in the elaboration and conceptualization of the collective enterprise of promoting a national identity" (Chanady, 36). As the author points out, her critique of those Latin American major authors (who are part of the decolonizing tradition I mentioned above) does not propose a general rejection of strategies of collective self-affirmation, but the need to adopt a critical stance with respect to monologic strategies of identity (1990, 46). In the same spirit, and as an attempt to be alert about our own tradition and practice, I would like to call attention to a similar intellectual operation in contemporary colonial studies practice. It is my impression that although a number of studies (often the most interesting ones in the field) pay special attention to the cultural traditions marginalized by the *criollo* national narratives that dominate the ideological landscape of the continent, some of them seem to seek, primarily, the legitimation of the scholar's situation of enunciation. That is, some scholars (in many cases, of Latin American descent) study the marginalized cultures in order to represent themselves as producers of knowledge in a globalized world that privileges other producers of knowledge (for example, those who come from cultural traditions more in fashion in the context of the current global geopolitical situation) and other objects of study (for instance, the former colonies of the British Empire). Most of the time, however, that intellectual operation is not accompanied by a vindication of the situation of enunciation of, and knowledge production by, the indigenous or subaltern cultures that made the investigation possible. The appropriation of those knowledges marginalized by the West, of those forgotten traditions, may become—if it does not go hand in hand with a clear validation of those local knowledges as equal in rank with the one produced by Western scholars—another form of intellectual colonization. This is why we, Latin American colonial studies experts, must be permanently alert in order not to fall into the trap of such (appropriating) academic strategies.

As John Beverley has pointed out repeatedly, literary studies and other humanistic disciplines have contributed to the promotion and perpetuation of domination of subaltern subjects both in Latin America and the world (for example, 1999, 1; 1993, x). That is why it is necessary not only to revise the theoretical tools we bring to the analysis of our object of study, but also to permanently question our role as practitioners of a discipline that has traditionally been at the service of the dominant ideology—that is, at the service of the values and practices of the dominant groups. I hope that this preface contributes to a discussion that eventually leads to the decolonization of our field of studies—that is, a discussion of an ethical program for a disciplinary practice that does not need to appropriate the knowledge produced by the colonial subjects of the past and the oppressed subjects of the present. Let us try, then, not to become accomplices of the powers that be. Let us try, in other words, not to be the colonizers of the present.

NOTES

1. I am using the expression colonial situations in the sense given to it by Walter Mignolo:

> the situation in which an ethnic minority, technologically advanced and practicing Christian religion, imposed itself upon an ethnic majority, technologi-

cally less advanced and practicing non-Christian religions. Colonial situations are shaped by a process of transformation in which members of both the
colonized as well as the colonizing cultures enter into a particular kind of
human interaction, colonial semiosis, which, in turn, contributes to the con-
formation of the colonial situation (1989, 94).

2. Later in this introduction, I will refer again to the notion of colonial legacies (the
living consequences of colonial situations) as developed by Mignolo.

3. It should be pointed out that although there are differences between their respective
research agendas, both Walter Mignolo and Rolena Adorno announced the advent
of a new paradigm in Latin American colonial studies.

4. Since then, several important scholars in the field of Latin American Studies have
called attention to the postcolonial critics' ignorance (which at this point one assumes is a conscious choice) of the Latin American critical tradition: Sara Castro-
Klarén (1994, 230; and in Zevallos-Aguilar 1997, 969), John Beverley (1994, 272),
and Hugo Achugar (1997, 61), among others.

5. This case could be supplemented by Ricardo Kaliman's critique of the cultural studies paradigm (another theoretical construct originated in the center) which, in his
opinion, does not consider "interesting"—and, therefore, pays little attention to—
many of the cultural practices currently taking place in Latin America (1998, 262).
He goes so far as to suggest that cultural studies, as a critical project, is strongly influenced by the orientation imposed on it by the institution on which it depends for
its existence (262).

6. And as it could be heard in the hallways during the Latin American Studies Association (LASA) Conference in Chicago (September 1998).

7. Moreover, García Canclini's claim that one of the most efficient ways to resist globalization and neo-liberalism is to organize civil society so that its members can exercise their right to citizenship through consumption, leaves his argument open to
some objections. For instance, one could argue that such a plan fails to recognize
that the situations of social injustice are the consequence of economic and hegemonic structures that perpetuate the domination of the ruling classes; that consumption itself, no matter how oppositional and organized it can get, does not
challenge—cannot challenge—the deep roots and strong structures of economic
domination and exploitation. Again, those domination structures are the colonial
legacies of our present.

8. Hugo Achugar's position, that can be synthesized in the following sentence: "the
periphery is a privileged place from which to think the world" (1998, 97), has been
recently criticized by Abril Trigo, who—like Moreiras—is wary of locational politics (2000, 85–87). He ends his criticism of Achugar's and Nelly Richard's positions—which are not identical but, to say the least, share some concerns and
views—with the following statement: "The epistemological borders don't disappear because the intellectual happens to write from Montevideo instead of Pittsburgh" (87).

BIBLIOGRAPHY

Achugar, Hugo. 1997. "Leones, cazadores e historiadores. A propósito de las memorias de las políticas y el conocimiento." *Revista Iberoamericana* 180: 379–387.

———. 1998. "Fin de Siglo: Reflections from the Periphery." In *New World [Dis]Orders & Peripheral Strains. Specifying Cultural Dimensions in Latin American and Latino Studies.* Edited by Michael Piazza and Marc Zimmerman. Chicago: MARCH.

Adorno, Rolena. 1986. *Guaman Poma. Writing and Resistance in Colonial Peru.* Austin: University of Texas Press.

———. 1988. "Nuevas perspectivas en los estudios coloniales hispanoamericanos." *Revista de Crítica Literaria Latinoamericana* 14, 28: 11–28.

Beverley, John. 1993. *Against Literature.* Minneapolis: University of Minnesota Press.

———. 1994. "Writing in Reverse: On the Project of the Latin American Subaltern Studies Group." *Dispositio/n* 46: 271–288.

———. 1999. *Subalternity and Representation: Arguments in Cultural Theory.* Durham: Duke University Press.

Castro-Klarén, Sara. 1994. "Writing Subalterity: Guaman Poma and Garcilaso, Inca." *Dispositio/n* 46: 229–244.

———. 1996. "El Cuzco de Garcilaso: el espacio y el lugar del conocimiento." In *Asedios a la heterogeneidad cultural. Libro de homenaje a Antonio Cornejo Polar.* Edited by José Antonio Mazzotti y U. Juan Zevallos Aguilar. Philadelphia: Asociación internacional de peruanistas.

Chanady, Amaryll. 1990. "Latin American Discourses of Identity and the Aproppriation of the Amerindian Other." *Sociocriticism* 6, 1–2: 33–48.

Cevallos, Francisco, et al., eds. 1994. *Coded Encounters: Writing, Gender, and Ethnicity in Colonial Latin America.* Amherst: University of Massachussetts Press.

Cornejo Polar, Antonio. 1997. "Mestizaje e hibridez: los riesgos de las metáforas." Apuntes. *Revista Iberoamericana* 180: 341–344.

Cueva, Augustín. 1981. "El método materialista histórico aplicado a la periodización de la historia de la literatura eruatoriana: algunas consideraciones teóricas." *Casa de las Américas* 12. 127: 31–36.

De la Campa, Román. 1999. *Latin Americanism.* Minneapolis: University of Minnesota Press.

García Canclini, Néstor. 1990. *Culturas híbridas. Estrategias para entrar y salir de la modernidad.* México: Grijalbo.

———. 1995. *Consumidores y ciudadanos. Conflictos multiculturales de la globalización.* México: Grijalbo.

Harrison, Regina. 1989. *Signs, Songs, and Memory in the Andes: Translating Quechua Language and Culture.* Austin: University of Texas Press.

Jara, René, and Nicholas Spadaccini, eds. 1989. *1492/1992. Re-Discovering Colonial Writing.* Minneapolis: Prisma Institute.

———. 1992. *Amerindian Images and the Legacy of Columbus.* Minneapolis: University of Minnesota Press.

Kaliman, Ricardo. 1998. "What Is Interesting in Latin American Cultural Studies." *Journal of Latin American Cultural Studies.* 7, 2: 261–272.

 Klor de Alva, J. Jorge. 1995. "The Postcolonization of the (Latin) American Experience: A Reconsideration of 'Colonialism,' 'Postcolonialism,' and 'Mestizaje.' " In *After Colonialism. Imperial Histories and Postcolonial Displacements.* Edited by Gyan Prakash, 241–75. Princeton, NJ: Princeton University Press.

———. 1992. "Colonialism and Postcolonialism as (Latin) American Mirages." *Colonial Latin American Review.* 1, 1–2: 3–23.

Larsen, Neil. 2001. "The 'Hybrid' Fallacy, or, Culture and the Question of Historical Necessity." In *Beyond Hybridity.* Edited by Leslie Bary, and Gustavo Verdesio. Minneapolis: University of Minnesota Press [forthcoming].

Latin American Subaltern Studies Group. 1994. "Founding Statement." *Dispositio/n* 46: 1–11.

Lopreto, Gladys. 1996. "*. . . que vivo en esta conquista.*" *Textos del Río de la Plata, Siglo XVI.* La Plata: Editorial de la Universidad de la Plata.

Mariátegui, José Carlos. 1988 [1928]. *Seis ensayos de interpretación de la realidad Peruana.* México: Era.

Mignolo, Walter. 1995. *The Darker Side of the Renaissance. Literacy, Territoriality and Colonization.* Ann Arbor: University of Michigan Press.

———. 1993. "Colonial and Postcolonial Discourse: Cultural Critique or Academic Colonialism?" *Latin American Research Review* 28, 3: 120–134.

———. 1989. "Colonial Situations, Geographical Discourses and Territorial Representations: Toward a Diatopical Understanding of Colonial Semiosis." *Dispositio* 14, 36–38; 93–140.

———. 1989b. "Literacy and Colonization: The New World Experience." In *Re/Discovering Colonial Writing. Hispanic Issues 4.* Edited by R. Jara, and N. Spadaccini, 51–96. Minneapolis: The Prisma Institute.

———. 1986. "La lengua, la letra, el territorio (o la crisis de los estudios literarios coloniales)." *Dispositio,* 11, 28–29; 135–160.

Mignolo, Walter, and Elizabeth Hill Boone. 1994. *Writing Without Words. Alternative Literacies in Mesoamerica and the Andes.* Durham and London: Duke University Press.

Moraña, Mabel. 1997. "El boom del subalterno." *Revista de crítica cultural* 15: 48–53.

————. 1989. "Para una relectura del barroco hispanoamericano: problemas críticos e historiográficos." *Revista de Crítica Literaria Latinoamericana* 29: 219–31.

————. 1988. "Barroco y conciencia criolla en Hispanoamérica." *Revista de Crítica Literaria Latinoamericana* 28: 229–51.

Moreiras, Alberto. 1997 [2000]. "Introduction: From Locational Thinking to Dirty Atopianism." *Dispositio/n* 22, 49: iii–vii.

Ortega, Julio and José Amor y Vázquez, Eds. 1994. *Conquista y contraconquista. La escritura del nuevo mundo.* México: Brown University, El Colegio de México.

Palermo, Zulma. 1997 [2000]. "Semiótica del vacío y de la espera." *Dispositio/n* 22, 49:

Rabasa, José. 1997. "Of Zapatismo: Reflections on the Folkloric and the Impossible in a Subaltern Insurrection." In *The Politics of Culture in the Shadow of Capital.* Edited by Lisa Lowe, and David Lloyd, 399–432. Durham, NC.: Duke University Press.

Rabasa, José, and Javier Sanjinés. 1994. "Introduction: The Politics of Subaltern Studies." *Dispositio/n* 19, 46: v–xi.

Rama, , Angel. 1984. *La ciudad letrada.* Hanover, NH: Ediciones del Norte.

Fernández Retamar, Roberto. 1989 [1973]. *Caliban and other Essays.* Trans. by E. Baker. Minneapolis: University of Minnesota Press.

Richard, Nelly. 1997. "Intersectando Latinoamérica con el latinoamericanismo: saberes académicos, práctica teórica y crítica cultural." *Revista Iberoamericana* 63, 180: 345–361.

Sarlo, Beatriz. 1997. "Los estudios culturales y la crítica literaria en la encrucijada valorativa." *Revista de Crítica Cultural* 15: 32–38.

Seed, Patricia. 1991. "Colonial and Postcolonial Discourse." *Latin American Research Review* 26, 3: 181–200.

Trigo, Abril. 2000. "Why Do I Do Cultural Studies?" *Journal of Latin American Cultural Studies* 19, 1: 73–93.

Vidal, Hernán. 1976. *Literatura hispanoamericana e ideología liberal: surgimiento y crisis.* Buenos Aires: Hispamérica.

Williams, Jerry, and Robert E. Lewis, Eds. 1993. *Early Images of the Americas: Transfer and Invention.* Tucson. London: University of Arizona Press.

Zevallos Aguilar, Ulises J. 1997. "Teoría Poscolonial y Literatura Latinoamericana: Entrevista con Sara Castro-Klarén." *Revista Iberoamericana* 176–177: 963–971.

On the Issues of Academic Colonization and Responsibility when Reading and Writing About Colonial Latin America Today

Alvaro Félix Bolaños

"... apenas oyeron el nombre de Miguel de Cervantes, cuando se comenzaron a hacer lenguas, encareciendo la estimación en que así en Francia como en los reinos sus confinantes se tenían sus obras, la *Galatea,* que algunos dellos tienen casi de memoria, la primera parte désta [*Don Quijote*] y las *Novelas.* Fueron tantos sus encarecimientos, que me ofrecí llevarles que viesen al autor dellas, que estimaron con mil demostraciones de vivos deseos. Preguntáronme muy por menor su edad, su profesión, calidad y cantidad. Halléme obligado a decir que era viejo, soldado hidalgo y pobre, a que uno respondió estas formales palabras: "Pues ¿a tal hombre no le tiene España muy rico y sustentado del erario público?" Acudió otro de aquellos caballeros con este pensamiento, y con mucha agudeza dijo: "Si necesidad le ha de obligar a escribir, plega a Dios que nunca tenga abundancia, para que con sus obras, siendo el pobre, haga rico a todo el mundo" (Miguel de Cervantes 1979 [1605], 311).[1]

[Once they heard the name of Miguel de Cervantes, they started to commend the great regard in which his works were held in France and its neighboring kingdoms, among those *Galatea,* which some of them almost knew by heart, the first part of this one [*Don Quijote*] and the *Novelas.* Their supplications were so many that I volunteered to take them to see the author of these works, which they greatly appreciated. They asked me about his age, his occupation, his qualities and quantities. I felt compelled to tell them that he was old, a soldier of lesser nobility, and impoverished, to which one of them answered with the following very words: "So, Spain hasn't rewarded such a man nor sustained him with public funds?" And another one of these gentlemen wittily retorted with the following opinion: "If poverty has compelled him to write, let us hope God does not allow him to see abundance so, with his works, while being poor, he can make the whole world rich."]

19

The previous Cervantes's quote tells of a conversation supposedly held in Madrid on February 5, 1615, between Licenciado Márquez Torres, author of the approval of the text for the second part of Cervantes's *Don Quijote,* and some members of a French diplomatic delegation. Its relevance to my contention here has to do with the notion it expresses of the necessity and permissibility of someone being indigent for the sake of not only high forms of literary expression, but also the enjoyment it provides to prosperous gentlemen who know how to appreciate it. The capacity of creating excellent writings for the leisurely reader becomes, according to this passage, a national, or even universal patrimony, which could rightfully be defended by those individuals who derive delectation from it, even if that entails the permanent disenfranchisement of one chosen individual, in this case, the author. It could be argued that Cervantes's intention with his sarcasm here simply signals a sad irony: the every day frustrations of the impecunious professional writer increases his or her sagacity and lucidity (a topic developed later by Romanticism), but the type of relation established between the miserably poor author and the well-off reader is undeniably one of social and economic disparity which is desired as permanent—and not by he who holds the short end of the arrangement.

In this passage, the privileged reader's defense of his or her right to enjoy literature becomes a defense of material destitution and privation of others. As we will see, the relevance of this notion has to do with the created feasibility of a conceptual operation that complaisantly admits the affliction and misfortune of some members of society for the sake of the existence of a sort of otherworldly discourse enjoyed by a select few. Such relevance also has to do with the currency of this assumption today in the consideration of certain discursive forms universally classified as "literary." Furthermore, it has to do with the notion of consenting to insensitivity towards the pauperism and misfortunes of others in the name of a literary refinement, especially in a continent like Latin America where there has been, and still is, a permanently disenfranchised majority.[2]

I

What is the difference between writing today about contemporary Latin American texts and culture and writing about colonial Latin American ones? If there is any difference, should it matter and why? The elucidation of these questions will hopefully shed light on my issue of "responsibility" of scholars dedicated to Latin American texts written hundreds of years ago. Many literary critics occupied with contemporary Latin American literature tend to consider the historical present of the Latin American republics as a finished, fully grown result of an earlier, timid, formative colonial phase. Furthermore, critics occupied with the colonial past study it mainly in terms of its contribution to its future (that is, our own present), and as an immature period destined to fade into the formation of the more perfect modern era. And this notion of an evolution from imperfect to a contemporary, more perfect cultural status rests, in turn, on the idea of the American territories as an empty space gracefully filled and fulfilled since 1492 with a "superior" European cultural endowment which gave rise to a new Euro-American cultural synthesis. Such synthesis is generally identified as universal for the entire population of the territory previously controlled by Spain (including the empowered white elite known as *criollos*,[3] the different kinds of racial mixes like *mestizos, mulatos, zambos,* etc., and the Indians and blacks), even though it is a cultural synthesis modeled exclusively after the views and tastes of the very inheritors of the culture, wealth, and privileges of the conquistadors.

There is, of course, a big difference between both kinds of writings indicated above and it has to do with the kind of relation the critic is able to establish between the colonial period and the era of the new Latin American republics. Does the critic relate to the colonial Latin American past (and its cultural accomplishments) as an overcome interval, which has no real or strong links with our present? Or does she or he relate to it as a historical process the repercussions of which still linger today? If the colonial period makes sense only as a social formation already disappeared, then the question of studying colonial history and culture runs the risk of becoming a mere celebration of overcoming not only an imperfect phase, but also its ingenious seminal contributions to the mature society of this moment. In the case of the great majority of literary critics, the colonial literature studied is assessed only in relation to its capacity to propitiate the very much admired present literary status quo (specially after the commercial success of the so-called Boom of the Latin American novel); whereas when this capacity is not found in the colonial literary works, these are simply regarded as registries of antecedent, not grown up phases of literary development. This operation in itself seems, and could be, quite innocuous until it is applied to social and cultural contexts. When these contexts are found useless to explain contemporary highly regarded social and political situations, they are relegated to spaces of curiosities like museums. And, as we all know, museums, perceived as windows to times already gone and surpassed, allow for a safe contemplation of things, regardless of how strange, exotic, or dangerous they were.

There is, of course, a process of accumulation of experiences in creating cultural artifacts over time (for instance those expressed in the form of architectural structures or verbal artifacts), and in this process we can see developing forms deemed simple at first and more sophisticated later on. But such a perception of progressive improvement rests on the particular desire of the observer to find an explanation to the present status of an esteemed social activity worthy of his or her critical attention. A *letrado* or an intellectual who traces the development of an isolated skill and writes about that tracing generally chooses to see it as proof of a "natural" pursuit of perfection common to all things in a society. For instance, if literature evolves from "primitive" verbal formations like the Mozarabic *jarchas* in the Spanish Middle Ages to more "advanced" ones like Carmen Martín Gaite's *El cuarto de atrás* (1978), or from Columbus's awkward *Diary* (1492–93) of his first voyage, to García Márquez's *One Hundred Years of Solitude* (1967), their respective societies must also have experienced this process of becoming perfect. But are the *jarchas* and the narratives on the conquest that simplistic? Can their cultural and social environments also be considered simplistic? Or are they perceived as such simply because that is what the inquiring intellectual wants to see? The possibility of tracing a continuous improvement of artistic skills in targeted individuals need not indicate a similar progression in the social and economic relations among all the individuals in the society in question.

Does colonial literature conform to a primitive state of formation existing only to be overcome by our twenty- and twentieth-first-century Latin American writers' advancements in literary skills? Are the colonial cultural and political formations totally absent from the present state of things in Latin American society and culture? The answer to these two questions is "no." In the case of the first question, the connections so far made between colonial writing and the literary (*criollo*) developments after independence from Spain have responded to a critical and ideological operation that imposes on sixteenth- and seventeenth-century texts twentieth-century literary sensitivities and expectations. As Walter Mignolo pointed out, finding literary quotas in the so-called *crónicas de Indias* today is less a discovery of origins and more a violence of classification over the colonial text (1982, 57, note 1). Or as Margarita Zamora put it (developing this same idea several years later): "The supposed novelesque (in the modern sense) characteristics that might be found in these texts can only appear novelesque when viewed in retrospect" (1987, 345).

And in the case of the second question, the colonial cultural and political formations are not absent today because in Latin America, like in the United States (especially in the South), there are too many lagging social and cultural ills that were supposed to be cured with the advent and validation of their new republics. In the U.S. case, they were supposed to be solved through Independence from England and the American Civil War, and in the Latin American case through independence from Spain. But such social maladies (injustice derived from uneven distribution of wealth, power, and privileges) still linger in these societies today. Searching for the origins of literary traditions and particular modes of writing in the context of inquiring for the artistic essential traces of a given geopolitical territory is an intellectual operation very similar to inquiring about traces of human groups. For instance, the study of anthropology tends persistently to acquire its data in the form of a search for primordial beginnings. As James Clifford has stated "It is assumed that evidence from "simple" societies will illuminate the origins and structure of contemporary structural patterns" (1986, 110). But the idea of a linear development of social groups from simple to complex forms is just that: an assumption very similar to the one held by literary historians and prompted by our own presumptuous view of today's state of affairs as a more perfect result of something that came before.

Is there any relation between the colonial social status quo, which served as context for the colonial Latin American texts we (the critics) present to contemporary audiences, and the social status quo that such audiences experience today? How does one ignore a link between the immediate and frequently miserable situation of indigenous communities throughout the Americas, and the present and invariably opulent Western societies, while considering the relation between indigenous populations and the conquistadors in the sixteenth century? For instance, ignoring any relation between the conquistador-*Araucanian* struggle in the sixteenth century and the fight of the Mapuche Indians against violent neo-liberal economic policies in Chile today is always an option, but one that requires the same kind of detachment from the plight of the disenfranchised that the French diplomats showed toward the Spanish indigent writer. Many might think that a great deal has been already said about the appalling social and human trauma brought about by the conquest, but I believe that the issue in this regard is not how much should we speak about it, but that we do not forget to do so.

In the case of Latin American literature these questions are relevant, among other reasons, because both "literature" and the "writer" have been revered as national conscience-building forces that help unify national territories and as such many people listen very carefully to what they have to say. They have also been sources of pride, glory, and political clout since the space of the intellectual has habitually been associated with political power.[4] The pen has alternated with the scepter in some cases (such as Domingo Faustino Sarmiento, José Manuel Marroquín, and Rómulo Gallegos who became presidents of their countries, and Gustavo Alvarez Gardeazábal who recently became the governor of his province), or has been conspicuously close to it (Mario Vargas Llosa and Pablo Neruda ran for office). Writers and literary critics have always enjoyed this kind of ascendancy and have become both national symbols, as in the cases of José Enrique Rodó, Pedro Henríquez Ureña, Arturo Uslar Pietri, Angel Rama, Octavio Paz, Gabriel García Márquez, and many others.

Do literary critics, who speak about Latin American literature and enjoy an increasingly broad and devoted audience, have a responsibility for both the selection of texts made available for such audience and the criteria for such selection? What does being responsible with the endorsement of selected texts mean? The answer to these questions could be as numerous as the amount of critics we care to examine, but one issue inevitably comes up when considering the question of responsibility: politics and its implications in the intellectual realm.[5] Among the many commentators who have constantly reflected on the meaning and importance of literary works there is a vast—and somewhat silent group—that has always reached, and still reaches, an immense audience, especially students and teachers: the writers of histories of literature and the editors of anthologies.[6]

These literary commentators who also assemble popular and widely available critical overviews, make selections of texts with one chief intention: to popularize and assess the literary production of a given geopolitical and geographical area and/or period. These exhibitions and appraisals of such representative selections amount to a definition of the respective people's cultural capabilities which, in turn frequently defines both the cultural profile and the social organization that allows for the existence of the literary production under scrutiny. Since these scrutinies are usually carried out with the intentions of memorializing intellectual prowess (hardly any encompassing literary survey is done to denigrate the literature of a region), this celebration also affects the cultural, social, and political contour of the society in question. Celebrating literature and its conditions of production is frequently a judgment on the kind of status quo involved and, as such, it is in most cases a celebration of that society's political state of affairs, which the critic deems acceptable, if not admirable. Assessments of literature made in too many anthologies and histories of Latin American literature are then hardly alien to politics.

Some of the critics explicitly present a view of textual production in Latin America as processes of study the realization of which implies the transformation of an undesirable kind of society into a desirable one. But these "liberal" critics do not comprise the majority of speakers for this wide and devoted audience mentioned before. The critics who are somewhat pleased with, or not bothered by, a status quo whose foundations were crafted in the colonial period do. The explanations given by most critics about what was written, what was meant by it, and what it means to us now in the literary production of Latin America (questions which the histories of Latin American literature intend to answer) have been issued from the location of the *letrado,* as it was known in the colonial period, and *intelectual,* as it is known today. Such locations correspond to a privileged vantage point where discourse and power merge and from which the lot of Latin American communities frequently have been, and still are, designed, redesigned, or obliterated.[7] Such location has always endowed the intellectual with an authority that makes possible and sustains the ample audiences they enjoy. "The voice of the masters" (González Echevarría 1985), as a well-known critic wants to have it, equals the utterances of successful critics, and since the audiences for them are always available and in increasing numbers, it matters to ask what the utterances convey. The place from which the "master" talks is not only very frequently a sheltered and placid one, but it is also a place from which to ensure the reproduction of these same places in the future. Such a place is too frequently associated with a sublime, essential activity, that of the writing and reading works of literary value for the edification and enjoyment mostly of those who have access to them.

One common operation in writing and reading about colonial Latin American realities is what I would call "textual cleansing," and it is exercised, at least, at two different and connected historical moments: (1) in the colonial times during the process of textual production by the writer; and (2) today by reading and teaching the text produced while reproducing this cleansing effect. This operation deliberately glosses American *loci*, and has been done in/about the *Indias Occidentales* and Latin America from the time the Spanish settled in the newly invaded land until today. An early case in point is Bernardo de Balbuena's praise of México after the conquest:

> Oh tú heroica beldad, saber profundo, / que por milagro puesta a los mortales / en todo fuiste la última del mundo; / criada en los desiertos arenales, / sobre que el mar del Sur resaca y quiebra / nácar lustroso y perlas orientales. (1941, 5) [Oh, you heroic beauty, profound knowledge, who by miracle were offered to mortals, in all you were last in the world, raised in sandy deserts, to which the *Mar del Sur* [Pacific Ocean] sends and shatters waves of white spume and oriental pearls.]

This glossing operation turns a site of invasion, plunder, massacres, and violent transfer of authority into an embellished clean setting that deliberately ignores the real conflictive relations among Natives and Europeans which took place from 1519 when the Spanish arrived in México to 1602–03 when the poem was composed. The same kind of glossing is most frequently found today in the process of creating a literary canon for particular territories and time frames identified with particular geopolitical spaces.

The aspiration of such an operation is to present samples of an all-encompassing, eternal, and essential capacity of special men to create beautiful literary works for an edifying contemplation during leisure time. The emphasis placed on beauty and virtuous edification as a justification for this kind of contented activity allows for a fracture between the concept of writing, as ethereal and splendid activity and space, and the crude realities of everyday life. The joy of satiating the human appetite for formal perfection and beauty becomes a natural and necessary endeavor that will reaffirm in those contemplating souls their connection with a quintessential human condition. The ability to enjoy or produce the intricacies of refined literature is, for that matter, a sign of being truly and properly a pure and identifiable subject, "human being," that is to say, a European or *criollo*, well-educated, well-off, urban gentleman, a *letrado,* an intellectual associated with a bigger entity called *Literatura latinoamericana.*

A case in point is Germán Arciniegas (to give an example of my country of origin). He is one of the most revered intellectuals in Colombia whose opinions on cultural history have been made available to a wide audience in local newspapers and in his numerous publications. His opinions have also been considered as a kind of spiritual guidance for the historical consciousness of the Colombian people.[8] In his 1979 review of *Desierto prodigioso y prodigio del desierto* (a hybrid seventeenth-century literary text written by Pedro de Solís y Valenzuela in 1650 and discovered only in 1962), Arciniegas makes a disturbing general characterization of the cultural region of central colonial Colombia: "Si el fondo de lo mexicano lo daban las guerras que conducía Cortés desde Tenochtitlán a Honduras, y el fondo del Perú los cuchillos y pólvora de los Pizarros y Almagros, *por los lados de Tunja* [were the text was composed] *todo eran místicas reflexiones en la muerte, vidas de San Bruno, charlas de cartujos, historias en verso, gongorismos desbordados*" [If the (historical) backdrop of México was provided by the wars waged by Cortés from Tenochtitlán to Honduras, and the one in Perú by the Pizarros and Almagros' knives and gun powder, *around Tunja all had to do instead with mystical reflections on death, the life of Saint Bruno, Carthusian monks chats, historical narrative, baroque verses . . .*].[9]

In Arciniegas' view, an active cultural legacy from the colonial Tunja region concerns itself only with lofty spiritual matters, not with crass dealings of commoners or unrefined individuals who do not spend their time singing in a European language the beauty of a land they do not—or no longer—enjoy (poor and poorly educated Indians and *mestizos* have always comprised the majority of the population of this region). As Arciniegas would have it, the Colombian central Plateau and its surroundings during the colonial period is one that can be solely and adequately characterized as a place of absorbed, ingenious, diligent, and well-off men who, in a placid countryside interrupted only by monasteries, recreate and imitate Mother Spain's Renaissance literary traditions. There are neither traces of the violence of the conquest, nor of the silent and harsh everyday collisions among different (culturally, racially, economically, politically, and gender-based) human groups who relate unequally to social and economic privileges; there are no signs of quarrels or divisions in the population of Spaniards and Euro-Americans whose cultural identity has been chosen by them then, and by Arciniegas in our times, to represent the cultural profile of the broad region called the New Kingdom of Granada. There is simply an Arcadia, full of nature-loving gentlemen, who by singing in verses in their ample leisure time, reflect on nature, beauty, and the mysteries of their material and spiritual existence.[10]

Such a cleansing notion is related to an obsession with the definition of the real character of a literature of Latin America very much linked to the obsession with the search for origins mentioned before. It is a lingering essentialist idea, inherited from Romanticism, in which a stable Latin American (literary) identity can be measured and assessed as part of a very long and venerable Pan-Hispanic cultural tradition. This conception, as a pernicious legacy of colonialism, is precisely the kind of colonizing intellectual operation we hope to contribute to dismantling with this volume of essays. The search for clear origins and stable essences of Latin American cultures presupposes the eradication of numerous non-European cultures into a Hispanic sameness, an eradication that more often than not involved the physical integrity of the practitioners of those cultures. As Antonio Cornejo Polar has explained discussing the heterogeneity of Latin American literature, these are the results of a destructive "colonial condition" "que destrozaba al sujeto y pervertía todas las relaciones (consigo mismo, con sus semejantes, con los nuevos señores, con el mundo, con los dioses, con el destino y sus deseos) que lo configuran como tal" [which destroyed the subject and perverted every relation he or she had (with herself, his fellow people, leaders, lords, destiny, and desires) and which had given him or her, his or her own identity] (1994, 19).

With such homogenizing postulation about the realm of literature many sectors of the Latin American population are consequently left out; from those who do not speak, read and/or write the European languages involved, to those who know them inadequately. They are all absent, as is subsequently, their negligible plight; unless they, as speakers of a particular "picturesque" linguistic trait, offer some "exotic" and interesting touch to a European literary tradition taking root in the Americas. Indians and African slaves, as subjects systematically overlooked, marginalized or downplayed in the historical and literary colonial writing of Latin America, have frequently found their way into contemporary literary criticism as mere mediums to enrich European literary languages. All the substantiality and validity of their existence as miserably colonized subjects gives way to a primary responsibility: to propitiate with their "exotic" presence the improvement of the European languages for their literary utilization in the Americas. Such a notion allows a critic like Luis Sáinz de Medrano (whose manuals of literature I have seen in the hands of our college students in Florida and Louisiana) to advance a carefree characterization of Spanish American literature as follows:

la presencia del factor negro, [que] ha representado un aporte del mayor interés a la literatura. En cuanto a lo indígena, ha tenido un valor de sustrato indiscutible en muchas obras y ha aflorado con deslumbradora originalidad en otras. Empleando un término nerudiano podríamos también definirla como literatura con *impurezas*. (1976, 119) [. . . the presence of a Negro element has provided a very interesting contribution to literature. As to the indigenous element, it has had an undeniable layer in many works and has surfaced with overwhelming originality in others. By using a [Pablo] Neruda's expression we could also define it as a literature with *impurities*.]

My problem with this kind of statement is not its information value, because certainly the presence of African and Native American speakers of non-European languages did in fact contribute to expand the vocabulary, syntactic variants, and conceptual usage of the European languages cultivated in the New World. Neither is there an explicit statement in Luis Sáinz de Medrano's (1976) texts indicating that the presence of millions of African and Native American subjects in the colonial period is validated *only* in their capacity to enrich a literary European language like Castillian. My problem with this kind of characterization resides in its power to present as "natural" the marginal position of non-European ethnic groups and their cultural idiosyncrasies, who are only portrayed as contributors to the "inevitable" development of the European culture in the Americas.

The Latin American territory has been, and still is, a place of pervasive and extreme violence in the everyday contact among people divided by social class, ethnic backgrounds, political views and access to privileges, all inside an immense cultural diversity very difficult to define under one single linguistic, cultural, political mantle. And the pervasiveness of such violent relations pertains to our modern times as to the times of the colonial struggles for those same reasons mentioned before. Assessments about textual productions, in order to be responsible, have to take into account such cultural and political complexity, and have to have sensitivity, or simply a sense of plain consideration for yesterday's and today's others. A glossing of those texts, in which social conditions are ignored or obliterated for the sake of aesthetic textual traits, will simply allow us to ignore the compelling realities of our history or be oblivious, for the sake of the *bellas letras,* to the plight of the Other (which we believe still exists).

II

In dealing with literature and the different social and cultural subjects in Latin America, recent critical works have not abandoned the old and drastic division between the social realm and the artistic one. Instead it has been turned into a totally exclusive contradiction. Faced with the impossibility of obliterating issues of slavery, exploitation, invasion of American territories, or racism, and the legacy of European colonialism in contemporary Latin American societies, recent attempts to assemble summaries of Latin American literature have had to contend with the double issue of "literature and social realities," which in the end is a euphemism for "literature and politics." But those attempts have not involved a transformation of old criteria, like the ones previously outlined, but a reconfirmation of them. Literature, as an insatiable, exaction-demanding entity, seeks contributions from reality for its own nourishment. As Sainz de Medrano has crudely put it, it accepts even "impure" offerings, like the ones provided by African or Native American groups.

[handwritten marginal note: BUT AS LONG AS THEY ARE OTHERS ONLY !]

Literature and politics, or creative textual elaborateness and basic realities cannot go together, unless the intellectual writer or reader wants to allow a depreciation of literature itself. In reworking this opposition, new significance has been given to that elated and morally befitting argument the French gentlemen gave Márquez Torres in Madrid in 1615. Literature is a dignified activity secluded from the ordinary chores and miseries of daily life, even though those miseries provide the writer with the spark to write well. Translated to the arena of many contemporary critics, Latin American literature becomes a highly acclaimed dissipation, which had to be constantly defended from spurious influences throughout its development in a racially, culturally, and socially conflictive scenario such as the Latin American one. An effective way to do that is by keeping literature from the blemishing of politics, lest it can turn into the simplicity of history.

A prominent and widely read critic of Latin American literature like José Miguel Oviedo starts by admitting that "la literatura es indudablemente un fenómeno social" (1995, 28) [literature is undoubtedly a social phenomenon], but the assessments of such nature tend to be exaggerated in two opposite directions. On the one hand, by what he calls "sociocrítica," which finds value in the texts only by appraising their merits as historical testimonies, or as "meros elementos de una ideología personal, de clase o de época, lo que permitiría colocar las obras en las distintas trincheras donde se libra la batalla por la liberación cultural" (28) [simple elements of an ideology (being personal, of social class, or of certain period), which would allow one to place the literary works in the different trenches where the battle for cultural liberation is fought]. This approach pays attention only to the informative aspect of literature, which is the most ephemeral, and which reduces literature to a simple weapon in said battle.

The other extreme, Oviedo continues, is presented by the "hiperformalistas" who have also reduced the study of literature, according to Oviedo, to a set of charts, mathematical formulas, logical models, and delineations. Such an approach implies studying literature as a reality torn from its roots, as if it were a system or mechanism that functions with autonomy typical of pure scientific objects in a lab (1995, 28). In light of such a polarization Oviedo offers his own alternative in which the acceptance of the social nature of literature should be just "un punto de partida, no de llegada" [a point of departure, not a destination]. But such an apparently healthy tendency towards a middle ground does not brook a simple question like: where does this point of departure lead us? The answer is: to the understanding of literature's essential value which, according to Oviedo "está en otra parte" (28) [it is located somewhere else]. That so-called somewhere else refers to an ideal, privileged region in which social reality has no place despite its importance in the production of literature itself. In Oviedo's own words: "Su origen es social, con claras connotaciones históricas y cargas ideológicas, su significado profundo se sitúa más allá:

precisamente en lo que *añade* a su tiempo y lo excede. Del subsuelo histórico extrae su alimento y estímulo, pero se levanta como algo que aquél no puede explicar del todo (1995, 28). [{Literature's} origin is social, with clear historical connotations and ideological burdens {but} its profound significance is located further onward: precisely in what it *adds* to its age to exceed it. From the historical subsoil it extracts its nourishment and stimulus, but it elevates itself from it, as something which that subsoil cannot explain thoroughly].

This essential *addendum* that literature is able to produce, like an extraordinary and marvelous capacity to single itself out from the commonness of general writing, corresponds also to a distinguished space to which only chosen individuals can accede, that is, those gentlemen who have the special cultural formation to truly appreciate that literature. With this kind of argument, what Oviedo ends up doing is authorizing a sort of thoughtless reading of literature, one in which the reader is ethically empowered to ignore the cultural and social subsoil and devote it to searching for that marvelous addendum. With this same argument Oviedo not only recreates the aforementioned division between social reality and true literature but also reduces social and cultural realities to simple instruments for the better appreciation of that *added*, sublime element that comprises legitimate literature.

Put in this way, my contention here could be taken as prejudicial against the cultivation of beauty, especially when we are dealing with many verbal artifacts constructed with esthetic purposes. But my dispute is not with the pursuit of esthetical beauty nor with the availability of leisure time to do so, since such a capacity is not a privilege of Euro-Americans in the newly conquered American lands but of any people of any culture, period and social class; my complaint has to do with the widely held opinion of contemporary commentators that the verbal construction of a privileged minority, with all its specific views of the world, can be counted as representative of all the different kinds of individuals in a given territory, and by the very dubious omissions that the sole pursue of genealogies of beauty frequently entails. Leisure and its aesthetic practices, on the other hand, should be a fundamental part of all social classes in a society, but that is not the case; as a result, presenting the exquisite artistic products of a segment of the population who have access to that leisure as reflecting the feelings and outlooks of different peoples sharing a given territory—many of whom do not have access to such leisure—is an irresponsible assertion or, at best, a naïve illusion.

III

The great ascendancy and exposure of Oviedo's type of view is closely related to the strength enjoyed by the narrow and violently homogenizing perspective of Hispanism established in the United States by the Spanish philological and stylistic schools. These schools have benefited from persistent waves of Hispanic immigrants prompted either by national conflagrations such as the Spanish Civil War (1936–39), the Cuban Revolution (1959), military repression in Chile (1973) and in Argentina (1974), and so forth, or by individual searches for better research conditions and higher paying jobs as educators. Despite the variety of origins and political tendencies of these immigrants, the fact remains that most Spanish schools of this sort, when they arrived, have been not only quite conservative, but also, as it has been pointed out, "virulently antispeculative and antitheoretical" (Avelar 1999, 51).

Without intending to monumentalize here the critical contributions to colonial Latin American studies presented so far by very active scholars such as Rolena Adorno, Walter Mignolo, Hernán Vidal, and Antonio Cornejo Polar (whose recent death we very much lament), their reflections on the relations between cultural production and the social and economic power have presented an alternative to the dominant Hispanism.[11] In doing so, they have shattered the attractive notion of historical, ideological, and cultural homogeneity advocated by the old schools and expressed in generalizing concepts like Patricia Seed's "colonial discourse."[12] Their positions on these issues have intended to protect the decolonizing and combatant thrust of colonial Latin American studies from the dangers of institutionalization.[13] If not constantly addressed, the tendency toward institutionalization would result in the upholding of the status, the opposition to which gave origin to their colonial Latin American studies in the first place.

This danger is particularly real in the departments of Spanish and Romance languages in the American universities where we, the majority of the practitioners of these studies work, and where the triumphant neo-liberal policies of globalization currently exercise great pressure over the teaching of Castillian language. Spanish (as opposed to French, Italian, or Portuguese) is the most popular language among North American students, and the respective departments or sections are the only ones still steadily growing. As Avelar put it: "The underlying assumption here is that Spanish will be crucial for conquering unexplored markets in Latin America as well as fully incorporating into consumption the growing Spanish-speaking population of the United States (1999, 50)." What this means is that in the departments of Spanish or Romance languages, and in the graduate programs where we conduct our teaching, research, and writing, most of our students of Spanish and respective administrators have expectations directly linked to the development of modern capitalism, and particularly to the expansion of neo-liberal policies that seek to affect the majority of the Hispanic population in Latin America and the United States itself. This raises the question of Hispanic immigrants to the United States, particularly in the last decades, which range from those seeking immediate opportunities compatible with their low level of income and education, and those with more years of schooling who seek to pursue a higher education and/or eventually, like many of us, hold higher paying jobs in American institutions.

Hispanic studies in the United States, especially those linked to departments of foreign languages, have resorted traditionally to this pool of Hispanic immigrants to develop, sometimes with great results, their graduate programs in Spanish.[14] Many of us have followed this system by pursuing doctoral degrees and taking advantage of the teaching assistantship system in the departments of Spanish (which allows also low-income intellectual immigrants to study in this country), and by eventually joining the faculty of graduate and undergraduate programs throughout this country. From a more advantageous position than in Latin America or Spain (due to the greater availability of resources such as grants, libraries, archives collections, symposia, travel monies, etc.), many of us interested in Colonial Latin American studies have initiated in the last twenty years, and in the context of an active and constant dialogue with North American scholars, a re-reading of primordial colonial narratives from diverse regions of Latin America.

The tendency of these rereadings has been generally more critical than celebratory, their focus has been frequently the geopolitical region of origin of the intellectual immigrant, and their interdisciplinary approaches have considered the texts studied not merely as aesthetic artifacts, but also as sites of tensions between discourse and power. For these same reasons it is frequently found that our contributions emulate critical projects of another type of immigrant—this time from the East—like Edward Said or Homi Bhabha—who have reflected, with postcolonial theoretical tools, on the cultural and political conditions of their respective regions of origin by questioning European colonialism regarding them. Aside from Antonio Cornejo Polar, Sara Castro Klarén, and Walter Mignolo, whose contributions have greatly advanced the field of colonial Latin American studies in the United States and Latin America, this group of Hispanic immigrants is enhanced by scholars such as José Rabasa, Gustavo Verdesio, Roger Zapata, Mabel Moraña, Mario Cesareo, Mariselle Meléndez, José Antonio Mazzotti, Verónica Salles-Reese, Luis Fernando Restrepo, and Alvaro Félix Bolaños, to name just some of those whose contributions are already found in book form (see bibliography).

In spite of the many advances in modern theoretical tools such as cultural theory in the study of colonial Latin American discourses made by Hispanic, North American, and European scholars today (including individuals such as Rolena Adorno, Maureen Ahern, Stephanie Merrim, Karen Stolley, Kathleen Ross, Kathleen Myers, Jerry Williams, Sabine MacCormack, Patricia Seed, Mary Louise Pratt, John Beverley, Peter Hume, Jorge Klor de Alva, Stacey Schlau, Antony Higgins, Neil Larsen etc.), most of the readings and studies made in universities—here and in Latin America—are still affected by the premises of Hispanism. How successful have epistemological and methodological contributions such as the concepts of "lettered city" (Rama 1984), "sociocultural heterogeneity (Cornejo Polar 1994), "colonial semiosis" (Mignolo 1989), "colonial discourse for sixteenth- and seventeenth-century Spanish America" (Adorno 1993) been if we take as an indication of this success a diminishing of tendentious notions of Hispanism in readings and criticism made today by the average reader? How are colonial Latin American texts read today by the selected group of scholars that write widely consulted guides for the study of Latin American literature?

This situation poses a challenge to every Latin Americanist: to strengthen and maintain the decolonizing thrust of colonial Latin American studies by taking these alternative critical approaches to the level of the less sophisticated, albeit most numerous, group of readers with whom we interact in our classrooms and advising sessions: our undergraduate and graduate students of Spanish language and Spanish American literature.[15] A challenge like this also poses a series of questions: how can we (immigrant and native scholars in the United States and scholars in Latin America) participate in this—in my view—necessary process of decolonization? What implications does the immigrant Latin Americanist condition of many of us have in the development of this process? What kind of relation should there be between the institutionalized departments and centers of Spanish and Latin American studies (on which many of us depend economically) and the decolonizing readings proposed by scholars like Mignolo, Adorno, Cornejo Polar, and Vidal, among others? Do we all—native or immigrant educators in this country—have any significant control in this relation?

Why would the U.S. university system reward with high salaries, excellent benefits, and superb conditions to conduct research and teaching those successful scholars carrying out these decolonizing projects? How far would we, as scholars, allow this decolonizing project to go before they affect the privileged and the generally comfortable position acquired in the U.S university system? What kind of relation does the generally conservative and complaisant Hispanism have with this decolonizing process? And finally, under the vigorous economic, ideological, and political pressures of commercial projects like NAFTA in the North American continent, how can we oppose the tendency to reduce colonial Latin American studies to a simple celebration of the virtues of the Castillian language, a language that during the colonial period and today has been widely taught for the sake of imperial or corporate interests?

IV

The great diversity of the Latin American population (with its different cultures, races, miscegenations, histories, and distributions of wealth and privileges) usually prompts among scholars of all origins, an urgent need to homogenize that diversity when considering the cultural history of this territory. One of the earliest and most renowned attempts to homogenize the literature of the Latin American territory around the Iberian culture was Marcelino Menéndez Pelayo's in his history and anthology of Latin American poetry in the nineteenth century. Adopting the celebratory mode characteristic in most literary histories and anthologies, Menéndez Pelayo's contribution was commissioned by the *Real Academia Española* in 1892 in order to pay tribute to Spain's triumphs in the Americas by publishing such an anthology and a literary history on the fourth centenary of Christopher Columbus's first voyage.

This literary celebration and canonization made by Spaniards and *criollos* implies a clear segregationist approach when dealing with such a multicultural and multiethnic territory as Latin America.[16] As Menéndez Pelayo points out, the title of the work shows clearly its "natural" limits. "Trátase sólo de la poesía castellana en América" [it deals only with Castillian poetry in America] (1948, 9). Poetry in the Portuguese language is prudently excluded for reasons of academic territoriality,[17] but many other languages spoken in this same territory—and their respective aesthetic expressions—are excluded without scruple on the grounds of the supposed inferiority and degeneracy of the native cultures that produced them. In such an openly colonizing and violently homogenizing operation all the aesthetic verbal artifacts of the territory formerly known as *Indias Occidentales* are equated with the literature composed and written in Castillian language, a literature that reflects only a Spanish cultural legacy crafted around the Spanish imperial experience in America, and conceived generally from the viewpoint of the victors in such experience.

I consider relevant to bring up Menéndez Pelayo's archaic case at this point because his project still has great acceptance today. In remembering Menéndez Pelayo here, I am referring to one of the most recent affirmations of the canon of Latin American literature which, although more cautious and subtle, is still based in central notions of Hispanism of the Menéndez Pelayo type such as: (1) cultural and linguistic unity of a literature capable of representing the Latin American territory; (2) Latin American literature as descending from European cultural traditions; and (3) the enrichment of this European tradition when entering into contact with different cultural traces in the Latin American territory. For reasons of its great importance, visibility and availability before a vast, growing and regular readership of Latin American literature, I want to turn my attention to the introductory justifications of the prestigious *The Cambridge History of Latin American Literature* (*CH*), edited by Roberto González Echevarría, and Enrique Pupo-Walker in 1996.

Applying a universal concept of culture to the entire Latin American territory entails great efforts in homogenizing characteristics of that territory based on different appreciations of its historical, social, and racial vicissitudes. For instance, José Martí looked for a common history and destiny of this territory (which he called "Nuestra América") by including all its human and cultural elements (*criollos*, Indians, blacks, and local knowledges) in his search of a future and better society (Martí 1980, 9–18). Menéndez Pelayo, for different reasons, also unified this territory in which, according to him, a mediocre extension of Spanish culture flourished and had to be tolerated; José Enrique Rodó and José Vasconcelos see this same territory unified by Mediterranean cultural traces in an Iberian version, which offers the possibility of racial unity around a cultural ideal more Latin than Anglo-Saxon. González Echevarría and Pupo-Walker, on the other hand, attempt this unification in a fashion similar to Menéndez Pelayo's although insisting on the notion that the current Spanish American literary products are exceptional developments of the literary tradition in Castillian language in Spanish America. When considering the entire Latin American territory, González Echevarría and Pupo-Walker include the literature in the Portuguese language of Brazil, but the inclusion of this European language does not obstruct the eurocentric homogenizing effect described here. Quite the contrary, it reaffirms it since it incorporates in their history and anthology a language of a second colonizing and imperialist power during colonial times.

Besides their efforts to pin down a cultural identity definable in absolute terms, in all the cases mentioned there is a drastic homogenization that obliterates the overwhelming linguistic and cultural diversity of this vast territory. The general preface to the *CH* starts by comparing this History with Menéndez Pelayo's, and thus placing it in this old tradition of Hispanism.[18] According to the editors' explanation, the *CH* is a sort of testimony of the origin and development of the respectability acquired by Latin American literature vis-à-vis Spanish and European literary expectations. In other words, the entire textual production of the Caribbean, Meso-American, Andean, Amazonian, and River Plate regions can be explained in relation with their adaptation to Western readers' aesthetic norms and tastes. This literature of a single language and derived from a central European tradition is also, and essentially, a cosmopolitan literature.[19] We are then talking only about the literature written in European languages (especially Castillian) and circulating mainly among a well-educated urban population, who reads, speaks, and writes those languages well. In a plain definition, that brings to mind Menéndez Pelayo's style when he speaks about Latin American poetry as an extension of the Spanish literature, González Echevarría and Pupo-Walker declare: "The burden of Latin American culture is a Western culture that extends back to the Middle Ages, when the foundations of the Spanish empire in the New World were set" (1996, xvi).

Not all the contributions related to colonial Latin American literature in this *CH* share the editors ideological orientation (the articles by Rolena Adorno, Stephanie Merrim, Thomas Skidmore, and Karen Stolley are good examples), but the influence of this orientation is more pervasive than the influence of these exceptions. Although González Echevarría and Pupo-Walker make great efforts to be inclusive by bringing into the *CH* literatures from diverse geographical, cultural, and racial spaces, as well as both genders (there are articles on colonial, Brazilian, black, Chicano, and women literatures), the neat definition they make of their project confirms the pervasiveness of the old tradition of Hispanism institutionalized by Menéndez Pelayo. "In short, the editors feel that our *History* is a reassessment and expansion of the canon of Latin American literature, seen in a broad, new-world context" (1996, xiii).

What is the problem—it could be asked—with gathering together a group of texts written in the same language and produced in an immense territory unified by Spanish colonization during three centuries? After all, due precisely to this common denominator, those texts share cultural and historical traditions that facilitate the kind of Pan-Hispanic unification sought here by these editors. In my view there are two problems with such project: first, this is a desired and easily imagined unity based on the common cultural Westernization endured throughout the territory known today as *América latina;* but it is, at the same time, an aspiration as illusory as the Pan-Latin American unifications imagined by José Enrique Rodó and José Vasconcelos. The second problem is that when the issue is presented this way, it is easy to fall into the assumption that Western cultural traditions (in Spanish version) enjoy an essential centrality capable of providing points of reference to understand the diverse cultural productions of this vast Latin American region.

The problem of the unity of Latin American literature amidst the very different regional characteristics is resolved by González Echevarría and Pupo-Walker by resorting to the concept of "tradition" in which they take, as points of reference, homogenizing works produced by the most celebrated authors of the territory.[20] Successful writers (García Márquez, Octavio Paz, Borges, etc.), with a literature written in Castillian language and from a European tradition, surpass national frontiers and local thematic tendencies: "the stronger authors and works—the editors say—cross frontiers or dwell on the homology. They constitute a kind of overreaching literature to which all aspire" (xiii).

Nevertheless, the concept of "tradition," as an individual's construction (or of a homogeneous group of individuals), responds to the creation of a sort of personal genealogy. It is a desired creation of origins from which the individual or group believes or desires to descend. Such construction depends heavily on a contemporary validation of those antecedents considered as the base for the celebrated literary products considered exemplary today. The construction of a "tradition" is an ideological effort of justification of a literary status quo or a discursive tendency deemed worthy of reproduction in the future. Based on such notion of tradition, the editors of the *CH* find a strong link between the Latin American cultural past and the celebrated literary tradition of the present. "If the Iberian Middle Ages, Renaissance, and Baroque are such a powerful presence in Latin American literature, then this literature shares a living past with its metropolitan counterparts" (xiv).

Once the tradition that will be the object of study of this *CH* has been defined, the editors proceed to characterize the study of colonial literature as one dedicated mainly to elucidating the colonial sources of contemporary masterpieces.[21] Therefore, the purpose of literary criticism—according to these editors—is to contribute to create a single and encompassing literature for the entire territory. "The recuperation of the colonial period, when Spanish America was one, is part of this struggle to constitute a continental literature with a common origin and discourse" (xiii). The great increase in colonial literary studies, so much celebrated by these editors, does not include the critical contributions of colonial semiosis nor the postcolonial theory. Those cannot be included because they question not only colonialism (and its epistemological operations in texts produced and read yesterday and today), but also the very notion of Pan-Hispanism (so dear and crucial for these editors), which intends to explain away the diverse cultural configuration of the Latin American territory.

It has not been my purpose here to finish off with the study of European literature nor of its influence in the literature produced in the Latin American territory. Neither am I proposing to oppose the production of macrostudies like the *CH*.[22] What I want to point out is that very frequently these kinds of studies chimerically aspire to define the literature of the entire cultural and geographic Latin American space, and in such rigid attempt they reproduce simplifications of this complex social and cultural territory in the same way the Spanish and Euro-American colonizers did for so many years. I also intend to indicate that studies like those by Menéndez Pelayo and González Echevarría and Pupo-Walker are occupied solely with the European literary tradition in the Latin American territory, and that their approach ignores—or reduces to mere supplementary factors—other cultural traditions.

An alternative has to consider a notion of literary studies that takes into account cultures, languages, and their traces still present in the territory in question, which in the Latin American case, implies the consideration of rhetorical, axiological, epistemological, semantic, and thematic influences in the texts of different cultures. Caribbean, Andean, Meso-American, River Plate cultures—among others—should be included, and some could be native (like the American aboriginal ones), and some immigrant (like the Iberian and African ones). Two common arguments against this kind of proposal are that we, as teachers of literature and/or as literary critics usually have command only of European languages, and that the likelihood that educational institutions would create departments of Nahuatl, Navajo, Quechua, or Aymara languages is minimal.

As to the first argument, we can start by presenting to our audiences models of study that do not ward off the existence of other verbal aesthetic productions because they are not transmitted by European languages—as Hispanism and Pan-Hispanic tendencies do—and we can always direct our audiences to the proper (and growing in numbers) specialists and bibliographies on those subjects. As to the second argument, there is a growing interest in the United States and in Latin America in developing programs in native American languages. Some of those programs include: Kaqchikel Maya (Department of Anthropology, at Tulane University), Yucatec Maya (Duke/University of North Carolina Program in Latin American Studies), Nahualtl Summer Language Institute (Yale University), Bolivian Quechua (Latin American Center UCLA), Bolivian Quechua in Cochabamba (Latin American Studies Program, Cornell University), Summer Intensive Quichua Institute (University of Wisconsin-Madison), Intensive Quechua in Cusco-Perú (Latin American and Caribbean Studies, University of Michigan). In The Latin American case: Cetlalic Escuela Alternativa (The Tlahuica Center for language and Cultural Exchange, Cuernavaca, México). The study of native languages has increased throughout Latin America with the incorporation of social, cultural, and political indigenous issues in regional and national political agendas.[23] Studies of colonial Latin American discourse involving non-European cultural and epistemological legacies have begun to be undertaken by an increasing number of scholars not committed to the old Pan-Hispanic project, although its influence has hardly surpassed the limits of the specialized intellectual circles.[24]

"La colonia continuó viviendo en la república" [the colonial status continued living in the republic], said José Martí in his essay "Nuestra América" over a century ago. Curiously, or regrettably, the colonial maladies he encountered as obstacles for the improvement of the conditions in which the Latin American population lived in the nineteenth century still have currency today: arrogance of the metropolitan centers, contempt for native traditions, excessive attention and veneration of Western cultural traditions, and marginalization and hostility towards indigenous groups.[25] When considering a living cultural universe, like the one found in the colonial period, the unification of a diverse linguistic and cultural territory under a single European language is a colonialist project to be dismantled, no longer in Martí's republic, but in the globalization of our new millennium. One way to start is by considering in our reflections on literature and culture, based on Eurocentric epistemological patterns, the vast heterogeneity of Latin America, and its reality of sheer misery and injustice. By not abandoning the chimerical homogenization proposed by Hispanism when dealing with this, frequently and exceptionally depressing Latin American reality, we run the risk of falling into the illusion that extracting only artistic traces from its complex discourses is feasible without falsifying reality. "Por eso nada tan burdamente pérfido como estetizar—o literaturizar—una realidad minuciosa y radicalmente inhumana" [That is why there is nothing more crudely perfidious than turning into aesthetics—or literature—an exhaustively and radically inhuman reality] (Cornejo Polar 1994, 23).

The vast and complex textual production in the territory we know as Latin America, whether within European or non-European modes of expression, has been realized for centuries inside the insidious dynamic that Walter Mignolo called a "Colonial Situation" (1989), and Cornejo Polar a "Colonial condition" (1994), and whose legacy still operates today. The textual cleansing operation exercised when reading and teaching colonial Latin American texts, the aesthetization of socially and politically complex literary discourses, as well as the violent homogenization of cultural diversity have been promoted and encouraged not only by colonial and now corporate powers, but also in great part by the very nature of the social space in which we, as teachers of Latin American literature, operate. This social space is an academic locus that has been largely developed in the schools of philology and history of Castillian language and literature, and which has been devoted to celebrate and monumentalize the destiny of Iberian languages in the American territories. This same locus tends to naturalize our own personal condition as middle or upper class, well-educated individuals who, like the French diplomats in Madrid in 1615, enjoy a space to contemplate literature and defend our hold on such space. Let us hope that what can be an understandable defense of our empowered position to direct our audiences' understandings of texts of the past, does not degenerate (as happened with those French diplomats who wanted Cervantes to continue being poor) into a contribution to the naturalization of the material or cultural disenfranchisement of past or contemporary "Others."

V

José Rabasa's article is a reprint (first published in 1994) that opens up this collection as an emblematic essay. From its title we took the idea for the title of this collection. Rabasa examines a pre-Columbian text produced under European control (mid-sixteenth-century *Códice Mendoza),* and a 1692 account by a *criollo* writer on a violent Indian uprising and its brutal repression by Spanish authorities (Carlos de Sigüenza y Góngora's *Alboroto y motín de los indios de México).* Rabasa looks at indigenous active and passive resistance to Westernization and the treatment of violence in colonialist discourse. He opposes notions of "monumental history" that impose ideas of our present in the past and proposes an archaeology of the historiography of pre-Columbian Meso-America and of its impact on disenfranchised indigenous peoples of later times.

In a similar vein, Cora Lagos also studies *Códice Mendoza* (which recounts the history of México-Tenochtitlán from its foundation in 1345 until its destruction in 1520). She looks at the confrontation of indigenous pictographic and

European alphabetical writing systems and its dynamics of power and violence. The codex is seen as a resistant pictographic structure transmitted through the medium of orality whose presence destabilizes the idea of the European alphabet as the main (or only) element of communication/contact in colonial contexts.

Luis Fernando Restrepo's contribution considers the writings of/about a sixteenth-century *mestizo* (mixed-raced), don Diego de Torres, *cacique* (Amerindian chief) of Turmequé, in the New Kingdom of Granada (present-day Colombia). He first considers how this historical figure has been narrativized as a colonial subject and as an element of an imagined community's narrative time from the colonial period to the twentieth century. He then focuses on Diego de Torres's texts and two maps produced for the Crown as a counter-colonial discourse that underscores the complex process of narrating the self and a community. Rafael Landívar's *Rusticatio Mexicana* (a little read colonial text, and much less in its original language, Latin), is the focus of Antony Higgins' study entitled, *(Post-) Colonial Sublime*. He examines the text's treatment of an imposing and portentous nature and of political events that have to be controlled. Notions of a baroque and neoclassic divinity aid the examination of these controlling strategies in the text and in the author's inspiration. It is also aided by a discussion on the nature of the sublime. This essay manages to discuss both technical details of Landívar's poetic composition and his political stand he amply expressed throughout his poem.

Stacey Schlau in her essay, *Gendered Crime and Punishment in New Spain*, studies two sixteenth- and seventeenth-century cases of inquisitional repression over women who sought subjectivity in history through spiritual transcendence. By examining texts of the inquisitional trials of Barbara Echegaray and Teresa Romero Zapata (both accused and convicted of being *Ilusas*), this essay traces the sociopolitical and religious construction of what Schlau calls "gendered heresy," which particularly targeted poor urban *criollo* women. In her analysis of the strategies of repression of women's social and religious transgressions, Schlau points out the self-righteous rhetoric with which the male accusers composed the trial documents, a rhetoric that displayed rigid stereotypical notions about women. A set of articles from the eighteenth-century Peruvian newspaper *Mercurio Peruano* written by males about females occupies Mariselle Meléndez's attention. Her contention is that the patriarchal society of that time (like in our contemporary states) considered women's social and spatial mobility, as well as female racial and cultural differences, as a threat that had to be closely monitored and controlled. The diverse, multiple, and conflictive configuration of the society since the colonial period makes women's mobility and managing of their bodies a great concern for the male empowered sector of the population.

The study of the development of a *criollo* Spanish-American identity, as expressed in sixteenth- to eighteenth-century epic poetry (a topic that has been neglected before) is what engages José Antonio Mazzotti's contribution. A Creole elite in the Peruvian case equates the Dragon (Francis Drake) and "heretical" non-European groups in the development of this identity. His essay shows how some members of that *criollo* elite used literary forms to enact their desire of social harmony in sixteenth- to eighteenth-century Lima. The authors and works in which Mazzotti finds these trends and strategies of national identity are Pedro de Oña and his *Arauco domado* (1596), Juan de Miramontes and his *Armas antárticas* (1921 [1608]), and Pedro Peralta Barnuevo and his *Lima fundada* (1732). By doing so they established from the late-sixteenth century on a discursive pattern that would pervade in the enlightened period and would model, if not the rhetoric of Independence, at least the strategies of social control and organization of the Republic.

Álvaro Félix Bolaños, on the other hand, takes a look at a well-known seventeenth-century historical treatise, *El carnero,* written by *criollo* writer Juan Rodríguez Freile. This text has been considered by most literary critics as an ambiguous discourse (a text hesitating between authorial imagination and objective referentiality) attempting to become an expression of a European literary genre in the American territory. The European literary genre that *El carnero* supposedly struggles to turn into is identified very frequently with the picaresque novel and such identification requires one to consider Freile's text as a narrative of only, or mainly, Spaniards and *criollo* subjects. Bolaños' essays deconstructs this premise and pays attention to the native subjectivity that is so ubiquitous in the text and so persistently downplayed or ignored by Freile himself and endorsed by most commentators since the seventeenth century.

According to Gustavo Verdesio, the physical and cultural appropriation of the American landscape, as a violent axiological and epistemological act performed by sixteenth-century European writers about the *Indias Occidentales,* is a colonizing intellectual operation in complicity with colonialism that still prevails today, even in the works of fiction writers and critics who claim to oppose it or question it (Juan José Saer and Abel Posse). The rewriting of Latin American history supposedly attempted by these fiction writers, and uncritically endorsed by most commentators today, amounts to reducing the role of pre-Columbian subjectivity to aiding in the legitimation of the privileged position of enunciation of the *criollo* subject, a subject that emits his/her discourse from a modern nation-state built by *criollo* elites. Such a rewriting of history does not alter much the conquistadors' view.

NOTES

I appreciate different commentaries offered by Julio Schvartzman, Jerry Williams, Luis F. Restrepo, Antony Higgins, Edward Baker, and Jonathan Tittler. Special thanks to the Humanities Scholarship Enhancement Fund of the University of Florida for providing a space to write this chapter.

1. See "Aprobación" by *licenciado* Márquez Torres, part II, in Cervantes (1979).

2. I disagree with the tenets of Hispanism as will be seen, but at the same time I am a reader, a teacher, and a lover of literature in Spanish language, hence my quotation of Cervantes.

3. I understand the term *criollo* as a member of a segment of the population (in the *Indias Occidentales* yesterday, and in Latin America today) that has preserved and reproduced a Western cultural legacy, a kind of social organization, a system of distribution of wealth and power that came from the Iberian peninsula and has benefited Europeans, Euro-Americans, and other Westernized elites since the colonial period. Well-intended definitions of *criollo* have departed from the premise that social, racial, and economic differences are somehow erased or diminished in Latin American when such a term is properly applied in cultural assessments. "*Criollo*, en lengua española, es un término que designa distinciones de carácter cultural. Los criollos somos los que, sea cual sea el color de nuestra piel, nos hemos criado de este lado del charco y hablamos y pensamos en español con sutiles matices americanos" (Arrom 1971, 26) [*Criollo*, in Spanish language, is a term that designates distinctions of the cultural kind. We, the criollos, are those who, regardless the color of our skin, have been raised on this side of the lake [the Atlantic Ocean] and speak and think in Spanish with subtle American tones].

4. This privileged position of the intellectual goes back to the colonial period, as Angel Rama has illustrated. A vast and always growing group of *letrados* was formed to be in charge of ensuring that the Spanish Monarchy's business of colonization ran smoothly. The demands of this colonial administration and the evangelization of Indians created both a staggering number of *letrados* concentrated mainly in the cities and what Rama calls "la ciudad letrada." (Rama 1984).

5. The great ascendancy that the Latin American intellectual—particularly the novelist—has over the destiny of his/her respective geopolitical regions is best illustrated (for the nineteenth century) by Doris Sommer's seminal study. "If nations were to survive and to prosper, they had to mitigate racial and regional antagonisms and to coordinate the most diverse national sectors through the hegemony of an enlightened elite; that is through mutual consent rather than coercion" (1991, 123). That mitigation and coordination was aptly aided by national fictions of racial and cultural unity in a social system that benefited mainly the empowered *criollo* elite.

6. González Echevarría (1996, 7–32) gives a good overview of the initial production of literary histories and anthologies of literature in Spanish language in the former Spanish territories in America.

7. Rama's work reminds us—as Verdesio puts it—that we, the intellectuals, are inheritors of a hegemonic culture that demolished the existence of untold local oral cultures and, in writing the history of such destruction, turned those communities into objects appropriated by the written word (Verdesio 1997, 242).

8. Juan Gustavo Cobo Borda attributes to Arciniegas's works a power to inspire in his fellow Colombians *mayor agudeza*, [greater judiciousness] and as a result

they acquire *"libertad y autonomía cultural"* [freedom and cultural autonomy] (1987, 15). An even more enthusiast admirer calls him "Maestro" with capital "M," "ser extraordinario" [extraordinary human being], "el más *grande* escritor colombiano del *siglo*" [the greatest Colombian writer of the twentieth century] (Tamayo Fernández 1998, 19).

9. "El Tiempo", Bogotá, 11 de mayo de 1979 (emphasis added). Why do I put so much emphasis on Arciniegas's opinion expressed in a humble local newspaper article, instead of on his books about the history of the contact between America and Europe (for instance, his 1937 *América tierra firme* or his 1975 *América en Europa*)? Because the daily *El Tiempo* has a wide audience in Colombia, and be cause the pressure of the particular celebration that Arciniegas is making, as well as the limitations of space, force him to expose his essential notions about cultural history and to clearly outline desirable reading selections for the general public. The average Colombian reader is more frequently exposed to the cultural and literary sections *El Tiempo* (and *El Espectador*, *El País*, or *El Colombiano*, for that matter), than to specialized books such as Arciniegas's.

10. On the violent and gruesome conquest of the region in which the city of Tunja was founded, see Fray Pedro Simón's *Segunda noticia historial*, chapter xxvi, Vol. III, 260), and Juan de Castellanos's *Cuarta parte, Canto sexto*, 1202. On the conquest of the *muzo* Indians (adjacent to the Tunja area) see Rodríguez Baquero (1995), on the quarrels among Spaniars and *criollos* in this same region, see Rodríguez Freile (1978).

11. The general assumption of these Latin Americanist scholars is that philological and aesthetic criticism is inadequate to study colonial texts. Such inadequacy had to do with the exclusive emphasis it places on the development of aesthetic qualities of the Castillian language, which in turn allows for the concentration of attention solely on: (1) the person of the author and the literary work as a pure entity (which essentializes aesthetic verbal skills of Western or Westernized subjects); (2) textual typologies (which turn European literary genres into preferred objects of critical attention); and (3) the notion of literary schools or movements (which demanded the creation and affirmation of a literary canon and the tracing of the so-called literary traditions in European languages). Alternative methodologies developed lately (as Adorno has illustrated [1988]), include the replacement of the notion of "literature" (as a practice limited to the European and aesthetic) by the notion of "discourse" (which includes silenced voices); the question of the "Other" (as a multilingual and multicultural subject); the contributions of different disciplines like history, anthropology, and different approaches like feminist and cultural theory; the issue of positionality (social, cultural, economic, and political stand of the authors); and the factors of colonization as a social and cultural context of great influence in the production and reception of the texts or discourses studied.

12. I am referring to Patricia Seed's 1991 review article entitled, "Colonial and Postcolonial Discourse," on five interdisciplinary studies in historical and literary texts, relating to the Spanish colonialist experience; in this article, she made a sort of institutionalization of the new methodology of colonial studies. Seed baptized

this methodology with the term "Colonial and Postcolonial Discourse" and the omissions she made and the rigidity of her definitions unleashed a healthy debate with Walter Mignolo, "Colonial and Postcolonial Discourse," (1993), Hernán Vidal "The Concept of Colonial and Postcolonial Discourse," (1993), and Rolena Adorno, "Reconsidering Colonial Discourse . . ." (1993) published two years later.

13. There is no doubt that these intellectuals' individual intentions with their respective critical projects are decolonizing; but two factors might interfere with that good intention if they were to grow complaisant (1) the multiple, and some times chaotic, forms that their collective criticism adopts (colonial semiosis, social and cultural heterogeneity, subaltern studies, etc.), which might end up essentializing the "Other" or losing sight of it; and (2) every critic's individual comfortable conditions linked to very prestigious teaching institutions not necessarily interested in developing anti-hegemonic processes.

14. This large pool of immigrants comes mainly from Spain and Latin America and include individuals of different critical approaches: Vicente Lloréns, Américo Castro, Tomás Navarro Tomás, Pedro Salinas, Jorge Guillén, Luis Cernuda, Emir Rodríguez Monegal, Roberto González Echevarría, Sara Castro-Klarén, Raquel Chang-Rodríguez, José Miguel Oviedo, Julio Ortega, Walter Mignolo, and many others.

15. I am aware of my own risky homogenizing notion of an "average reader," which I identify now with our own students. This group has not only to include the increasing number of teachers of literature in Spanish language at the high school and college levels in this country, but also those who consult regularly relevant and available anthologies and literary histories. It should also include administrators who make decisions to create or close academic programs.

16. In Menéndez Pelayo's view this project was a joint endeavor of Spaniards and some Spanish-Americans of good will, all united by a common respect for "la integridad de la lengua patria, y por el culto de unas mismas tradiciones literarias, que para todos deben ser familiares y gloriosas" [the integrity of the mother tongue, and the respect for common literary traditions, at the same time glorious and well known by all] (1948, 7).

17. Menéndez Pelayo cites a 1836 work by Fernando Wolf that already dealt with Brazilian literature as a first reason to exclude it from his work. The second reason is his refusal to "mezclar lenguas distintas en una misma obra" [to mix different languages in the same book] (1948, 9).

18. "With *Modernismo* Spanish-American literature came of age, while the *Antología* [Menéndez y Pelayo's], compiled and prefaced by the most authoritative critic of the language, gave it institutional substance and academic respectability. The present *History* appears in the wake of the most remarkable period of expansion and international recognition ever enjoyed by Latin American literature" (González Echevarría, Pupo-Walker 1996, xi).

19. "Latin American literature is today at the pinnacle of the international literary

movements that began with the avant-garde in the 1920s. Those movements, as well as their aftermath, are cosmopolitan in essence" (1996, xii).

20. "Tradition is the sum of works that a writer or group of writers conceives as antecedent, as origin, as the connection with a literary past from which they issue. Tradition is a binding, living, and dynamic past. Its existence may or may not be explicit, but it is necessarily and always implicit" (González Echevarría 1996, 7).

21. "One reason for this increase in colonial studies is that modern Latin American authors have discovered in the works of the colonial Baroque, or in the chronicles of the discovery and conquest, the starting point of the literary tradition to which they belong" (1996, xv).

22. The *Cambridge History* is, after all, a product of our departments of Spanish and Portuguese in this country and none of us is about to propose to do away with them. What we can do, and here lies our general intention with this whole volume, is to maintain a critical attitude from inside the system where we are frequently and comfortably inscribed, so that we do not end up reproducing and glorifying with our research and teaching social and cultural organizations that foster inequality and injustice now and in the future.

23. In the case of Colombia, for instance, and as a result of the 1991 Constitution, the "Ministerio de Educación Nacional" has developed programs in indigenous languages called "Etno-educación" targeting indigenous communities. These initiatives mirror long-standing efforts by local indigenous communities who want to keep their ancestral language alive.

24. Besides the critics mentioned before it is important to include many studies published in the *Latin American Indian Literatures Journal,* and two recent interdisciplinary studies on the Mayan-Kiche narratives (particularly those contained in the manuscript known as "Popol vuh"): Carlos Lopez's (1999) and Mary H. Preuss's (1988).

25. These same maladies, that bring to mind classic violent clashes between "civilization" and "barbarism," gain actuality in Colombia's bloody civil war today. As Antonio Caballero (1999), a Colombian columnist, put it: "La guerra tiene su origen en los conflictos sociales del campo, jamás resueltos pacíficamente" [the war has its origin in the countryside social conflicts, never resolved peacefully]. This city/countryside struggle, in which urban Westernized power and arrogance looks down upon, and obliterates, local oral cultures, and alternative political aspirations, is a current example of the social and political conflicts illustrated in Rama's paradigm, "the lettered city," only with atrocious and, sometimes, unimaginable violence.

BIBLIOGRAPHY

Adorno, Rolena. 1988. "Nuevas perspectivas en los estudios literarios coloniales hispanoamericanos." *Revista de Crítica Literaria Latinoamericana* 14, 28: 11–27.

————. 1993. "Reconsidering Colonial Discourse for sixteenth- and seveteenth-century Spanish America." *Latin American Research Review* 28, 3: 135–145.

Arciniegas, Germán. 1979. "Sobre el Desierto prodigioso y el prodigio del desierto." In *El Tiempo.* Bogotá: May 11.

————. 1975. *América en Europa.* Buenos Aires: Editorial Sudamericana.

————. *América tierra firme.* [1937] 1944. Buenos Aires: Losada.

Arrom, José Juan. 1971. *Certidumbre de América. Estudios de letras, Floklore y Cultura.* Madrid: Editorial Gredos, S.A.

Avelar, Idelber. 1999. "The Clandestine Ménage à Trois of Cultural Studies, Spanish, and Critical Theory." In *Profession 1999,* 49–58. New York: The Modern Language Association.

Balbuena, Bernardo de. 1941. *Grandeza Mexicana y fragmentos del Siglo de Oro y El Bernardo.* México: Ediciones de la Universidad Nacional Autónoma.

Bolaños, Alvaro Félix. 1994. *Barbarie y canibalismo en la retórica colonial. Los indios pijaos de Fray Pedro Simón.* Santafé de Bogotá: CEREC.

Caballero, Antonio. 1999. *Revista Semana.* Santafé de Bogotá, febrero 15 de 1999, electronic edition # 999. *http://semana.com.co/*

Cesareo, Mario. 1995. *Cruzados, mártires y beatos: emplazamientos del cuerpo colonial.* West Lafayette, IN: Purdue University Press.

Cervantes Saavedra, Miguel de. 1979 [1605, 1615]. *El ingenioso hidalgo don Quijote de la Mancha.* México: Editorial Porrúa.

Clifford, James. 1986. "On Ethnographic Allegory". *Writing Culture. The Poetics and Politics of Ethnography.* Eds. James Clifford and George Marcus. Berkeley: University of California Press. 98–121.

Cobo Borda, Juan Gustavo. 1987. *Arciniegas de cuerpo entero.* Bogotá: Planeta Colombiana Editorial S.A.

Codex Mendoza. 1992. Edited by Frances F. Berdan and Patricia Rieff Anawalt. Berkeley: University of California Press.

Columbus, Christopher. 1989. *The Diary of Christopher Columbus's First Voyage to America 1492–1943.* Edited by Oliver Dunn and James E. Kelley, Jr. Norman and London: University of Oklahoma Press.

Cornejo Polar, Antonio. 1994. *Escribir en el aire. Ensayo sobre la heterogeneidad sociocultural de las literaturas andinas.* Lima: Editorial horizonte.

García Márquez, Gabriel. 1968. *Cien años de soledad.* La Habana: Casa de las Américas.

González Echevarría, Roberto. 1996. "A Brief History of the History of Spanish American Literature." In *The Cambridge History of Latin American Literature.* Vol. I, Discovery to Modernism, 7–32. Cambridge, New York: Cambridge University Press, 1996.

————. 1985. *The Voice of the Masters : Writing and Authority in Modern Latin American Literature*. Austin: University of Texas Press.

González Echevarría, Roberto and Enrique Pupo-Walker, eds. 1996. "General Preface." *The Cambridge History of Latin American Literature*. Vol. I, Discovery to Modernism, Cambridge, xi–xvii Cambridge, New York: Cambridge University Press.

Higgins, Antony. 2000. *Constructing the* criollo *Archive. Subjects of Knowledge in the* Bibiotheca Mexicana *and the* Rusticatio Mexicana. West Lafayette, Indiana: Purdue University Press.

Landívar, Rafael. *Rusticatio Mexicana*. 1987. Edited by Faustino Chamorro González. San José, CR; Asociación Libro Libre.

López, Carlos M. 1999. *Los Popol Wuj y sus epistemologías. Las diferencias, el conocimiento y los ciclos del infinito*. Quito, Ecuador: Ediciones Abya-Yala.

Martí, José. 1980. "Nuestra América." *Nuestra América*, 9–18. Buenos Aires: Editorial Losada, S.A.

Martin Gaite, Carmen. 1979. *El cuarto de atrás*. Barcelona: Ediciones Destino.

Mazzotti, José Antonio. 1996. *Coros mestizos del Inca Garcilaso. Resonancias andinas*. Lima: Fondo de Cultura Económica.

Menéndez Pelayo, Marcelino. 1948. *Historia de la poesía hispano-americana*. Santander: Aldus, S.A. de artes gráficas.

Meléndez, Mariselle. 1999. *Raza, género e hibridez en* El lazarillo de ciegos caminantes. Chapel Hill: North Carolina Series on the Romance Languages and Literatures.

Mignolo, Walter. 1982. "Cartas, crónicas y relaciones del descubrimiento y la conquista." In *Historia de la literatura Hispanoamericana. Epoca colonial*. Vol. I. 57–116. Madrid: Ediciones Cátedra, S.A.

————. 1989. "Colonial Situations, Geographical Discourses and Territorial Representations: Toward a Diatopical Understanding of Colonial Semiosis." *Disposito*. 14: 36–38.

————. 1993. "Colonial and Postcolonial Discourse: Cultural Critique or Academic Colonialism?" *Latin American Research Review* 28, 3: 120–134.

Moraña, Mabel. 1996. *Mujer y cultura en la colonia hispanoamericana*. Pittsburgh: Instituto Internacional de Literatura Iberoamericana, University of Pittsburgh.

Oviedo, José Miguel. 1995. *Historia de la literatura hispanoamericana. Desde los orígenes a la emancipación*. Madrid: Alianza Editorial.

Preuss, Mary H. 1988. *Gods of the Popol vuh : Xmukane, Kucumatz, Tojil, and Jurakan*. Culver City, CA: Labyrinthos.

Rabasa, José. 2000. *Writing Violence in the Northern Frontier. The Historiography of Sixteenth-Century New Mexico and Florida and the Legacy of Conquest.* Durham and London: Duke University Press.

————. 1993. *Inventing America. Spanish Historiography and the Formation of Eurocentrism.* Norman, OK, and London: University of Oklahoma Press.

Rama, Angel. 1984. *La ciudad letrada.* Hanover, N.H.: Ediciones del norte.

Restrepo, Luis Fernando. 1999. *El Nuevo Reino imaginado. Las* Elegías de varones ilustres de Indias *de Juan de Castellanos.* Santafé de Bogotá: Instituto Colombiano de Cultura Hispánica.

Rodó, José Enrique. 1948. *Ariel.* Madrid: Espasa-Calpe, S.A.

Rodríguez Baquero, Luis Enrique. 1995. *Encomienda y vida diaria entre los indios de Muzo (1550–1620).* Santafé de Bogotá: Instituto Colombiano de Cultura Hispánica, Giro Editores Ltda.

Rodríguez Freile, Juan. 1979. *El carnero.* Edited by Darío Achury Valenzuela. Caracas: Biblioteca Ayacucho.

Sáinz de Medrano, Luis. 1976. *Historia de la literatura hispanoamericana (hasta el siglo XIX).* Vol. I. Madrid: Guadiana de Publicaciones, S.A.

Salles-Reese, Verónica. 1997. *From Viracocha to the Virgin of Copacabana. Representation of the Sacred at Lake Titicaca.* Austin: University of Texas Press.

Schlau, Stacey and Electa Arenal, editors. 1989. *Untold sisters: Hispanic Nuns in Their Own Works.* Albuquerque: University of New Mexico Press.

Seed, Patricia. 1991. "Colonial and Postcolonial Discourse." *Latin American Research Review* 26, 3: 181–200.

Sommer, Doris. 1991. *Foundational Fictions. The National Romances of Latin America.* Berkeley: The University of California Press.

Tamayo Fernández, Martalucía. 1998. *Germán Arciniegas: el hombre que nació con el siglo (una autobiografía escrita por otro).* Santafé de Bogotá: Fundación Universidad Central.

Vasconcelos, José. 1948. *La raza cósmica.* México: Espasa-Calpe Mexicana, S.A.

Verdesio, Gustavo. 1996. *La invención del Uruguay: La entrada del territorio y sus habitantes a la cultura occidental.* Montevideo: Editorial Graffiti and Editorial Trazas.

————. 1997. "Revisando un modelo. Angel Rama y los estudios coloniales." *Angel Rama y los estudios latinoamericanos.* Edited by Mabel Moraña. 235–248. Pittsburgh: Instituto Internacional de Literatura Iberoamericana.

Vidal, Hernán. 1985. *Socio-historia de la literatura colonial hispanoamericana: tres lecturas orgánicas.* Minneapolis, MN: Institute for the Study of Ideologies and Literature.

————. 1993. "The Concept of Colonial and Postcolonial Discourse: A Perspective from Literary Criticism." In *Latin American Research Review.* 28, 3: 113–119.

Zamora, Margarita. 1978. "Historicity and Literariness: Problems in the Literary Criticism of Spanish American Colonial Texts." *Modern Language Notes* 102, 2: 334–346.

Zapata, Roger. 1989. *Guaman Poma, indigenismo y estética de la dependencia en la cultura peruana.* Minneapolis, MN: Institute for the Study of Ideologies and Literature.

Pre-Columbian Pasts and Indian Presents in Mexican History

José Rabasa

This paper is the first in a series of studies on how the pre-Columbian past has been collected in different moments in Mexican history and what has been the relationship between these forms of knowledge and policies towards Indians. On the one hand, these studies will examine forms of ordering the pre-Columbian past (that is, modes of knowing, organizing, and interpreting artifacts), while on the other, they will study forms of containing disorder in the corresponding Indian presents (that is, modes of subordination, control, and counterinsurgency). Idealized perspectives of the pre-Columbian period have had contemporaneous views that denigrate and undermine historical Indians (the many recent pages on the political insufficiency of the Zapatistas is one of the many instances). Indian resistance includes both passive forms of rejecting Westernization as well as armed rebellions. In studying forms of creating order and containing disorder, we must keep in mind writing violence in colonialist discourses.

The concept of writing violence in colonialist discourses suggests a definition of Latin American Subaltern Studies that, on the one hand, would develop an inventory of the Culture of Conquest that continues to produce subalternity, while on the other, would define the terms of a discourse that could dialogue with other rationalities to those dominant in the "West."[1] Subaltern studies, therefore, would retake the histories of uprisings, insurgencies, rebellions, and national identities without subjecting them to criteria that privilege moments where elites have organized them according to their political programs. This perspective would enable us to break away from teleological schemata that situate the meaning of the past in terms of an approximation to (a questionably more developed) modern present. We would thus avoid privileging an elite Third World intellectual cadre that would have immediate access to the subaltern—quite the contrary, it would register the signs that inscribe "me," the Third World intellectual (or, for that matter, the First World sympathizer) as a collaborator of colonialist discourses. As John Beverley has put it: "Subaltern studies begins with a critique of the adequacy of any

51

intellectual construction of the subaltern since, nolo volens, the constitution of the intelligentsia itself and intellectual discourse and its institutions is not unrelated to the production of subalternity itself" (personal communication). Colonialist writing practices, then, do not just pertain to the (early) colonial period, but inform contemporary modernization programs that folklorize forms of life and deplore the loss of old—thereby confining Indian cultures to the museum and the curio shop.

In the span of a decade after the conquest of Mexico, Meso-American civilizations came to be conceptualized as a form of antiquity by missionaries and crown officials. War, the burning of books, and the persecution of spiritual leaders forced a way of life into clandestinity. Indigenous cultures, in the lingo of the early missionaries, became antiguallas (ancient history, old customs)— an array of cultural practices that Indians held in esteem regardless of their proscription by the Catholic Church. The missionary's impulse to eradicate (to extirpate idolatries and superstitions), paradoxically, was intimately bound to a will to preserve (to resurrect the grandeur and moral order of old). Mexican historiography of the pre-Columbian period has been from its inception Janus-like: it at once has preserved a memory of old and severed contemporary Indian presents from history. (This exclusion from history, as we will see later on, should be understood as constituting a mode of living history rather than as verifying a recalcitrance to modernity). Ancient Mexico is conceptualized as dead—which does not exclude a ghost-like continuity that forevermore threatens the social order or progress—and becomes a patrimony of the patria, the fatherland, as early as Fray Diego de Durán's *Historia de la Nueva España e islas de Tierra Firme* (ca. 1580), and of the nación, the nation, since the Independence from Spain in 1821. It is not so much a question of Indians having historical significance only insofar as they could be integrated into the church or the nation, but of using their history against them. Colonialist discourses first proscribe Meso-American cultures and then reduce the effects of the destruction—the Indian present—to shadows of the ancient grandeur.

México's Clio, from the reconstruction of the pre-Columbian world in the *Codex Mendoza* (c. 1540) to the collection of past and present indigenous artifacts in the Museo Nacional de Antropología e Historia in México City (1964), has tended to privilege antiquarian historiography. Antiquarianism, I must add, does not preclude building monuments to better preserve the meaning of its findings. Those familiar with Nietzsche's, *The Use and Abuse of History*, will not fail to recall his preference for the term polypsest over palimpsest in his discussion of antiquarian history. Antiquarian historians would not only read the scribbles of the past, but also reconstruct the past from its multiple rubbings, erasures. For the antiquarian identifies the history of his town, the nation with the history of the self: "He greets the soul of his people from afar as his own, across the dim and troubled centuries." But the antiquarian also brings about one more erasure as it "undervalues the present growth" (Nietzsche 1979, 18). Consequently, collections of the pre-Columbian pasts have had corresponding subaltern Indian presents. The story of the collection of past and present indigenous artifacts, moreover, tends to be told in progressivist terms that privilege the emergence of the social sciences (see Boon 1993b; Errington 1993; Florescano 1993). Against a monumental history that reads the past to find a kernel of the present and projects a present mentality into the past, my project seeks to elaborate an archaeology of the historiography of pre-Columbian Meso-America and its effects on the indigenous population. This archaeology, however, does not pretend to have access to a more objectivist view of the past, but is fully motivated by a desire to understand how indigenous people have been and continue to be marginalized through the expropriation of their culture and history. These are the tasks of a book length work in progress that obviously goes beyond the scope of a single paper.

In what follows, I limit myself to illustrate my project with two instances of writing violence in Mexican history: (1) The production of *Códex Mendoza* in the mid-sixteenth century: this text enables us to trace how the *tlacuilos*, as writers of history, were subordinated to Spanish historiography by a Spanish interpreter; (2) Carlos Sigüenza y Góngora's *Alboroto y motín de los indios de México*: Sigüenza's account of the 1692 riots in México City and Tlaxcala enables us to isolate forms of subaltern insurgency in spite of, perhaps because of, his racist phantasms.[2] I have chosen these two very unique and different texts precisely because they enable me to address two related and distinct modalities of collecting and recollecting the past. Their readings in this essay are intended as examples of the type of work my project envisions, rather than finished studies of either text or historical moment. These instances exemplify two archaeological tasks implicit in the definition of subaltern studies that I have been elaborating in this paper: *a* to draw an inventory of the systems of thought that have informed the collecting of the pre-Columbian past; and *b* to identify life forms and rationalities in documents whose purposes were not to record them as such but to provide information for their eradication or neutralization.[3] By conceptualizing "pre-Columbian pasts and Indian presents," I seek to define a terrain for reading Mexican history against the grain. It is no longer a question of opposing the masses (Indian presents and their representation) to the great men (pre-Columbian pasts and their collectors), nor simply of writing history from the bottom up, but of avoiding, indeed, destroying the grounds that privilege up in interpretation.

Although my project bears similarities to the work of Enrique Florescano (1987) and Serge Gruzinski (1993), it differs from theirs in that I do not aim to document degrees of acculturation or describe processes of occidentalization as consequences of literacy, but rather to examine forms of life that are often seen as undeveloped or historically ineffective. If one fetishizes the letter of the alphabet by positing it as the most evolved system of writing, one also fetishizes the alphabet by defining the meanings that it produces as univocal—for there might be several pictographic versions of an event in any given community, strictly defined rules of what can be said about a pictograph, alphabetical inscriptions of oral texts that do not erase their own logic, and writers and painters who do not know what they write and paint. On the other hand, who would lack some form of acculturation or hybridity after contact? Subalternity cannot be thought outside colonialism or capitalism. As Dipesh Chakrabarty has argued, "stories about how this or that group in Asia, Africa or Latin America resisted the 'penetration' of capitalism do not constitute 'subaltern' history, for subaltern histories do not refer to a resistance prior and exterior to capital" (Chakrabarty, 16).

THE CÓDICE MEDOZA AND THE ENCOMIENDA

The *Codex Mendoza* consists of three parts that provide a pictographic account of: (1) the history of México-Tenochtitlán (Figure 1); (2) México-Tenochtitlán's tributaries (Figure 2); and (3) the life cycle of the average Aztec at the time of the conquest (Figure 3). It is important to note that the third part also contains information regarding personal services and labor tribute (Figure 4). Scholars have generally agreed that *Codex Mendoza* was produced by several *tlacuilos* (painter-writers) and that it is representative of the best colonial school of painters. Prototypes for the historical and tribute components have been identified by Elizabeth Boone (1992) and Frances F. Berdan. Gordon Brotherston, on the other hand, has pointed out that the "Féjérvary exactly anticipates the *Codex Mendoza*, which deals first with the conquest and levying of tribute items and then with birth, growth, and the duties of the citizen of Tenochtitlán" (1992, 67). The different components abide in different degrees to pre-Columbian writing conventions. It is generally agreed that the historical component does not contain formal deviations from similar pre-Columbian texts. Frances F. Berdan, following Donald Robertson, has pointed out that the scribe of the *Matrícula de Tributos,* a pre-Columbian prototype of the tributary section, composed the sequence of town glyphs and the corresponding tributes " 'against the direction of reading,' while the *Mendoza* scribe wrote them with or toward the direction of the reading" (Berdan, 57; Robertson, 105). Brotherston's observation that *Codex Féjérvary* anticipates the third section of *Codex Mendoza,* the so-called ethonographic part, is not self-evident from a perusal of the pictographic conventions in the *Féjérvary.* But even if there were no pre-Columbian prototypes for this section, the use of (what would at least be interpreted as) an indigenous form of writing would authenticate the information regarding personal service and labor tribute. Rather than isolating this section as ethnographic (Calnek 1992), we ought to see the whole *Mendoza* as the result of an ethnographic project and as an example of the rhetorical use (in this case by the Spaniards) of pictographic writing.

Codex Mendoza testifies to the continuation of a pictographic tradition as well as to the epistemological need to fill in the gap created by the burning of books in the early missionary campaigns of the 1520s and 1530s. The *Mendoza* is an imaginary elaboration that at once provides historical information about the past and reproduces, as it were, a document from the past. It marks a turning point in colonial history where ethnography fulfilled an ancillary function to define governmental policies, to aid judges, and to inform missionaries. *Codex Mendoza*, however, was produced for a European audience rather than to solve legal disputes among Amerindians or to identify superstition and idolatry.

After the conquest, *tlacuilos* became indispensable to the information retrieval project of reconstructing the pre-Colombian past in such documents as the pictorial sections of Sahagún's *Florentine Codex*, the tribute records in the *Codex Osuna*, and the account of the Tlaxcalan participation in the Conquest in the *Lienzo de Tlaxcala*. Iconic script, moreover, recorded information from within the indigenous cultures that a purely alphabetical text could not contain. Spanish missionaries and authorities were concerned with creating a code to understand the Indian mind from within and thus further its occidentalization. Beyond this will to objectify and extirpate indigenous cultures, indigenous people used alphabetical writing and "European-style" painting in forms that were not directly and explicitly part of the colonial order meant to repress them. Contemporary scholars, however, tend to emphasize degrees of purity in their classification of indigenous pictographic documents. In this regard, studies of the strokes of the main *tlacuilo* of the *Mendoza* indicate an adoption of cursive line that manifests acculturation (Howe 1992). But rather than seeing the *Mendoza* as a more or less authentic example of pre-Columbian writing or evaluating the correctness of the information it contains, here we will observe how the production of texts in the native tradition fulfills the rhetorical function of authenticating data—pictographic texts would seem to contain more reliable data about the pre-Columbian social order.

We lack detailed information regarding the production of the *Mendoza*. We also ignore the interests that informed its production as well as the identity of the interpreter who wrote glosses, supplemented the pictographic text with an alphabetical narrative and provided descriptions and explanations of the nature of iconic script. At the end of the alphabetical narrative, the interpreter complains that the *tlacuilos* had taken too long to produce the text:

diez dias antes de la partida de la flota se dio al ynterpretador esta ystoria para que la ynterpretase el qual descuydo fue de los yndios que acordaron tarde y como cosa de corrida no se tuvo punto en el estilo que convenia ynterpretarse. (Vol. 4:148)

Figure 1.

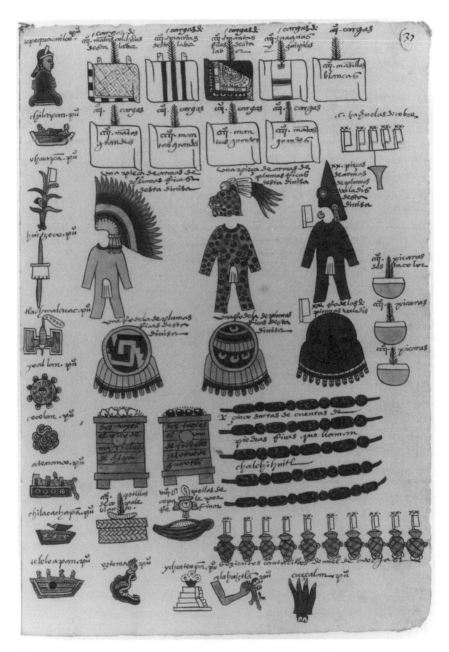

Figure 2.

Figure 3.

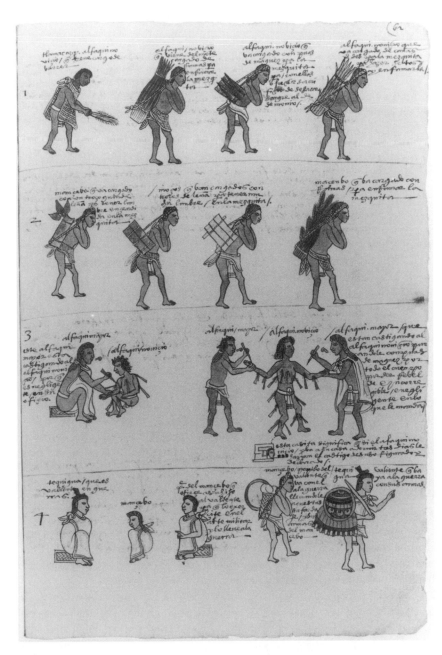

Figure 4.

[the interpreter was given this history ten days prior to the departure of the fleet, and he interpreted it carelessly because the Indians came to agreement late; and so it was done in haste and he did not improve the style suitable for an interpretation.]

These remarks are extraordinary for the light they shed on the seriousness of interpretation in colonialist discourses. The interpreter underscores the accuracy of his translation into Spanish:

y aunque las ynterpretaçiones ban toscas no se a de tener nota sino a la sustançia de las aclaraciones lo que significan las figuras / las quales ban byen declaradas por ser como es el ynterpretador dellas buen lengua mexicana. (Vol. 4:148)

[and although the interpretations are crude, one should only take into account the substance of the explanations that explain the drawings; these are correctly presented, because the interpreter of them is well versed in the Mexican language.]

The interpreter implies that the substance of his comments, the facts, as it were, are correctly documented in his glosses and alphabetical narrative. It is a question of style, of the appropriate historical genre, that is at stake in this commentary.

The interpreter confesses that his use of Moorish terms like *alfaqui* and *mezquitas* rather than *sacerdote* and *templo*, "fue ynadvertencia del ynterpretador poner tales nombre que son moriscos" [it was a mistake for the interpreter to use the Moorish words] (Vol. 4:148). But more problematic than these misnomers is the style he was forced to adopt because of the rush: "porque no se dio lugar al ynterpretador de nyngun vagar / y como cosa no acordada ny pensada se ynterpreto a uso de proçceso" [because the interpreter did not take time or work at all slowly; and because it was a matter neither agreed upon nor thought about, it was interpreted according to legal conventions] (Vol. 4:148). Legal accounts or relaciones as a genre would approximate a degree zero of employment insofar as the writer limited himself or herself to stating the particulars and abstained from drawing their universal significance—that is, from historical interpretation. The "uso de proçceso," furthermore, points to the legal framework in which pictographic documents were used.

But the passage also insinuates that the interpreter did not know why the text was solicited in the first place, "como cosa no acordada ny pensada." Clearly he was a latecomer in the chain of production. Given the structural similarity with Féjérvary, we need not assume an active Spanish agency organizing the content of the text according to a set of questions. From a legal perspective the information regarding who paid tribute is relevant; however, the specific kind (such as warrior suits made of feathers) lacks relevance given Spanish needs. On the other hand, from a political perspective, the record of labor tribute in the third section was crucial. The value of this data for the Spaniards would reside in its form rather than its contents: who paid tribute to whom and in what kinds. The interpreter complains of not having had enough time to reflect on the contents of the pictorial text, but also, perhaps more important, not enough time to provide a proper narrative because he ignored the purpose of the text.

We are asked to supplement the limitations: "El estilo grosero e ynterpretaçion de lo figurado supla el letor" [The reader must excuse the rough style in the interpretation of the drawings in this history] (Vol. 4:148). The English translators have chosen "to excuse" (that is, to dissimulate, to pretend that it is not there) as the meaning of the Spanish word *suplir,* but this verb also means to integrate what is missing as well as to put oneself in the place of the other. (The definition is, according to the *Diccionario de la Real Academia:* "Cumplir o integrar lo que falta en una cosa, o remediar la carencia de ella. // 2. Ponerse en lugar de uno para hacer sus veces.") The reader is called to take the place of the interpreter and thus supplement his faulty interpretation. In the horizon of interpretation, an oral text (that is, the deliberations by those who know or will make sense of why the text was produced) will supplement writing, will add materials, and take the place of the interpreter. The differentiation of pictographic from alphabetical writings as requiring an oral interpretation, as not containing a univocal content, would seem to be breached (in spite of the interpreter's views on the question) in this appeal to the reader to supplement.

Although the style of the Spanish commentary resembles legal conventions, the intent and nature of the interpreter's alphabetic text is to draw out the significance of the contents. The generic constraint of the relación to an account of particulars does not mean that the genre did not lend itself to allegoresis (stating one thing and meaning another); in this case its "rough style" was circumstantial. The interpreter calls for more interpretation rather than a zero degree of employment. Given that the text contains a history, he suggests an implicit narrative resolution with universal significance. One wonders, however, whether the historical nature of the text resides in the pictographic account or in the alphabetical section that needs to be supplemented by the readers. If the pictographic text is a history, the interpreter's deficiency would merely consist of a weak reading.

But then what was the purpose of glossing and translating? To simply facilitate a reading for Charles V? But what was the urgency, if the purpose of the text was simply to interpret iconic script for the King? Why produce a text that approximates the writing convention of pre-Columbian traditions? Was this a mere rhetorical effect to reinforce a political argument? My guess is that the *Codex Mendoza* was part of a series of documents produced to legitimate

the Encomienda in New Spain either on the eve of, or in the immediate years
after, the promulgation of the New Laws of 1542 that outlawed the institution
of Indian tribute to Spaniards. The New Laws abolished the Encomienda, but
they were not accepted passively. Viceroy Blasco Núñez de Vela was killed
when he attempted to enforce the New Laws in Peru. In New Spain there was
a series of protests and a vast number of letters were written by members of the
religious orders to defend the legality and economic value of individual encomienda as well as of the system as a whole. Since *Codex Mendoza* was lost to
a French corsair on its way to Spain (eventually becoming part of André
Thevet's collection of American artifacts), we ignore what effect it would have
had either before or after the promulgation of the New Laws. By 1546, however, the New Laws had undergone a series of amendments that revoked laws
that had prohibited the inheritance of *encomiendas* and dissolved the disposi-
tion that took Indians away from *encomenderos* who mistreated them.

The *Mendoza*'s description and account of the tribute paid to Tenochtitlan
establishes a tradition where the Encomienda would be a continuation of and
not an alien structure to the Amerindian world. By documenting rigorous
order in the third section, the reader may supplement both iconic and alphabetical texts with a reflection on how the exercise of colonial domination and
exploitation were not alien to the pre-Columbian order. Clearly, *Codex Mendoza* validates tribute paid to *encomenderos* in the form of labor and personal
service. The history of México-Tenochtitlán gives us a clue to its ideological
elaboration. As the narrative moves into the last Mexican ruler, Moctezuma
(there is no mention of Cuahutémoc whom Cortés hanged after the fall of
Tenochtitlán in 1521), the history of Mexico-Tenochtitlán surreptitiously
turns into the history of New Spain. The validity of New Spain as a political
institution is grounded in a past that it destroyed:

> y estando en el dicho señorio amplio mas en todo estremo el ynperio
> mexicano / dominando sobre todos los pueblos de desta Nueva Es-
> paña en que le dauan y pagavan grandes tributos y de balor de mucha
> Riqueza. (4,34)

> [and during his reign he greatly extended the Mexican empire, ruling
> over all the towns of this New Spain, so they gave and paid large and
> richly valuable tributes.]

Rather than merely seeing the capitalization of Riqueza as an isolated cal-
ligraphic anomaly, we ought to observe that it recurs with other R-words such
as in "muchos estremos y Respetos," "majestad que les Representaua," and "Reconoçimiento de vasallaje" (4,34). Thus, the history of México-Tenochtitlán
becomes the antiquity of New Spain and legitimates the new political order

while subordinating the indigenous population to the new Spanish lords. The colonial order must impose the discipline that gave Moctezuma *Respeto* (respect), *majestad que Representaua* (sovereignty that he represented) and *Reconoçimiento de vasallaje* (recognition of vassalage).

The subordination of the Indians can best be grasped in the summary mention that the interpreter makes of the *tlacuilos:* "el qual descuydo fue de los indios que acordaron tarde" [because the Indians came to agreement late] (*Codex Mendoza* 4: 148). We must avoid the temptation of reducing the *tlacuilos* to mere artisans that knew not what they wrote; this position would reiterate the interpreter's undermining of the *tlacuilos*. In doing this, we collaborate with the culture of conquest that informed the production of this text. Rather than pressing the *tlacuilos*, that is, their text, to deliver the goods, to read it as a source of data, we ought to put its silences into play with the power dynamics that inscribed the *tlacuilos* as incompetent. This statement ultimately foregrounds the new intellectual elite that claims authority "por ser como es el ynterpretador dellas buena lengua mexicana" [because the interpreter of them is well-versed in the Mexican language] (4,148). We can read in the *tlacuilos*'s disagreements a lack of stable information (i.e., the old books had been burned) but more interesting—at least to me—a cautious reserve (e.g., clandestine cultural practices).

Sixteenth-century efforts to reconstruct life before contact not only had the administrative and ideological implications of *Codex Mendoza*, regarding the Encomienda and the payment of tribute, but also responded to a lack of knowledge regarding the everyday life of the Indian present. Franciscan missionaries such as Olmos, Motolinía, and Sahagún, the Dominican Durán, and the Jesuit Juan de Tovar justified collecting information about the pre-Columbian period on the void of knowledge caused by the systematic burning of books and censorship of religious practices that drove native leaders into clandestinity. Diego Durán's *Historia de la Nueva España e islas de Tierra Firme* is a particularly good source to analyze historical antiquation as a will to eradicate Nahua culture (i.e., subjecting indigenous knowledge as superstition and idolatry) and to appropriate the institution of history (constituting the Nahuas as incapable of writing their own history). A "reading in reverse" of Durán and other missionary ethnographies, however, would allow us to observe forms of resistance to processes of occidentalization. *Alboroto y motín de los indios de México* establishes connections between passive resistance and insurrection. The antiquarianism of the *Mendoza* resides in the production of a document from the past that legitimates the Spanish colonial order and its oppression of Indians; in the case of *Alboroto y motín*, histories of the pre-Columbian past and the conquest locate places of memory in the city and provide a code for interpreting an Indian present. *Alboroto y motín* is a long, detailed letter to the admiral Don Andrés Pez that described the heavy rains that destroyed the crops, the food shortages that followed, and the eventual uprisings.

OF BOOKS AND RAGE

A classic site where a pre-Colombian past and an Indian present are juxta-posed is the scene, on a July afternoon in 1692, in which don Carlos de Sigüenza y Góngora abandoned his desk and books to look out the window at a multitude of rebellious Indians in the streets of México City:[4]

> A nada de cuanto he dicho que pasó esta tarde me hallé presente, porque me estaba en casa sobre mis libros. Y aunque yo había oído en la calle parte del ruido, siendo ordinario los que por las continuas borracheras de los indios nos enfadan siempre, ni aun se me ofreció abrir las vidrieras de la ventana de mi estudio para ver lo que era hasta que, entrando un criado casi ahogando, se me dijo a grandes voces:—¡Señor, tumulto! Abrí las ventanas a toda prisa y, viendo que corría hacia la plaza infinita gente a medio vestir y casi co-rriendo entre, los que iban gritando: ¡Muera el Virrey y el Corregi-dor que tiene atravesado el maíz y nos matan de hambre!, me fui a ella. (123)

> [I was not present at all that I have related that happened this after-noon because I was at home over my books. Although I had heard part of the noise on the street it did not even occur to me, since ordi-narily on account of the habitual drunkenness of the Indians we are continually disturbed by uproars, to open the glass partitions of the window of my study to see what it was about until a man servant came in almost choking with excitement and shouted to me, "Sir, a riot!" I opened the windows in all haste and seeing that an infinite number of people were running toward the Plaza I also went half-dressed and almost running amidst those who kept shouting "Down with the Viceroy and the Corregidor who have stopped our corn and who are killing us with hunger!"][5] (Leonard, 256)

Here we have the tranquillity of the Creole savant, the collector of pre-Columbian artifacts and precious histories from the sixteenth and seventeenth centuries being disturbed by a "mob" of subalterns who were assaulting the de-posits of corn and setting the city in flames. Our consummate antiquarian rushes to the palace to rescue the archives of the nation from the fires. He de-scribes himself in heroic terms:

> . . . ya con una barreta, ya con una hacha, cortando vigas, apalan-cando puertas por mi industria, se le quitaron al fuego de entre las manos no sólo algunos cuartos del palacio sino tribunales enteros y de la ciudad su mejor archivo . . . (130)

[. . . with a bar and with an ax I cut beams and pried open doors by my own efforts and not only some apartments of the Palace but whole halls and the best archives of the city were rescued from the fires . . .]. (268)

This passage has given place to readings of Sigüenza which tend to either highlight his love for the nation (Zárate) or denounce his lack of solidarity with the Indians (Iglesia). Others have seen in the *Alboroto y motín* a brand of criollismo (Paz, 1982), a pro-Spanish defense of privilege (Cogdell, 1994), and even a resistant carnivalesque text (Moraña 1994b).

The task of subaltern studies, however, would consist of recuperating the strategies of mobilization, the interracial allegiances, the role of women, the anticolonial positionings, and the tactics of rumor that remain sedimented in Sigüenza's text. But in doing this sort of reading we should remain careful not to forget that we are dealing with an ideological elaboration and therefore should avoid claiming access to reality itself. For we witness Sigüenza's phantasms, not the uprising itself. It is not a love of Indian things that Sigüenza loses in the rebellion of 1692. We should trace instead his fear of insurgency by people of color (along with marginal Spaniards) and racial hatred. And in this respect, Sigüenza's denunciations of the unruliness of the "Indians"—as well as denunciations in the other versions of the story that blamed the uprising on the Spanish authorities—would manifest typical/tropical modes of containment and semantic control. Ranajit Guha's essay "The Prose of Counter-Insurgency" (1988) has isolated the rhetorical strategies used not only by colonial officials, but also by nationalist historians to delimit the meaning and significance of subaltern insurgency. These range from condemnations of their tactics to negations of their political nature. Dismissals of the political character of the 1692 uprising can be traced in conservative critics like Octavio Paz, but it is also endemic to Gramscian readings that would highlight the limitations of peasant revolts.

Although *Elementary Aspects of Peasant Insurgency*—Guha borrows the title from a passage by Gramsci—tends to attribute a lack of sufficient political development to subalterns (without defining peasant rebellions, however, as pre-political [Guha 1983; cf. Hobsbawam]), this book lays out the practice of "writing in reverse" as a mode of reading the specific rationales that inform peasant insurgency. Thus, Guha's book traces rebellion in the use of language, differentiates insurgency from crime, maps out forms of struggle in burning, eating, wrecking, and looting, analyzes the language used to understand transmission, and critiques the territorial constructs of the local, the ethnic, the nation, and so forth. These conceptual rearrangements prove invaluable for a reading of Sigüenza's account and other documents pertaining to the 1692 riots in México City and Tlaxcala.

The populace, the plebe, was composed of

... indios, negros criollos y bosales de diferentes naciones, de chinos, de mulatos, de moriscos, de mestizos, de zambaigos, de lobos y también de españoles que en declarandose zaramullos (que es lo mismo que pícaros, chulos y arrebatacapas) y degenerando de sus obligaciones, son los peores entre tan ruin canalla. (113)

[... Indians, Creoles, bozales from various nations, Chinese, mulattoes, moriscos, mestizos, zambaigos, lobos, and Spaniards as well who, in declaring themselves zaramullos (which is the same as knaves, rascals, and cape-snatchers) and in falling away from their allegiance, are the worst of them all in such a vile rabble.] (240)

In this impulse to classify races and their miscegenation (along with the *mestizos* and mulattoes, Sigüenza identifies *zambaigos*—Indian and Chinese—and *lobos*—Indian and African), the Spaniards are the worst lot, because they do not assume the responsibilities of their race to the colonial order. If all the castes were yelling, "¡Muera el virrey y quantos lo defendieren!" [Death to the Viceroy and all those who defend him!], it is the Indians who yell "¡Mueran los españoles y los gachupines (son los venidos de España) que nos comen nuestro maíz!" [Death to the Spaniards and the Gachupines (applied to those who have come from Spain) who are eating up our corn!] But it is the Indian women, however, who play a particular role in the circulation of rumor and the definition of an anti-colonial agenda:

—Ea señoras! ó se decían las indias en su lengua unas a otras, —¡vamos con alegría a esta guerra, y comoquiera Dios que se acaben en ella los españoles, no importa que muramos sin confesión! ¿No es nuestra esta tierra? Pues ¿qué quieren en ella los españoles?—(123)

["Ah, señoras" the Indian women kept saying to each other in their own language, "let us go joyfully into this war. If God wills that the Spaniards be wiped out in it, it does not matter if we die without confession! Isn't this our land? Then what are the Spaniards doing in it?"] (257)

The Indian women denounce the colonial situation and defy any threat of punishment in the afterworld, "no importa que muramos sin confesión" [it does not matter if we die without confession].

Sigüenza does not comment on this anti-colonial shout, which records the uprising as a godless act. And, of course, he does not see himself as a colonized subject, but concedes that as far as the Indians are concerned, the Spanish occupation of the New World is a colonial situation.[6] By singling out the Indian women as emitting this cry in their tongue, he would seem to suggest that the castes and the marginal Spaniards could not identify themselves with this specific articulation of anti-colonial sentiment. Their plight and source of unrest resulted from socioeconomic injustices and obviously, as far as the castes were concerned, from the racism of the dominant peninsular and Creole Spaniards. As such, the castes' rioting must be understood in terms of racial differentials prevalent in what Mary Louise Pratt has called contact zones (Pratt 1992). Sigüenza seems to make a distinction between white Spaniards and people of color: "reconocí con sobrado espacio (pues andaba entre ellos) no ser solos indios los que allí estaban sino de todos colores sin excepción alguna" [I readily recognized (for I walked right among them) that not only Indians were present but all the colors without exception whatsoever] (124, 259). Although the term *"todos colores"* could include Spaniards, the emphasis on color highlights the gravity of the events in that the castes solidarized with the Indians. Sigüenza goes on to add that the Indians gained the following of the other castes (of all those who frequented the *pulquerías*) by carrying around an Indian woman that pretended to be dead. The display of the "corpse" served to mobilize the masses in the market. Looting ensued and the main governmental buildings were set in flames. The rioters targeted buildings that were locations of power or residences of officials as the viceroy and the corregidor. Although the stands at the marketplace were ransacked, there was no indiscriminate burning of private residences.

Let us now look into the role of rumor in mobilizing the crowd and the phantasms it generates in Sigüenza's text. Sigüenza wonders about the discourses that circulated among the Indians during the night: "¿Quién podrá decir con toda verdad los discursos en que gastarían los indios toda la noche?" (1984, 119). The rumor prompts the phantasm of Indian women calling a drunken mob to kill the viceroy, loot, and take over the city: "Creo que, instigándolos las indias y calentándolos el pulque, sería el primero quitarle la vida luego el día siguiente al señor virrey; quemarle el palacio sería el segundo, hacerse señores de la ciudad y robarlo todo" (119). Whether this is exactly what the Indians said in the midst of the night should not concern us, but that Sigüenza conveys the efficacy of rumor by wondering about other worse iniquities, "otras peores iniquidades." Rumor suggests the phantasm of an irrational mob:

> . . . y esto, sin tener otras armas para conseguir tan disparatada y monstruosa empresa sino las del desprecio de su propia vida que les da el pulque y la advertencia del culpabilísimo descuido con que vivimos entre tanta plebe, al mismo tiempo que presumimos de formidables. (119)

[. . . and they had no other weapons to succeed in such a foolish and monstrous undertaking than those of the indifference to their own lives which pulque gives them, and the consciousness of the exceedingly culpable carelessness with which we live among a great populace which, at the same time, we suspect of being dangerous.] (251)

Rumor circulates information that terrifies the Spaniards with the prospect of a city ruled by Indians. But by signaling the efficacy of rumor, my analysis borders with a justification of the worst fears regarding the "irrationality" of the Indians. My point, however, is to evoke a cry that says enough, a threatening "orale!" as exemplified today by Subcomandante Marcos in one of his recent comunicados: "El México de abajo tiene vocación de lucha, es solidario, es banda, es barrio, es palomilla, es raza, es cuate, es huelga, es marcha y mitín, es toma tierras, es cierre de carreteras, es 'no les creo!' es 'no me dejo,' es 'orale!' " (*La Jornada,* 22 September 1994). This popular language cannot be translated without distortion. For instance banda or palomilla would call for gang, but Marcos emphasizes a vocation for solidarity. The "no les creo" [I don't believe you], "no me dejo" [I will not take it] sums up the "orale!," to which something like "enough" would hardly do justice. Sigüenza's account seems to dismiss the feasibility of taking over the city, but expresses the determination of the Indians to engage the Spaniards. Pulque, says Sigüenza, is to be blamed for arousing the Indians. The difference between the efficacy of rumor and its phantasm is that the hysteria of Sigüenza leads him to imagine a generalized and indiscriminate violence. But there is no evidence of an indiscriminate murder of Spaniards in Sigüenza's text; on the contrary, Spaniards do murder Indians to take away stolen merchandise. Sigüenza partially blames the uprising on the vulnerability and ostentatiousness of the Spaniards who live in a city without walls separating them from the Indian quarters. In the aftermath of the rebellion Sigüenza recommended that Indians should be forbidden from living in the center of México City and be confined to several barrios on the periphery; the viceroy ordered on July 11, 1692 that within twenty days all Indians should move to their barrios (See Leonard, 136–38).

Murmur was also a preferred mode of communication. At Mass, a few days before the uprising,

. . . al entrar [el virrey] por la iglesia se levantó un murmullo no muy confuso entre las mujeres (pues lo oyeron los gentileshombres y pajes que le asistían, ¿cómo pudo su exelencia dejar de oirlo?) en que feamente le execraban y maldecían, atribuyendo a sus omisiones y mal gobierno la falta de maíz y la carestía de pan. (120)

[. . . a not very indistinct murmur arose among the women (if the gentlemen-in-waiting and the pages who were in attendance heard it how could His excellency fail to do so?) as he entered the church; they were execrating and cursing him in an ugly fashion attributing the shortage of corn and the high price of bread to neglect and poor management on his part.] (251–52)

For Sigüenza the viceroy did nothing more than pretend he did not hear the grumble, the "orale!" Women had been murmuring and circulating rumors since the seventh of April. This "secret," hence, illegitimate communication eventually developed into a public outcry. Sigüenza gives us a version of the riot's origins in which he accuses the Indian women of monopolizing corn for tortillas, and then buying pulque with the money. The men, seeing that their women were favored over Spanish women (Sigüenza specifies that Indian women were the only ones who knew how to make tortillas), attributed the preferential treatment to Spanish fear of Indian wrath. Thus, a strategic frightening of the Spaniards preceded the rebellion, "se determinaba [la plebe] a espantar (como dicen en su lengua) a los españoles" [(the populace) made up its mind to scare off the Spaniards (as they say in their own language)] (116, 245).

There are several issues to sort out in this passage. Why did Sigüenza emphasize that the Indians say "espantar en su lengua?" One wonders whether he was translating or simply documenting the use of the Spanish word in Nahuatl. In the passage cited above, he also underscored that the Indian women used their language when they contested the Spanish colonial claims over their lands. These specifications on the use of (most likely) Nahuatl implies that Spanish might not have been the common language to communicate across racial and ethnic lines, or at least that Nahuatl was generally understood. Anthropologists and linguists have documented that Indians in both the Andes and México tend to speak Spanish when drunk. Indeed, drunkenness goes hand in hand with the use of Spanish to condemn colonial regimes, as can be witnessed in a passage from Lizarraga's *Descripción breve del Perú:*

. . . y cuando están borrachos entonces hablan nuestra lengua, y se preguntan cuando los cristianos nos hemos de volver a nuestra patria, y porque no nos echan de la tierra, pues son más que nosotros, y cuando se ha de acabar el ave maría, que es decir cuando no les hemos de compeler a la doctrina. (quoted in Saignes 1989, 102)

[. . . and it is when they are drunk that they speak our tongue, and they ask each other when are we the Christians going to go back to our fatherland, and why don't they throw us out of their land, since they are more than us, and when will the Hail Mary end, which means when will we not compel them to hear the doctrine.]

This is the same colonial situation and anti-Christian sentiment that we find in Sigüenza, but the use of Spanish has a specific political motivation: to make sure that the Spaniards know how they feel about their oppression. The difference might reside in that in this instance violence remains exclusively on an imaginary plane, whereas in Sigüenza's account the Indians are already rioting. Although riots are both an actualization and an imaginary of violence, as a "place of rage" they are not limited to verbal attacks but also include burning buildings, looting, drinking pulque, and espantar the Spaniards with the threat of racial warfare.

In their observations on the consumption of alcoholic beverages, colonial officials and missionaries usually juxtaposed statements about a democratization of drunkenness after the colonization. Drunkenness, moreover, was associated, from the very early colonial period, with idolatrous practices. These commonplaces also recur in Sigüenza. For instance, he describes the consumption of pulque in one day as greater than the amount that was consumed in one year in the pre-Columbian past: "abunda más el pulque en México sólo en un día que en un año entero quando la gobernaban idólatras" [pulque is more plentiful in a single day in México City than in a whole year when the capital was governed by idolaters] (134, 274). More souls, according to Sigüenza, were sacrificed to the devil in the *pulquerías* of Colonial México than bodies in the temples of old. Thus, ancient México remained a paragon of morality, if not an object of desire, vis-à-vis the degeneracy of the contemporary Indians. There were, nevertheless, some Indians that retained the nobility of the past in their support of the prohibition of pulque: "y aun de los propios indios los pocos que conseruaban algo de nobleza antigua" [and even by a few of the Indians themselves who had kept something of their former nobility] (134, 275). Here he seems to privilege an Indian elite that tended to look after its own interests rather than feel solidarity with Indian subalterns. It is an elite concerned with retaining privileges that would keep them from labor drafts.[7]

Given that this nobility was subservient to the Spanish order, it is hard to understand Sigüenza's remarks about an Indian conspiracy. His account is only a brief version: "Las armas falsas, los miedos, las turbaciones de todo México . . . pedía para su expresión relación muy larga" [The false alarms, apprehensions and excitement in all México . . . would require a very long account for adequate expression] (134, 275). Other Spaniards trusted that the Tlaxcaltecas would come to their aid, but Sigüenza discounted an assumed continuous fidelity to the Crown since the Tlaxcaltecas rebelled the week after. The letter by an anonymous witness documents the exclusively subaltern nature of the Tlaxcala riots: "fué sola la plebe é indios masaguales [*macehualli*] los que hicieron la hostilidad, estando de parte de su Alcalde Mayor los caciques y nobles" [it was only the populace and the masaguale Indians [*macehualli*] who created the hostilities, for the caciques and the nobility were on the side of the *Alcalde Mayor*] (García, 250). This letter also confirms Ranajit Guha's observation on how the specter of a conspiracy "has its source in the psychosis of the dominant groups" (Guha 1983,225): "y esto que fue sola sospecha, llegó a co-brar fuerza, diciendo estaban convocados muchos pueblos y que tenían deter-minado el incendio de la ciudad" [and this that was only suspicion, grew in force, saying that many towns had gathered and had the determination of burning the city] (Garcia, 248). The momentum did build up; however, the or-ganizing principle should not be understood as a secret confabulation, but as resulting from the same conditions of exploitation and oppression.

An aspect of this oppression was the subjection of native religions and knowledges. Idolatry and magic played an important role in the imaginary of violence, at least in Sigüenza's phantasms. In his account, Sigüenza describes effigies of Spaniards in clay that were pierced with knives and lances also made of clay, bearing signs of blood on their necks as if their throats had been cut, which would manifest the anti-colonial feelings that preceded the riots. These figures were found, according to Sigüenza, in the same place where Hernán Cortés's forces had been destroyed on the night he fled Tenochtitlan in 1520. Here Sigüenza alludes to Indian histories that recorded this event and dedi-cated it to their major god, Huitzilopochtli, the god of war. This recollection of the defeat of Cortés's forces as they fled the siege of Tenochtitlan manifests a memory continuum in the Indian's historical consciousness (cf. Ross 1988). This site of historical remembrance, if ominous for the Spaniards, was a source of joy for the Indians: "como ominoso para nosotros y para ellos feliz" (117). Indians retained a memory of old in present practices of their beliefs.

And here Sigüenza reconnects the scene of reading the books of old with the current events and an ethnography of the present:

> . . . no habiéndose les oluidado aún en estos tiempos sus supersti-ciones antiguas, arrojan allí en su retrato a quien aborrecen para que, como pereció en aquella acequia y en aquel tiempo tanto español, le suceda también a los que allí maldicen. Esto discurrí que significaban aquellos trastes por lo que he leído de sus historias y por lo que ellos mismos me han dicho de ellas cuando los he agregado. (117)

> [. . . since they had not forgotten their ancient superstitions even in these days, they throw there in effigy those whom they hate in order that the Spaniards, whom they now curse, may suffer the same fate as those of the earlier date who perished in the canal. I inferred that this was the significance of those objects, judging by what I have read of their histories and by what they themselves told me about them when I have gathered them up.] (246)

Sigüenza underscores the authority of his interpretation by alluding to his historical readings ("he leído de sus historias") and ethnographic research ("lo que ellos mismos me han dicho").

To Sigüenza's credit, he preferred the version—actually testifies as an eye witness—that traces the beginnings of the uprising to the Indians themselves and not to the castes or the poor Spaniards. The mobilization of the multitude presupposed an accurate analysis of the lack of corn, "No discurrían estos sin fundamento" [The latter were not without some basis]—moreover, a strategic use of "palabras desvergonsadas" [lewd words], "pleitecillos que entre si trataban sin lastimarse" [petty quarrels among themselves in which they did not hurt each other], and "grandes corrillos" [large groups of loungers] were like "premisas de algún tumulto" [portents of a mob] (117, 247). This letter testifies to the strategic deployment of noise, *Ruido,* in building an uprising. Obviously, Sigüenza did not sympathize in the least with the insurgency initiated by the Indians, but in spite of his disapproval, perhaps because he intended to record its logic for counterinsurgency, his version of the events exemplifies and complements the rebellions studied by Guha in *Elementary Aspects of Peasant Insurgency.* Traditional readings of insurgency in Latin America have tended to emphasize a lack of a political program and have praised the political acumen that the leaders of independence movements displayed in the nineteenth century when they were able to regulate the mobilization of subalterns who by then had had a long history of insurgency. One of the tasks of subaltern studies, however, is to retake these histories of uprisings, insurgencies, rebellions, and national identities without subjecting them to criteria that privilege moments where elites have organized them according to their political programs.

IN THE MANNER OF A SHORT CONCLUSION

The *Codex Mendoza* has enabled us to trace the production of a document that not only represented the pre-Columbian past, but also reproduced a text that would be taken for an authentic native document. If the *tlacuilos* were copying from pre-Columbian prototypes, why did the viceroyal authorities bother to produce a "copy" rather than send a pre-Columbian text? My guess has been that the production of the text by post-conquest subjects would have a greater impact, since the subjects affected by the Encomienda would seem to ratify its compatibility with ancient structures. In the end it did not matter what the *Mendoza* said about the kinds of tribute; what mattered was the fact that the system existed—especially in the form of labor tribute and personal services. The *tlacuilos* in not agreeing among themselves suggest a form of silence, of eschewing inquiry by missionaries, of "resisting the heat"—as Doris Sommer would put it (Sommer 1993). As an ethnographic document, *Codex Mendoza* is not concerned, however, with documenting idolatries and superstitions for their eradication—or, for that matter, resistance—but with establishing a socioeconomic precedent that would legitimize the Encomienda. This collection of the pre-Columbian past, therefore, bears an immediate relationship to policies towards Indians. But the Indian present is not only subordinated to Spanish rule politically and economically, but also intellectually. The interpreter casts the *tlacuilos* as inept and thus appropriates the institution of history. The key to recollecting the past—the task of interpreting the collection itself—now pertains to the Spanish specialist who presumes to understand pictographic writing and to be fluent in Nahuatl. In this text, we witness how the constitution of an intellectual elite is inseparable from the production of subalternity.

Sigüenza belongs to a later, fully consolidated intellectual elite that takes as a given—as a natural order the subalternity of the Indian population; his commendation of the remains of an indigenous nobility strikes me as paternalistic. Sigüenza collects pre-Columbian artifacts and early histories as an end in itself. He is an antiquarian in the strict sense of the term—the preservation of old documents informs his will to collect the past. It is the pre-Columbian past as the antiquity of New Spain that fascinates Sigüenza, and not its significance to his contemporary Indians, who are, moreover, perceived as an unruly mass with no (positive) resemblance to the ancient grandeur. But recollecting the past also enables him to decipher idolatrous and magical practices, as well as the significance Indians gave to specific locations within the city. Beyond the archival Spanish written sources, these places of memory testify to living indigenous oral histories. Both *Codex Mendoza* and *Alboroto y motín* provide materials for an inventory of the Culture of Conquest that produces subalternity, but *Alboroto y motín* also documents other rationalities to those dominant in the "West." Sigüenza's text, moreover, suggests how forms of passive resistance became fully articulated in the numerous rebellions that broke out in different parts of New Spain during the seventeenth century.

Scholars have tended to see these acts of insurgency as not political, as irruptions of violence without rationality, as sources of energy that had to wait for the political leadership of Creole elites of the independence movements. If the meaning of history always comes from the future, the emergence of the nation in the nineteenth century privileged these readings of insurgent movements as undeveloped. The Zapatistas today function as a return of the repressed that reminds us that other rationalities could have very well informed other insurgencies in other times.

NOTES

Early versions of this paper were read at the symposium on "Private Culture/Public Policy," organized by Norma Alarcón, at the University of California at Irvine Humanist Research Institute, June 8–12, 1994; the colloquium on "Other Circuits of Theory," organized by David Lloyd and Lisa Lowe, at the University of California at Irvine

Humanist Research Institute, July 13–16, 1994; and as a lecture in the series "Writing Conquest and Frontier Expansion," at Tulane University, November 14, 1994. I benefited greatly from the comments at these occasions. John Beverley, Lana Liebsohn, and Javier Sanjinés read earlier versions of this essay and gave me useful suggestions. I am, however, solely responsible for any errors of fact or judgment.

1. Readers of Gayatri Chakravorty Spivak's essay "Can the Subaltern Speak?" have generally failed to foreground a recommendation to learn how to speak to the subaltern, rather than limit the import of her question to an affirmative or negative response. We might all be willing to listen to the subaltern, but how would we know that the subaltern agrees on what we are hearing? The "learn-to-listen" solution invariably ends up in a we/them structure that ultimately betrays an anthropological will to objectivity that obviates dialogue.

2. Judith Halberstam, "Imagined Violence/Queer Violence," *Social Text* 37: 187–201. Another mode of addressing the "imaginary of violence" is the notion of "places of rage."

3. The archaeological dimension is informed by Michel Foucault's work in *The Order of Things: The Archaeology of Knowledge,* and his essay "What is an Author?" This essay is especially pertinent for comparative study of authority in collecting pre-Columbian pasts. In this regard I am indebted to the comparativist approaches in James A. Boon, *Other Tribes, Other Scribes* (New York: Cambridge University Press, 1982).

4. Ironically, Sigüenza y Góngora's books on Mexican antiquities have been lost. We know of Sigüenza y Góngora's historiography of ancient México from later historians who referred to him as "la autoridad del distinguido anticuario" [the authority of the distinguished antiquarian] (Orozco y Berra [1880]: I: 71) and "uno de los más beneméritos de la historia de México, porque formó a grandes expensas una copiosa y selecta colección de manuscritos y de pinturas antiguas" [one of the most worthy historians of México, because he formed at great expense a copious and select collection of manuscripts and ancient paintings] (Clavigero 1945 [1780–81]; I: 92).

5. I follow William G. Bryant's modernized edition of the *Alboroto y motín de los indios de México* (Sigüenza 1984). For a paleographic edition, see Sigüenza, *Alboroto y motín de los indios en México* (México City: Talleres Gráficos del Museo Nacional de Arqueologiá, Historia y Etnografía, 1932). The English version is by Irvine Leonard. Irvine Leonard, *Don Carlos de Sigüenza y Góngora* (Berkeley: University of California Press, 1929), 256. I have modified Leonard's translation when I have felt it necessary. Hereafter page numbers correspond to these editions. If I abstain from using terms such as "mob" and "riot" in my discussion of the events, I retain those terms in the translations of Sigüenza's use of *tumulto* (mob), *motín* (riot), and *alboroto* (disturbance), which are part and parcel of his counterinsurgent discourse. Ranajit Guha in *Elementary form of Peasant Insurgency,* in particular chapters 3 and 4, has discussed the use of these terms as a form of negating the political character of subaltern insurrections. We have become especially sensitive to language in the wake of the 1992 Los Angeles uprising, as the use of the term riot has systematically undermined the possibility

of conceiving any political motivation beyond the characterization of an irrational mob.

6. I emphasize this last point to counter recent scholarship that has questioned whether there ever was colonialism in the New World (Klor de Alva 1992; Adorno 1993). If Spanish colonialism in the sixteenth and seventeenth centuries differs from the English or French imperial enterprises in the nineteenth century, it does not follow that there is not much to gain by comparative study from both regional and temporal perspectives.

7. A classic instance is Fernando de Alva Ixtlilxochitl's description of a group of Indians led to their repartimiento (labor draft to perform work for Spaniards) by their governor, don Juan de Aguilar, Ixtlilxochitl's grandfather. According to Ixtlilxochitl they were singing songs by Netzahualcoyotl in which they recalled their noble origins (1975–1977, 2, 267–69). Their nobility should have kept them from the repartimiento: "la desdicha ha llegado a tanto que como si fueran maceguales y villanos los llevan a repartir a Tacuba . . ." [the extent of their misfortune is so great that they are taken to Tacuba as a labor draft [a repartir] as if they were *maceguales* [commoners] and peasants . . .] (2, 270).

BIBLIOGRAPHY

Adorno, Rolena. 1993. "Reconsidering Colonial Discourse for Sixteenth- and Seventeenth-Century Spanish America." *Latin American Research Review* 28, 3: 135–145.

Alva Ixtlilxochitl, Fernando. 1975–1977. *Obras históricas.* Edited by Edmundo O'Gorman. 2 Vols. México City: Universidad Nacional Autónoma de México.

Berdan, Frances F. "The Imperial Tribute Roll of the *Codex Mendoza.*" *Codex Mendoza* 1: 93–102.

Boon, James A. 1982. *Other Tribes, Other Scribes: Symbolic Anthropology in the Comparative Study of Cultures, Histories, Religions, and Texts.* New York: Cambridge University Press.

Boone, Elizabeth Hill. 1992. "The Aztec Pictorial History of Codex Mendoza." *Codex Mendoza* 1: 35–54.

Boone, Elizabeth, ed. 1993a. *Collecting the Pre-Columbian Past.* Washington, D.C.: Dumbarton Oaks Research Library and Collection.

———. 1993b. "Collecting the Pre-Columbian Past: Historical Trends and the Process of Reception and Use." In *Collecting the Pre-Columbian Past.* Edited by Elizabeth Boone, 315–51. Washington, DC: Dumbarton Oaks Research Library Collection, 1993a.

Brotherston, Gordon. 1992. *Book of the Fourth World: Reading the Native Americas Through Their Books.* Cambridge: Cambridge University Press.

Calnek, Edward. 1992. "The Ethnographic Content of the Third Part of *Codex Mendoza.*" *Codex Mendoza* 1: 81–91.

Chakrabarty, Dipesh. 1993. "Marx After Marxism: Subaltern History and the Question of Difference." *Polygraph* 6, 7: 10–16.

Clavigero, Francisco Javier. 1945 [1780–81]. *Historia antigua de México.* 4 Vols. México City: Editorial Porrúa.

Codice Mendoza. 1992 [c.1540]. Edited by Frances F. Berdan, and Patricia Rieff Anawalt. 4 Vols. Berkeley: University of California Press.

Cogdell, Sam. 1994. "Criollos, Gachupines, y 'plebe tan extremo plebe': Retórica e ideología criollas en Alboroto y motín de México de Sigüenza y Góngora." In *Relecturas del Barroco de Indias.* Edited by Mabel Moraña, 245–79. Hanover, NH: Ediciones del Norte, 1994a.

Durán, Diego. 1967 [c.1580]. *Historia de la Nueva España e islas de la Tierra Firme.* Edited by Angel María Garibay K. México City: Editorial Porrúa.

Errington, Shelly. 1993. "Progressivist Stories and the Pre-Columbian Past: Notes on Mexico and the United States." In *Collecting the Pre-Columbian Past.* Edited by Elizabeth Boone, 209–51. Washington, DC: Dumbarton Oaks Research Library Collection, 1993a.

Florescano, Enrique. 1993. "The Creation of the Museo Nacional de Antropología of Mexico and Its Scientific, Educational, and Political Purposes." In *Collecting the Pre-Columbian Past.* Edited by Elizabeth Boone, 49–81. Washington, DC: Dumbarton Oaks Research Library Collection, 1993a.

———. 1987. *Memoria mexicana.* México City: Editorial Joaquín Mortiz.

Foucault, Michel. 1984. "What is an Author?" *The Foucault Reader.* Edited by Paul Rabinow. 101–20. New York: Pantheon Books.

———. 1973. *The Order of Things: An Archaeology of the Human Sciences.* New York: Vintage Books.

———. 1972. *The Archaeology of Knowledge.* Translated by A. M. Sheridan Smith. New York: Harper Torchbooks.

García, Genaro. 1907. *Tumultos y rebeliones acaecidos en México: Documentos inéditos o muy raros para la historia de México.* Vol 10. México City: Viuda de C. Bouret.

Gruzinski, Serge. 1993. *The Conquest of Mexico: The Incorporation of Indian Society into the Western World, Sixteenth-Eighteenth Centuries.* Translated by Eileen Corrigan. Cambridge: Polity Press.

Guha, Ranajit. 1983. *Elementary Aspects of Peasant Insurgency.* Delhi: Oxford University Press.

———. 1988. "The Prose of Counter-Insurgency." In *Selected Subaltern Studies.* Edited by Ranajit Guha and Gayatri Chakravorty Spivak, 45–86. New York: Oxford University Press.

Halberstam, Judith. 1993. "Imagined Violence/Queer Violence: Representation, Rage, and Resistance." *Social Text* 37: 187–201.

Hobsbawm, Eric. 1959. *Social Bandits and Primitive Rebels. Studies in Archaic Forms of Social Movement in the 19th and 20th Centuries.* Glencoe, Illinois: The Free Press.

Howe, Kathleen Steward. 1992. "The Relationship of Indigenous and European Styles in the *Codex Mendoza:* An Analysis of Pictorial Style." *Codex Mendoza* 1: 25–33.

Iglesia, Ramón. 1944. "La mexicanidad de Don Carlos de Sigüenza y Góngora." In *El hombre Colón y otros ensayos.* México City: El Colegio de México.

Klor de Alva, J. Jorge. 1992. "Colonialism and Postcolonialism as (Latin) American Mirages." *Colonial Latin American Review* 1, 1/2: 3–23.

Leonard, Irving A. 1929. *Don Carlos de Sigüenza y Góngora: A Mexican Savant of the Seventeenth Century.* Berkeley: University of California Press.

Moraña, Mabel, ed. 1994a. *Relecturas del Barroco de Indias.* Hanover, NH: Ediciones del Norte.

———. 1994b. "Introducción." In *Relecturas del Barroco de Indias.* Edited by Mabel Moraña. Hanover, NH: Ediciones del Norte.

Nietszche, Friedrich. 1979. *The Use and Abuse of History.* Translated by Adrian Collins. Indianapolis: Library of Liberal Arts, Bobbs Merrill.

Orozco y Berra, Manuel. 1880. *Historia antigua y de la conquista de México.* 4 Vols. México City: Tipografía de G. A. Esteva.

Paz, Octavio. 1982. *Sor Juana Inés de la Cruz, o, las trampas de la fe.* Barcelona: Seix Barral.

Pratt, Mary Louise. 1992. *Imperial Eyes: Travel Narrative and Transculturation.* New York: Routledge and Kegan Paul.

Rabasa, José. 1993. "Writing and Evangelization in Sixteenth-Century Mexico." In *Early Images of the New World: Transfer and Invention.* Edited by Robert E. Lewis, and Jerry M. Williams, 65–92. Tucson: University of Arizona Press, 1993.

Robertson, Donald. 1959. *Mexican Manuscript Painting of the Early Colonial Period: The Metropolitan School.* New Haven, CT: Yale University Press.

Ross, Kathleen. 1993. *The Baroque Narrative of Carlos de Sigüenza y Góngora.* Cambridge: Cambridge University Press.

———. 1988. "Alboroto y motín de México." *Hispanic Review* 55: 181–90.

Saignes, Thierry. 1989. "Borracheras andinas: ¿Por qué los indios ebrios hablan en español." *Revista Andina* 7, 1: 83–123.

Sigüenza y Góngora, Carlos. 1984. *Alboroto y motín de los indios de México: Seis obras.* Edited by William G. Bryant. Caracas: Biblioteca Ayacucho.

———. 1932. *Alboroto y motín de los indios en México, 30 de agosto de 1692.* Edited by Irving A. Leonard. México City: Talleres Gráficos del Museo Nacional de Arqueología, Historia y Etnografía.

Sommer, Doris. 1993. "Resisting the Heat: Menchu, Morrison, and Incompetent

Readers." In *Cultures of US Imperialism*. Edited by Amy Kaplan, and Donald E. Pease. Durham: Duke University Press.

Spivak, Gayatri Chakravorty. 1988. "Can the Subaltern Speak?" In *Marxism and the Interpretation of Cultures*. Edited by Cary Nelson, and Lawrence Grossberg. Urbana: University of Illinois Press.

 Zárate, Julio. 1950. *Don Carlos de Sigüenza y Góngora*. México City: Vargas Rea.

Confronting Imaginations

Towards an alternative reading
of the *Codex Mendoza*

Cora Lagos

"Blatant colonialism mutilates you without pretense: it forbids you to talk, it forbids you to act, it forbids you to exist. Invisible colonialism, however, convinces you that serfdom is your destiny and impotence is your nature: it convinces you that *it's not possible* to speak, *not possible* to act, *not possible* to exist."

—Eduardo Galeano

Orality makes people verbose and lively, great entertainers and performers, free from the constraints of script and scripture.

—Johannes Fabian

How are cultures created, altered, destroyed, and maintained? What types of experiences are necessary, and what amount of disruption of the old society is required for the individuals in a culture to submit to domination and externally imposed cultural destruction? When we consider México, conquered and ruled by the Spanish from the sixteenth to the nineteenth centuries, we inevitably confront these questions, not out of some perverse desire for the exotic and archaic, but as part of trying to comprehend the impact on the Americas of the presence of Europe from the sixteenth century until today. The revolution in the modes of expression and communication, the conquest's impact on the memories and dreams of the survivors, the transformation of the imagination and subjectivity, and the role of the individuals and social groups in the development of forms of syncretic expressions, all remain necessary issues of exploration for anyone interested in the study of the colonization of México.

These topics need closer critical scrutiny. Despite notable exceptions, anthropologists have systematically ignored the impact of the period in which Spain dominated and transformed México, or have simply treated this as an accomplished fact, relegated to superficial treatment. In the same manner, the pre-Hispanic archaeology and history has been placed in catalogs to be forgotten or classified and converted into mere museum pieces, kinds of "souvenirs" of a remote past. At the same time, the majority of historians have simply ignored the revolution in the modes of expression that took place in sixteenth century México—the transition from pictographs and oral transmission of culture to the scriptural alphabet, forgetting perhaps that this was one of the main projects of Spanish domination. Yet, in just a few decades the indigenous nobility not only discovered writing, but also often combined it with their own forms of expression based on images that they cultivated, producing an important set of texts. The alphabetization and introduction of new pictographic techniques was a less spectacular method of colonization than the images and descriptions we have of war and conquest or the supposed ballads they converted into legends; but perhaps the colonization of the imaginary was one of the conquest's most insidious and violent practices, among the worst that any individual has ever had to experience.

This paper examines the confrontation of pictographic and alphabetical writing systems in sixteenth- and seventeenth-century Meso-America. In examining these writing systems I focus on the dynamics of power and violence in colonialist cultural impositions. These systems of inscription underlie fundamentally different ways of understanding the world. One of the main components in the colonization was the teaching of alphabetic writing which sought to reeducate and train the body and senses as well as to implement a new logic and semantics. To understand this attempt to reconstruct the colonized self, I intend to study a Meso-American codex in particular, the *Codex Mendoza*, with the goal of problematizing the production of this type of texts with respect to the implementation of alphabetic writing and the relation of this to the pictographic system and its transmission through the medium of orality.

My work also tries to question how the terms "orality," "writing," and "image"/"painting" have been naturalized.[1] These concepts are historically specific and value-laden. Evolutionary and classificatory writing theories (Walter Ong 1982, Jack Goody 1963, Joyce Marcus 1992) set up alphabetic script as the most accomplished form of writing. However, it is my contention that one needs to go beyond these theories by studying alternative systems of inscription not contemplated by Western categories. Resistance to the imposition of writing and theorizations that destabilize the idea of the letter as the main element of communication/contact in colonial contexts will allow me to question the fetishization of alphabetic script (Jacques Derrida 1976, and Peter Wogan 1994). This work will enable me to better understand the relationship between painting and writing in the past but it will also allow me to intervene in the politics of language that are still being practiced in the present. A reading that does not privilege alphabetic writing will have profound implications on the understanding of contemporary indigenous alternative forms of history. These binary classifications do not allow us to historizice the indigenous present cultures. My work endeavors not only to continue this ongoing debate about classificatory-evolutionist studies, but also to explore the multiple ways in which these Meso-American codices were changed from living works of art and knowledge into museum pieces and extinct histories.

This process began during the European Renaissance which searched for universal knowledge and articulated a philosophy of consciousness based on the scriptural alphabet perceived as an indispensable element in the production of history and the colonizing project. The "illiterate" subjects were constructed as people without history—without writing—and their cultural manifestations were considered incongruent with Western epistemology. Writing, construed as a more evolved technology, was a fundamental part of the process of colonization and epistemological violence against the methods of thinking Europeans considered "illiterate" and "irrational." Therefore it cannot be denied that the celebration of the letter and the complicity of the book was a development that retained in many ways a fetishized, mystical character, almost like a magical amulet.[2]

Walter Ong is one of several scholars who limit writing to a system of syllables or letters. So for Ong (1982), David Diringer (1962), and others, writing is in general a concept unified and restricted to the book. He believes the revolution in printing implies a new visual perception of the world: "a sight oriented sensorium." At the same time, Ong claims that the advantage of printing is to place "speech in space" in permanent form; this has caused a transformation of human perception into a form more "spatialized" or "visual" towards language and the material world's surroundings. According to Ong, starting with the seventeenth century, a transition can be observed towards a visual sensibility that results in a philosophy of language as synonymous with writing: "Views of language themselves had grown more and more spatialized. Language belonged essentially to the world of writing, not to speech" (64).

The implicit valorization of writing over orality in Ong and also Diringer extends further, it seems to me, in the theories of Jack Goody, which assume binary distinctions between orality and writing: "Looked at in the perspective of time, man's biological evolution shades into prehistory when he becomes a language-using animal; and history proper begins. . . . Writing gives rise to logic and objective history . . . writing permits the 'immutable' and impersonal mode of discourse" (1963, 305). Goody emphasizes the consequences of writing (writing considered as "recorded speech") in opposition to orality, referring in the first instance to logical thinking and later to the writing of history. The technological determinism of theories about literacy, such as Goody's, romanticize and construct the oral from rigid categories that mark it as a space of incoherence and contradiction: the oral as incapable of transmitting "objective" consciousness, as (mis) representing societies without memory—without history. Goody proposes a linear, teleological, and evolutionary development of phonetic writing that already establishes a hierarchy—superiority—and representation (visual against auditory) of the systems of writing in which the Greek alphabetic writing is positioned as the "maximum" moment in the "cerebral" development of the abstract.

It is interesting to note Michel de Certeau's (1984) observation that distinctions between conceptions of "writing" and "orality" derive from particular cultures beginning principally in the seventeenth century, utilizing a form of symbolic opposition developing in the emerging field of ethnography. For his part, Johannes Fabian describes orality as an invention of anthropologists such as Goody who base their definitions on "anterior" cultures and homogeneously raise the category of "lack of literacy": "Investigating literacy is part of the phenemon anthropology tries to comprehend" (1992, 64).

According to Fabian, the oral communities have been described, among other things, as societies that for centuries lacked the benefit of the letter. For Fabian, imperialist practices have been intrinsically associated with theories about writing and the ethnographer has acted as a collaborator. Fabian proposes destabilizing the type of associations surrounding the oral/written, object/subject dichotomies which are "lessened" if the outside reader is to be considered as an integral part of the written, thereby already moving towards breaking with these binary oppositions: "As I have argued, and tried to exemplify, oralization, that is, a recourse to audible speech, actual or imagined, is an essential part of our ability to read texts. Yet our "ideology" of literacy seems to put a taboo on revealing what we actually do when we read, for fear that oralization might subvert the authority of the written text" (1992, 89).

One of the seminal works of the last thirty years in exploring the split in theory between orality/writing has been *Of Grammatology* by Jacques Derrida (1976). Derrida's approach is enormously influential in the revision of this binary convention because of its intent to deconstruct the traditional Western preference for speech over writing and for ending the conception of the written word as a mere representation—visualization—of the spoken word. This includes his view that the perception of phonetic writing as a criterion to evaluate "progress" from an evolutionary perspective of culture is an ideological construction. The possibility of an "archi-writing," that is, the precondition of speaking frees us from the traditional binarism of speaking/writing, phonetic/nonphonetic writing that, according to the author, only serves to illustrate the naturalizing ideology of technology utilized by the West in contrast with other societies.

On the other hand, Walter Mignolo criticizes Derrida's framework as already containing ethnocentrism. According to Mignolo, Derrida questions these categories as a vehicle for destabilizing the foundations of Western thinking but not for condemning the use of writing as an instrument of colonial power. For Mignolo, Derrida's project cannot be used to work with nonverbal systems of writing, with "literacies in conflict" in colonial Latin America (1994, 293). I believe that Walter Mignolo is not fully considering the critique that Jacques Derrida makes of Claude Levi-Strauss and his political ethnocentrism, therefore forgetting that Derrida challenges the binarism of the "absence" of the written in orality and proposes alternative productions of nonverbal writing, trying to present a moment anterior to the differences: "they have [orality and writing] as their ultimate reference . . . the presence of a value or of a meaning that is supposed to be anterior to difference" (119). I think that Elizabeth Hill Boone offers a very useful interpretation of Derrida in her prologue to *Writing Without Words*, when she notes that instead of finding absences in Derrida work's, his approach can be used as a major part of the "reformation of a definition of writing" (1994a, 4). I consider the work of Derrida as fundamental for the purpose of studying the systems of nonverbal writing—pictographs—in Meso-America and the position and functions of these in the colonization and construction of subjectivities. Derrida's critical practice permits the inclusion of other systems and helps the ending of "writing" as a privileged site in that, for him, already there is no intrinsic relationship with speaking: "phonetic language *does not exist*" (118). The perspective offered by Derrida permits the consideration of different systems of writing, including among others, the Meso-American.

And if we intend to begin to problematize—to move out of—the "metaphysical oppositions" and study the dynamics of violence between different rationalities in the colonization of America, the theoretical positions of Mikhail Bakhtin (1986) and Michel de Certeau (1984) must form part of our intended deconstruction of the structures of power. Bakhtin argues that "orality" has never been completely eliminated even in the most "literary" texts and that we need to remember the reader as a crucial part of comprehension (this emphasizes the importance of the multiple receptions of texts) and the interaction of each individual with respect to the texts (60–102). Michel de Certeau presents writing as a normative practice, as a discipline that intends to purify all the nonregulated (non-policed) social practices for the efficient functioning of systems/institutions. It is necessary to mention the importance for Bakhtin, as much as for de Certeau, of other modes of alternative scriptural production, of the filtering of orality in the process of writing, of the penetration of unified genres, and of the horror of the "solitary erections of the oral" in the economy and processing of writing.

These critiques permit us to achieve a reading beyond the writing in it; the attack on the exclusive system of alphabetical writing in some emblematic way transforms itself into a challenge to all institutions of regulation in which the metaphor of writing on the body is symptomatic of the broad conflict that comes from the different systems of writing and refers to all the machinery of controlling subjectivities: "From initiation ceremonies to tortures, every social orthodoxy makes use of instruments to give itself the form of a story and to produce the credibility attached to a discourse articulated by bodies. . . . They are the figures of an experimental knowledge won through pain of the bodies that change themselves into engravings of these conquests" (de Certeau, 145–149).

The frameworks offered by de Certeau, Bakhtin, and Derrida help make us more aware of the colonizing nature of the traditional ways in which systems of writing have been studied and placed within a hierarchy of values. This allows us to study the question of writing from a more conscious position. We should think from the perspective of some of these critics, or as in the work of Peter Wogan (1994), about alternative forms of writing such as body tattoos, tracks in the woods, constellations, monuments, pictograms. This demystifies the idea of writing and the book perceived as a fetishized object. It follows from considering all these moments or productions as texts, as alternatives in which the categories of script, orality, and the pictorial cannot be maintained as absolute ones. Therefore we may need to constantly consider the range of situations that are never completely reducible. Many examples come to mind such as when "colonized" subjects appropriate the alphabet in their resistance; when *mestizos* and indigenous people re-write in Spanish or Nahuatl their own history within a Western mode, when pictographic texts are already shaped by their relations to the colonial experience, and when written documents and titles from colonial times are utilized today in rituals, becoming part of indigenous contemporary culture and heritage.[3]

The codices are a body of productions designed to reconstruct indigenous history after earlier pre-Hispanic documents were destroyed. These were created for various reasons: as a new restructuring of the Amerindian memory authorized by Spanish institutions, as a response to the necessity to negotiate legal and economic claims with institutions in the colony, and as a method of negotiating the cultural identity under new circumstances (Leibsohn 1994). And through having a significant number of alphabetic texts written in Nahuatl for Amerindians, "the legacy of the ancient system was still in force— in Central México and the Valley of Oaxaca—at least until the seventeenth century" (Mignolo 1994, 299).[4]

The *Codex Mendoza,* created on European paper, was produced between 1541 and 1542 by order of Virrey Mendoza almost a century after the conquest.[5] This codex forms part of the group of texts authorized as a reproduction of preconquest history. It was presented pictorially and with text and glosses. It effects a recounting of the history of México-Tenochtitlán from its foundation (1345) until its destruction (1522) and after colonization and it consists of three parts that provide pictographic information concerning the history of México-Tenochtitlán, including information about tributes of México-Tenochtitlán and the cycles of life in the time of the conquest. According to Serge Gruzinski (1992), this codex was produced by various *tlacuilo* that were subordinated—at least they appeared to be—to the Spanish historiography of the interpreter. The *Codex Mendoza* was to be admired by King Carlos V, rather than used to resolve legal disputes or to identify superstition or idolatry at a local level (Gruzinski 1992).

Once again we can observe a text where the pictographic side possesses great power and validity in the production of meaning—independent of writing—in the colonial epoch. According to Elizabeth Hill Boone, it presents a capacity for standardization and a structure of conventions that permits it "to be intelligible across ethnic and linguistic boundaries throughout and beyond the imperium . . . the manuscript painters structured the histories they told" (1994b, 51). The creation of an important body of codices suggests the impossibility—or at least the difficulty—of translating meaning and at the same time the necessity of utilizing the pictographs in spite of the fierce campaign of alphabetization: "it would unduly restrict the significance of these documents [the codices] to reduce them to inventories, primarily because the combination of things signified in the design of an ideogram enabled the Indians to express highly complex concepts and to handle the most abstract notions and the most imaginary constructions" (Gruzinski 1992, 12). It can also be noted that in the *Codex Mendoza* the pictorial text was made before the written interpretation (Gruzinski 1992) and can also be presented as an entity totally unconnected to, and independent of the interpreted written work. Because of this, the writing is reduced to a secondary level in this type of project, demonstrating, as Gruzinski and Boone point out, the centrality of orality and painting despite the incorporation of European elements and the constant supervision of interpreters and agents of alphabetization.

When we analyze these types of productions, we open a space with many questions and few answers. But it is important for us to continue investigating manifestations of culture that remind us at each moment that the pictorial images are not simply "decorations" that are annexed and already extinguished by the writing on the texts. However, projects such as the sixteen-volume encyclopedia *Handbook of Middle American Indians* (1964–76)—which are intended to catalogue the corpus of the colonial Meso-American codices within Western epistemological categories—in many ways either erase difference by considering the production of pictographs only as archaeological artifacts. Therefore, before beginning a study of a particular codex, it is important to pose certain questions with respect to the production of colonial texts in

general. This requires deconstructing the underlying assumptions as predictable, homogeneous, and colonized textualities. The corpus of codices that
are the texts with a pictographic component present great semantic complexity
and, on some occasions, are even contradictory and opaque projects or simply
products of a new site of signification, of new discourses of power, and of
emerging sensibilities.

We must avoid the classification and evolutionary studies that have been
the common practice in the works many anthropologists and archeologists
have produced in the last few years about the systems of inscription before and
after colonization. To some degree these works reproduce the system of hierarchization and concepts of Western progress (more or less evolutionary) for
nonverbal systems. As an example, the text of Joyce Marcus (1992) about
Meso-American systems of writing considers the Mayan system to be the
"most developed" of the region, because it is observed to be the "most evolved,"
which implies it is closest to the syllabic-alphabetic writing (with the highest
ratio of ideograms). If we apply this type of theory to the *Mendoza*, we mini-
mize the capacity to produce meaning across the pictorial, and we reduce it to
a mere artistic museum piece that needs to be catalogued by Western archaeol-
ogists. As Thomas Cummins points out, the codices refer us to a system of
inscription of Meso-American images that cannot be conceived of as "an-
tique"—as *antiguallas*. The colonial codices were not thought of as simulacra
of a time passed that was meant to be recreated and archived posteriorly.
Rather, "pictorial images . . . had a different role than recording and dissemi-
nating information and ideas; they established and authenticated them. After
all, the invention of writing was one of the key cultural differentiations that
Europeans made between themselves and the peoples of the New World,
whereas pictorial images were something they held in common" (Cummins,
249). It is interesting to develop an approach like that of Thomas Cummins
that opens a spectrum of possibilities for the conceptualization of these types
of textualities where the written is in some way demystified and where the
"tyranny of the alphabet" encountered resistance that was not insignificant.
The idea, then, is to investigate texts that, admittedly, show evidence of the
constraints imposed by a colonial project but, at the same time, also show how
difficult it is for ethnographic discourse to erase the "colonized subject" or
translate/represent manifestations of subaltern culture—which have their own
rationality—that oppose the occidental world view.

Thinking of the *Codex Mendoza* as a paradigmatic model for the functioning of the pictorial image in the colonial situation helps because it is in the
image more than in the writing where the contact between cultures is performed. In opposition to the studies previously mentioned, where the pictorial
side is a simple annexed text, marginal to the writing, I intend to study the pictorial images not merely as decorative texts that accompany the written text,

but as the nexus, the common space where information is established and authenticated. The creation of an important corpus of codices with significant pictorial content suggests the impossibility of translating meaning without demonstrating the capacity to utilize the systems of Meso-American inscription that survived despite the fierce campaign of alphabetization and the dissemination of a European aesthetic.

The last words written by the interpreter of the *Codex Mendoza* before this "history" was sent to become the property of King Carlos V are suggestive: "Diez dias antes de la partida de la flota se dio al ynterpretador esta ystoria para que la ynterpretase el qual descuydo fue de los yndios que acordaron tarde y come cosa de corrida no se tuvo punto en el estilo que convenia ynterpretarse" (the interpreter was given this history ten days prior to the departure of the fleet, and he interpreted it carelessly because the Indians came to agreement late; and so it was done in haste and he did not improve the style suitable for an interpretation). Who is this interpreter that constantly apologizes because "the interpretations are crude?" Do we really need to keep trying to identify through the calligraphy whether the interpreter is Gomez de Orosco, with his long Fs, or if it is Juan Gonzalez with his distinctive Gs or some other *mestizo* Nahualato, or possibly an Indian brought in by Father Bernardino de Sahagún? Perhaps these last words, with the reference by the interpreter to the distance between the Indians production of these pictographic texts and the alphabetic description of them "sin estilo, de corrida"—without style, in a rush—suggests the need to rethink the relation between writing and the image during the colonial epoch. This type of commentary can permit us to recognize ambiguities and mistakes. It demonstrates the difficulty of reading the pictographs from outside their context. Besides, we should remember that the pictographic text to which the interpreter refers is already a text produced in a different moment, a palimpsest of different times and world views: the pictographs were ordered by the Spanish crown to be placed next to their alphabetic description.

We must notice this quote of the interpreter which, in each sentence, appears to apologize and to describe his embarrassment for the clumsiness of his translation. The interpreter does not provide a narrative but rather a set of descriptions which he himself characterizes as "crude" which merely illustrate the pictorial. What is the significance of this desire to dialogue with different rationalities at the same time as trying to neutralize them? Why is there the idea of returning to the past through writing about it? Can it be thought of as an attempt to construct Amerindian culture as an *antigualla* through trying to reproduce its past? Why write alphabetically in the margin of the pictorial texts, to produce a metatext and not simply write without the pictorial representations? Perhaps, we can understand the reproduction of the codices as a strategy for both authenticating history and using it against the indigenous communities. If we consider, for example, the first page of this codex in which the foundation of Tenochtitlán is described as merely a decoration incapable of being intelligible and of conveying its original meaning, we lose the symbolism and the capacity of capturing and transmitting the memory these images have. On the other hand, to think that these images are transparent and easy to translate and to describe them in written words is absurd; there are already multiple levels in them that incorporate diverse sources of consciousness. We cannot forget that these images were once spoken, sung, and performed. The words that describe this event are at the end of the first page: "The Mexicas were brought to the seat of the City . . . and after many years of traveling from land to land they stopped in a place. In a grand crossroads in the middle of barren land, they encountered a land of clean water and resources and in this crossroads they discovered the *meshiti* a great stone or pineapple flourishing near a great tunnel in which a flow of eagles has been maintained who graze in the space of the poor nest of—and—many feathers of diverse colors" (*Codex Mendoza*, Folio 71V).

With respect to the content of the images in this kind of codices, James Lockhart (1976, 1993) describes them as something more than representations of things that existed in another space and time. Instead he and other scholars believe these may provide some glimpses of the indigenous spiritual world. Lockhart's perspective reminds us of the barriers of time mediating between the thinking of the Mexicas and that of the Europeans that we do not have the capacity to fully understand. The interpreter takes the image of an eagle perched on a rock and surrounded by bones and feathers, which represents the foundation of Tenochtitlán and describes it simplistically as just another historic moment of the Mexica people when they settled on a marsh. Its significance for them was much greater. Because of this we should question once more the articulation of the pictorial by the verbal. The description of the interpreter with respect to this first page appears to be indifferent to the coexistence of these different "mythic spaces," or perhaps his repeated blushing and apologies would suggest a consciousness of the limits of the system of writing at the very moment of its expression/articulation of the pictorial.[6]

On the other hand, we can always infer that pictographic texts such as the *Codex Mendoza* were developed as part of the strategies of colonization which intended to recreate a continuity of historical events (in the European mode, indifferent to other imaginaries) across the pictorial permitting authentic information to be written in a history in which the past and present are conflated without any contradictions: "For the things of the past are never viewed in their true perspective or receive their just values; but values and perspectives change with the individual or the nation that is looking back on its past" (Nietzsche 1957, 19). As a clear example of this, the *Codex Mendoza* presents an inventory of the tributes to Tenochtitlán before the coming of the Spanish that can denote an intention to present the system of *encomiendas* (attacked

and criticized by many) as a continuation of the tributary system during the
colonization, making this system familiar as an indigenous practice of the area.
It is important to note that these codices were produced in the period in which
the formulation of the *Nuevas Leyes* attempted to regulate and organize the *encomienda* system. And in addition to the detailed inventory of tributes Serge
Gruzinski points out that:

> The *Codex Mendoza* unfolds a film of daily life in the Nahua world.
> Birth, marriage, education, war, justice, prevention of crime, drunk-
> enness, adultery, theft, were all in turn conjured up in pictures. The
> lower classes and daily life made a notable apparition: the peasant
> with his stick (*coa*) and his basket (*huacal*), the artisan, the carpenter,
> the stonecutter; even deviants of all kinds, the thief, the hobo, the in-
> veterate gambler. It is as if there suddenly emerged into pictorial exis-
> tence layers of the population and types in which tlacuilo of other
> periods seem to have paid little heed, being inclined to work on the
> imposing images of gods and the powerful than on the delineation of
> the lowly. . . . The third part of the *Codex Mendoza* attests to the fact
> that pictographic expression could also view the world and the society
> from which it emerged, by recording what it would have judged too
> ordinary or too obvious to be painted. (Gruzinski 1993, 32)

According to Gruzinski, the *Codex Mendoza* displays a "film" of daily life
of the Nahua world presenting images that describe scenes related to birth,
family life, war, justice, prevention of crime, and adultery. And contrary to the
pre-Hispanic pictographic texts, the lower classes make a significant appearance: the farmer, the artisan, the carpenter, the athlete, the drunk, among others, are presented in "snap shots" throughout the images of the codex. It
appears as if, in the pictorial texts, there is a sudden emergence of the lower
classes, their everyday life, and even their existence, which the *tlacuilo* had not
paid attention to in times previous to the conquest (they were dedicated more
than anything to portray the gods and the ruling classes). This sudden inclusion of scenes of domestic life can therefore direct us to the subaltern subjects
that are now represented and invented under another optic. The *tlacuilo* distance themselves from their own way of representing their reality, because they
now have to operate within a different rationality.

The "snapshots" that Gruzinski mentions describe the domestic scenes removed of all context (the pre-Hispanic visual images always were included in a
context), make us aware of pictographic moments, supervised and designed as
texts that are presented in a way that seems to be indifferent to pre-Hispanic
conventions. Maybe we can interpret this mode of representation as the disappearance of the *tlacuilo* imaginary outside of what is revealed and retained of

their culture in the new space of signification. These new images help us realize that the pictographic text in these codices acts as another instant of violence in the colonization process: it intends to recreate and to verify a continuity of historic events through the pictorial system, which "authenticates" information. It may be interpreted, then, as the production of a history through images in which the past and present converge without any contradictions.

At the same time, the images of activities of the lower classes could suggest to us the intention to construct the subjects as domestic, submissive—regulated—accustomed to pay tribute and ready to accept the colonial order and religious conversion. Previously their images were primarily concerned with spiritual matters or depicting the activities and interests of the nobility. These new images could show the project of representing secular and subordinated future citizens of the crown.

And if we wish, in conclusion, to continue reading against the grain, to continue trying to consider these pictographic images as something more than an authorized invention of Virrey Mendoza for justifying the tributary system and the implementation of personal service, we should perhaps look for the possibility of reading resistances, including silences and self-censorship. I return to the last quote of the codex to rethink this complex scenario, "diez dias antes de la partida de la flota se dio al ynterpretador esta ystoria para que la ynterpretase el qual descuydo fue de los yndios que acordaron tarde y coma cosa de corrida no se tuvo punto en el estilo que convenia ynterpretarse" (*Codex Menodoza*, Folio 71V). How can we know that what they produced, now on European paper, was a faithful reproduction of their practices and history before the conquest? Why did they hold back, what type of self-censorship—resistance—was at play in this activity? What type of clandestine activities can we surmise? It is not only important to come up with answers, but to continue the work of conceiving these texts as dynamic, multifaceted spaces where Meso-American cultures and their system of inscription do not submit or accept the "tyranny of the alphabet" so easily. Because through the image there is an articulation of the differences and oppositions that continually subvert the integrity and the authority of the colonial alphabetic text. Maybe, we can consider these moments of contact as a scenario of systems in conflict where the subject that is alphabetized, converted, and neutralized can begin to be heard and read from these disagreements, these silences and these secret actions.

How does the reading and questioning of these texts help us understand and critique the present? And how does reading the past help us understand present social, political, and individual conflicts? As I referred to earlier, my perspective is not to create a study intended to speak for, and enter into the past, but to try to think of the past and the present as a plurality of temporalities that coexist in the moment in which we read and think about colonial problematics.

Thus what allows medievalist historians to historicize the medieval or the ancient is precisely the fact that these worlds are never completely lost. It is because we live in "time-knots" that we can undertake the exercise of straightening out some part of the knot (which is what chronology is). Subaltern pasts—aspects of these time-knots—thus, act as a supplement to the historian's past and in fact aid our capacity to historicize (Chakrabarty, 39).

In this quote, Dipesh Chakrabarty integrates to some degree two of the principal concerns in this article. On the one hand, to problematize this investigation with respect to what Chakrabarty defines as writing the "minority history" or the "subaltern past" and also, to always consider it as related to, and relevant for the problems of the present. In my work, I neither intend to reduce the "subaltern past" to a subset deep within traditional historiography nor to reduce it to a predictable and already situated type of discourse; for this study my intention is to read voices "of the minorities" in a codex such as the *Mendoza* that express the complexity of these productions in the Mexican colonial epoch. To problematize this text permits my reading to try to avoid reification, stagnation, and the binaries of the *Codex Mendoza*'s opposition to "minor" or "marginal" narratives of the past and the present. Chakrabarty prevents us from simplifying this type of investigation by naively believing that it can systematically change previous historical research by easily replacing the corpus of materials or studying it from new and different perspectives (1997, 41). Theorization such as Chakrabarty's reminds us of the importance of being careful and not repeating the same type of hierarchical constructions and generalizations typical of other historical studies. We must accept the limits of the discipline to endeavor this type of investigation. José Rabasa (1993), for his part, has argued that infinite deconstruction should be our goal: "The task of subaltern studies, as we define it in this essay, would seek to conceptualize multiple possibilities of creative political action rather than defining a more mature political formation. Subaltern studies, therefore, would not pretend to have a privileged access to subalterns—rather would define intellectual work as one more intervention in insurgent movements. . . . *Protagonism* would thus be subjected to infinite deconstructions" (N/P).[7] For this reason, in this article I try less to reread these forgotten texts as skeletons of the past than to offer a perspective that focuses on their multiple "historical realities." In this way, I also intend to contribute to think about, and question the present. The term "time-knots" that Chakrabarty borrowed from Ranajit Guha reminds us of the plurality of temporalities of which the present is constituted; the project of investigating these "subaltern pasts" can help us at the same time to visualize and exhibit the multifaceted, the "incommensurable," and the chaotic nature of our present.

Statements such as that of Comandante Ramona of the Zapatista Army of National Liberation (EZLN), "we have not been able to speak in 500 years," reminds us that the present is primarily constituted by an accumulation of things of the past that reflect it in the current situations. The silences, the doubts, the subtle resistances that I try to read in a colonial text such as the *Mendoza* begin now to become embodied and to have a voice and a name, but not without having already paid a price in horrible violence. The reference that José Rabasa makes to the emergence of a "hegemony of the diverse" in México is manifested also throughout Latin America and in the United States. These new discourses and new activisms can be heard, read, and seen now in, among many other places, the Zapatista communiqués from the Lacandona forests in the internet; the new production on the part of young Mexicans of new codices, *"amates de resistencia"*—resistance amates—, the movement of the "new Indian" organized by young Argentines as a form of protest against the massive incursion of North American capitalism, the multiple testimonies, autobiographies, oral narratives, performances, poems, murals, textiles that women from all the cardinal points have been producing, are all new forms of protest against the political and social situations that have oppressed subalterns for the last five centuries.

The denunciations in the past about the situation of colonial oppression that once were suggested—almost whispered—by the drawings of the *tlacuilo* or written by an indigenous, a *mestizo,* a *criollo* or even a European subject are now much more vocal and open. In the present, these types of textualities have multiplied and identities have exploded into multiple positions and types of protests for subjects facing different situations of colonial and postcolonial oppression. Let me return to the first epigraph of this essay: "Blatant colonialism mutilates you without pretense: it forbids you to talk, it forbids you to act, and it forbids you to exist. Invisible colonialism, however, convinces you that serfdom is your destiny and impotence your nature: it convinces you that *it's not possible* to speak, *not possible to act, not possible to exist,"* which reminds us again that the present should never forget either the less dissimulated colonialism of the past or the no less obvious colonialism of the present. And at the same time we should continue to unmask—no matter if through the study of writing, the oral, the pictorial or other media—the not so invisible "invisibilities" of the multiple mechanisms of oppression of the past and present.

NOTES

1. I refer to such terms with only a brief introduction, yet I should problematize them. It is impossible to use these terms absolutely, since there is already a colonial context present, alternative manifestations and cultures, different contexts, and different

subjectivities. I do not wish to make an exhaustive study of writing, orality and painting or to present the "tyranny of the alphabet" as the most important vehicle/instrument in the process of colonization. However, I believe it is fundamental to question the theories that have been produced about this theme. Nevertheless, it is also important to study facts, texts, and theories that help us to enter in this infinite and controversial field. I should acknowledge that I will examine a range of theoretical discussions as they apply to this text in particular.

2. According to Walter Mignolo (1995), the book was converted into one of the symbols of the European imperial/religious enterprise from the sixteenth century onward. For more information about the "materiality of writing" and the book as artifacts of power see his book *The Darker Side of the Renaissance* (Ann Arbor: The University of Michigan Press).

3. The references to these documents and titles are provided by the essay of Joanne Rappaport, "Writing History" (Chicago: Chicago University Press, 1994). The essay presents examples of titles and documents in indigenous alphabetic writing that are used today for validation of their culture and territory. Rappaport proposes considering the written and the oral as forms of knowledge that interact in the present time and that therefore it is not easy to separate oral manifestations from writing.

4. I do not wish to essentialize and give the impression that only pictographs can "express" the indigenous rationality. The *Leyenda de los cinco soles* is a clear example of a text written in alphabetic form written by an indigenous Mexican about the Nahua cosmology that demonstrates that the use of the alphabet does not imply the writing and acceptance of a new epistemology. The text recreates their cosmology reading pictographic images and recording the memory of oral narratives. I believe I also should point out the hermeticism of this text that translates with extreme difficulties in reading and comprehension for the reader not familiar with these materials.

5. *The Codex Mendoza,* Edited by Frances F. Berdan and Patricia Reiff, 4 vols. (Berkeley: University of California Press, 1992).

6. As a side note, the image of the eagle perched on the cactus reminds us of the national emblem of México that has remained on the Mexican flag until today.

7. José Rabasa offers in this article a panorama and problematization of the localized movements of resistance and their repercussions on a global level (and vice versa) that have emerged in México during these last years.

BIBLIOGRAPHY

Adorno, Rolena. 1988. "El sujeto colonial y la construcción de la alteridad." *Revista de crítica literaria latinoamericana* xvi, 28: 55–68.

Bakhtin, Mikhail. 1986. "The Question of Speech and Genres." *Speech Genres and Other Essays,* 60–102. Austin: University of Texas Press.

Bhabha, Homi, K. 1994. *The Location of Culture.* London and New York: Routledge and Kegan Paul.

Boone, Elizabeth Hill. 1994a. "Introduction: Writing and Recording Knowledge." In *Writing Without Words: Alternative Literacies in Mesoamerica and the Andes.* Edited by Elizabeth Hill Boone, and Walter Mignolo. Durham and London: Duke University Press.

———. 1994b. "Aztec Pictorial Histories: Records Without Words." In *Writing Without Words: Alternative Literacies in Mesoaemerica and the Andes.* Edited by Elizabeth Hill Boone and Walter Mignolo. Durham and London: Duke University Press, 1994.

Chakrabarty, Dipesh. 1997. "Minority Histories, Subaltern Pasts." *Perspectives* 35, 8: 39.

Codex Mendoza. 1992. Edited by Frances Berdan, and Patricia Reiff. 4 Vols. Berkeley: University of California Press.

Cummins, Thomas. "From Lies to Truth: Colonial Ekphrasis and the Act of Crosscultural Translation." 249

de Certeau, Michel. 1984. "The Scriptural Economy." *The Practice of Everyday Life,* 132–152. Berkeley: University of California Press.

Deleuze, Gilles, and Guattari, Felix. 1987. *A Thousand Plateaus: Capitalism and Schizophrenia.* Translated by Brian Massumi. Minneapolis, MN: University of Minnesota Press.

Derrida, Jacques. 1976. *Of Grammatology.* Translated by Gayatri Chakravorty Spivak. Baltimore and London: The Johns Hopkins University Press.

Diringer, David. 1962. *Writing.* New York: Praeger.

Foucault, Michel. 1973. *The Order of Things.* New York: Pantheon.

Fabian, Johannes. 1992. "Keep Listening: Ethnography and Reading." In *The Ethnography of Reading.* Edited by Jonmathan Boyarin, 89–105. Berkeley: University of California Press.

Goody, Jack. 1963. "The Consequences of Literacy." *Comparative Studies in Society and History.* 1, 3:

Gruzinski, Serge. 1993. *The Conquest of Mexico: The Incorporation of Indian Societies Into the Western World,* 16–18th. Centuries. Cambrige, UK: Polity Press.

———. 1992. *Painting the Conquest: The Mexican Indians and the European Renaissance.* Paris: Flammarion.

Leibsohn, Dana. 1994. "The Paradise Garden Murals of Malenalco: Utopia and Empire in 16th Century Mexico." *Americas* 51, 3: 433–435.

———. 1993.

Lockhart, James. 1976. *Beyond the Codices: The Nahua View of Colonial Mexico.* Translated and edited by Arthur J. O. Anderson, Frances Berdan and James Lockhart. Berkeley: University of California Press.

Marcus, Joyce. 1992. *Mesoamerican Writing Systems: Propaganda, Myth, and History in Four Ancient Civilizations.* Princeton: Princeton University Press.

Mignolo, Walter. 1995. *The Darker Side of the Renaissance: Literacy, Territoriality & Colonization.* Ann Arbor: The University of Michigan Press.

―――. 1994. "Afterword: Writing and Recorded Knowledge in Colonial and Postcolonial Situations." In *Writing Without Words: Alternative Literacies in Mesoamerica and the Andes.* Edited by Elizabeth Hill Boone and Walter Mignolo. Durham and London: Duke University Press.

Nietzsche, Friedrich. 1968. *The Will to Power.* Translated by Walter Kaufmann and R. J. Hollingdale. New York: Random House

―――. 1957. *The Use and Abuse of History.* Translated by Adrian Collins. New York: Macmillan Publishing Company.

Ong, Walter. 1982. *Orality and Literacy: The Technologizing of the Word.* London: Methuen.

Rabasa, José. 1993. *Inventing America.* Norman and London: University of Oklahoma Press.

―――. N/P. "Beyond Representation? The Imposibility of the Local" In *Notes on Subaltern Studies in Light of a Rebellion in Tepoztlán, Morelos.*

Rappaport, Joanne. 1994. "Writing History." In *Cumbe Reborn,* 10–36. Chicago: Chicago University Press.

Wogan, Peter. 1994. "Perceptions of European Literacy in Early Contact Situations." *Ethnohistory* 41, 3: 70–90.

Narrating Colonial Interventions

Don Diego de Torres, *Cacique* of Turmequé in the New Kingdom of Granada

Luis Fernando Restrepo

An inquiry into colonialism past and present is ultimately a matter of the hegemony of the Western notion of time. Western temporality or its experience of time (in)forms the story of colonialism. But no hegemony is total nor uncontested. Opposed, juxtaposed, or intertwined to Western temporality we can find multiple temporalities arising at any given moment from the heterogeneity of lived experience. These different and competing notions of time are experienced and made meaningful through narrative forms. The narrativization of time in contexts of colonization is thus a strategic site for a critical inquiry and for intervention. Opening and locating hegemonic time may prove useful to the postcolonial project of decolonization: to reveal the Othering of non-Western time narratives and to reinscribe the suppressed, marginalized time of the Other. Johannes Fabian (1991) and Homi K. Bhabha (1990) have already rendered valuable insight about these processes, the denial of "coevalness" of colonial discourse and the homogenizing holism of national narratives, respectively.

A postcolonial reading of Paul Ricoeur's (1980) concept of "narrative time" may also shed light into the cultural processes involved in the colonization of the Americas. Briefly stated, narrative time refers to a public (collective) experience that embraces, through a narrative process, past, present, and future time. Such process makes it possible not only to *plot* imperial and national projects, but also to read the end in the beginning and vice versa. It is at once a founding act (present) that draws from memory (the past tuned into human time) to project it into the future.[1] In a few words, narrative time refers to a hegemonic reading of time experience (past, present, and future) oriented towards the future. Its teleology, however, is not based on linear, abstract time, but on a deeper, collective experience of it. We still have to see if this is a

97

particularly Western reading of temporality. In any case, what is important from a postcolonial perspective is to see narrative time as colonial discourse and to conceive and account for counter hegemonic readings of this public imperial and national time.

How can postcolonialism surpass the epistemic violence of colonial and national narrative time? Bhabha suggests that we must attempt to *write* the heterogeneous, nonsequential energy of lived historical memory and subjectivity (Bhabha 1990, 293). In other words, we need to think time "otherwise" and to think that which we were "obliged" to forget by the pedagogic colonial and national narratives.

With this general postcolonial project in mind, the present essay focuses on the relationship of narrative, subjectivity, and colonialism by examining the writings of and about a sixteenth-century *mestizo* (mixed-race), don Diego de Torres, *cacique* (Amerindian chief) of Turmequé, in the New Kingdom of Granada (present-day Colombia). First, I will examine how this historical figure has been narrativized from the colonial period to the twentieth century. Don Diego de Torres is narrativized as a colonial subject; he is also turned into an important element of an imagined community's narrative time. Second, I will focus on Diego de Torres's texts and two maps produced for the Crown as countercolonial discourse that underscores the complex process of narrating the self and community. But both processes (colonial discourse and don Diego's interventions) are not separated but intertwined. Therefore, we must address this conflictive interstice of the colonial subject.

Don Diego's story has been studied by Colombian historian Ulises Rojas. His now classic study *El cacique de Turmequé y su época* (1965) examines the political context of the New Kingdom of Granada during don Diego's time and offers us an ample collection of documents related to the *cacique* and sixteenth-century colonial society. The present study is based on many documents transcribed by Rojas. However, a postcolonial reading of the same texts offers us new insight into don Diego's colonial interventions.

Don Diego de Torres was born around 1549 to a Spanish conquistador and *encomendero* (Trustee of Indian tribute), Juan de Torres, and a Chibcha noble woman, Catalina de Moyachoque, niece of the Cacique of Turmequé. Don Diego grew up in the Spanish city of Tunja, where he attended the Dominican's school, but he also must have maintained close ties to Turmequé, for he was later considered a legitimate *cacique*. He may have been, in fact, a *capitán*, a lower rank authority, according to Rojas (1965). His Chibcha name was *Rurmequeteba*. In Chibcha it meant the *capitán* (*teba*) of Rurmequé (Rojas 1965, 133).

As the son of the *encomendero* of Turmequé, he also must have had strong yet uneasy relations with the Turmequé community. For one part, *encomenderos* were by law forbidden to live in their *encomiendas* (alloted Indian community); they often preferred to live in the Spanish cities. They had, however, close and continuous links to the allotted Amerindian community. In Tunja, the *encomenderos'* impressive mansions with ample arcades and courtyards were not only made to express power and prestige, but also to accommodate the necessities of a livelihood that mediated between the country and the city. They provided enough room for the circulation and storage of tax goods such as textiles and agricultural products (Corradine 1990). On the other hand, Diego's relation to his mother's community must have been somehow problematic considering the Crown's legislation forbidding *mestizos,* blacks and "vagrants" to live in Indian towns (Morner 1967, 46).

In 1565, the *encomienda* of Turmequé consisted of fifteen hundred taxpaying Indians and sixty "personal" Indian servants (this figure excludes women, children, and elders). Juan de Torres died in 1570 and his Spanish-born son, Pedro de Torres, inherited the *encomienda,* rather than Diego. This was not at all unusual. It was common for *mestizos* to receive less inheritance, or even nothing if they were "illegitimate" (Ares 1997). In addition, the Crown had prohibited awarding *encomiendas* to *mestizos* since 1549 (Ares 1997, 40). But if don Diego's right to the *encomienda* was lost, he still was considered part of Turmequé. His maternal uncle was the *cacique.* Therefore, when he died, according to the Chibcha matrilinear tradition, Diego de Torres was the legitimate heir to the *cacicazgo.* This was accepted by the people of Turmequé (as far as we know). Even colonial authorities recognized this, since the *Audiencia* of Santafé ratified the people of Turmequé's petition to nominate him as their *cacique* (Rojas 1965, 9). His half-brother, however, soon complained to the *Audiencia* that don Diego was "inducing the Indians to disobey" (cited in Rojas 1965, 11). In 1575 the *Audiencia* decided to remove don Diego from his *cacicazgo* because: "They understood that there were no *mestizo caciques* in Perú or in New Spain. They also thought that this measure prevented major inconveniences and future cases due to the bad "tendencies" of the *mestizos*" (cited in Rojas 1965, 14). This started a long legal battle in which don Diego was persecuted, imprisoned, and later exiled from the New Kingdom. After escaping prison, he traveled to Spain in 1575 to present his case to the Council of the Indies. He also presented a similar petition for another *mestizo* of the New Kingdom of Granada, Alonso de Silva, *cacique* of Tibasosa.[2] A year later, the Council upheld the *Audiencia's* decision. In a new hearing with Philip II in 1578, the King overturned the Council's decision and recognized don Diego's right to the *cacicazgo* of Turmequé. Both Rojas (1965) and Gálvez Piñal (1974) have stressed that don Diego's interventions were a decisive factor in the Crown's appointment of Juan Bautista Monzón as *visitador* (official inspector) to the New Kingdom of Granada. The Crown's efforts to exercise greater control of the New Kingdom may not have been as succesful as expected. For decades there was a strong opposition to the New Laws (1542) regulating *encomiendas,* for instance. Don Diego seemed to provide the kind of arguments that the Crown needed to limit the power of the *encomenderos*. The alliance of King-Monzón-don Diego is far from permanent and horizontal, and it illustrates well the complex issue of subalternity, a topic that has been central in the postcolonial discussion (Guha 1988; Spivak 1988; Said 1994; Gandhi 1998) in general and also in the Americas (Seed 1991; Mignolo 1993; Vidal 1993; Latin American Subaltern Studies Group 1993; and Mallón 1994). Don Diego as a legitimate *mestizo* and *cacique* was part of an empowered elite. Yet he also occupied an ambivalent and subordinated position in colonial society. The Crown's legislation is often contradictory regarding *mestizos*. It seems to express well the ambiguous place they occupied. For example, the Crown's favorable decision regarding don Diego's case, suggests that, if not expressly recognized, it seemed to consider *mestizos* as valuable *passeurs culturels* or mediating agents. On the other hand, the same year (1578) it passed legislation barring *mestizos*, who had been crucial in the evangelization in Indian communities, from being ordained as priests (Ares 1997, 48).[3]

In 1579 don Diego returned to the New Kingdom with a Royal decree overruling the *Audiencia's* removal of his *cacicazgo* and awarding him royal protection. However, rumors that he was organizing an Indian revolt forced him to flee to Spain once again (more on this alleged revolt below). But this time the Crown decided not to allow him to return to the New Kingdom, confining him to the court, where he remained until his death. From this seemingly endless legal battle, we have today ample documentation about don Diego's plight and the world he lived in.

At the time of the Spanish arrival (1536), the Chibcha people of the central Andean region consisted of a confederation of communities whose population, according to Juan Friede, neared half a million (1984, 97). They were organized in two major groups, the *Zipa* and the *Zaque*. To the southwest, on or around present-day Bogotá (*Bacatá, Mequetá* in Muisca), ruled the *Zipa*. The *Zaque's* center was located to the northwest, where the city of Tunja (*Hunza*) was founded (Friede 1984, 98). It is not coincidental, therefore, that in the sixteenth century, when the *encomienda* was the central structure of colonial society, both Bogotá and Tunja were the most important Spanish cities in the New Kingdom of Granada. Initial Spanish rule maintained part and modified other elements of Chibcha political structure to establish the *encomienda* system as a form of indirect rule. First they abolished the top political figures (*Zipas*) from the two main confederations, Bogotá and Tunja. They maintained, however, the local leaders, called *caciques* (an Arawak term imported to the mainland) and *capitanes* by the Spaniards.[4] Yet several measures taken during the following decades altered substantially the Chibcha social fabric: mining and the *mita urbana* (labor for hire) altered internal relationships, Spanish-like urban settlements were implemented to facilitate evangelization and policing, and the *resguardos*, a reservation system set up during the final decades of the sixteenth century, relocated Chibcha communities near Spanish towns or *haciendas* to provide a labor pool (Gonzalez 1970).

NARRATING DON DIEGO'S INTERVENTIONS

From the colonial period to the twentieth century the story of *el cacique* of Turmequé has drawn the attention of colonial officials, historians, and writers more than any other *mestizo* in the region. Don Diego's story seems to be the emblematic story of *mestizaje* in the New Kingdom of Granada. Although we know that his story comprises more than an individual situation, it may be problematic to view his experience as representative of all *mestizos*, since recent studies reveal that there were largely two groups of *mestizos* during the sixteenth century, the "illegitimate" and marginalized on one hand, and, on the other hand, a small group of *mestizos* from powerful Indian and Spanish families who had been integrated, with certain limits, to Spanish society (Ares 1997).[5] Granted that don Diego's case may not be representative of all *mestizos*, the different texts that register his presence still reveal larger social concerns. These preoccupations, colonial and national, can be highlighted by examining how don Diego's interventions in colonial society are narrativized. But I want to stress that this narrativization per se is an act of colonization, of inscribing him as a discursive figure within the narrative time of the state, both colonial and national.

MESTIZAJE AND THE PROSE OF COUNTERINSURGENCY

Don Diego's return from Spain to the New Kingdom of Granada in 1579 with Royal protection and a decree supporting his *cacicazgo* generated strong responses in the region from both the Spanish and Indians. Don Diego went first to Turmequé where he reportedly met with several *caciques*. Tunja officials were alarmed. They decided to cancel Holy Week celebrations, to guard the town, and to confiscate arms and horses "a todo género de gente naturales y mestizos y gente común extravagante" [to all sort of Indians, mestizos, and common people] (Rojas 1965, 114). From this point on we have several reports, rumors, and accusations that don Diego was planning a major revolt. For example, on April 8, 1580, in a letter to the president of the *Audiencia*, Tunja officials stated that "estan tan prevenidos los naturales, después que vino Don Diego de Torres, por tenerlo todo alterado . . ." [Indians are stirred after don Diego's arrival, there is great unrest] (Rojas 1965, 127). The *Audiencia* wrote to the King explaining that they ordered don Diego's detention "por ser hombre mañoso y tenerle todos los indios mucho respeto y fuera desto ser belicoso y muy diestro en las armas y buen hombre de acaballo" [because he was a tricky man and well-respected by the Indians. He is a troublemaker and a skillful rider and soldier] (Cited in Rojas 1965). The *Oidores* considered best to remove don Diego from the New Kingdom of Granada "por la poca confianza que del y de los demás mestizos se puede tener" [because he and the other *mestizos* cannot be trusted] (Rojas 1965, 129). They took this opportunity to request that no *mestizo* be allowed to serve as Crown officials (Rojas 1965, 130). Whether the accusations of don Diego's revolt were founded or not is not the main concern here. I want to focus instead on how and when the figure of the *mestizo* emerges in social discourse. Berta Queija Ares has documented that in Perú the attitudes towards *mestizos* changed dramatically during the 1560s and 1570s. During the previous two decades mixed-race people were mainly referred to as "hijos de españoles e indias" [of Spanish and Indian parents] (Ares 1997, 38). Around 1550 the term *mestizo* started to appear frequently in wills and other legal documents as a descriptive phrase added to the usual phrase: "O *mestizo, como aquí se les llama*" [or *mestizos,* as they are called here] (Ares 1997, 42). While the first *mestizos* were seen as an integral part of Spanish society, later they were perceived more and more as an alien and dangerous element. They occupied a space symbolically undefined: associated with the vagrants and the Indian world.[6] The Crown's efforts to "incorporate" into Spanish society *mestizo* children seems to be based on the same concern.[7]

The texts that refer to *mestizos* as a dangerous element may be considered part of what Ranajit Guha (1988) calls the prose of counterinsurgency. In one way or another these texts call for the state's intervention. They seem to make sense only as a code of pacification. These documents view subalterns in negative terms, as a law and order concern. As a result, they tend to suppress subaltern consciousness. For instance, peasant revolts are often narrated using the language of natural disasters, such as fire and storms. In the New Kingdom of Granada, for example, Fray Francisco de Segura, the parish priest for the *encomienda* of Guacha, near Tunja, wrote a letter to the King on June 10, 1582 referring to don Diego:

> Que los indios de este pueblo estan tan alzados como lo estan los de la [illegible] como ha ellos no les falta otra cosa sino matanzas . . . esto ha sido despues que vino un mal mestizo despana que les predico libertad despues que vino la bos del vistador palo cuales le hizo entender el dicho mestizo que ya no avian de pagar demoras ni habian de reconocer cristiano algunos y dizen que ya no han de pagar demora ni ha de tener doctrina y insiten a los indios comarcanos que haga lo mismo que si les va a pedir demora que ha de matar a quien se la fuera a pedir. Aunque vaya con vara de justicia. Que no ha de poner obediencia en doctrina ni han de entrar en la iglesia en su vida y otras maldades y desvuerguenzas. (AGI Escribanía de Camara, 826B)

[The Indians of this town are rebelling as the others[?]. They are close to start killing people . . . this happened after a bad mestizo arrived from Spain preaching freedom. News about the Crown's *visitador* had spread when this *mestizo* told them that they did not have to pay tributes and that they will not have a parish priest. They told the other Indians in the region to kill whomever asks them for tribute, even if he comes with the official staff. Also that they should not obey the parish priest. They are asked never again to enter the church and other evil and shameful things.]

In this text, Indian actions are responses to a perceived external stimulus, the "bad" *mestizo*. If indigenous consciousness is suppressed, that is not the case of the *mestizos*. Their actions are represented as conscious interventions. The problem, however, is that the prose of counterinsurgency sees these *mestizos* in terms of order and social control, and this revolt as the result of the "bad" influence of an individual, not as a collective action.[8] But perhaps these mediating agents' texts and actions articulate more than individual concerns. What I am suggesting here is that perhaps we can gain some insight into the colonial process by considering the issues of subalternity and *passeurs culturels* together. In don Diego's case, to what extent did his reports to the Crown (*memoriales de agravios*) articulate a mediated collective discourse? I will return to this question when I address the subject positions assumed by don Diego in the *memoriales de agravios* (formal complaints) sent to the Crown.[9]

The prose of counterinsurgency can be also found in different texts in which *mestizos* emerge as part of the narrative of the colonial or national state. Two Tunja historians centuries apart narrate don Diego's case in these same terms. That is they inscribe his story within a larger narrative. Juan de Castellanos' *Elegías de varones ilustres de Indias* (1589–1601) yields an epic vision of the history of the New Kingdom of Granada that supports the privileges of the *encomenderos* (Restrepo 1999). It is no coincidence that the story of don Diego is marginal here, since the poem projects a social order ruled by a military elite, the veterans of the conquest who "deserve" privileges. Castellanos seldom refers to *mestizos* and only a few lines of this long poem are dedicated to don Diego and the other *mestizos*. Castellanos contends that accusations of don Diego's revolt are not true, and that he and the people of the region are loyal to the Crown (Castellanos 1886, 202). In this way, this narrative manages to incorporate don Diego's intervention—which sought to redefine Spanish-Indian relationships—into the colonial project. In other words, counter-hegemonic discourse is absorbed by the narrative of the state.

In the twentieth century, don Diego's intervention is known mainly for the already mentioned work of Ulises Rojas, *El cacique de Turmequé y su época* (1965). Rojas text attempts to integrate in one narrative a personal story and a wider collective text: primarily a political history rather than a social history of the New Kingdom of Granada. The biographical narrative provides the main pathos, while the other articulates the narrative of the state. In one sentence, we see both projects intertwined:

> El valiente, sufrido y noble Cacique de Turmequé, que por su condición humilde, despertó el interés y recibió el favor de ser atendido por el corazón magnánimo de un Monarca que en su largo reinado no aspiró a otra cosa que al bienestar y felicidad de los vasallos de sus extensos dominios de la América meridional. (Rojas 1965, 347)

> [The daring, suffering, and noble Cacique of Turmequé, whose humble condition touched the heart of a great King, who reigned for many decades only seeking the welfare and the happiness of his subjects in his American domains.]

Rojas' liberal humanism comes to terms with colonial violence condemning not the system but its "abuses." Rojas' work is ultimately a story of national (be)longings for an Indian past that can only be mourned: "Al llegar a este punto, las vidas de los descendientes de don Diego de Torres desaparecen de la escena histórica para cubrirse, como toda su desventurada raza, con el piadoso manto del anonimato" [At this point, the lives of don Diego de Torres' descendants disappear from the historical scene, covered, as the rest of his unfortunate race, by the kind blanket of anonymity] (Rojas 1965, 515). Rojas envisions Amerindian culture in a remote past and most of his historiography is centered on Spanish-American society into which the figure of the *cacique* is incorporated.

MESTIZO ROMANCES

Two texts from different centuries have narrated don Diego's intervention in terms of a romance, Juan Rodríguez Freyle's *El carnero* (1636) and Gertrudis Gómez de Avellaneda's nineteenth-century short story "El cacique de Turmequé: Leyenda americana."

Rodríguez Freyle's *El carnero* is a hybrid text that offers a brief narrative of the history of the conquest, catalogues of colonial and ecclesiastical authorities, and a collection of stories or "cases" that occurred during the first century of Spanish occupation. Rodríguez Freyle's prose is overtly moralizing but also clearly ironic and satirical, repeatedly undermining the authority of New Kingdom's officials. Cases of corruption, witchcraft, and adultery are perhaps what thrust the narrative forward. The case of don Diego, discussed in chapters 13 and 14, is no exception. As a matter of fact, according to Rodríguez Freyle, the alleged revolt was concocted by Orozco, a crown official (*fiscal*), to fulfill his mistress's demand to apprehend Juan Bautista Monzón, don Diego's political ally. The figure of Salomé is echoed in Rodrígez Freyle's misogynic discourse.[10] She asked him:

> Que le había de dar la cabeza de Monzón, o que no le había de atravesar los umbrales de su casa; con lo cual le pareció a Orozco que ya quedaba privado de sus gustos. Este fue el principio y origen de la prisión del Licenciado Monzón, y de los muchos alborotos que tuvo esta ciudad, y pérdida de muchas haciendas, y daños, como adelante veremos. (Rodríguez Freyle 1942, 184)

> [to bring her Monzon's head, or he could not come to her house anymore. Orozco though that he could not fulfill his pleasures anymore. This was the beginning and the origin of Monzon's prison, and the upheavals that occurred in this city, and the many losses that it caused, as we will see ahead.]

Don Diego' interventions at a local, regional, and transnational level all are marginalized in this story focused primarily on Spanish society. The colonial project per se is not questioned, rather its corrupt officials and citizens.

The second romancing of don Diego's intervention, entitled "El cacique de Turmequé: Leyenda americana," comes from the romantic writer Gertrudis Gómez de Avellaneda. Born in Cuba in 1814 to an impoverished Spanish aristocrat and a wealthy Creole mother, Avellaneda traveled to Spain in 1836, where she became an established writer. Among her works are *Sab* (1841), an abolitionist novel; *Guatimozín, ultimo emperador de México* (1846), an idealized vision of the pre-Columbian past; and several poems and plays. Although no date is provided for "El cacique," it is most likely that Avellaneda wrote it in Spain. A moving story about an exiled *cacique* seems to reflect Avellaneda's own experience of exile.

Avellaneda's text is mainly a story of star-crossed lovers, don Diego and Estrella, *la capitana*, an attractive married woman also known as "the incomparable one." Avellaneda follows Rodríguez Freyle's text, which she considers "history." In addition, she expresses that she does not want to distort its accuracy in her emplotment of the story (Avellaneda 1981, 270). Avellaneda offers a positive yet idealized view of don Diego and of *mestizaje*:

> Pero más aún que por su origen augusto, era notable por su figura, que ostentaba la singular belleza producida comunmente por el cruzamiento de razas. Con dificultad se podría encontrar otro hombre en quien se amalgamasen tan armónicamente los más nobles rasgos de los hijos de la Europa meridional, con los característicos de las castas superiores americanas; constituyéndole un tipo magnífico, que no vacilamos en calificar como el bello ideal de los *mestizos*. (Avellaneda 1981, 250)

[But more than for his noble origin, he had a remarkable figure, which had the special beauty often produced by the mixture of races. There could hardly be any other man who had embraced so harmoniously the features of the descendants of Europeans with the characteristic features of the high castes of Amerindians. He was a magnificent type that we do not hesitate to consider as the beautiful ideal of the *mestizos*.]

All the conflicts of the contact zone lived by don Diego and other *mestizos* are ironed out. In the nineteenth century, a time of high nationalism, the ambivalent figure of the prose of counterinsurgency was turned into an ideal for social integration. In the story, *La capitana*'s affair is discovered by her husband, and he allegedly poisons her. The story concludes with an exiled and impoverished *cacique*, who remembers with tears his lost love. Don Diego's interventions are turned into melodrama. This failed romance instills a longing for a national narrative not much different from other national romances of the period discussed by Doris Sommer (1990).

There is also a recent work on don Diego which combines both Rojas' liberal humanism and Avellaneda's melodramatic narrative, drawing also from Freyle's misogynous discourse and Castellanos' epic tone. María Luz Arrieta de Noguera's *La fuerza del mestizaje o el cacique de Turmequé* (1991) is a short novel for young audiences that casts don Diego as a chivalric hero, who rides horses and wins military tournaments (37–45). According to the novel, civil unrest in Tunja during this time is caused by the actions of "bad" women and the wandering jew (*el judío errante*). Doña Inés de Hinojosa's illicit affairs become the metonymy for social disorder and amorality. It is significant that she is described as a *mestiza* from Caribbean Indians. This association is important because here we see how colonial discourse confuses the figures of the *femme fatale* and the savage (Caribs). Philip II is portrayed as a benign father to don Diego and all Amerindians. At the end of the story, don Diego's second trip allows him to marry a woman he met and fell in love with on his first trip. His return is attributed to a miracle of *Santiago de Compostela*. A melancholic epilogue narrates don Diego's death in Spain in 1590 and proclaims him the precursor of Colombia's Independence movement.

CONFLICTIVE INTERSTICES OF THE COLONIAL SUBJECT

Postcolonial theory has developed and/or adapted a complex array of concepts to better understand the issue of subjectivity (i.e. subject positions and subalternity) in contexts of colonization. Post-structuralism and feminism have been instrumental in this matter, although the theoretical base has somehow undermined the certainty of the postcolonial project of decolonization. Who is the subaltern? How can he/she be appropriately represented? Who can represent him/her? The attempt to cease epistemic violence through non-essentializing or objectifying discourse on the subaltern is ultimately the question of a responsible intellectual endeavor. How effective such intellectual labor may be, in terms of decolonization, is questionable given that current postcolonial critique—or the hegemonic component of it—is mainly an academic and literary project (Ahmad 1996). It is likely that this will generate a higher degree of reflexivity across disciplines within academe, but it can hardly represent a frontal and fatal blow to Western/neocolonial structures and practices of knowledge. This is no basis for the dismissal of postcolonialism, but an acknowledgement of the need for a greater and more significant political involvement to make the postcolonial project historically meaningful. However, as long as we keep working towards the integration of the political and theoretical thrusts of postcolonialism, there is no reason to abandon our present inquiry into the complex process of subjectification and subalternity. With that said, let us return to don Diego's intervention.

Previous literature on don Diego has seen him in terms of a rational, self-sufficient individual. He has been seen as a highly acculturated *mestizo* who, in his legal interventions, does not reveal us much about Amerindian cultures, particularly when compared to Guaman Poma de Ayala and El Inca Garcilaso in Perú or Fernando de Alva Ixtlilxochitl in México.[11] A close analysis of his texts and maps can help us see don Diego differently. It may also offer us a better understanding of the issue of subjectivity in the context of colonization. One step in this direction is to examine critically don Diego's submissive and loyal address to the Crown in the legal documents. This may be more a matter of protocol. In the following example, we can see how don Diego strategically situates himself in relation to his audience. Lope Clavijo, an ecclesiastical authority from Bogotá's cathedral, asked don Diego to preach to the Indians in Chibcha, since they seemed to listen to him. Don Diego complied but he did it in a way that significantly changed his address. Don Diego declared:

> [Se le pidió que] les hiciese una plática de represión al cacique y a los indios de aquella ciudad a quienes habían hecho reunir en la plaza, para que dejase[n] ciertos ídolos que allí tenían y les dijese la intención de S.M., y que así lo hizo y por más recatarse, con saber bien su lengua, no quiso hacer el dicho parlamento sino por intérprete hablando él en castellano y declarándolo en el idioma de los indios Pedro de Sanabria, delante del señor Arcediano y de muchos otros españoles que estaban presentes y que mucho se holgaron de oírlo. (Cited in Rojas 1965, 111)

[He was asked to preach to the *cacique* and the indians of that city, who were gathered in the main square, to abandon certain idols that they had and to explain to them the Crown's intentions. He did so and to be more careful, knowing their language, he decided that he would only give the speech through an interpreter. He spoke in Spanish and Pedro de Sanabria in the Indian language in front of the ecclesiastical official and other Spaniards present who were pleased with what they heard.]

Why don Diego did not speak in Chibcha to the Indians? To be more careful (*recatarse*), he states. This word's meaning is very suggestive: "Andar con aviso y cuydado de alguna cosa que le puede suceder [. . .]no se fiando de todos" [to be aware and careful lest something may happen . . . not trusting everyone] (Covarrubias 1998 [1611], 898). It seems that don Diego is more concerned with pleasing the Spanish audience. This is stressed by the fact that he does not mention how the Indian audience receives his message. He states instead that the Spaniards were pleased (*se holgaron mucho*). We can assume that don Diego was aware that this act changed, for the indigenous people, the meaning of what he was now telling them through an interpreter in the presence of the colonial authorities. How was he seen, speaking Spanish, by the Indian audience: as a *cacique*, a *mestizo* or a Spaniard? We may never know that. This particular situation reveals somehow that there don Diego was both performing "being" Indian for the Spanish audience and "being" Spaniard or playing "good Indian" for the Indian audience. Thus, we can see the politics of identity as a complex practice of performances and of ambivalent maskings.

This performing subject can be seen also in don Diego's *memoriales de agravios,* where he assumes different subject positions. These positions may be multiple and contradictory: "Such positions can be purely structural, based on class, age, gender, sexual orientation, ethnicity, race, and so on, taken singly or together in various combinations. Rather than being positioned in a single unified manner, individuals live at the intersection of multiple subject positions [. . .] These positions can be relatively consistent, contradictory or both" (Rosaldo 1994, 244).

In the *memoriales,* Don Diego frequently refers to the miserable Indians (*miserables indios naturales*) in third person, as if he were not one of them but rather an external observer. On other occasions, however, he presents himself as Indian by using first person singular or plural. In 1584 he declares:

. . . los miserables naturales que nunca alcanzan remedio ni justicia de sus agravios, consumiéndose cada día como se consumen y acaban [. . .] Jamás V.M. tendrá hacienda ni justicia, ni vuestros vasallos vivirán en orden ni gobierno [. . .] y vendrán a cada día a menos vuestros vasallos y rentas reales y nosotros miserables en nuestras personas y vidas [. . .]. (cited in Rojas 1965, 430)

[the miserable Indians are never treated with justice. They are disappearing every day. Never Your Highness will have wealth nor justice, nor your subjects will live in law and order . . . and every day you will have less subjects and less income, and we the miserable will be less and less . . .]

The text shifts from an external self that speaks on behalf of Indians (*los miserables naturales*) to a collective Indian self (*nosotros miserables*). Don Diego's interventions embrace a collective identity also present in twentieth-century *testimonios* such as Rigoberta Menchu's (Restrepo 1996b). These coalitions, even though they may be partial or for a limited time, must be seen not as external processes of a transcendental subject, but as internal processes that constitute the subject itself. We surpass in this way the notion of an autonomous individual to consider the complex process of collective and individual identities in a colonial context. It is revealing to examine those circumstances where different subject positions are in conflict.

This happens, for example, when don Diego affirms his alterity—as a *cacique*—and he inscribes himself within colonial discourse as a loyal subject of the King:

Esto es católica Majestad, lo que pasa y se usa con aquellos miserables indios que son fieles vasallos de V.M. como los demás naturales de Castilla . . . y en descargo de mi conciencia como uno de los caciques de aquella tierra, hago esto por la obligación que tengo. (1584 *Memorial de agravios*, cited in Rojas 1965, 451)

[This, Your Royal Majesty, is what happens and is done against those miserable Indians that are your loyal vassals as the others of Castile. . . . To alleviate my conscience as one of the *caciques* of that land, I do this because it is my duty.]

The fact that don Diego affirms his "difference," a *cacique natural*, does not happen *ex nihilo*. It occurs, rather, in the context of the exercise of power, in which, as Homi K. Bhabha has argued, the production of alterity is a necessary process of colonization: "The objective of colonial discourse is to construe the colonized as a population of degenerate types on the basis of racial origin, in order to justify conquest and to establish systems of administration and instruction" (Bhabha 1986, 154). It was imperative for the colonial Spanish state to inscribe the mark of alterity to Amerindians and other social sectors. In this context, we have to understand the category of *mestizo*, which is used in the documents in don Diego's case. This category's meaning became increasingly a negative attribute in mid-sixteenth century, as discussed above, and the word itself was for some time associated with mixed-bred animals (Covarrubias

1998 [1611], 751). It is perhaps for these reasons that don Diego omits this category when referring to himself. In contrast, he claims, as the Inca Garcilaso, that he is the descendant of noble Indian and Spanish parents. In this way he strategically inscribes himself in the moral and political Spanish universe, using to his advantage the ideological framework of the colonizer to situate himself in a position of power.[12]

What we have here is ultimately the double process of identity formation in a context of colonization. On the one hand, the state's strategy, which is not simply a monologue, is an interpellation of specific social segments (these segments, however, are not assumed to exist outside discourse). On the other hand, this process also involves the intervention of the interpellated subject, who seeks to reappropriate and control his or her own identity and to articulate with it his or her place in the colonial public sphere. As a result, we have a "minority discourse."[13] David Lloyd distinguishes between ethnic and minority discourse:

> [W]here an ethnic culture can be conceived as turned, so to speak, towards its internal differences, complexities and debates, as well as to its traditions or histories, projects and imaginings, it is transformed into minority culture only along the lines of its confrontation with a dominant state formation which threatens to destroy it by direct violence or by assimilation. Minority discourse is articulated along this line and at once registers the loss, actual and potential, and offers the means to a critique of dominant culture precisely in terms of its own internal logic. (1994, 222)

Don Diego's texts are clearly not an ethnic discourse, generated for an internal audience, but rather part of the power and identity negotiating process in a colonial context where the ethnic element, his nativism, has been politicized. Two maps that don Diego attached to his *memorial de agravios* illustrate well this point.*

In his 1584 petition to the Crown, don Diego included two maps of Tunja and Bogotá provinces (the two main Chibcha political areas). We must take into account that land struggles are not only about canons, soldiers, and bullets, but also involve narratives, ideas, forms, images, and imaginings (Said 1993, 7). Both maps submitted by don Diego make visible an indigenous territory that circumscribes both Spanish cities. Official cartography, in contrast, suppressed Amerindian presence. Such is the case in Diego Velasco's map, published in 1601.** This map is full of *silences*, of vast empty spaces. As in music and in poetry, cartographic silences are quite meaningful. A conquering state imposes a silence on minority or subject populations through their manipulation of place names.

---

*see illustrations of these maps in Eduardo Acevedo Latorre
**see Acevedo Latorre (57).

Whole strata of ethnic identity are swept from the map in what amount to acts of cultural genocide (Harley 1988, 66). In this view, don Diego's maps represent a counter-hegemonic discourse that challenges the narrative time/space of the empire. In contrast to Velasco's map, the maps of don Diego offer us highly visible indigenous territories: Machetá, Gachetá, Choachí, Chocontá, Cajicá, Guatavita, Tocaima, Subaté, Simijaca, and many more. The maps simultaneously inscribe the presence and disappearance of the Amerindian world: written on the map's margin we read: "En este valle hubo sesenta y seis mil indios cuando llegaron los españoles; ahora lo que se ve en este papel es todo yermo" [In this valley there were sixty thousand Indians when the Spaniards arrived, now it is all empty].

The importance of Chibcha toponymies in this essay about colonial subjectivity is that neither space nor subject are transcendental categories. They are historical categories and the relationship between geographical space and identity is not unidirectional but dialectical. For instance, the basic Chibcha social unit was the *uta*, which was defined in terms of lineage and territory (Villamarín 1979, 31–32). In contexts of colonization, territorial conflicts are often expressed in terms of identity.[14] The perspective in the maps that don Diego sent to the Crown are ambiguous. For example, the anthropomorphic sun, and the orientation of the map (towards the east) could be either Chibcha, European, or hybrid features.[15] This ambivalence is not present in the *memoriales*. The toponymies themselves are never decoded for a European audience. They remain an ethnic or "internal" discourse. We know from other documents that they enclosed territorial meaning, signaling internal divisions; Soacha, for example, meant "limit of the land" (Castellanos 1886). But here we also find a minority discourse. Don Diego presents Chibcha population in Spanish terms, as towns (*pueblos de indios*) whose icon (signifier) is a parish church. For a metropolitan audience, don Diego represents Chibcha population as a Christian and urban society, inscribed within the realm of the empire to achieve full royal protection. He does the same in the *memoriales*. Don Diego complains, for example, that "de cómo los indios no son tratados como personas libres como lo son y como S.M. manda" [Indians are not treated as free people as they are and as Your Highness has ordered] (Cited in Rojas 1965, 422). This is, however, a strategy with limited potential. It may serve well to acquire a legal status within the colonial machine (protection and political representation, for example), but to depend on the rights provided by the colonizer implies conforming to public sphere as defined by the dominant culture. It is, ultimately, an inscription within the narrative time of the state.

Don Diego's petitions, however, are not limited to denounce abuses. He blames the King himself, and suggests some structural changes that are necessary for the "descargo de vuestra real conciencia" [to alleviate your royal conscience] (cited in Rojas 1965, 422). Can we consider this as an act that more than accepting is challenging the colonial system? In this respect Lloyd's comments are illustrative:

[M]inority politics moves beyond the affirmation of civil rights within the present state formation towards a fundamental questioning of the reason of state itself as a critical stage in the pursuit of the conditions by which radical self-determination of various social formations could become possible. (1994, 235)

On several occasions, don Diego questions the purported reason of the Spanish state, its Christianizing mission and its sense of justice. At one point he confronted colonial authorities when the reasons of the state were not followed appropriately. This was the case in 1582 when he fled to the mountains. From there he wrote to Archbishop Zapata: "[C]uando se teman y obedezcan los mandatos reales como es razón, me entregaré y pondré a las manos del que viniere a saber y conocer desta causa" [When royal decrees are feared and obeyed as they should be, I will turn myself in to whomever is in charge of this case] (Cited in Rojas 1965, 307). Clearly, he was questioning the basis of the colonial system, although not proposing overtly its dismissal, at least not in the existing documents, for obvious reasons. It would mean political suicide and overt rebellion. In such a case, repression would likely follow. As Ranajit Guha has rightly argued, to rebel under colonial rule meant to go against the structures through which the world was made meaningful. This we do not find in Rumequeteba's intervention. Instead, Don Diego, as a *passeur culturel,* is known to us precisely for his strenuous attempts to reconcile and negotiate conflictive worlds and to balance unequal relations of power in a colonial context. That, however, does not rule out the possibility that revolt was discussed in those reported meetings with several Chibcha *caciques.*

NOTES

1. I only offer a sketch of one aspect of Paul Ricouer's rich and deep discussion that draws from philosophical inquiries about time and narratology. For the concept of narrative time, he draws primarily from Martin Heidegger's existential analysis of time, but he also revises Aristotle, Saint Augustine, and others in his three-volume work entitled *Time and Narrative,* 1984 (Chicago: University of Chicago Press).

2. This alliance of two wealthy *mestizos* is important in the context discussed below regarding the different subject positions assumed by don Diego. *Mestizos* in the New Kingdom and Perú formulated collective responses to the Crown's legislation barring them from many privileges, such as bearing arms. They considered such legislation an offense to their dignity. See for example the letter to the King by Miguel López de Patearroyo, Diego García Manchado, and Cristóbal López, Tunja, April 19, 1580 [AGI, Escribanía 824] (Cited in Rojas 1965, 137–143); also, in Perú, we find several collective petitions asking the Third Provincial Council to reconsider the ban on ordaining *mestizo* priests. One petition was

signed by 165 *mestizos* from Lima, Cuzco, Arequipa, Oropesa, and Loja (Ares 1997, 51).

3. In the New Kingdom, Bishop Fray Luis de Zapata ordained several *mestizos* as priests since he considered them useful because they knew native languages [AGI Audiencia de Santa Fé 266 Doc. No. 1133 in FDHNRG] (Friede 1976, V: 338). Two priests from the Dominican and Franciscan Orders complained to the Crown months later that they had been ousted from their parish. They argued that, since these *mestizo* priests were ordained, the blind were leading the blind [AGI, Audiencia de Santa Fé 234 document no. 1139 in FDHNRG] (Friede 1976, V:359).

4. At the intermediate level, precontact Chibcha political hierarchy is not well known. Carl H. Langebaek (1987) differentiates between high-ranking leaders the *uzaques* or noble military leaders, and *capitanes,* the lower political figures who controlled the *utas* or communities. Juan Villamarín affirms that there were two intermediate Chibcha political figures: the *sintivas,* whom the Spaniards called *"capitanes,"* and the *sijipcua,* called *"caciques"* (Villamarín 1979, 33).

5. Berta Queija Ares refers to the *mestizo* population in Perú. The case seems to be similar in the New Kingdom of Granada as we can see from a Dec. 3, 1581 document from Tunja's town officials summoning all *mestizos.* Nearly forty-five *mestizos* were registered, and some listed their trades and occupations: tailors, shoemakers, mill workers, merchants, carpenters, blacksmith, and so forth. (AGI, Escribanía de Cámara, 826C).

6. For example, Tunja officials appoint Juan Rodríquez de Vergara to search and disarm *mestizos* and others: os informeis, sepáis y averiguéis qué mestizos, indios, negros, y mulatos e otras cualquier personas que sean que anden vagando . . . [Search and find *mestizos,* Indians, Blacks, Mulatos and vagrants] (Rojas 1965, 124). Magnus Morner (1967) and Ares (1997) agree that the first generation of *mestizos* were more integrated into Spanish society than later generations.

7. A 1565 Royal decree ordered that two houses in Santa Fé de Bogotá and Tunja be destined "[para] recoger los dichos mestizos y que allí se les pusieren personas que los doctrinasen y enseñasen en las cosas de nuestra Santa Fe Católica y a vivir políticamente, mostrándoles en cosas de virtud, por que con esto se remediarían muchos de ellos, especialmente las mestizas que tienen mucha necesidad de ser recogidas" [to confine these *mestizos* and to appoint priests who will teach them the Catholic ways and how to live within the law. They should teach them virtuous things, since it will reform many of them, specially the *mestizo* women who have much need to be confined]. AGI, Audiencia de Santa Fé, 553. Document no. 851 in Friede 1976)

8. This fact can be further illustrated by the following May 22, 1586, document in which criminal charges are brought against don Diego because he: "que ha puesto en muchos peligros alborotando los Yndios y naturalles della y haciendoles lebantar y alçar y persuadiendoles que no le han de pagar servicios personales [. . .] Ni cumplir tasas ni los demas mandamientos." [has brought many dangers instilling Indians to revolt, and persuading them not to serve Spaniards, pay taxes or obey them]. (AGI, Escribanía de Cámara 824A doc. 5. Folios 10–11).

9. Ulises Rojas (1965) transcribes these *memoriales.* In *Fuentes documentales para la*

historia del Nuevo Reino de Granada (FDHNRG); Juan Friede (1976) also transcribes one of these *memoriales.*

10. Salomé is a representative figure of the *femme fatale.* Through seduction, she convinces her lover to behead Saint John and bring the head to her on a platter.

11. My concern is not, however, with a historicist viewpoint, but rather with how these authors engage discursively with both cultural worlds and the strategies they use to address the metropolitan audience in the context of power relations. It may be a project that recasts pre-Columbian history in Christian terms, as Fernando de Alva Ixtlilxchitl does (Velazco 1998).

12. According to Mary Louise Pratt, "Transculturation and autoethnography," (1994, 25), this is a strategy used by several Amerindians to negotiate power in contexts of colonization.

13. David Lloyd borrows this term from Gilles Deleuze and Felix Guattari's well-known work *Kafka: Toward A Minor Literature* (1986). In this work, the authors examine how Kafka, in a political move, chose to write in German and not in his vernacular language as a political act. He appropiated the dominant code and took it to its limits. The act of writing in itself is considered paramount by Deleuze and Guattari. The power machine cannot be done away with nor is there the possibility of escaping it. Writing, nonetheless, is a practice which opens lines of fugue, non-objectified spaces within the machine.

14. See for instance the cartographic histories studied by Dana Leibsohn, "Primers for Memory," (1994). Another example is the *Popol Vuh,* whose narrative circumscribes a territory. Gordon Brotherstone, for instance, argues that the *Popol Vuh* can be considered as a *título primordial,* a deed or right to the land (1992).

15. I thank Tom Cummins and Joanne Rappaport for noting that these features also could be European.

BIBLIOGRAPHY

Acevedo Latorre, Eduardo. MD. *Atlas de mapas antiguos de Colombia. Siglos XVI a XIX.* Bogotá: Arco.

Ahmad, Aijaz. 1996. "The Politics of Literary Postcoloniality." In *Contemporary Post-colonial Theory: A Reader,* 276–93. New York: Arnold.

Archivo General de Indias (AGI). Sevilla. Escribanía de Cámara 824A, 826B.

Ares Queija, Berta. 1997. "El papel de los mediadores y la construcción de un discurso sobre la identidad de los mestizos peruanos (siglo XVI)." In *Entre dos mundos: fronteras culturales y agentes mediadores.* Edited by Berta Ares Queija and Serge Gruzinski. Sevilla: Consejo Superior de Investigaciones Cientificas.

Arrieta de Noguera, María Luz. 1991. *La fuerza del mestizaje o el cacique de Turmequé.* Bogotá: Biblioteca Familiar.

Bhabha, Homi K. 1993 [1990]. "Dissemination: Time, Narrative, and the Margins of the Modern Nation." In *Nation and Narration*. Edited by Homi K. Bhabha, 291–322. London and New York: Routledge and Kegan Paul.

———. 1986. "The Other Question: Difference, Discrimination and the Discourse of Colonialism." In *Literature, Politics and Theory*. Edited by Francis Baker et al., 160–172. New York: Methuen.

Brotherston, Gordon. 1992. *The Book of the Fourth World: Reading the Native Americas Through Their Literature*. New York: Cambridge University Press.

Castellanos, Juan de. 1914 [1589]. *Elegías de varones ilustres de Indias*. Madrid: Biblioteca de Autores Españoles.

———. *Historia del Nuevo Reino de Granada*. 1886 [1601]. Madrid: Colección Escritores Castellanos.

Corradine, Alberto. 1990. *La Arquitectura En Tunja* Bogotá: Imprenta nacional de Colombia.

Covarrubias, Sebastián de. 1998 [1611]. *Tesoro de la lengua castellana o española*. Barcelona: Ad Litteram.

Deleuze, Gilles, and Felix Guattari. 1986 [1975]. *Kafka: Toward a Minor Literature*. Minneapolis: University of Minnesota Press.

Fabian, Johannes. 1991. *Time and the Work of Anthropology*. Philadelphia: Harwood.

Friede, Juan. 1984. "La conquista del territorio y el poblamiento." In *Manual de historia de Colombia*. Edited by Jaime Jaramillo Uribe, 117–222. Bogotá: Procultura.

———. 1976. *Fuentes documentales para la historia del Nuevo Reino de Granada* (FDHNRG). Bogotá: Biblioteca Banco Popular.

Gálvez Piñal, Esperanza. 1974. *La visita de Monzón y Prieto de Orellana al Nuevo Reino de Granada*. Sevilla: Escuela de Estudios Hispano-Americanos.

Gandhi, Leela. 1998. *Postcolonial Theory: A Critical Introduction*. New York: Columbia University Press.

Gómez de Avellaneda, Gertrudis. 1981. "El cacique de Turmequé: leyenda americana." In *Obras* 5. Madrid: Biblioteca de Autores Españoles.

González, Margarita. 1970. *El Resguardo en el Nuevo Reino de Granada*. Bogotá: La carreta inéditos.

Guha, Ranajit, and Gayatri Chakravorty Spivak, eds. 1988. *Selected Subaltern Studies*. New York: Oxford University Press.

Harley, J. B. 1988. "Silences and Secrecy: The Hidden Agenda of Cartography in Early Modern Europe." *Imago mundi* 40: 57–71.

Hulme, Peter. 1994. "Postcolonial Theory and the Representation of Culture in the Americas." *Ojo de Buey* 2, 3: 14–25.

Langebaek, Carl H. 1987. *Mercados, poblamiento e integración étnica entre los muiscas siglo XVI*. Bogotá: Banco de la República.

Latin American Subaltern Studies Group. 1993. "Founding statement. Boundary" 2, 20(3): 110–121.

Leisbohn, Dana. 1994. "Primers for Memory: Cartographic Histories and Nahua Identity." In *Writing without words*. Edited by Elizabeth Hill Boone, and Walter Mignolo, 161–187. Durham, NC: Duke University Press.

Lloyd, David. 1994. "Ethnic Cultures, Minority Discourse and the State." In *Colonial Discourse/Postcolonial Theory*. Edited by Francis Barker et al., 221–238. Manchester: Manchester University Press.

Mallón, Florencia. 1994. "The Promise and Dilemma of Subaltern Studies: Perspectives from Latin American History." *American Historical Review* (Dec):1491–1515.

Mignolo, Walter. 1993. "Colonial and Postcolonial Discourse: Cultural Critique or Academic Colonialism?" *Latin American Research Review* 28(3):120–134.

Mörner, Magnus. 1967. *Race Mixture in the History of Latin America*. Boston: Little and Brown.

Pratt, Mary Louise. 1994. "Transculturation and Autoethnography: Peru 1615/1980." In *Colonial Discourse/Postcolonial Theory*. Edited by Francis Barker et al., 24–46. Manchester: Manchester University Press.

Restrepo, Luis F. 1999. *Un Nuevo Reino imaginado. Las Elegías de Varones ilustres de Indias De Juan de Castellanos*. Bogotá: Instituto Colombiano de Cultura Hispánica.

———. 1996b. "Bounding the Self: Subject Positions and Contestation in Rigoberta Menchú's *testimonio. Torre de Papel* 6, 1: 37–49.

Ricoeur, Paul. 1984 [1983]. *Time and Narrative*. 3 Vols. Chicago: University of Chicago Press.

———. 1980. "Narrative time." In *On Narrative*. Edited by W. J. T. Mitchell, 165–166. Chicago: University of Chicago Press.

Rodríguez Freyle, Juan. 1942 [1636]. *El carnero*. Bogotá: Biblioteca Popular de Cultura.

Rojas, Ulises. 1965. *El cacique de Turmequé y su época*. Tunja: Academia de la boyacense de la Historia.

Rosaldo, Renato. 1994. "Social Justice and the Crisis of National Communities." In *Colonial Discourse/Postcolonial Theory*. Edited by Francis Barker et al., 239–252. Manchester: Manchester University Press.

Said, Edward. 1993. *Culture and Imperialism*. New York: Vintage.

Seed, Patricia. 1993. "More Colonial and Postcolonial Discourses." *Latin American Research Review* 28(3): 146–152.

———. 1991. "Colonial and Postcolonial Discourse." *Latin American Research Review* 26(3): 181–200.

Sommer, Doris. 1990. *Foundational Fictions*. Berkeley: University of California Press.

Velazco, Salvador. 1998. "La imaginación historiográfica de Fernando de Alva Ixtlilxo-chitl: etnicidades emergentes y espacios de enunciación." *Colonial Latin American Review* 7, 1:33–58.

Vidal, Hernán. 1993. "The Concept of Colonial and Postcolonial Discourse: A Per-spective Form Literary Criticism." *Latin American Research Review* 28, 3: 113–119.

Villamarín, Juan. 1979. "Chibcha Settlement under Spanish Rule: 1537–1810." In *Social Fabric and Spatial Structure in Colonial Latin America.* Edited by David J. Robin-son, 25–84. Syracuse: Syracuse University Department of Geography.

———. 1972. "Encomenderos and Indians in the Formation of Colonial Society in the Sabana de Bogotá, Colombia 1530 to 1740." Ph. D. diss. Brandeis University.

(Post-)Colonial Sublime

Order and Indeterminacy in Eighteenth-century Spanish American Poetics and Aesthetics

Antony Higgins

In this chapter, I will attempt to situate certain aspects of Spanish-American literature with respect to postcolonial theory.[1] First, I will consider some of the specific features of Spanish-American political and aesthetic history, as they converge with and differ from those of the British and Francophone colonial and postcolonial territories. Second, I will attempt a critical analysis of the aesthetic categories and models that have predominated in theorizations of Spanish-American postcolonialities, in particular, Baroque aesthetics. Finally, I will focus on the generally effaced discursive formation of the sublime in Spanish-American literary discourse and try to sketch an outline of its role in the emergence of the thought of *criollo* elites in the eighteenth century, most notably in the *Rusticatio Mexicana*, a landscape poem written by Rafael Landívar, a *criollo* Jesuit from Guatemala.

ANGLO- AND FRANCOPHONE POSTCOLONIAL STUDIES

As a point of departure, I would like to sketch out the key features of postcolonial theory as it has developed with respect to its initial object of study, that is, the literatures and cultures produced by individuals and groups from the different territories affected by British and French imperialism. As the title of the anthology edited by Patrick Williams and Laura Chrisman—*Colonial Discourse and Post-colonial Theory: A Reader*—indicates, work on colonialism and imperialism in literary studies has been divided between colonial discourse analysis and postcolonial theory. The first of these, initiated by Edward Said's

Orientalism, and further developed in the works of scholars such as Peter Hulme (1992) and Beatriz Pastor (1988) on the writings of explorers and *con- quistadores,* scrutinizes the unfolding ideology of imperialism during the early modern period, spanning from the late fifteenth century to the nineteenth century.[2] Notwithstanding the insights of the first movement, it has been, in part, as a result of a disenchantment with the emphasis Said and others have tended to place on discourses of European mastery, and their simultaneous fix- ing of the non-European in a position of irreducible and impotent alterity, that there has emerged the varied body of studies that have come to be grouped to- gether under the banner of postcolonial theory.

Although it has become difficult to speak of a single, unifying current of postcolonial theory, particularly in view of the continuing metaphorical dis- semination of the term beyond the notion of territorial expansion, we can per- haps sketch a framework out of the interventions of its two most conspicuous exponents after Said: Homi K. Bhabha and Gayatri Chakravorty Spivak.[3] First, one can discern in both thinkers a concern to locate and theorize in- stances of resistance and agency in peoples which have lived histories of mate- rial and symbolic colonization, which have been *subjected* by forms of power that are determined, or overdetermined, by transnational economic and politi- cal relations of exploitation. Second, efforts to situate and mobilize such kinds of agency and resistance move between the form of the revolutionary and/or postcolonial nation-state, on the one hand, and the figures of the migrant and/or subaltern, displaced and/or subjected by forces of economic, gender, and racial oppression, on the other.

Just as the utopian projects of the socialist states which had grown out of the former European colonies in Africa, Asia, and the Americas during the 1950s to 1970s, waned in the 1980s and 1990s, and with them the idea of an international postcolonial bloc, so the narrative of the postcolonial nation-state as agent of resistance to imperialism has been displaced by the micro-narra- tives of migrant subjectivities as the principal focus of postcolonial theory.[4] Si- multaneously, in a more properly theoretical domain, this shift in focus towards a subject endlessly displaced and split from itself, is also an outgrowth of the unpacking of the concept of the subject of Western metaphysics per- formed by structuralism (Lacan) and poststructuralism (Derrida, Foucault).

Aijaz Ahmad (*In Theory* 1992) and Neil Larsen ("DetermiNation" 1995) may be correct in reading this move as primarily a symptom of the collapse of the socialist international project and, by extension, a function of the location of the principal exponents of postcolonial theory in elite educational institu- tions of the metropoli, such as Columbia University (Spivak 1988) and the University of Chicago (Bhabha 1994).[5] I am generally in sympathy with the efforts of Ahmad and Larsen to reemphasize class as a category of analysis. However, I think that their critiques tend to gloss over the careful work done by Spivak, in particular, in seeking to interrogate and articulate the often out-wardly opaque connections between relations of class and gender oppression. In their analyses both Ahmad and Larsen represent postcolonial theory as a mode of thought which is suspect for its failure to negotiate adequately with Marxism and for its dependence on post-structuralism, which they read as a cipher for a politics that is, at best, ineffectual and, at worst, ultimately conser-vative.[6] What troubles them most is the localization of resistance in an unsta-ble, protean subject, endlessly split from itself, rather than in the putatively coherent agency of a class formation.[7] Their suspicion of Bhabha's readings and celebrations of migrant subjectivities seem to be well founded, to the ex-tent that his privileging of the complex, hybrid cultural articulations per-formed by the immigrant populations of the large European and North American cities appears, to this reader, to be tied up with a problematic invest-ment in high modernist aesthetics.

The logic of Bhabha's thought is shaped primarily by the writings of Roland Barthes, Walter Benjamin, Jacques Derrida, Martin Heidegger, and Jacques Lacan. It is not surprising, therefore, that he tends to attribute an idealized counter-hegemonic agency to canonical works of high mod-ernism—such as James Joyce's *Ulysees*—and to the works of those members of the postcolonial literati lucky enough to have been granted a place in the Western pantheon, such as Salman Rushdie (223–29). My own ambivalence about Bhabha's work is not, therefore, born out of a rejection of post-structuralism per se, but the manner in which, within his attempts to theorize postcolonial forms of counter-hegemony, he ends up privileging an aesthetics which is generally the province of small elites in its production, reception, and effects.

The work of Spivak is characterized by a more concerted engagement with issues of power, especially in her efforts to bring post-structuralist thought, par-ticularly that of Derrida, into encounters with issues of the transnational and the postcolonial. I refer to the triad of essays comprising: "Can the Subaltern Speak?"; "Subaltern Studies: Deconstructing Historiography"; and "A Literary Representation of the Subaltern: A Woman's Text from the Third World," her brilliant discussion of Mahasweta Dewi's short story "Breast Giver."[8] In these essays, she builds on, and simultaneously critiques, the work of the Southeast Asian Subaltern Studies collective. She scrutinizes the fissures in the order of the postcolonial nation-state, and rewrites the story of how it ultimately serves the interests of a bourgeois *comprador* class eager to find a place within the transnational economic order by exploiting those sectors of their societies con-signed to difficult, low-paid work as a result of their gender, class, caste, and/or skin pigmentation. Pursuing this line of argument, she makes the aforemen-tioned move away from the "grand narrative" of the nation to the micro-narratives of those groups which have largely built, or reproduced, the nation through their labor—in both senses—but which have been effaced from the accounts produced by Indian nationalist historiography.[9] Thus, her work in this area gives a sense of the force of necessity, conflict, and struggle in the lives of migrants and subclasses, largely as a result of her commitment to contributing to the elaboration of critical encounters between Marxism and feminism.

Oriented primarily around the different coordinates marked out in the work of Bhabha and Spivak, postcolonial theory has thus sought to displace the nation-state as a potential agent of constatation to imperialism in favor of conjunctural instances and situations of symbolic indeterminacy in which the ordering position of the subject of Western metaphysics and reason is destabilized.[10] Such instances may be found to occur at moments when Western paradigms of representation become disoriented in the face of the symbolic excess and heterogeneity of non-Western cultures, during the different stages in the history of European and North American imperialism.[11] Alternatively, it manifests itself in moments of confusion and instability, in cultural articulations of or by postcolonial peoples, sometimes in acts of mass insurrection, at others in the hybrid cultural forms negotiated by transculturated subjects, both in the so-called Third World and as migrants transplanted to the metropolis.[12]

Spivak's work, together with that of the Southeast Asian Subaltern Studies group, demonstrates a concern for both the *internal* dynamics of postcolonial spaces, and their continuing relationships with transnational capital and culture.[13] Although I do not mean to bracket off the transnational plane, I will focus primarily, in the rest of this paper, on the issues surrounding the relations between political, economic, and cultural elites, on the one hand, and subaltern groups on the other, in colonial and postcolonial Spanish America. Specifically, my concern is not only to interrogate how such elites configure a postcolonial order, primarily through unfolding programs of internal colonialism and domination, but also how forms of resistance can be found to be simultaneously contesting and disrupting those programs.

NARRATIVES OF SPANISH AMERICAN POSTCOLONIALITY

Some of the problems involved in theorizing postcoloniality in Spanish-American contexts stem from basic historical differences with respect to the dynamics seen in Africa and Asia. First, the area known as Spanish America was colonized at a much earlier stage (1492–1550s) than the parts of Africa and Asia into which the major European powers expanded from the late-eighteenth century into the 1930s. Consequently, it is an oversimplification to discuss the Spanish expansion in the same terms as the British and French imperialisms, that is, as the extension of capitalism beyond Europe and into other parts of the globe. Any analysis of the Spanish case has to maintain a sense of the tensions and contradictions between a messianic religious component and impulses towards economic expansion and accumulation.[14] Second, the Spanish-American revolutions leading to independence occur in the nineteenth century and are inspired largely by the American and French models, a configuration with marked differences from the period of the 1940s to the 1960s, during which most of the previously colonized parts of Africa and Asia achieved independence from the European powers. Correspondingly, these are actions carried out, at least theoretically, in the name of many of the core principles of the bourgeois revolutions—civil rights, property rights, taxation, representation—rather than the Marxist programs that inspired many of the movements of the 1950s to the 1970s. In addition, the groups which led those nineteenth-century revolutions and subsequently attempted to implement systems of liberal government, with mixed results, tended to be dominated by *criollos,* that is, individuals born in America and identified as being of purely European descent, who were largely drawn from landowning and merchant elites.[15] The subsequent history of the Spanish-American nation-states is, for the most part, that of the various attempts of those elites to carry out programs of modernization and impose forms of order on the racial and linguistic heterogeneity of their populaces.

Generally, therefore, it seems to me that one of the most important areas for the work of postcolonial studies in Spanish America is that which comprises the multiple histories of the relations and conflicts between the national elites and the spaces and subaltern groups they seek to order and transform. This entails analyzing forms of action, texts, and discourses produced in the face of such projects as the racially inflected modernizing program of Argentine liberalism in the nineteenth century, the authoritarian regime of modernization overseen by Porfirio Díaz during the late nineteenth and early-twentieth centuries in México, the mechanisms of the official kinds of *indigenista* literature and anthropology in post-revolutionary México, and the hardship and violence that has formed part of the implementation of draconian neoliberal economic policies throughout the continent since the early 1970s.

Historically, the dominant aesthetic category used in discussions of colonial and postcolonial Spanish-American literatures is that of the Baroque. Accounts of the history of Spanish-American literature have been divided between those which view the Baroque as the art of the Counter-Reformation and of a conquering, colonizing culture in the Americas—Marxist and some liberal critics—and others, mainly Spanish-American scholars and public intellectuals, who have wished to reconstrue the Baroque, in its complexity and privileging of syntactic inversion and metaphorical displacement over referentiality, as a form which represents the peculiar diverse mixtures of the cultures of the region.[16] These are primarily those writers who produce Spanish-American variants on high modernism—such as José Lezama Lima, Octavio

Paz, and Severo Sarduy—and the critics who have disseminated and canonized Hispanic Baroque and neo-Baroque writing, such as Pedro Henríquez Ureña, Alfredo Roggiano, and more recently Roberto González Echevarría.[17]

The latest rereading of the Spanish-American Baroque is that of Mabel Moraña, who has rethought the terms of the discussion, and represented Gongorine writing as being of a kind that by its very ambiguity simultaneously acts as the official discourse of imperial power and serves as the medium through which *criollos* and *mestizos* articulate contestatory forms of expression in the seventeenth and eighteenth centuries (1994, "Barroco"; 1989, "Para una relectura").[18] This reconceptualization of the terms of the discussion has perhaps now become the canonical reading and overlaps, to some extent, with parts of Bhabha's work.[19]

By contrast, the category of the sublime has remained largely absent from the key debates in Spanish-American literary history and theory. While it enjoys a position of importance within English and North American literature and criticism, it is barely discussed in Hispanism, largely since Baroque aesthetics stands in the places that the sublime occupies in the other traditions, and performs many of the same functions.[20] That is, the Baroque is read as a discourse through which official power is articulated and, at the same time, as the medium for its contestation. In the face of this, it seems that it might be illuminating to rethink the trajectory of Spanish-American letters, and of a dialectic of hegemony and resistance, order and heterogeneity, in terms of the sublime.

In the rest of this chapter, I will consider here the situation of some texts produced by *criollo* Jesuits from New Spain during the eighteenth century, members of a generation influenced by the new philosophical and scientific thought of the time. Specifically, I focus on two figures, Francisco Javier Alegre and Rafael Landívar, since their works bear witness to the crisis of a regime in which the Company of Jesus played a key role until its expulsion from America in 1767. My interest in these writers is twofold. First, they wrote at a key time in the history of colonial Spanish America, when the viceregal order was showing increasing signs of strain in the face of discontent among *criollos* and native uprisings such as the Tupac Amarú rebellion in Perú. Second, their works are marked by a concern with shifts taking place in Western poetic theory and practice, as the potentially destabilizing concept of the sublime was introduced into a field that had been dominated and framed by the ordering, harmonizing principle of the beautiful, as conceptualized in neoclassical poetics.

COLONIAL SPANISH-AMERICAN POETICS

The trajectory of poetic theory and practice during the first two centuries of the Spanish Empire in America has been extensively analyzed by scholars.[21] Discussions of the initial process of conquest and colonization offer up the image of a mixture of scholastic and Neoplatonic discourses configuring the textual regime that came to subvent the new Spanish order established in most regions by the middle of the sixteenth century.[22] Together with rhetoric, the poetic genres shaped by humanism, most specifically epic, lyric, and evangelizing theater were important instruments of the expanding matrices of colonialism and empire. From the first there was a concern that textual production should conform to a classical concept of representation, in which harmony, proportion, clarity, and decorum were the primary norms. Such a concept can be found to inform the rhetoric of Francisco Cervantes de Salazar and the lyric poetry of Bernardo de Balbuena. The numerous fictional representations of the praxis of conquest and the material and cultural reconfiguration of the "Indies" project a world in the process of being made to conform not only to the ideologies of Catholicism and mercantilism, but also to the order of classical poetics and rhetoric, as it had been reconstructed by Italian and Spanish scholars and poets.[23]

While the new regime was consolidated within the span of a century, the coordinates of this poetics would, nevertheless, frequently be stretched and destabilized in the face of the ethnic, linguistic, and racial heterogeneity which the authorities endlessly struggled to subdue. Such circumstances then become one of the determining factors in the shaping of a differentiated order, that of the Baroque period or style, particularly in the fracturing of the aforementioned norms in poetry written in the Gongorine mode in America, defended most notably in Espinosa Medrano's *Apologético,* and extensively discussed by the critics mentioned above.[24]

Less clear is the trajectory of poetic theory and practice in Spanish America during the eighteenth century. While *gongorismo* remains the dominant mode of poetic diction through the first half of the 1700s in México and Perú, other residual and emergent modes begin to displace it in the work of certain elite groups, both Spanish and *criollo.* However, modern literary historiography has tended to gloss over the segments of these emergent modes of writing that are articulated within the terms of neoclassical and/or enlightened thought.[25] Since the ideological coordinates of much of this criticism are configured by a putatively antirepresentational Modernist aesthetics and by the various schools of formalist criticism, it has projected onto the texts of this period prejudices against any type of literature that is viewed as narrow in its concept of mimesis, normative in its approach to poetry, and bound to any notions of a utilitarian function for art.[26] As a counterpoint to such readings of eighteenth-century Spanish-American literature, I will develop here an analysis of what I take to be a more complex conjuncture, one marked by the beginnings of a complex dynamic that moves between the categories of the beautiful and the sublime.

In Spanish and Spanish-American poetics of the fifteenth, sixteenth, and seventeenth centuries the theorization of the stimulus for creation had been articulated around a concept of inspiration that could only be divine in nature, an inspiration that then had to be submitted to the discipline of a learned body of precepts assembled from Horace and Aristotle's writings on poetry and the treatises of Cicero and Quintilian on rhetoric.[27] These are the coordinates of two of the earliest Spanish-American defenses of poetry, the anonymous *Discurso en loor de la poesía* (1608) and Bernardo de Balbuena's *Compendio apologético en alabanza de la poesía* (1604). In the second half of the seventeenth century, as the discourse of *gongorismo* became more dominant, Spanish-American poetic thought would accord greater importance to the concept of *ingenio*, according a stronger role of agency to the author—of which the greatest example was held to be Góngora—trained in the arts of the conceit and hyperbaton, a thesis defended most systematically by Espinosa Medrano in his *Apologético*.[28]

During the eighteenth century thinking on this issue in Western Europe generally, and to a lesser extent in Spain, again shifted under the influence of John Locke's investigation into the workings of the human faculties, and Sir Isaac Newton's rethinking of cosmology.[29] In Enlightenment discussions the concept of the sublime became secularized and subjectivized. First, it appeared particularly in northern European nature poetry as a medium for theorizing the representation of phenomena and scenes that could not be encompassed within the terms of the concept of the beautiful (charm, harmony, order, and proportion): waterfalls, volcanoes, raging seas, and violent weather conditions.[30] Second, it served, most famously in Edmund Burke and Immanuel Kant, as the cipher through which the position of the individual, free and autonomous, could be instantiated, apart from both society and nature, particularly through the act of submitting even in its most overwhelming manifestations to the acts of conceptual and linguistic representation.[31] Third, it played a key role in the gradual shift from the scheme of normative *poetics* to the scrutinization of the effects produced by the natural or artistic object in the reader or spectator, that is, *aesthetics*.[32]

Within the scheme of viceregal Spanish America it was not possible for the discourses of subjetivization and secularization to emerge with such force. Nevertheless, as course outlines of the period and Francisco Javier Alegre's notes to the *L'Art poétique* attest, the Mexican intellectual elite was becoming appraised of the writings of thinkers as diverse as Joseph Addison, Sir Francis Bacon, Descartes, Sir Isaac Newton, Alexander Pope, and Voltaire.[33] Indeed, it appears that conflicts within the most important education institutions of the Jesuit order in New Spain arose out of the initiatives of certain educators, in particular Rafael Campoy and Agustín Castro—who translated Bacon's *Advancement of Learning* (1605) into Latin, in incorporating the new currents of thought into the curriculum of the colleges.[34]

FRANCISCO JAVIER ALEGRE'S TRANSLATION OF BOILEAU'S *L'ART POÉTIQUE*

In a manifestation of the contradictory oscillations of colonial Spanish-American intellectual and literary history, it is the institutional corpus of the

Jesuit order that oversees the most dynamic push towards new modes of knowledge and poetics in New Spain during the eighteenth century. This change is, in part, a function of a mutation of the trajectory of European intellectual history during the Enlightenment, to the extent that the potentially revolutionary sectors of viceregal society at the time—*criollos* and some *mestizos*—seeing themselves excluded from institutions of government by the newly implemented Bourbon reforms, came to concentrate their energies in economic affairs and in careers in education and the production of knowledge within the network of colleges and universities in New Spain, primarily at the Jesuit Colegio de San Pedro y San Pablo and Colegio de San Ildefonso. This "enlightened" generation of Jesuits came to prominence in the 1750s and 1760s, continuing their activities in Italy after being expelled from America in 1767. In the areas of philosophy and science, they were influenced by the developments in scientific thought set in motion by Descartes and Newton. Additionally, in the realm of poetics, some time after the interventions of Ignacio Luzán in Spain, these primarily *criollo* Jesuits promoted a renewed respect for neoclassical precepts.[35] Some of the outstanding members of this group were Rafael Campoy, who taught a course of philosophy incorporating the new thought, Francisco Javier Clavigero, author of the *Historia antigua de México*, Francisco Javier Alegre, noted for his knowledge of classical Greek and Latin texts, and Rafael Landívar.[36]

The most revealing document pertaining to this shift in thought is Francisco Javier Alegre's translation of Nicolas Boileau-Despréaux's *L'Art poétique* (1674), the primary exposition of normative poetics in eighteenth-century Western Europe. Probably the most outstanding scholar of humanistic learning among the group of Mexican Jesuits, Alegre was a teacher of rhetoric. After the expulsion of the Jesuits, he continued his activities as a scholar in Italy.[37] He completed the translation of the *L'Art poétique* around 1776, although his own statements indicate that he was already familiar with the poetic treatise prior to the expulsion of the order from America in 1767.[38] Alegre's translation offers insight into a complex conjuncture in the history of poetics, primarily through modifications to the original text produced by his rendering of it into Spanish and by the extensive notes in which he amplifies and comments upon Boileau's recommendations for poetic practice.[39] His principal concern is for a return to the principles set down by Horace in his *Ars poetica*, namely, those of mimesis, clarity of style, decorum, and the formula of *dulce et utile*, and by Aristotle, in his discussion of epic poetry and tragic theater.[40] However, at the same time the potentially destabilizing category of the sublime also appears, albeit still within a primarily neoclassical framework. The key features of Alegre's supplementary remarks might be summarized in the following terms: first, like Boileau, he argues for a stricter observation of Horace's principles of poetry; second, he stresses the need for adherence to Aristotle's norms for theater; third, he, at the same time, defends the comedies of Félix Lope de Vega and Calderón De La Barca against the criticisms leveled

at them by Boileau and others; fourth, he defends Spanish literature, especially
that of the sixteenth and seventeenth centuries, against the denigrating remarks made by eighteenth-century English, French, and Italian scholars and
poets (1989, 3–4, 36–37, 53–54, 93–100, 131–32).

Alegre's position as a representative of Hispanic letters living in Italy
obliges him to negotiate a complex movement between neoclassical, normative
discourse and a concern to defend the specific cultural heritage of which he
feels himself to be a part. He rationalizes the inconsistencies of Spanish
Baroque theater on the grounds of the following: (1) the sheer quantity of
works written by Lope, which made errors and excesses inevitable; and, (2) by
recourse to an argument for the expression of the specificities of national genius over and above the exigencies of normative, classical poetics (94, 118,
131–32). While such positions may appear to be in contradiction with the poetics articulated in Boileau's text, and with the universalist ideology of the
Company of Jesus, the coherence of Alegre's thinking can perhaps be best dis-
cerned in his statements about the lyric, and especially the poetry of Luis de
Góngora y Argote, which had inspired a mode that remained dominant in
New Spain even into the mid-eighteenth century. Alegre does not reject Góngora out of hand, but quotes and praises segments of his works that conform
most closely to the classic ideals of elevated, but also clear and harmonious,
style (1889, 22, 24, 26, 65). These works are praised in accordance with the
same rationale used to eulogize the more canonical poets of the sixteenth century, in particular Garcilaso de la Vega, Fray Luis De León, and Bartolomé and
Lupercio Leonardo De Argensola (13, 19–22, 28, 56). Significantly, he is
heavily critical of the *Soledades* and the body of poetry that Góngora's most
ambitious works inspired (22–23, 59).

Notwithstanding his criticisms of Góngora, Alegre does allow for a certain amount of license with respect to precepts and rules, particularly in his in-
vocations of the concept of the sublime. Within a framework dominated
primarily by the principle of the beautiful, Alegre makes several significant references to the sublime. Citing Horace's principle of *Ut pictura poesis erit*, he insists that the sublime should be clear and seem unaffected, an idea expressed
most famously in *On Sublimity*, the treatise probably composed in the first
century A.D. and mistakenly attributed to Greek critic Longinus.[41] Like most
of the theoretical writing on the sublime written in the first half of the eighteenth century, still under the dominant influence of the Longinian text, Alegre's text evinces an understanding of the concept that functions mainly in
terms of its denotation of a writing style reserved for the most elevated genres
and topics (36, 55, 99–100). In fact, it is most likely that he was familiar with
the concept through Boileau's translation of *On Sublimity*.[42] He associates sublimity with literary characters of high social rank and with the more exalted,
public genres of poetry, epic, and tragedy (30, 98–99). However, his choice of

words in discussing these questions does also indicate a familiarity with the concept's mobilizing role within contemporary discussions of the respective roles of precepts, on the one hand, and inspiration, or poetic *furor*, on the other in the construction and organization of the work of poetry. Commenting specifically on the role of inspiration and genius in the writing of poetry, Alegre observes: "Los genios nimiamente exactos y metódicos no son los más á propósito para la poesía, y mucho menos para la lírica, que pide más viveza, *rapto y entusiasmo* que alguna otra." (59; emphasis added) In Alegre's comments, therefore, the notion of high style does appear to share ground now with that of rapture or transport (*rapto*), although this second, aesthetic and rhetorical inflection does seem to remain subordinate to the first, still within the overall scheme of a normative poetics.[43]

RAFAEL LANDÍVAR'S *RUSTICATIO MEXICANA*

More properly, it is in a poem by one of Alegre's colleagues, Rafael Landívar's *Rusticatio Mexicana*, that the respective weight of the different semantic nuances in the concept of the sublime undergoes a greater shift. Born in 1731, Landívar began his schooling in Antigua, Guatemala, and completed his education at the Colegio Máximo de San Pedro y San Pablo, in México City. After finishing his studies, he returned to Guatemala, which at the time comprised most of the territory now known as Central America, and a part of New Spain, to assume the post of rector of another Jesuit institution, the Colegio de San Francisco de Borja in 1765. After the expulsion of the Jesuits from America, he settled in Italy with the majority of the Mexican members of the order. He wrote the *Rusticatio* in this situation of exile, publishing a first edition in Modena in 1781 and an expanded version in Bologna the following year.[44] The poem, which is made up of 5313 Latin hexameters written after the style of Virgil's *Georgics,* is divided into fifteen cantos, and an appendix. In it Landívar offers detailed descriptions of natural landscapes, agriculture, cattle raising, and different species of animals in New Spain. The first three cantos, upon which I will focus primarily, form part of the genre of landscape poetry, portraying some of the region's most awe-inspiring natural scenery. Cantos four through eleven offer detailed representations of the main areas of economic production in New Spain: dye making, sugar production, gold and silver mining, and cattle raising. The final four cantos are devoted to features that cannot readily be inserted into the scope of organized production and economy: natural springs, exotic animals and birds, and forms of leisure and popular spectacle.

The *Rusticatio* stands as the culmination of the *criollo* Jesuits' cultivation of ancient Greek and Latin language and culture. It also provides insight into the

change in the educational program at the Mexican Jesuits' elite learning institutions that took place in the middle of the 1700s, whereby emerging secular,
or secularizing, disciplines of knowledge, most notably natural history, were incorporated into curricula. Of most interest for the scope of this paper is the
emergence of the discourse of the natural sublime in the *Rusticatio*, albeit still
within an overall framework configured by a normative poetics oriented primarily around the concept of the beautiful. Specifically, the poem opens up
Spanish-American letters to a modern aesthetics of the sublime, although
Landívar cannot fully articulate or embrace the broader scheme of both its literary and political ramifications.[45] There are two key features of this aesthetic:
first, the articulation of the position of the poet as creative agent who must engage in a dialectic movement between the creative force of inspiration and the
scheme of poetic rules in order to produce the work of art; second, the problematic of representing, linguistically, natural spaces that are not easily submitted to the workings of mimesis and reason.[46]

Insofar as he writes his poem from a position of exile in Italy, faced with
the fragmentation of the order's system of knowledge and authority, Landívar's
text represents a conjectural moment in which one paradigm—that of the
Spanish imperial political order and of scholastic pedagogy—breaks up, and
another slowly and uncertainly assumes shape—that of a national, regional political order, founded on the new philosophical and scientific modes of knowledge that philosophers and scientists were beginning to use to demystify the
world. These circumstances impose certain limits on the deployment of the
sublime effected in the *Rusticatio*. First, it cannot emerge as a dominant mode,
as the principal force of artistic creation, but is subordinated, albeit uneasily, to
the discourse of the beautiful. Thus, when the sublime is invoked, in Landívar's
depictions of nature, it is ultimately overcome through a restoration of images
characterized by charm, harmony, and order.[47] To this extent, Landívar inhabits a rationalist, Enlightenment *poetics*, one in which nature, both human and
environmental, is to be represented in accordance with a normative system of
precepts, and thus mastered, controlled, rendered productive and useful, rather
than a romantic *aesthetic*, in which freer rein is to be given to the emotions and
nature is represented as indomitable, irreducibly wild.[48] Second, within this
framework the sublime cannot be mobilized to establish the autonomy of the
individual, alienated from society and its discourses and techniques of control,
as is postulated in Edmund Burke's *A Philosophical Enquiry*.[49] Instead, in the
Rusticatio the sublime is harnassed and ultimately put to the service of the
beautiful, and the notion of harmonious social order which is its political
corollary, one which emphasizes the role of the loyal, conscientious citizen
within such an order.[50]

Written at a time when uncertainty surrounds the configuration of political authority and the grounds for legitimate knowledge—the destruction of
the Jesuit infrastructure, growing tensions between Spanish officialdom and

criollos and *mestizos*—the *Rusticatio* emerges as an attempt to theorize a frame-work for knowledge and representation subvented by a centering subject of reason. In the *Monitum* with which Landívar prefaces the text of the *Rusticatio* he foregrounds the problem of representing to European readers that which is unfamiliar to them or which appears to be irreducibly other. Although he does not explicitly use the word "sublime," he does here outline the terms of a situation in which the writer seeks to achieve mastery over things that are opaque and difficult, rendering them intelligible through the labors of representation and translation. Landívar remarks:

Vereor tamen, ne dum ista percurreris, aliqua interdum suboscura offendas. In argumento quippe adeo difficili omnia latino uersu ita exprimere, ut uel rerum ignaris sub aspectum cadant, arduum quidem est; ne dicam impossibile. Nihilominus claritati, qua potui diligentia, ut prouiderem, plurimum in iis, quae nunc primum in lucem prodeunt, allaboraui; uulgata uero ad incudem reuocaui; in quibus plura mutaui, nonnulla addidi, aliqua subtraxi. Sed uerendum est adhuc, ne incassum desudauerim, neque eorum satis desiderio fecerim, qui in rebus etiam suapte natura difficillimis nullum uellent laborem impendere. Solacio tamen mihi erit, quod hac super re Golmarius Marsiglianus cecinit:

Heu! quam difficule est uoces reperire, modosque
addere, cum nouitas integra rebus inest.
Saepe mihi deerunt (iam nunc praesentio) uoces:
Saepe repugnabit uocibus ipse modus.[51]

[I fear, moreover, that in reading this you will at times find some things which are obscure. Since to express it all in Latin verse on such a difficult theme, in such a manner that it might be understandable, even to the ignorant, is difficult, if not impossible. In spite of everything, in order to achieve clarity I have toiled a great deal, with such diligence as I was capable of, on what here comes to light for the first time: that which is common knowledge I returned to the anvil; I have changed many things, added some, suppressed others. Nevertheless, it is still to be feared that I might have sweated in vain and not complied sufficiently with the desires of those who, even in things which are by their very nature very difficult, do not wish to expend the slightest effort. However, of solace to me will be the words which Golmario Marsigliano sang about a similar thing: "Oh, how difficult it is to find the words, and fit them to the meter, to things that are wholly new. Often I will lack (I foresee it now) the words, often the meter itself will rebel against the words."][52]

Landívar outlines here the terms of a problematic of representation which is laden with contradictions and conflicts. On one level he elaborates a defense of neoclassical poetics against the imputed lack of decorum in Baroque poetry, particularly in its Gongorine mode. At the same time, he articulates a concern about the opaque and distorting features of language, and the discursive constructs which European writings and representations have transposed onto the American real.[53]

Landívar's poem demonstrates a familiarity with the thought and methods of natural history as it had developed as a discipline in the eighteenth century through the work of scientists like Carolus Linnaeus and Georges-Louis Leclerc de Buffon. At the same time, in his painstaking analyses of the workings of large-scale natural phenomena—such as volcanoes—and the distinguishing characteristics and behavior patterns of animals—he devotes canto six to a study of the life of a beaver community—Landívar manifests a concern to produce a corrective representation of America and, in the process, establish the credentials of *criollos* to stand in the position of a subject ordering the representation and knowledge of the region.

In order to track how such a position of subjectivity is configured in the *Rusticatio Mexicana,* it is relevant to consider Landívar's descriptions of sublime objects in New Spain. The first kind of natural phenomena he depicts are volcanoes, chiefly that of el Jorullo, in the region of Michoacán, where volcanic activity had begun on September 29, 1759, and continued intermittently for several years after that. This part of the poem stages an encounter of an ordering neoclassical conception of representation with spectacles of material unruliness and excess, an encounter with indeterminacy out of which the form of a coherent subject of poetics and knowledge will be constituted. Landívar opens this segment with a declaration of intent:

Nunc quoque Xoruli Vulcania regna canendo
persequar, et nigras montis penetrabo cauernas,
qui mala tot populis, clademque minatus acerbam
diuite florentes populauit germine campos,
flammarumque globos, et ruptis saxa caminis
impatiens uomuit, gelida formidine gentes
concutiens, póstrema orbis quasi fata pararet.

Nam quamuis animum delectent floribus horti,
claraque fertilibus labentia flumina pratis;
sunt tamen interdum, uigili quos horrida uisu
aspectare iuuat longe, et reputare tuendo.
                    (canto 2, lines 1–11)

Now I will continue, singing of the volcanic realms of el Jorullo, and I will enter the dark caverns of the mountain which, having threatened so many people with cruel ruin, pillaged the blooming fields of abundant crops, and impatiently vomits balls of flames and broken, burning rocks, terrifying people with icy horror, as if the final doom of the world were being prepared.

For although blooming gardens and clear streams flowing between fertile meadows delight the soul, there are those who take pleasure in watching and studying horrible sights with vigilant eyes, from a distance, and reflecting.

Landívar's opening remarks explicitly set down the terms of the experience of the sublime object, counterposing the allure of that which is horrifying with the charm of the beautiful, as described in Burke's *Enquiry*.[54] The introductory section of the canto is followed by a series of stanzas which evoke the different features of the lands around the volcano prior to the recent eruption. The overall image of the valley of el Jorullo, a large expanse of agricultural lands, crossed by several rivers and dotted with forests, conforms to that of a conventional pastoral, marked by the tranquility, harmony, and order taken to be characteristic of the beautiful. On these lands the *hacendado* grows sugarcane, and raises sheep, cattle, horses, and fowl (1987, 2.24–44). In the middle of this landscape there stands the house of the *hacendado* and a small church (2.59–64). Together, these images make up the picture of the economy of a *criollo* landowning class, largely autonomous from the mechanisms of the Spanish state.

Having sketched this *criollo* pastoral, Landívar begins his description of the natural disaster which throws it into crisis. Rather than evoke the eruption in apocalyptic, mystified terms, he gives a scientific, step-by-step account, beginning with the first murmurs heard coming from beneath the earth (2.114–27). He relates how the indigenous peasants try to flee their lands in search of safer ground (2.128–66). He then recounts, in minute detail, the eruption proper, describing how balls of fire were hurled into the air and the skies were filled with black smoke (2.167–79). The violence of the eruption culminates in the formation of a mountain of rock, created by the accompanying earth tremors and the force of the flames and ashes thrown out of the volcano (2.184–94).

However, the canto does not conclude with these images of destruction. In a subsequent sequence of stanzas Landívar analyzes the short- and long-term consequences of the eruption in the area of the valley of el Jorullo. First, he describes the initial havoc wreaked on the agricultural lands and architecture of the lowland areas. The trees have been blackened and stripped of their foliage, the once grassy pastures and fruit burnt, and most of the cattle killed (2.207–13). The house of a local *hacendado* and an elegantly decorated church, the latter possibly a symbol of the waning of Baroque aesthetics, have been reduced to rubble (2.214–19). Human agency is depicted as having been overcome by natural forces, symbolized in the movement of wild animals out of the forests and into the severely damaged towns and villages of the area (2.220–34). Additionally, the climactic conditions of the region are described as having been altered by the prolonged presence of a black cloud, filled with sulphur fumes, which has caused frequent thunderstorms (2.235–66).

Continuing his scientific analysis, Landívar notes that the volcanic eruption also produced aftereffects in the land. First, he notes that it caused dramatic changes in the temperature of the water in its rivers, making them hot at night and cold during the day, in a seeming inversion of the natural order (2.267–87). Second, he describes how the volcanic activity has contributed favorably to the workings of the valley's ecosystem. He concludes his poetic account of the eruption and its effects on an optimistic note, buoyed by the information garnered from scientific observation:

> Accedunt nec parua tamen solacia tantis
> excidiis; sua nam campis sua gratia maior.
> Vallis enim primum nimio feruentior aestu,
> repleuit postquam Xorolus cuncta ruinis,
> graminaque infensus maculauit caede cruenta,
> nec Libyco eneruat languentia membra calore,
> frigore nec Scythico torpent ad munia palmae;
> aere sed gaudent populus, pecudesque benigno.
> Sic laetos quamquam apoliauit germine campos,
> terraque per lustrum nullis fuit apta ferendis
> fructibus, at uero ex illo tot tempore fetus,
> antiquam ut uincant praesentia commoda damnum.
> (2.288–99)

[Yet, even so, there is no slight consolation in the face of these disasters, for the fields take on a greater glory. Indeed the valley which before was too hot, now that el Jorullo has filled every place with ruin and angrily stained the meadows with bloodshed, does not wilt faint bodies with the heat of Lybia, nor does Scythian cold make hands too numb for work, but men and beasts alike rejoice in a mild climate. Although the fertile fields were thus despoiled of plant life, and for many years the land was rendered unsuitable for agriculture, since that time production has been so great that the new advantages offset the former losses.]

The negative power of the volcano is thus represented as a force that can reconstitute an environment, rendering it more productive than before. The images of ruin recede with the passage of a lustrum (five years), and the *hacendado,* the shepherds, and the indigenous peasants are able to return to their labors. The volcano stands as a destabilizing force that cannot be mastered or controlled. Nevertheless, its violence and chaos can be submitted to the work of representation and rendered comprehensible through Landívar's mapping of its workings. Armed with such knowledge of the volcano's mechanics and effects, both positive and negative, the region's inhabitants can organize their labors around it.

In this canto, I read Landívar as staging an instance of what Neil Hertz calls the "moment of blockage," namely, an instance in which the experience of the indeterminacy or failure of the attempted representation of sublimity, and the resulting "anxiety" and uncertainty of the representing subject are ultimately overcome through the reestablishment of its coherence in the face of the seemingly overwhelming boundlessness of the object.[55] Specifically, Landívar's enactment of this drama sets in motion a process in which a form of mastery and stability coalesces in the position of a subject who seeks to demystify the workings of natural phenomena through the application of scientific reason and, at the same time, restores the ordered, harmonious terms of the beautiful in the aftermath of the experience of the sublime object. In this fashion, the *criollo* intellectual is implicitly posited as the ordering center of American poetics and space.

The workings of the interaction of the beautiful and the sublime in Landívar's poem are again set in motion in canto three, in his representations of another set of sublime objects, the waterfalls of the region of New Spain. A key segment in this canto is his depiction of a body of falling water in his home province of Guatemala. After a long section in which he traces the path of waters back to their source, Landívar describes how the waters hurl themselves down from a high cliff at great speed (3.137–207). He writes:

Tunc latices fluuius tumulo delapsus ab alto
distrahit in minimas uenti spiramine guttas
inque leuem totus casu dissoluitur imbrem.
Vndique lympha uolat, ceu nubes cana, per auras.
Plena tamen gelida, terret quae subter, abyssus
perstrepit horrendum, circum spumante barathro,
undaque curuatis ripas corrodit auara
absorbens torto disiunctas gurgite cautes.
Ceu mare, cum ualidi permiscent aequora uenti,
nunc undas tumidum faciles iaculatur in astra,
ut caelum credas iamiam contingere pontum;
nunc fundum retegit, dissectis fluctibus, imum

tartareas ardens sonitu terrere cauernas:
tunc rabido cautes caedit, murosque furore,
absorbetque cauas sinuoso uortice pinus:
non aliter uallo saxi praeecinta cuati
unda ferit crudas, deglutitque anxia rupes.
                                    (3.241–58)

[Then, the waters, having slipped down from the high precipice, are
scattered by the force of the wind into very small drops which, as they
fall, dissolve into light mist. On every side water flies through the air
like a white cloud. In the same fashion, the abyss, filled with icy waters,
brings terror to the regions below and the foam-covered pit makes a
horrible roar. Its greedy waves eat away the curved banks, devouring the
rocks torn loose by the whirlpools. Just as the sea, when the powerful
winds agitate its surface, now quickly lifts its swelling waves towards
the stars, until you might think its waters to be about to touch the sky,
and then parts its waves and uncovers the ocean's floor, eager to
frighten the caves of Tartarus with noise, and then, with uncontrolled
fury, breaks down cliffs and walls, and swallows up boats in its swirling
eddy, so the surging waters, confined by the walls of the rocky depres-
sion, anxiously strike the rough rocks and swallow them up.]

Guatemalan nature is here portrayed as a dynamic space, in which some
features are unstable and subject to shifting processes of large-scale destruction and of reconversion into new formations. The waterfall is shown to be a
powerful force which is simultaneously able to project itself into the sky and
crash down on to the rocks below, reshaping them at every moment. At the
bottom of the valley, the waters form a whirlpool which erodes the cliffs
around it and drags rock fragments down into its vortex. Having depicted
these images of violence, Landívar shifts focus to more tranquil visual spectacles. The first of these is the sight of the rainbows that frequently appear as a
result of the interaction of the falling waters with the sun's rays. He conveys
this process through recourse to classical mythology, depicting Iris as descending from the sky and sitting in the waters under Phoebus' rays of sun-
shine, which split the light up into the individual components of the color
spectrum (3.258–66). Thus, sublimity gives way to beauty, in the form of an
image of harmony and proportion.

Landívar then describes the course taken by the waters after they flow out
of the gorge in which the falls are located. They are dispersed into smaller,
weaker streams that run quietly, and in more controlled fashion, down a canal
(3.267–70). They barely make a murmur as they flow down into the Pacific
Ocean, where their sweet waters are mixed with, and subdued by, the harsher
brine (3.271–76).[56] The canto concludes with two stanzas that celebrate the

grandeur of the rocky portico which houses the waterfall. It is represented as an important symbol the experience and knowledge of which binds the elite members of Guatemalan society together. Annually, they gather at the site to perform a ceremony. Landívar describes it as follows:

Nobilis huc properat Guatimala tota quotannis
tempore quo rigidis torpent Aquilonibus artus,
brumaque immiti tabescunt gramina campi.
Pensilibus scalis ad saxea tecta relati
ponte domant fluuium, donec sub rupe recepti
concaua suspenso perlustrent lumine saxa.
Omnia mirantur, montemque, amnemque, specusque.
Ore tamen presso nutus, et signa sequuntur,
siue salutatum pubes exoptet amicum,
seu uelit ad tectum prono iam Sole reuerti.
                    (3.278–87)

[To this place all of noble Guatemala hastens every year, at the time when the stiff north winds numb the body and the grass is withered in the field by the harsh winter. Having let themselves down to the stone roof by means of hanging ladders, they cross the river by bridge and, entering the rocky cavern, they scan the vaulted chamber with astonished eyes. They marvel at everything: the mountain, the river, and the cavern. With a hushed voice, they communicate only by means of nods and signs, whether one anxiously longs to greet a friend, or wishes to return home at sunset.]

The experience of observing this natural landscape functions as a means of association for the members of the highest sector of Guatemalan society (*nobilis*), presumably *criollos* for the most part. The stanza evokes a ritual according to which they travel there from the city of Guatemala (Antigua), gather together, and descend into the grotto at the beginning of every winter. Observing the breathtaking sight of the cliff, the waters, and the cavern, they are bound together, rather than alienated from one another, by the feeling of astonishment it produces in them.[57] Significantly, the noise of the torrents drowns out any attempt at linguistic communication between the spectators. Nevertheless, they are able to communicate and associate with each other through the transmission and reception of visual signs, by moving their hands or nodding their heads. Thus, although Landívar's spectators have moved into the realm of the sublime, manifested primarily in the characteristics of wild force, loud noise, and the viewer's feeling of astonishment, the effect is ultimately subordinated to the order of the beautiful, producing the sense of a unity not yet fully realized linguistically or politically.

The valley's incorporation into the terms of the beautiful is consolidated in the final stanza of canto three. Landívar declares that the spectacle it offers surpasses the Nile valley and the seven wonders of the ancient world in its beauty, reverting from the semiosis of the sublime to that of a more unambiguously neoclassical pastoral.[58] He portrays a concluding scene in which nymphs find shade in spaces enhanced by the sweet fragrances of the mountain and the singing of the birds (3.288–95). Transformed into a sign (*portentum*) by Landívar, the valley now assumes a discursive status over and above its material form as an object, a status similar to that which has been conferred on the seven ancient wonders by fame (*fama*).

The staging of the experience of these two kinds of sublime objects— volcanoes and waterfalls—thus serves to postulate the notion of an organic social order in New Spain, with the potential to stand in a position of economic and political autonomy with respect to the existing regime of the Spanish Empire. This functions by means of two discursive operations. First, these representations serve to mobilize a protean form of intellectual subjectivity which can oversee and order the heterogeneity of American space. The coordinates of this subjectivity shift and move over the course of the encounter with sublime objects, finally becoming fixed at the moment of the silent association effected between the young Guatemalans as they contemplate, rapt, the huge gorge, from a position deep inside it. Second, the process of signification is restabilized in the closing movement of the transition from the register of the sublime to that of the beautiful, manifested in the final, panoramic views of the rejuvenated agricultural lands around el Jorullo and of the grotto into which the waterfall flows, now reinserted into the kind of organic, harmonious order required by neoclassical poetics. The collective awe of the Guatemalan "nobles" before the spectacle of the gorge stands as a manifestation of the workings of a notion of aesthetic evaluation, or taste, shared by the members of a gentlemanly elite.[59]

In this chapter, I have attempted to argued for a continuing focus in colonial and postcolonial studies not only on transnational relations of economic and cultural production, but also on the conflicts and relations between postcolonial elites and the heterogenous array of bodies and geographies upon which they seek to impose the ordering principles that constitute the "nation." In particular, I have tried to analyze how the aesthetics of the sublime, as it is deployed in eighteenth-century landscape poetry, serves as a medium through which the emergent power of a *criollo* class formation is theorized. The *Rusticatio Mexicana* stages a process in which a moment of indeterminacy serves as a means to stabilize a position of authority, initiating a dynamic that later unfolds during the nineteenth century in the struggles between *criollo* elites and the heterogeneous populaces over which they seek to establish and maintain hegemony.

NOTES

1. For an interesting discussion of some of the issues pertaining to postcolonial theory and Spanish America, see the interview conducted by Juan Zevallos-Aguilar with Sara Castro-Klarén, "Teoría poscolonial y literatura latinoamericana: entrevista con Sara Castro-Klarén," *Revista Iberoamericana* 62, 176–77 (1996): 965–71. Patricia Seed offers useful discussions of the development of Latin American colonial and postcolonial studies in two articles: "Colonial and Postcolonial Discourse," *Latin American Research Review* 26, 3 (1991): 181–200; "More Colonial and Postcolonial Discourses," *Latin American Research Review* 28, 3 (1993): 146–52.

2. Peter Hulme, *Colonial Encounters* (London: Routledge and Kegan Paul, 1992); Beatriz Pastor, *Discursos narrativos de la conquista* (Hanover: Ediciones del Norte, 1988).

3. Other critics worth mentioning include: Bill Aschroft, Gareth Griffiths, and Helen Tiffin, authors of *The Empire Writes Back* (London: Routledge and Kegan Paul, 1989). A useful overview of postcolonial theory and criticism is provided by Bart Moore-Gilbert, *Post-colonial Theory: Contexts, Practices, Politics* (London: Verso, 1997), 5–33, 185–203.

4. See, for example, Homi K. Bhabha, *The Location of Culture* (London: Routledge and Kegan Paul, 1994), 223–26.

5. Aijaz Ahmad, *In Theory: Classes, Nations, Literatures* (London: Verso, 1992); Neil Larsen, "DetermiNation: Postcolonialism, Poststructuralism and the Problem of Ideology," *Dispositio* 47 (1995): 1–16.

6. Ahmad, *In Theory*, 34–42; Larsen, "DetermiNation," 4–10.

7. Such critiques seem, however, to efface some notable divergences between Gayatri Chakravorty Spivak's thought and that of Bhabha, or to take Bhabha as a synecdoche for postcolonial theory, without engaging Spivak sufficiently. It is worth noting the shortage of references to Spivak in both critics' discussions of postcolonial theory. Ahmad does not engage with Spivak at all and Larsen mentions her only once in the text of his article and once in a footnote. See Larsen, "DetermiNation," 3, 14.

8. Gayatri Chakravorty Spivak, "Can the Subaltern Speak?," in *Marxism and the Interpretation of Culture*, eds. Cary Nelson and Lawrence Grossberg (Urbana: University of Illinois Press, 1988), 271–313; "Subaltern Studies: Deconstructing Historiography," and "A Literary Representation of the Subaltern: A Woman's Text from the Third World," in *In Other Worlds: Essays in Cultural Politics* (New York: Routledge and Kegan Paul, 1988), 197–221, 241–68.

9. I refer here to Spivak's insightful analysis of "Breast Giver," especially her discussion of the intersections of class and gender in the story. See Spivak, *In Other Worlds*, 258–64.

10. The complex relationship between nationalism and colonialism is analyzed most famously by Partha Chatterjee, *Nationalist Thought and the Colonial World: A De-*

rivative Discourse (Minneapolis: University of Minnesota Press, 1993), 1–22, 39–43, 167–70.

11. Bhabha, *The Location of Culture,* 86–92.

12. See Bhabha, *The Location of Culture,* 25–29 38–39, regarding the central role given to the concept of "negotiation" in Bhabha's thought. In dealing with related issues, the focus of the subaltern studies movement overlaps with those of postcolonial theory. However, its exponents do not only open up the issue of symbolic excess or surpluses of signification, but also more explicitly thematize the breakdown of discourse and the determining role of material conditions in the struggles of subaltern social groups. See, for example, Shahid Amin's "Ghandi as Mahatma," in *Selected Subaltern Studies,* eds. Ranajit Guha and Gayatri Chakravorty Spivak (Oxford: Oxford University Press, 1988), 288–342); and Gyanendra Pandey's "In Defense of the Fragment: Writing about Hindu-Muslim Riots in India Today," in *A Subaltern Studies Reader, 1986–95,* ed. Ranajit Guha (Minneapolis: University of Minnesota Press, 1997), 1–33.

13. Some of the key research produced by the group can be found in the anthologies mentioned in note 7. Guha lays out the terms of subaltern studies with respect to more established bodies of Indian historiography in "On Some Aspects of the Historiography of Colonial India," in *Selected Subaltern Studies,* eds. Ranajit Guha and Gayatri Chakravorty Spivak (Oxford: Oxford University, 1988), 37–44. Spivak offers a cogent commentary on the group's work, particularly with reference to the contradiction between its theoretical borrowings from European structuralism and post-structuralism, on the one hand, and its continuing investment in notions of subaltern consciousness in the essay "Subaltern Studies: Deconstructing Historiography," in *In Other Worlds* (New York: Routledge and Kegan Paul, 1988), 199–211. The first fruits of the research carried out by the Latin American Subaltern Studies Collective were recently published in a special number of *Dispositio/n,* edited by José Rabasa, Javier Sanjinés, and Robert Carr. See, in particular, the group's "Founding Statement," in *Dispositio* 46 (1994): 1–11.

14. See Hernán Vidal, "The Concept of Colonial and Postcolonial Discourse: A Perspective from Literary Criticism," *Latin American Research Review* 28, 3 (1993):114–19, Rolena Adorno, "Reconsidering Colonial Discourse for Sixteenth- and Seventeenth-Century Spanish America," *Latin American Research Review* 28, 3 (1993): 139–45; Beatriz Pastor, *Discursos narrativos de la conquista* (Hanover: Ediciones del Norte, 1988), ii-vi; Eric Hobsbawm, *The Age of Empire* (London: Weidenfield, 1987), 73.

15. For a full account of the history of this term's use in Spanish America, see José Juan Arrom, *Certidumbre de América* (Madrid: Gredos, 1971), 9–24.

16. Among the first group it is worth mentioning the now classic accounts offered by Leonardo Acosta, *El barroco de Indias y otros ensayos* (Havana: Casa de las Américas, 1984), 51; Jaime Concha, "La literatura colonial hispano-americana: problemas e hipótesis," *Neohelicon* 4, 1–2 (1976): 46; and John Beverley, "Barroco de estado: Góngora y el el gongorismo," in *Del "Lazarillo" al Sandinismo* (Minneapolis: The Prisma Institute, 1987), 79–82.

17. Pedro Henríquez Ureña, *Obras completas,* 7 (Santo Domingo, Dominican Republic: Universidad Nacional Pedro Henríquez Ureña, 1979), 167–72; Alfredo Roggiano, "Para una teoría de un Barroco hispanoamericano," in *Relecturas del Barroco de Indias,* ed. Mabel Moraña (Hanover: Ediciones del Norte, 1994), 1–3, 9–11; Roberto González Echevarría, *Celestina's Brood. Continuities of the Baroque in Spanish and Latin American Literature* (Durham: Duke University Press, 1993), 4–5, 195–96.

18. Mabel Moraña, "Barroco y conciencia criolla en Hispanoamérica," *Revista de Crítica Literaria Latinoamericana* 14, 28 (1988): 229–51; "Para una relectura del barroco hispanoamericano: problemas críticos e historiográficos," *Revista de Crítica Literaria Latinoamericana* 15, 29 (1989): 219–31.

19. I see a close affinity between Moraña's theorization of the discourses of colonial Baroque poetry and religious oratory as complex, polysemic forms of expression in which *criollos* and *mestizos* encoded their criticisms of the viceregal order and the role of the aforementioned concept of "negotiation" in Bhabha's thought. See Mabel Moraña, "Barroco," 234–38, and "Para una relectura," 227–29.

20. On the trajectory of the sublime within eighteenth-century English literature, see Samuel H. Monk, *The Sublime: A Study of Critical Theories in XVIII-Century England* (Ann Arbor: University of Michigan Press, 1960), 1–42, 85–100, 113–33, 141–52; and Andrew Ashfield and Peter de Bolla, eds., introduction, *The Sublime: a Reader in British Eighteenth-century Aesthetic Theory* (Cambridge: Cambridge University Press, 1996), 1–16.

21. Notable, in this respect, is Antonio Cornejo Polar's study of the *Discurso en loor de la poesía:* "El texto. Estudio," *Discurso en loor de la poesía,* ed. Antonio Cornejo Polar (Lima: Universidad Mayor de San Marcos, 1964), 120–216. See also the following analyses of Espinosa Medrano's *Apologético:* John Beverley, "Máscaras de humanidad," *Revista de Crítica Literaria Latinoamericana* 22, 43–44 (1996): 46–48, 52–54; Eduardo Hopkins, "Poética de Espinosa Medrano en el Apologético en favor de don Luis de Góngora," *Revista de Crítica Literaria Latinoamericana* 4, 7–8 (1978): 105–09, 111–17; and Mabel Moraña, "Apologías y defensas: discursos de la marginalidad en el Barroco hispanoamericano," in *Relecturas del Barroco de Indias* (Hanover: Ediciones del Norte, 1994), 42–48.

22. Hernán Vidal, *Socio-historia de la literatura colonial hispanoamericana: tres lecturas orgánicas* (Minneapolis: Institute for the Study of Ideologies and Literature, 1985), 89–90, 111–13.

23. Of central importance for the shaping of Spanish thought on poetics and rhetoric during the fifteenth and sixteenth centuries are Antonio Nebrija, who oversees the early dissemination of the principles of the humanist program, Garcilaso de la Vega, who incorporates the mode of the new Italian poetry into Castilian, and, amongst poetic treatises, López Pinciano's, *Filosofía antigua poética,* ed. Alfredo Carballo Picazo, 3 vols. (Madrid: CSIC, 1953). Useful accounts of the trajectory of poetic thought in Spain can be found in A. Porqueras Mayo, *La teoría poética en el Renacimiento y el Manierismo españoles* (Barcelona: Puvill Libros, 1986), 33–71; and Antonio García Berrio, *Formación de la teoría literaria moderna* (Madrid: Cupsa editorial,

1977). See also Weinberg's monumental account of the Italian Renaissance's recuperation and reinterpretations of the main classical works on poetics: Bernard Weinberg, *A History of Literary Criticism in the Italian Renaissance,* 2 vols. (Chicago: University of Chicago Press, 1961).

24. See Beverley, "Máscaras de humanidad," 46–48; Hopkins, "Poética de Espinosa Medrano," 111–17; González Echevarría, *Celestina's Brood,* 158–69.

25. Typically, the Mexican and Peruvian inflections of this thinking are oriented more towards inititiatives in different spheres of scientific investigation than any political project concerned with civil rights and representative, democratic systems of government. On this see A. Owen Aldridge, "Introduction. The Concept of the Ibero-American Enlightenment," in *The Ibero-American Enlightenment,* ed. A. Owen Aldridge (Urbana: University of Illinois Press, 1971), 12–14; José Carlos Chiaramonte, *Pensamiento de la Ilustración: Economía y sociedad iberoamericanas en el siglo XVIII* (Caracas: Biblioteca Ayacucho, 1979), xiv–xx; Karen Stolley, "The eighteenth century: narrative forms, scholarship, and learning," in *The Cambridge History of Latin American Literature,* eds. Roberto González Echevarría and Enrique Pupo-Walker, vol. 1 (Cambridge: Cambridge University Press, 1996, 338–40; and Arthur P. Whitaker, "Changing and Unchanging Interprtations of the Enlightenment in Spanish America," in *The Ibero-American Enlightenment,* ed. A. Owen Aldridge, 27–28.

26. For a discussion of the neglect of the eighteenth century in Spanish-American literary historiography, see Stolley, "The eighteenth century," 337–38, 374.

27. On this, see Antonio Cornejo Polar, "El texto. Estudio," 154–60; Ernst Robert Curtius, "Theological Art-Theory in the Spanish Literature of the Seventeenth Century," in *European Literature and the Latin Middle Ages,* trans. Willard R. Trask (Princeton: Princeton University Press, 1990), 552–58; García Berrio, *Formación de la teoría literaria moderna,* 229–83; and Porqueras Mayo, *La teoría poética en el Renacimiento y el Manierismo españoles,* 33–71.

28. Juan de Espinosa Medrano, *Apologético,* ed. Augusto Tamayo Vargas (Caracas: Biblioteca Ayacucho, 1982), 29–32, 47–49, 57–60, 68–70.

29. Catherine Henry Walsh, *The sublime in Spain* (Ph. D. diss., University of California, Los Angeles, 1992; Ann Arbor: UMI, 1993), 37–39, 49–50.

30. On this, see Monk, *The Sublime,* 203–20.

31. See Ashfield and de Bolla, *The Sublime,* introduction, 1–9, Monk, *The Sublime,* 1–9, 203–29.

32. Ibid., 4–9, 46–60, 85–100, 134–52. See also Jean-François Lyotard, "The Sublime and the Avant-Garde," in *The Lyotard Reader,* ed. Andrew Benjamin (Oxford: Blackwell, 1989), 202–07.

33. Francisco Javier Alegre, *"Arte poética* de Mr. Boileau," in *Opúsculos inéditos latinos y castellanos del P. Francisco Javier Alegre,* ed. José García Icazbalceta (México City: Imprenta de Francisco Díaz de León, 1889), 37, 101, 105. See also Bernabé Navarro, *Cultura mexicana moderna en el siglo XVIII* (México City: UNAM, 1964), 109–33.

34. On this, see Juan Luis Maneiro and Manuel Fabri, *Vidas de mexicanos ilustres del siglo XVIII*, (México City: UNAM, 1989), 24–27, 68–69.

35. Arnold Kerson, *Rafael Landívar and the Latin Literary Currents of New Spain in the Eighteenth Century* (Ph. D. diss., University of California, Los Angeles, 1963; Ann Arbor: UMI, 1968), 34–49; Allan F. Deck, S. J., *Francisco Javier Alegre: A Study in Mexican Literary Criticism* (Rome: Jesuit Historical Institute; Tucson: Kino House, 1976), 11–30.

36. Ibid., 20–30; Navarro, *Cultura mexicana moderna*, 109–33.

37. Deck, *Francisco Javier Alegre*, 35–45.

38. Alegre, "*Arte poética* de Mr. Boileau," 1–2. See Arnold Kerson, "Francisco Javier Alegre's Translation of Boileau's *Art poétique*," *Modern Language Quarterly* 41, 2 (1981): 154.

39. For a useful analysis of some of the changes produced in the text of the translation itself, see Kerson, "Francisco Javier Alegre's Translation," 161–64.

40. García Berrio offers a full exposition of the trajectory of Horatian poetics in Spain in *Formación de la teoría literaria moderna*. Useful accounts of the shifts in thinking during the eighteenth-century Spain are provided by Russell P. Sebold, "Neoclasicismo y Romanticismo dieciochescos," in *Siglo XVIII (I)*, vol. 6 *Historia de la literatura española*, ed. Guillermo Carnero (Madrid: Espasa Calpe, 1995), 139–64; and by Guillermo Carnero, Philip Deacon, and David T. Gies, "La poesía del siglo XVIII (I)," in *Siglo XVIII (I)*, ed. Guillermo Carnero, 230–58.

41. Alegre, "*Arte poética* de Mr. Boileau," 28; Longinus, *On Sublimity*, trans. D. A. Russell, in *Classical Literary Criticism*, eds. D. A. Russell, and M. Winterbottom (Oxford: Oxford University Press, 1991), 172–75.

42. In his notes to Boileau's, *Art poétique*, he makes explicit reference to this text. See Alegre, "*Arte poética* de Mr. Boileau," 99. Additionally, Maneiro and Fabri, in their biography of Agustín Castro, another member of this generation of Jesuits, indicate that he, too, was familiar with the works of Longinus: *Vidas de mexicanos ilustres*, 89. The frequency of such references in the texts of the Mexican Jesuits of the eighteenth century offers convincing evidence that *On Sublimity* was a text well-known among the group.

43. Alegre also uses the term *entusiasmo* in another interesting sentence, which is a nuance it acquires only from the late-seventeenth century on, coming out of debates about the nature and practice of religious belief, and later extending into discussions of poetry and art: "El entusiasmo poético no es trastorno, sino elevación de la fantasía" (38). The topic is treated by Locke within the overall framework of his investigation into human understanding: John Locke, *An Essay Concerning Human Understanding*, ed. Roger Woolhouse (London: Penguin Books, 1997), 614–22. Shaftesbury discusses it in connection to the inspiration of poets, orators and musicians. See Anthony Ashley Cooper, Third Earl of Shaftesbury, *Characteristicks*, in *The sublime*, eds. Ashfield and de Bolla, 77–79.

44. Kerson, *Rafael Landívar*, 95–102.

45. This is a development that one can track in the writings of ninenteenth-century authors such as Heredia, in his "En el Teocalli de Cholula" and "En una tempestad," in *Niágara y otros textos (poesía y prosa selectas),* ed. Angel Augier (Caracas: Biblioteca Ayacucho, 1990), 106–09, 134–35. For an interesting discussion of the role of the sublime in Heredia's poetry, see Ted E. McVay Jr., "The Sublime Aesthetic in the Poetry of José María Heredia," *Dieciocho* 17, 1 (1994): 36–38.

46. See Monk, *The Sublime,* 7–8, 17–18, 203–29.

47. The coordinates of the beautiful, as articulated within eighteenth-century literary thought tend to be those of order, finitude, and charm. On this, see Walter John Hipple Jr., *The Beautiful, the Sublime, and the Picturesque in Eighteenth-century British Aesthetic Theory* (Carbondale: Southern Illinois University Press, 1957), 210–13, and Monk, *The Sublime,* 6).

48. Thomas Weiskel offers a psychological analysis of the role of the sublime in English romantic literature. See *The Romantic Sublime* (Baltimore: Johns Hopkins University, 1976), 3–33, 34–62).

49. Edmund Burke, *A Philosophical Enquiry into the Origin of our Ideas of the Sublime and Beautiful,* ed. Adam Phillips (Oxford: Oxford University Press, 1990), 37–40. I see in Landívar's poem an operation similar to that which Walsh discerns in eighteenth-century Spanish writers such as Surís de Monpalau Capmany. See Walsh, *The sublime in Spain,* 94–95.

50. Burke explicitly identifies the beautiful with society and the sublime with the individual, a division repeated by Kant in his *Critique of Judgement.* See Burke, *A Philosophical Enquiry,* 36–40). Ferguson offers a thought-provoking discussion of the slippage between the concepts of the beautiful and the sublime in eighteenth-century literary and philosophical discourse, and of the privileging of the sublime over the beautiful in twentieth-century scholarship on the literature of that period. See Frances Ferguson, *Solitude and the Sublime* (London: Routledge and Kegan Paul, 1992), 3–9, 50–53.

51. Rafael Landívar, *Rusticatio Mexicana,* ed. and trans. Faustino Chamorro González (San José, Costa Rica, 1987), 8.

52. All translations of the text are my own. In the process of producing my translations I consulted the rendering offered by Graydon W. Regenos: *Rafael Landívar's "Rusticatio Mexicana,"* Philolological and Documentary Studies, I, 5 (New Orleans: Middle American Research Institute, 1948), 155–312.

53. As Antonello Gerbi has documented in *The Dispute of the New World,* the proponents of natural history constructed a series of images of American nature and species which tended to invert the terms of the accounts of the marvellous and abundant offered by explorers like Columbus in the fifteenth and sixteenth centuries. See Antonello Gerbi, *The Dispute of the New World,* trans. Jeremy Moyle (Pittsburgh: University of Pittsburgh Press, 1986), 4–34, 52–74). Buffon, for example, depicted America's natural environment as predominantly marshy and inimical to the survival of plants and animals. Within the systems of classification of species

established by Buffon and others American animals were depicted often as strange anomalies and as weaker variants of European models. See Georges Louis Leclerc Buffon, *Histoire Naturelle, Générale et Particulière* (Paris: F. Dufart, 1808), 1: 279; 20: 316–23, 423–26.

54. Of the attraction of the sublime Burke writes: "Whatever is fitted in any sort to excite the ideas of pain, and danger, that is to say, whatever is in any sort terrible, or is conversant about terrible objects, or operates in a manner analogous to terror, is a source of the *sublime;* that is, it is productive of the strongest emotion which the mind is capable of feeling." (36) In the same section he concludes: "When danger or pain press too nearly, they are incapable of giving any delight, and are simply terrible; but at certain distances, and with certain modifications, they may be, and they are delightful, as we every day experience." (36–37)

55. Neil Hertz, *The End of the Line: Essays on Psychoanalysis and the Sublime* (New York: Columbia University Press, 1985), 40–44; Immanuel Kant, *Critique of Judgement,* trans. James Creed Meredith (Oxford: Oxford University Press, 1952), 106–09.

56. On the role of sound as a feature of the sublime, see Hugh Blair, *Lectures on Rhetoric and Belles Lettres,* in *The sublime,* eds. Ashfield and de Bolla, 214; and Burke, *A Philosophical Enquiry,* 75–76.

57. This stands in contrast to the account offered by Burke described above, in which the beautiful is identified with society and the sublime with individuation. See Burke, *A Philosophical Enquiry,* 37–40.

58. It is important not to see the beautiful and the sublime as discrete, organic categories, wholly distinct from one another, and in the works of many eighteenth-century writers, the semantic differences between the two are often reduced, if not wholly collapsed. See Monk, *The Sublime,* 13, 69, 85–86. Frances Ferguson offers an interesting analysis of the relationship between the two concepts, particularly in the works of Burke and Kant. See Ferguson, *Solitude and the Sublime,* 30–32, 50–53.

59. I discern in Landívar's poem an approach similar to that of Boileau, that is, an attempt to maintain the sublime as a supplement to the beautiful, as an element that cannot yet destabilize or fragment the order of neoclassical poetics to the point of rupture. For a discussion of the embeddedness of the concept of the beautiful within a certain ideology of the social in the eighteenth century, see Monk, *The Sublime,* 10–41. Alternatively, a more radical reading might find here the bare outline of an effort to theorize a conception of aesthetic appreciation which would allow for the participation of a wider segment of society, one which would accord a stronger role for the less stable and ordered dynamics of the sublime. Such a reading would place Landívar's thinking closer to that of Kant, who articulates, at least theoretically, a more universalist understanding of aesthetic judgement, tied to the notion of its "communicability". See Kant, *Critique of Judgement,* 82–84, 226–27, and Ted Cohen and Paul Guyer, introduction to *Essays in Kant's Aesthetics,* eds. Ted Cohen and Paul Guyer (Chicago: University of Chicago Press, 1982), 5–6.

BIBLIOGRAPHY

Acosta, Leonardo. 1984. *El barroco de Indias y otros ensayos.* Havana: Casa de las Américas.

Adorno, Rolena. 1993. "Reconsidering Colonial Discourse for Sixteenth- and Seventeenth-Century Spanish America." *Latin American Research Review* 28, 3:135–45.

Ahmad, Aijaz. 1992. *In Theory: Classes, Nations, Literatures.* London: Verso.

Aldridge, A. Owen, ed. 1971. *The Ibero-American Enlightenment.* Urbana: University of Illinois Press.

Alegre, Francisco Javier. 1889. "*Arte poética* de Mr. Boileau." In *Opúsculos inéditos latinos y castellanos del P. Francisco Javier Alegre.* Edited by José García Icazbalceta, 1–132. Mexico City: Imprenta de Francisco Díaz de León.

Arrom, José Juan. 1971. *Certidumbre de América.* Madrid: Gredos.

Ashcroft, Bill, Gareth Griffiths, and Helen Tiffin. 1989. *The Empire Writes Back: Theory and practice in post-colonial literatures.* London: Routledge and Kegan Paul.

Ashfield, Andrew, and Peter de Bolla, eds. 1996. *The Sublime: A Reader in British Eighteenth-century Aesthetic Theory.* Cambridge: Cambridge University Press.

Beverley, John. 1996. " 'Máscaras de humanidad': sobre la supuesta modernidad del *Apologético* de Juan de Espinosa Medrano." *Revista de Crítica Literaria Latinoamericana* 22, 43–44: 45–58.

———. 1987. "Barroco de estado: Góngora y el gongorismo." In *Del "Lazarillo" al Sandinismo.* Minneapolis: The Prisma Institute.

Bhabha, Homi K. 1994. *The Location of Culture.* London: Routledge and Kegan Paul.

Buffon, Georges Louis Leclerc. 1808. *Histoire Naturelle, Générale et Particulière.* 127 vols. Paris: F. Dufart.

Burke, Edmund. 1990. *An Enquiry into our Ideas of the Sublime and the Beautiful.* Edited by Adam Phillips. Oxford: Oxford University Press.

Carnero, Guillermo, ed. 1995. *Siglo XVIII (I).* Vol. 6 of *Historia de la literatura española.* Madrid: Espasa Calpe.

Carnero, Guillermo, Philip Deacon, and David T. Gies. 1995. "La poesía del siglo XVIII (I)." In *Siglo XVIII (I).* Edited by Guillermo Carnero, 209–91.

Castro-Klarén, Sara. 1996. "Teoría poscolonial y literatura latinoamericana: entrevista con Sara Castro-Klarén." By Juan Zevallos-Aguilar. *Revista Iberoamericana* 62, 176–77: 963–71.

Chatterjee, Partha. 1993. *Nationalist Thought and the Colonial World: A Derivative Discourse.* Minneapolis: University of Minnesota Press.

Chiaramonte, José Carlos. 1979. *Pensamiento de la Ilustración: Economía y sociedad iberoamericanas en el siglo XVIII.* Caracas: Biblioteca Ayacucho.

Curtius, Ernst Robert. 1990. "Theological Art-Theory in the Spanish Literature of the Seventeenth Century." In *European Literature and the Latin Middle Ages*. Translated by Willard R. Trask. Princeton: Princeton University Press.

Deck, Allan F., S. J. 1976. *Francisco Javier Alegre: A Study in Mexican Literary Criticism*. Rome: Jesuit Historical Institute; Tucson: Kino House.

Derrida, Jacques, 1976. *Of Gramatology*. Translated by Gayatri Chakravorty Spivak. Baltimore: John Hopkins University Press.

Espinosa Medrano, Juan de. 1982. *Apologético*. Edited by Augusto Tamayo Vargas. Caracas: Biblioteca Ayacucho

Ferguson, Frances. 1992. *Solitude and the Sublime*. London: Routledge and Kegan Paul.

Foucault, Michel [1970] *An Archeology of Human Sciences*. New York: Vintage Books.

García Berrio, Antonio. 1977. *Formación de la teoría literaria moderna*. Madrid: Cupsa editorial.

Gerbi, Antonello. 1986. *The Dispute of the New World*. Translated by Jeremy Moyle. Pittsburgh: University of Pittsburgh Press.

González Echevarría, Roberto. 1993. *Celestina's Brood. Continuities of the Baroque in Spanish and Latin American Literature*. Durham: Duke University Press.

Guha, Ranajit, ed. 1997. *A Subaltern Studies Reader, 1986–1995*. Minneapolis: University of Minnesota Press.

Guha, Ranajit, and Gayatri Chakravorty Spivak, eds. 1988. *Selected Subaltern Studies*. New York: Oxford University Press.

Henríquez Ureña, Pedro. 1979. *Obras completas*. Vol. 7. Santo Domingo, Dominican Republic: Universidad Nacional Pedro Henríquez Ureña.

Heredia, José María. 1990. *Niágara y otros textos (poesía y prosa selectas)*. Edited by Angel Augier. Caracas: Biblioteca Ayacucho.

Hertz, Neil. 1985. *The End of the Line: Essays on Psychoanalysis and the Sublime*. New York: Columbia University Press.

Hipple, Walter John, Jr. 1957. *The Beautiful, the Sublime, and the Picturesque in Eighteenth-century British Aesthetic Theory*. Carbondale: Southern Illinois University Press.

Hobsbawm, Eric. 1987. *The Age of Empire*. London: Weidenfield and Nicolson,

Hopkins, Eduardo. 1978. "Poética de Espinosa Medrano en el *Apologético en favor de don Luis de Góngora*." *Revista de Crítica Literaria Latinoamercana* 4, 7–8: 105–18.

Hulme, Peter. 1992. *Colonial Encounters: Europe and the Native Caribbean, 1492–1797*. London: Routledge and Kegan Paul.

Kant, Immanuel. 1952. *The Critique of Judgement*. Translated by James Creed Meredith. Oxford: Oxford University Press.

Kerson, Arnold. 1981. "Francisco Javier Alegre's Translation of Boileau's *Art poétique*." *Modern Language Quarterly* 41, 2: 153–65.

————. *Rafael Landívar and the Latin Literary Currents of New Spain in the Eighteenth Century*. 1968. Ph.D. diss. Yale University, 1963. Ann Arbor: UMI.

Lacom, Jacques. 1977. *Ecrits*. Translated by Alan Sheridan. New York: Morton.

Landívar, Rafael. 1987. *Rusticatio Mexicana*. Translated by and edited by Faustino Chamorro González. San José, Costa Rica: Asociación Libro Libre.

Larsen, Neil. 1995. "DetermiNation: Postcolonialism, Poststructuralism and the Problem of Ideology." *Dispositio/n* 47: 1–16.

Locke, John. 1997. *An Essay Concerning Human Understandiing*. Edited by Roger Woolhouse. London: Penguin Books.

Longinus. 1991. *On Sublimity. In Classical Literary Criticism*. Translated by D. A. Russell, and Edited by D. A. Russell and M. Winterbottom, 143–87. Oxford: Oxford University Press.

López Pinciano, Alonso. 1953. *Filosofía antigua poética*. Edited by Alfredo Carballo Picazo. 3 Vols. Madrid: CSIC

Lyotard, Jean-François. 1989. "The Sublime and the Avant-Garde." In *The Lyotard Reader*. Edited by Andrew Benjamin, 196–211. Oxford: Blackwell.

Maneiro, Juan Luis, and Manuel Fabri. 1989. *Vidas de mexicanos ilustres del siglo XVIII*. Biblioteca del estudiante universitario 74. México City: UNAM.

McVay, Ted E., Jr. 1994. "The Sublime Aesthetic in the Poetry of José María Heredia." *Dieciocho* 17, 1: 33–41.

Mignolo, Walter. 1993. "Colonial and Postcolonial Discourse: Cultural Critique or Academic Colonialism?" *Latin American Research Review* 28, 3: 120–34.

Monk, Samuel H. 1960. *The Sublime: A Study of Critical Theories in XVIII-Century England*. Ann Arbor: University of Michigan Press.

Moore-Gilbert, Bart. 1997. *Postcolonial Theory: Contexts, Practices, Politics*. London: Verso.

Moraña, Mabel. 1994. "Apologías y defensas: discursos de la marginalidad en el Barroco hispanoamericano." In *Relecturas del Barroco de Indias*. Mabel Moraña, 31–57. Hanover: Ediciones del Norte.

————. 1989. "Para una relectura del barroco hispanoamericano: problemas críticos e histriográficos." *Revista de Crítica Literaria Latinoamericana* 29: 219–31.

————. 1988. "Barroco y conciencia criolla en Hispanoamérica." *Revista de Crítica Literaria Latinoamericana* 28: 229–51.

Navarro, Bernabé. 1964. *Cultura mexicana moderna en el siglo XVIII*. México City: UNAM.

Pastor, Beatriz. 1988. *Discursos narrativos de la conquista*. Hanover: Ediciones del Norte.

Porqueras Mayo, A. 1986. *La teoría poética en el Renacimiento y Manierismo españoles*. Barcelona: Puvill Libros.

Rabasa, José, Javier Sanjinés C., and Robert Carr, eds. 1994. *Dispositio/n 46*.

Regenos, Graydon W., trans. 1948. *Rafael Landívar's "Rusticatio Mexicana,"* by Rafael Landívar. *Philological and Documentary Studies,* I, 5: 155–312. New Orleans: Middle American Research Institute, Tulane University.

Roggiano, Alfredo. 1994. "Para una teoría de un Barroco hispanoamericana." In *Relecturas del Barroco de Indias.* Edited by Mabel Moraña, 1–15. Hanover: Ediciones del Norte.

Said, Edward. 1978. *Orientalism.* New York: Random House.

Sebold, Russell P. "Neoclasicismo y Romanticismo dieciochescos." In *Siglo XVIII (I).* Edited by Guillermo Carnero, 137–207

Seed, Patricia. 1993. "More Colonial and Postcolonial Discourses." *Latin American Research Review* 28, 3: 146–52.

———. 1991. "Colonial and Postcolonial Discourse." *Latin American Research Review* 26, 3: 181–200.

Spivak, Gayatri Chakravorty. 1988. "Can the Subaltern Speak?" In *Marxism and the Interpretation of Culture.* Edited by Cary Nelson and Lawrence Grossberg, 271–313. Urbana: University of Illinois Press.

———. *In Other Worlds: Essays in Cultural Politics.* New York: Routledge and Kegan Paul, 1988.

Stolley, Karen. 1996. "The Eighteenth Century: Narrative Forms, Scholarship, and Learning." In *The Cambridge History of Latin American Literature.* Edited by Roberto González Echevarría and Enrique Pupo-Walker, I: 336–74. Cambridge: Cambridge University Press.

Vidal, Hernán. 1993. "The Concept of Colonial and Postcolonial Discourse: A Perspective from Literary Criticism." *Latin American Research Review* 28, 3: 113–19.

———. 1985. *Socio-historia de la literatura colonial hispanoamericana: tres lecturas orgánicas.* Minneapolis: Institute for the Study of Ideologies and Literature.

Walsh, Catherine Henry. 1993. *The Sublime in Spain.* Ph.D. diss. University of California, Los Angeles, 1992. Ann Arbor: UMI.

Weinberg, Bernard. 1961. *A History of Literary Criticism in the Italian Renaissance.* 2 Vols. Chicago: University of Chicago Press.

Weiskel, Thomas. 1976. *The Romantic Sublime.* Baltimore: Johns Hopkins University Press.

Whitaker, Arthur P. 1971. "Changing and Unchanging Interpretations of the Enlightenment in Spanish America." In *The Ibero-American Enlightenment.* Edited by Owen A. Aldridge, 21–57. Urbana: University of Illinois Press.

Williams, Patrick, and Laura Chrisman, eds. 1994. *Colonial Discourse and Post-colonial Theory: A Reader.* New York: Columbia University Press.

Gendered Crime and Punishment in New Spain

Inquisitional Cases Against *Ilusas*

Stacey Schlau

> Popular understanding of and arguments about legitimate and ille-
> gitimate authority rested on profoundly gendered foundations. The
> deep interplays between the politics of gender and the gendering of
> politics suffused popular [and elite] culture
> —Steve Stern, *The Secret History of Gender*

In both Latin America and the United States the legacy of racist, classist, and
sexist norms from the early modern period continues to exist. Women are paid
less than men, and by and large have different employment. In the home, gender roles to a large extent determine the tasks that women perform: child care
and domestic labor. For women who work outside the home, especially those of
poorer and working classes, home and marketplace combine to create a "double
day" of work. Women's sexuality, still popularly confined to the paradoxical jux-
taposition of seduction and passivity, is subject to both verbal and physical male
violence. Despite differences, such as the religious basis of oppression in the
earlier period, the connections in women's, especially poor and working-class
women's, situation in the colonial and contemporary periods are evident in, for
instance, the abuse that Bárbara Echegaray, who is discussed later in this essay,
experienced as a child and the sexual harassment she endured as an adult.

Colonial Mexican society, like its late-twentieth-century descendent, contained great economic and social tensions. Divisions along class, race, and gender lines, themselves closely linked, were strictly enforced. To a large extent,
the juridical arm of the Roman Catholic Church, the Holy Office, or Inquisition,[1] regulated an elaborate race and gender classification system that determined normative behavior and the social category in which a given person

151

belonged. As J. Jorge Klor de Alva maintains, "In the New World the history of the Inquisition is primarily the story of the struggles over power and truth that marked the changing fortunes of the various ethnic, racial, and social sectors" (1991, 8). Thus, ostensibly religious criteria for the behavior of individuals in differing sectors disclosed social realities. In this essay, I focus on the sociopolitical, religious construction of a gendered heresy that particularly targeted poor urban Creole women.

Founded in New Spain in 1571, the Inquisition created a culture of fear, despite its lack of resources. That fear did not necessarily derive from Catholicism: Greenleaf's research suggests that insularity, exclusivism, xenophobia, even racial attitudes, were more important factors than religion in developing the climate of intolerance that prevailed from the fifteenth century to the 1800s (Greenleaf 1991, 271). Toward the end of the eighteenth century, when prisoners were no longer tortured and *autos de fe* no longer held, few were exempt from the grip of the Holy Office (Franco 1989, 58–59). The boundaries between church and government apparatuses were so blurred that, ". . . overriding political considerations of the state made the inquisitors responsible for enforcing a rapidly changing 'party-line' kind of orthodoxy, an almost hopeless task" (Greenleaf 259). Afraid of being caught in the machinery that implemented this ideology, *criollos* and *mestizos*, especially those of the poorer classes, walked a fine line between heterodoxy and orthodoxy.

People's daily lives, thoughts, hopes, dreams, and fears were subject to inquisitional scrutiny. Many scholars have pointed out that, "Thoughts as well as actions counted in the definition of sin" (e. g., Lavrin 1989, 52). Free will counted. How one used it defined sinner or saint: "This stress on freedom to choose between good and bad was central to the definition of sin. Sin is the voluntary—thus knowledgeable—breach of the rules of behavior set by the church, leading to the loss of divine grace by the soul" (Lavrin, 50).

Noemí Quezada implies that in power struggles between other officials and those of the Inquisition, it was the ecclesiastics attached to the Holy Office who wielded enormous power: "Priests who made arrests without the authorization of the Holy Office were also severely reprimanded, and if the civil authorities tried to make arrests, the inquisitors protested the encroachment on their jurisdiction" (1991, 48). The reality of inquisitional control thus was strongly felt by many sectors, including powerful ones.

Yet some contemporary critics ascribe quite limited power to the Inquisition. Irving A. Leonard, for instance, claims that Inquisitional power was not absolute, but diluted by: "jurisdictional and other conflicts with state officials, with business elements . . . and even with the hierarchy of the Church. . . . the Inquisition, representing both Pope and King, often encountered resistance in both lay and ecclesiastical elements of society, and its effectiveness was less complete than commonly believed" (1993, 100).

Additionally, he asserts that the Holy Office did not prosecute only religious crimes. Rather, "the Inquisition's energies went chiefly into adjudicating crimes and misdemeanors nowadays handled by municipal courts. Offenses . . . against "good morals" far outnumbered those against 'the purity of the Faith.' " (101).[2] He further asserts that "The judges frequently differed among themselves as to the guilt of the accused, or regarding proper retribution, and the prosecuting attorney usually abstained from injecting his biased recommendations" (103). Finally, he confirms that the Inquisition had a relatively small staff: "The New World tribunals were staffed by two Inquistors, or judges, a prosecuting attorney, and varying numbers of *consultores* [conoultantc], *calificadores* [officials who examined books and writings], and *familiares* [low-level officials]" (Leonard, 101).

Other critics support these assertions. Klor de Alva, for instance, suggests that "From the beginning of the colonial effort in New Spain, ambivalence about the Holy Office limited its utility as an instrument for the domination of natives" (3). And Richard E. Greenleaf even asserts that "as an agency of social control the Mexican Inquisition worked as all such agencies do: to constrain but not to intimidate" (1991, 271). Further, he goes so far as to defend the Holy Office: "Examination of thousands of Inquisition trial records has demonstrated to this writer that within the prescribed rules and regulations the inquisitors acted with zeal but also with fairness and common sense in the vast majority of cases" (269).[3] While this interpretation of inquisitional activities makes a startling claim, the research behind the apology is thorough.

The general objective of regulating orthodoxy and rooting out heterodoxy necessitated action on individual and social levels. This meant that the stated purposes of both the confessional and inquisitional interrogation were remarkably similar. The act of confessing to a spiritual director approximated that of testifying before church judges. A complex language for confession, which was also used in the courts of the Holy Office, had emerged by the seventeenth century. This speech altered "the emphasis from . . . repentance . . . and changed it to discipline. . . . It stressed not the ritual but the abiding nature of repentance, that it was for all the year round" (Tambling 1990, 71–72). As Jeremy Tambling has also pointed out, "Those addressed by a confessional discourse . . . [were] made to define themselves in a discourse given to them, and in which they must name and misname themselves; and . . . made to think of themselves as autonomous subjects, responsible for their acts" (2). Each person was required to engage in in-depth analysis of the self. The confessional (and the Holy Office) made the subject ". . . speak knowingly, in an intellectual sense, the language given by the Church" (Tambling, 70).

Spiritual examination of individuals was always connected to great economic, social, and racial tensions, contained in a fragile balance in colonial Mexican society. By the eighteenth century, México City had a huge poor population—only about one-third of whom were steadily employed. The threat of upheaval and social disorder terrified many of the elite, who, as Jean Franco notes, struggled to preserve control over public spaces (1989, 57–58).

Women constituted 20 to 30 percent of all inquisitional indictments in New Spain, but only about 16 percent of the total cases that came to trial had women defendants (Alberro 1987, 19). During the last decade of the sixteenth century and from 1640 to 1650, both periods in which suspected Jews were especially persecuted, however, women and men made up an equal percent of arrested persons (Alberro, 20). Gender stereotyping accounted for one reason for the relatively lower rates of arrest of women.[4] Since church officials considered the female gender inferior, they mostly ignored women's witchcraft, or love magic, as a product of ignorance and superstition, rather than a heresy inspired by the devil (Alberro, 21).[5] Casual disregard of women's magical practices constituted one crucial difference between Europe and America. By the sixteenth century, Elspeth Whitney claims, "Europe had a well-developed tradition of persecution of outsider groups . . . defined according to well-established stereotypes . . . these groups were accused of infanticide, cannibalism, and 'unnatural' sexuality and . . . were demonized by their alleged association with the Devil" (1995, 86)

In Europe, a major "outsider group," famously persecuted, were witches. In colonial México, on the other hand, primarily poor urban women (mostly of European extraction), not witches, were targeted for crimes similar to those listed by Whitney.[6]

Urban Creole women of the lower classes were particularly subject to the charge of *ilusión* (false religiosity), for which many were brought before the ecclesiastic tribunal in México City. Jean Franco asserts that trials of *ilusas* (women accused of illusion) increased as the power of the confessional as an instrument of social control decreased (1989, 59). Generally, but not always, *ilusas* publicly exhibited, even occasionally sold strange manifestations of/from their bodies, which they claimed were miracles affirming their holiness. They "often 'performed rapture and ecstasy' in public and exhibited their 'grotesque' bodies . . . their 'incorrect' behavior made them into a living and often unconscious parody of all that was held holy" (Franco, 55). Franco further argues that because *ilusas* had no learning, they used their bodies, the only instrument they owned (59).

While this may have been partly true, it is worth remembering that almost everyone lived under the direction of a confessor and therefore was subject to the will of another. Some *ilusas* were under even more immediate control of men than merely as confessants: María Rita Vargas and María Lucía Celis, for instance, lived in their mentor/amuensesis's house. And dominant values about women's bodies, internalized even by women accused by inquisitional officials, in addition to religious myth, contributed in specific ways to *ilusas's* attempts to gain "interpretive power."[7] Social norms were predicated on male power over women and violence was an outcome of that power. Steve J. Stern's comment about late colonial México is also true of the seventeenth century. He remarks that ". . . because patriarchs, would-be patriarchs, and women assumed that men held rights of punishment in a world of contested gender right and obligation, conflicts over gender claims inevitably sparked connected tensions over the rightful boundaries of violence" (1995, 77). Thus, women, especially women without the resources of the oligarchy, had much to fear. The gendered situational dynamics of all echelons of society consistently circumscribed female movements and methods of expressing themselves. As Carole Levin and Patricia A. Sullivan assert in another context, "Clearly, for a woman to speak with an articulate voice in the public arena makes her the object of worry and butt of jokes, and makes those around her worry about their vulnerability" (1995, 6).

Stern observes that "The premise of social order and authority at both the family and the polity levels of society was an organic hierarchy that vested power in fathers and elders, both literally and metaphorically" (1995, 315). Priests were of course, fathers in their role as spiritual guides, as well as elders because of the authority vested in them as church officials. *Ilusas*, who functioned outside established norms and rules, constituted a threat to this patriarchy. The many folios of the *acusaciones* against Teresa Romero Zapata and Bárbara de Echegaray form prime examples of how gendered notions of access to power and legitimacy operated in the Roman Catholic Church.

I.

Published in 1946, extracts of the inquisitional trial against Teresa Romero Zapata, which lasted from 1649 to 1659, contain three principal viewpoints: (1) some of the accused's testimony mixed with sermons by the judges, (2) a chronicle of meetings she requested over the course of the years she spent in jail, and (3) the *Acusación* (Charges) by the prosecuting attorney. The hybrid text, based on records of ecclesiastic secretaries, is linguistically heterogeneous.[8] Although we do not know with certainty that the words of the accused were transcribed accurately, the meticulousness and obsession with detail for which the inquisitional clerks were noted probably resulted in a precise rendering.

Class status heavily influenced the direction taken by Teresa Romero Zapata and her family. Although in the formal charge, the *fiscal* (prosecutor) calls Teresa Romero an *alumbrada* (Illuminist) whose visions, he writes, are "contra toda buena Teología, con proposiciones expresamente heréticas" (J.J.R. 1946, 54), the heretical aims he so vehemently attacks seem, even by his words, to have been primarily a result of poverty, a means of earning a living. The accused had engaged in the illusory activities, he remarks, "para salir de la miseria en que estaba" (1946, 404).

Born in Cholula and a resident of the capital, the self-styled Teresa de Jesús came from the poorest sector of society. Her three sisters also took religious names: the twins became Josefa de San Beltrán and María de la Encarnación, and the younger Nicolasa de Santo Domingo. All were arrested for feigned ecstatic experiences. Their father, Juan Romero Zapata, a peasant who had been thrown out of their hometown of Tepetlaotoc for stealing from Indians (1946, 407), and a would-be priest, advertised the trances.

Of Teresa de Jesús's life, the transcript gives some specific details. We know that she was eighteen-years-old when she was arrested and that her case took ten years to be resolved. Her genealogy and the low opinion that the inquisitors and prosecutor had of the family are included in the record. The Romero Zapatas came to México City in 1645, where they lived in a house "con suma miseria y pobreza" (408). Teresa Romero was said to have had two love relationships. The judges and prosecutor disapproved of both on racial grounds, belittling one partner as an *"indizuelo"* (dirty Indian) and the other as a *"mesticillo"* (little mestizo). A child was born from each.

José Bruñón de Vértiz, a priest who believed in the saintliness of the Romero Zapata sisters, aided them. He attempted to transcribe, word for word, everything Josefa de San Beltrán said during *"raptos"* (ecstasies), and even began a treatise on the subject in 1648 (1946, 37). Father Bruñón developed a theory and system of mysticism in which he described two kinds of ecstasies: the *vocal* (verbal), which was characterized by badly pronounced words in Spanish and Latin and the *continuado* (continuous), during which the person was outwardly silent and could not control muscular movements. Josefa, María, and Teresa all adhered to this framework in recounting their own trances.

The perspective of patriarchal orthodoxy is encapsulated in the *Acusación* (Charges). In these pages, the prosecutor reviews the complaints and evidence against the prisoner.[9] He alleges that Romero deceived in order to "encubrir sus deshonestidades, mala vida y costumbres, y robar para salir de la miseria en que estaba, y por envidia y emulación de otra hermana suya" (404). When he utilizes a series of gerunds to list her sins, beginning with "haciéndose predicadora" (making herself a preacher), in effect he emphasizes the process of self-incrimination. While nun leaders engaged in teaching and preaching all the time, the prosecutor's first charge discloses the thin line that women of differing classes walked:

> haciéndose predicadora . . . pariendo y mal pariendo, confesando y comulgando . . . engañando a su confesor . . . usando de extraordinarias y maliciosas cautelas para engañar . . . estando . . . con sus padres, hermanas y hermanos, cuya casa era de juego y entretenimiento . . . entrándose esta rea en las casas de los indios . . . siendo constante que un indizuelo pilguanejo . . . la habría estuprado . . . (405)

making herself a preacher . . . giving birth and giving birth badly, confessing and taking communion . . . deceiving her confessor . . . using extraordinary and malicious tactics to deceive . . . being . . . with her parents, brothers and sisters, whose house was a site of games and entertainment . . . entering this prisoner into houses of Indians . . . a dirty despicable Indian . . . having had sex with her . . .

Four major themes predominate in this quote: relationships among the sisters, false religious displays such as trances in public, unrestrained sexuality, and the deception of confessors.[10]

Romero had too much sex, and with the wrong people—nonwhite men. The prosecutor highlighted her relationship with the unnamed *"mestecillo"* (little mestizo), assuring the court that he fathered Romero's first child. The prosecutor insisted on the connection between what he considered her lust and the desire for dark-skinned men: "para ir con el indizuelo pilguanejo, y con el mestecillo y otros tales, a cumplir sus apetitos deshonestos . . ." [. . . to go with the dirty thieving Indian, and with the little *mestizo* and others such, to fulfill her dishonest appetites . . .] (415). Revealing overt racist and sexist attitudes, he maintained that ". . . achacó su preñado a diferentes hombres, ensartando cómplices con manifiestos falsos testimonios a mujeres virtuosas, siendo cierto que el malhehor [*sic*] fué dicho mesticillo, que más era tenido por chinillo o indizuelo . . ." [. . . she blamed her pregnancy on different men, implicating accomplices with manifestly false testimony to virtuous women, it being certain that the wrongdoer was said *mestecillo*, who was held to be Chinese or Indian . . .] (431). Accusing her of implicating innocent respectable women in her lies, which were designed to cover up an insatiable sexual appetite, the prosecutor specified the role that he saw the *mesticillo* played, encasing his absolute certainty of guilt in bigoted ambiguity about the color of his skin.

To further prove his contention of Romero as temptress, he gave the example of her becoming pregnant after having publicly dedicated her virginity to God. When asked why she had not kept the vow of chastity, "Le respondió que cuando hizo dicho voto era menor de edad y estaba fuera de su sentido" [She answered him that when she made that vow she was a minor and out of her mind] (432). At one point, the prosecutor even accused Romero of having been a go-between for lovers (432). Her appetites did not diminish in jail, he asserted, which constituted further proof of her unrestrained sexuality. During Easter week of 1650, he contended that Romero tried to maintain "dishonest relations." She contacted a lover, an act that constituted a "delicto digno de severo castigo, violando lo sagrado del secreto de dichas cárceles" [a crime meriting severe punishment, violating the sacred secrecy of said prison] (432). Her unrestrained appetite overwhelmed any discretion or need for secrecy. Perhaps he worried about the security of the inquisitional jails. Responding to Romero's attempted evasion of responsibility for her errors by placing blame on her confessors, the prosecutor sermonized: "era manifiesta injuria de esta embustera contra sus confesores, que de creer era que si ella les hubiera (y no engañádolos y burládolos como los engañó y burló) tratado verdad, la hubieran desengañado y guiádola para que fuese buena cristiana" [it was a serious injury by this lying woman against her confessors, for it was to be believed that if she had (and not deceived them and mocked them as she deceived them and mocked them) spoken the truth, they would have revealed her deception and guided her toward being a good Christian woman] (432).

Ten years later, he fumed, she still blamed them. But he turned the blame back on her, glossing over the apparent gullibility (or worse, opportunism) of Romero's spiritual directors, to focus instead on her ability and will to deceive. She damaged not only herself, but also them by not telling the truth, he insisted.

Reserving his harshest words for what he considered to be Romero's deception of confessors, the prosecutor offered the example of when Romero informed one that Jesus had told her to go to confession mute, so she only answered questions from the spiritual director by nodding yes or shaking her head no. The treatment of confessors exemplified the grave sin of not taking church sacraments seriously: "el haber abusado sacrílega e impíamente de los mesmos sacramentos de la confesión y eucaristía" [having abused, with sacrilege and without piety, the sacraments of confession and the Eucharist] (424). He constructed a dichotomy: on one hand, religious men filled with holy knowledge they wished to teach and on the other, the unrepentant, straying female sinner. Paradoxically, he ascribed a great deal of power, albeit negative, to Romero: she caused trouble throughout the country.

The prosecutor's case depended on proving Teresa Romero Zapata's falsehoods, which, following Catholic Church doctrine, he views as an integral part of woman's nature since Eve: "y dichas [locuciones] por una mujercilla tan embustera cual su género se habrían visto muy pocas semejantes" [and said statements by a woman who lied so much that her gender has seen very few like] (414). Repeatedly, he argued that she spoke "siempre con manifiestas contradicciones y sin satisfacer a la verdad de lo contra ella probado" [always with contradictions and without satisfying the truth of what had been proved against her] (438). Once, in order to avoid her angry father, for a month she pretended to be disabled, unable to get out of bed. Then, when she thought he had gotten over his anger, she feigned having been miraculously cured in a silent trance (68). Another time, she took credit for understanding the cause of an earthquake, which she claimed was the result of God's wrath because humankind had behaved badly (71).

Romero's visions, as recounted in the *Acusación* (Charges), included altercations with the devil; direct communication with God (e.g. 412), Jesus (e.g. 411), and several saints (Teresa, Michael, and Peter of Alcántara) [e.g. 422]. Some even offered lessons in mystical theology. During the trances, she handed out indulgences (433) and was given the stigmata (418). Miraculous signs of exemplarity, both events were meant to strengthen her case. And, like María de Agreda, she, who never left México, traveled: to Armenia to see Noah's ark, to Jersualem and Bethlehem to visit the site where Jesus was born; and to Japan, where she predicted she would gain the ultimate missionary reward, dying as a martyr (426).

While at times Romero engaged in long conversations with Jesus and other holy figures, at others she remained silent, absorbed for hours or once, nine days at a time (413). The intimate relationship she sought to sustain with Jesus ran the gamut from playing ball with the Niño Jesús (411) to listening to his affectionate maxims, directed at her: "como si la hablase el Señor, dijo: mi paz sea con vosotros; mi paz sea contigo borriquilla" [as though God spoke to her, he said: my peace be with you all; my peace be with you my little lamb] (412). Too much familiarity with saints also smacked of fakery: she called Saint Michael "tata Miguel" (417) [Daddy Michael] and claimed to have gotten a cigarette from Saint Paul (422). Her behavior brought her a great deal of attention, in the forms of money, gifts, and local fame, which probably led to the interest of the Holy Office. Sometimes she pretended she was crippled, perhaps to elicit pity. At others, she returned to childhood in trance, perhaps to reinforce her innocence (413, 415). The prosecutor, though, had another theory, based on common characterizations of women: "Y para acreditar más su enajenación de sentidos y potencias, fingía decir todo lo referido con notable sencillez y alegría . . . y hacía los chiqueos, quejidos, pucheritos y lágrimas de una criatura de dos años, llamando a este embuste, rapto continuado" [And in order to give more credence to her alienation of senses and abilities, she pretended to say all the above with notable simplicity and joy . . . and made the sounds, moans of, and cried like, a two-year-old child, called this lie, *rapto continuado*] (414). The presupposition of deception and disparaging language that concretely infantilized Romero both corresponded to standard gender ideology. Romero's daring to designate her trances *"rapto continuado"* (continuous trance), the category formulated by Father Bruñón, served to further damage her cause.

Continuing, the prosecutor accused her of several kinds of trickery in the public displays. During the ecstatic displays, the prosecutor alleged, "lo que hablaba . . . era lo que a la imaginación la venía de la alteza y grandeza de Dios, Misterios de la Santísima Trinidad, y lo que había oído, así en conversaciones de sacerdotes como oído leer en los libros devotos" [that she said . . . was what came to her imagination of the greatness and sublimity of God, mysteries of the Holy Trinity, and what she had heard in conversations among priests and heard read from pious books] (66).[11] Although her sources were sanctioned, her use of them was not. When she enacted public trances, he claimed, "dichas apariciones contenían irreverencias gravísimas, y en referirlas, como eran fingidas, la cogían en manifiestas contradicciones" [the said apparitions contained severe irreverences, and upon telling them, since they were faked, she was caught in obvioius contradictions] (420). She repeatedly pretended to be lame, but "estando en estos tullamientos, que ella llamaba rapto amoroso, y arrobada, si le daban alguna cosa, luego al instante se destullía" [And, the blood that flowed from her mouth, because, she said, of the force of her divine love was, he said, "alguna bebida colorada" (419) [some red-colored drink] (415). The prosecutor described in detail Romero's public displays of ecstasies, "como si fuera una comedia" (409) [as though it were a play]: "y que también se manifestaba ser todo embuste y fingimiento diabólico en la mesma publicidad . . . de los arrobamientos y apariciones, visiones y revelaciones que esta rea decía tener, en el citar para ellos, y hablar tanto [and that everything manifested as a lie and diabolical pretense in the very publicity . . . surrounding the trances and apparitions, visions and revelations that this prisoner said she had, in the setting of dates for them, and talking so much] (430). True mystics, one may infer, undergo their trances in private modesty, without advertising their experiences. Of course, the very fact that these acts were public made them suspect, even without taking into account their content. Unsanctioned by the Inquisition, left in the hands of those marginalized by gender and class, they were necessarily heterodox.

Other punishable sins abound. Teresa de Jesús often took communion without having confessed (e.g. 438). She presumed (dangerously) to be a preacher (405, 413). After God taught her seven methods of praying (397), she created another place in the afterlife next to purgatory, which she calls the *"penaculario"* (Penaculary), for those who were penitent at death but did not receive the sacraments. She must, of course, have been pronounced a heretic for such a dogmatic assertion (423).

Twice she pretended to fight with the devil, and to have been hurt in the process (67). According to the prosecutor, she even had public disputes with Satan (416). One scene, which the prosecutor named "fiction" and "illusion," summarized the performance aspect of Romero's spectacle: "como a las nueve del día comenzó la ficción de las peleas con el demonio, que duraron hasta casi media noche, en que era de maravillarse cómo no se cansaba en casi quince horas de hablar y de hacer tantas torerías con su cuerpo . . . con que se comprobaba la violencia de su ilusión" [at about nine o'clock in the morning the fiction of the battles with the devil began; they lasted until almost midnight, which was something to see, how she did not get tired in almost fifteen hours of talking and making silly movements with her body . . . with which the violence of her heterodoxy is proven] (417).

Other encounters with the devil fit standard representations. For example: "un bulto sin facciones, que se resolvió en una sombra . . . en diferentes formas que tomaba, de hombre galán y de niño . . . y una vez estando ella en la iglesia, se le transformó en un sapo grande que vió salir debajo de sus faldas [a shape without features, which became a shadow . . . in the different forms it took, of dandy and child . . . and once when she was in church, it transformed into a large frog which she saw come out from under her skirts] (388).

The devil returned many times, in many different forms, always goading her "a que pecase con él deshonestamente" (389) [to sin with him dishonestly]. According to the prosecutor, she claimed to have been a "mártir del demonio" (406) [martyr of the devil].

The erstwhile holy woman engaged in a wide range of religious activities without inquisitional authorization. Any kind of spiritual project was strictly regulated. Given her social status, Romero would never have obtained permission for her pursuits, but not to seek ecclesiastic sanction greatly strengthened the prosecutor's case.

Through religious books and priests's words, Teresa Romero was acquainted with the lives and work of Saint Catherine of Siena (401), Ana María de san José (388), Marina de Cristo (393), and Saint Teresa of Avila (388, 407). These holy women of Italy and Spain had exerted a great deal of power and influence during their lives and were widely imitated. Teresa Romero attempted to emulate them in three principal ways: by displaying mystical trances, writing a Life, and wearing religious dress.

Having been given the name Teresa at birth, with the alias Teresa de Jesús, she sought to emulate the Saint of Avila even more closely. Teresa Romero availed herself of the legends that sprung up about Saint Teresa almost immediately after her death in 1582. Once the Saint's canonization had been achieved in 1622, people were given permission for a wide variety of actions, thoughts, and feelings. The *ilusa* incorporated this lore into her spiritual life, in order to gain approval for unorthodox behavior. And during a brief period she achieved some acceptance: many called her a saint (408).

Unable to become a Carmelite nun, or perhaps simply because the Carmelite Order was considered a model of religiosity, Teresa Romero attempted to pattern herself after the most famous Hispanic woman religious of all, not only by taking her name, but in other ways. For a time, she even wore a Carmelite habit (407). Reaching for authority and exoneration, the accused woman insisted that Saint Teresa had communed with her: "que sus acciones, obras y palabras iban todas desde el cielo guiadas y enderezadas por Santa Teresa de Jesús . . . y la llevaba a que viere el convento de sus religiosas de esta ciudad" [that her actions, deeds and words were all guided and trained from heaven by Saint Teresa of Jesus] (422). The Carmelite mother authorized her temporary, but repeated entrance into a forbidden space. She could peek into the lives of "real" nuns. But she, and many others of her class, race, space, and time could not remain.

Romero simulated and perhaps had even heard parts of Saint Teresa's Life read.[12] Daring to dictate a spiritual autobiography might cement the contention of holiness. If the account of her life were vindicated, as Saint Teresa's finally had been, then her orthodox exemplarity might be guaranteed. But the transcribed words of the trial reveal instead deep ecclesiastic rage. The prosecutor's misogynistic comments about the *Vida* (Life), for instance, reflect dominant ideologies and norms. She claimed, he repeated sarcastically, "que Cristo, Señor Nuestro, la mandaba que se escribiese lo que la pasaba en los raptos para enseñanza y edificación de los fieles, siendo los escribientes el dicho su padre, un hermano de esta rea y otra cierta persona, y que lo que era más de notar, fué que dictaba esta rea lo que habían de escrebir sus escribientes" [that Christ, our God, ordered her to write down what happened in her trances for the education and edification of the faithful, the scribes being her aforementioned father, a brother of this prisoner, and another person, and what was most notable, was that this prisoner dictated what her scribes were supposed to write] (427). When the notebook was shown to a priest, he ordered it burned. Her father became upset, "sin duda porque perdió el instrumento para engañar" (undoubtedly because she lost the tool with which to deceive) the prosecutor alleged. Inquisitional officials abhorred the audaciousness of Romero's wanting her life recorded as a model for the faithful, and even more, boldness in telling her (male) secretaries what to write, when she herself was illiterate and a woman. She reached for too much subjectivity. Unfortunately, she achieved not what she must have wished for, but rather historical notoriety.

Caught in several outright lies, Romero attempted, perhaps in desperation, to save herself. She professed to have given God one of the three shirts she owned, but the prosecutor contended that she really gave it to "cierto mestecillo" (392) [certain little mestizo]. She had given birth to one child, and was pregnant in prison on September 18, 1649, when she called herself a *"doncellita"* (little virgin) and stated that she had never been married or had children (60). Yet a day earlier, on 17 September, 1649, in order to request a companion, she admitted to being eight months pregnant and to having refused to marry the father because, she said, they did not love each other (217). During her testimony, Romero availed herself of another tried and true tactic: she claimed to suffer from amnesia or ignorance. Early in the proceedings she testified that: "no se acuerda de cosa de las pasadas porque como eran fingidos los raptos, en habiendo pasado no se acordaba después de nada de lo que había dicho" [she does not remember anything of the past because, since the trances were faked, once they ended she remembered nothing of what she had said] (55). Since she presumed she was in prison because of the scandal caused by the false visions, she denied prior knowledge that she had sinned, asserting that "si supiera que era pecado grave o caso que tocaba a este Santo Tribunal, no lo hubiera hecho" [if I had known that it was a mortal sin or a case for this Holy Office, I would not have done it] (62). Thus, she constructed a case for mercy, built on the claim that she did not know she had sinned, and its logical corollary, that if she had known she wouldn't have done what she did. Therefore she begged for and expected leniency from the judges: "cuando con malicia y conocimiento de esto hubiera pecado ... se hubiera entrado por las puertas de la misericordia de este Santo Tribunal a pedirla, como la ha pedido y de nuevo la pide" [if she had sinned with malice and knowledge ... she would have entered through the doors of this Holy Office to ask for mercy, as she has asked and again asks] (62). Even if she had known she sinned, she asserted, she would have come forward to ask the same judges for compassion.

In a *Respuesta a la acusación* (435–38) [Response to the Charges], Romero responded to the prosecutor's attacks, but briefly and weakly, as if to confirm that he was right, a stance that her court-appointed attorney encouraged. Ill and weak from a decade in prison, it is no wonder that she tried out the rhetoric of capitulation on those who held the power of the ecclesiastic machinery. For instance, she hesitantly put forth, "que podía ser que hubiese cometido algunos de los delictos que en dicha acusación se decían contra ella, pero que no los había cometido con malicia" [that it could be that she had committed some of the crimes that were listed in the said charges against her, but she had not committed them with malice] (435). And, she admitted to having had a pact with the devil, but only because of his persuasive arts: "que el demonio la persuadía a que tuviese pacto con él" [that the devil persuaded her to make a pact with him] (437). The tactic backfired: her implicit reliance on the gendered explanation that women were more easily tempted to sin and so were more closely associated with the world, the flesh, and the devil turned out to confirm the dominant ideological stance of women's inferiority.

A judgment typical in New Spain for those (women) found guilty of *ilusión* (Illuminism) was proclaimed in 1659, a decade after the initial arrest. Teresa Romero Zapata was prohibited from using the name Teresa de Jesús; forbidden to associate with her former colleagues or to read books that might encourage false trances; allowed only a confessor appointed by the inquisitors; required to participate in an *auto de fe;* with other convicted prisoners, paraded through public streets half-naked and on a donkey or some other beast of burden; and sent to work in a hospital for ten years, after which she was banished from México City and Tepetlautoc and their environs (440–41). Because of her poor health, the judges witheld the execution of their sentence of two hundred lashes during the public display, although the whip was draped across her back (442). Public punishment for Teresa Romero and others like her "functioned as an educational ritual of inquisitorial power" and served another goal, "to avoid social transgression, disequilibrium, and rupture" (Quezada, 1991, 50, and 51). Inquisitional officials therefore deemed such demonstrations essential.

Further information about the fate of Teresa Romero Zapata, alias Teresa de Jesús, has not been uncovered. Her attempted emulation of holy women ultimately failed. The exaggerated, apparently distorted manifestation of saintliness led to her downfall. Despite the punishment, like Satan she remained unredeemed. Unlike him, her crime was the desire to achieve recognized holiness while at the same time earning a living. She was too marginalized from the mechanisms of social, economic, and religious power to be perceived as anyone but an *ilusa* (Illuminist woman) who required the father's discipline.

II.

In the brief that details his charges against Bárbara de Echegaray (1797), Bernardo de Prado y Ovejero writes with a ferocity derived from the same prevailing gender-typed assumptions as his predecessor, the earlier prosecutor. The accusations, similar to those against Teresa Romero (and many others): sexual laciviousness, resistance to confession and exorcism, falsehoods, and false mysticism. And, no less weighty: like Teresa Romero, she fooled her confessor into thinking her saintly, a sin which reversed the gendered power structure of which Steven J. Stern wrote. The document builds into a frenzied crescendo of scatological and sexual accusations, spewed forth in increasingly forceful, even violent nomenclature aimed at proving, even inventing, Bárbara de Echegaray as an *endemoniada* (possessed by the devil), an *ilusa*. Further, at first accused of consorting with the devil, in the succeeding pages Echegaray becomes the diabolical angel himself, captured in several different guises.

While Prado's rhetoric of hatred might be understood simply as a courtroom tactic, the *Acusación* (Accusation) is in some ways a personal narrative, one that exemplifies and supports a specific body politic. The voice of the prosecutor, his "I," dominates. Permeating the narrative, his judgments, sarcastic comments, theological analyses, and angry remarks aim at reasserting the social and religious status quo. He implicitly and explicitly justaposes the "good woman"—she who submits to men, personified in the Virgin Mary—to the "bad woman"—she who invokes her own subjectivity (within certain limits), exemplified through Eve.

Of course, Echegaray and other women judged *ilusas* did not envision overthrowing the established order. Not revolutionaries, but subversives, they attempted to push back a little the socioreligious boundaries, so as to carve out a space for their own positionality inside, rather than outside of the body politic. In other words, they combated their marginalization, using the only tool available to them: Catholic practice. But Prado's response to Echegaray's conduct underlines the rigidity of the world view, and practices against which they attempted to rebel and which allowed poor urban Creole women little room to maneuver.

One intriguing rhetorical device, which the prosecutor repeatedly employs, involves references to literary forms and modes that work to bolster his explanation of her behavior. He announces Echegaray's story at different times as a comedy, a farse, in which illusion becomes reality, a novel, and a tragicomedy. About her *Vida* (Life), written by the confessor, he avers, "en esta tragicomedia no haya otra cosa que tramoya, y aparato de virtud, y el asco, y fetidad de la luxuria de esta muger" [in this tragicomedy there is nothing but deceit, and the appearance of virtue, and the disgust, and smell of the lust of this woman] (cap. 15).[13] Later, he accuses her of fictionalizing: "No tienen otro fondo, ni posibilidad, que el empeño de mentir para componer esta Novela" (cap. 21) [They have no other background, or possibility, than the impulse to lie in order to compose this novel]. Here, fiction is conflated with lying. Finally, during the summary of her early years, he opines, "se fue a Puebla teatro principal en donde con la obscuridad, y tinieblas que busca el Pecador se executó esta Espantosa comedia" [she went to Puebla, main theater in which with the darkness and clouds that the sinner seeks this frightening comedy was performed] (cap 35). Naming literary genres highlights the enormity of the accused's guilt. The devious nature of this woman, and by extension all women, one of whose central characteristics is her facility in lying, is intimately linked to literature. While this rehetoric may only reveal the prosecutor's prejudices against literature, more probably he utilizes the ecclesiastic prohibition against certain genres and themes as a way of strengthening his case against Echegaray.

Through their challenge to gendered expectations of behavior and thought, five aspects of Bárbara de Echegaray's crime appear interrelated: *alumbrismo* (Illuminism) and *molinismo* (Molinism),[14] association with demons, pride and arrogance,[15] self-authorization, and counterfeit mysticism. When Prado asserts, for instance, that "la experiencia que hay en la Iglesia de Dios de haber introducido el Demonio muchos errores por medio de mugeres torpes y visionarias en cuio catalogo deve ocupar esta un lugar mui distinguido" [the experience that the Church of God has had of the devil having introduced many errors through indecent and visionary women] (cap. 97), for instance, he combines the charges of consorting with the devil, the inherent weakness of women, and the experience of false visions. By relying on the inquisitors' historical understanding of women as a gateway for the devil to operate toward the goal of destroying the faith, he touches on one aspect of their deepest code of beliefs.

The prosecutor accused Echegaray of heresy because, according to him, her revelations violated doctrine. They placed the visionary at the center of a religious universe in which she was affirmed as special, "favorecida de Dios" (favored by God). In his view, that mistake aligned her with false mystic cults and practitioners, which required review to establish the link. He asserted, "es necesario el trabajo de referirla en compendio, y presentar, aunque sea en indice, los principales pasages, que describen las heregias mas manifiestas, y la conducta mas conforme à la de modernos, y antiguos Pseudomisticos" [the work of summarizing is necessary, and presenting, even if in an index, the principal passages, which describe the most obvious heresies, and the behavior most like that of the modern and ancient pseudomystics] (cap. 15). Her guilt was plain as he described it, embedded in the already proven culpability of past and present heretics. Her ignorance of mystical theology worked against her. She had too sudden a conversion, he claimed. She used exercises for the illuminitative stage in the purgative, and she moved from the purgative to the illuminative too quickly.

Even more: she sought to define her own religiosity and enlisted the aid of the confessor to accomplish this. The desire for self-definition led to arrogance and pride. The prosecutor contended: "He aqui dos cosas notables, y monstru-osas; una, que el corazon corrompido havia de ser la regla de la mistica direc-cion; y la otra, la arrogancia, y sobervia, con que esta muger en la linea de padecer, y sufrir por Dios se toma el primer lugar entre todos los Santos, y Criaturas" [I have two monstrous and notable things here; one, that a corrupt heart must have been the rule for the mystical direction; and the other, the ar-rogance, and pride, with which this woman, saying she is afflicted and suffers for God, puts herself in first place among all the saints and humankind] (cap. 82). He harped on the idea that Bárbara de Echegaray wanted to define her own spiritual path, remain a "Directora de si misma" (cap. 50): "este pasage que aunque imaginario mas huele a la invencion, que a cosa de espiritu, manifiesta que esta [ilusa?] era la Maestra de si misma, y una falsa profetisa de las [vi?]siones, y grados de su alma, y favores del Señor" [this passage, which al-though imaginary smells more like invention than anything spiritual, demon-strates that this (ilusa?) was her own instructor, and a false prophetess of the (vi?)sions, and levels of her soul, and God's favors] (cap. 55). Since the illumin-ists and other quietist heresies favored direct communication with God, with-out priestly intervention, their doctrine directly attacked the Catholic Church, for which they were punished. The prosecutor in Bárabara de Echegaray's case capitalized on that chapter of Hispanic religious history when he built the linkage between her lack of submission to spiritual guidance and false visions.

Reproduced in chapters forty-eight through fifty of the Accusation, a visionary series that Echegaray experienced after she was excommunicated and declared an "Herege formal" (formal heretic), constituted a prime exam-ple of this tendency, Prado continued. The landscape and characters, tropes of Christian mysticism, were always the same. A gardener in front of a large tree spoke to the ecstatic, affirming her exemplarity and recognition by God. In the first, for instance, he insisted that it was not enough that she keep en-graved in her soul her vocation and the benefits of God; the spiritual life should be written down, "para mayor gloria de Dios" [for the greater glory of God] (cap. 49). The prosecutor insisted that "esta fue la primera imbencion con que o por propia malicia, o por engaño del Demonio burlo los decretos de la Iglesia, y autoridad del Santo Oficio" [this was the first invention with which, either out of malice or because of deceit from the devil, she mocked the decrees of the church, and the authority of the Holy Office] (cap 48). But Echegaray claimed spiritual exemplarity from the repeated ecstatic ex-periences. Through a mystical sleight of hand common among early modern women, Echegaray and her confessor found themselves ordered by the di-vinity to write her Life. Thus, Echegaray sought to define herself through writing.

But the prosecutor maintained that she was a charlatan and a fraud. He asserted that she faked miracles and deceived many people, especially her confessor, which appreared to be one of the gravest errors: "esta Visionaria alucino al confesor hasta hacerle creer que todo lo dicho era favor de Dios" [this false visionary deceived the confessor until she made him believe that everything said above was a favor from God] (cap. 52). He emphasized that she was guilty of "aparentando prodigios a que atribuir su Conversion, tanto mas expectables, quanto mayores eran sus delitos, y mas copiosas las gracias, y auxilios recibidos para su creencia afianzar la credulidad de muchos, y mucho mas del Confesor, y en ella los frutos de la Soberbia e hypocresia" [faking miracles to which to attribute her conversion, which crimes were as conspicuous, as they were serious, and the more copious the graces, and help received to support her belief with the credulity of many, and even more of the confessor, and in this the fruits of pride and hypocrisy] (cap. 11). Pride and hyprocrisy, cardinal sins, led Echegaray down the path of sin. The unsanctioned activity and self-referential spirituality must have driven her, in the prosecutor's view, to rejecting obedience and submissiveness to male authority, a particularly problematic character trait: "particularmente en el desprecio de la autoridad" [particularly in the disdain of authority]. Clearly, she seemed to him an uppity woman (cap. 11).

Heavily laced with sexual imagery, the prosecutor's description of Echegaray's false mysticism derives from the ideology of repression supported by the church: "no hay pasage [de la *vida*] sin resavio de lascivia, y que no presente falacias, y engaños muy groseros" [there is no passage (of the Life) without the flavor of lasciviousness, and that does not have fallacies, and gross deceptions] (cap. 60). Two aspects of the connection between illusion and lasciviousness remain salient: the demonization of those people whose spiritual practices sought to establish unmediated rapport with God and the rejection of the goal of enjoyment. As Asunción Lavrin has pointed out, "Ultimately, the will to gain pleasure from sexual activities was the key to defining any situation as sinful" (52). Prado went further: he conceptualized a link between sexual expression and quietist communication with the divinity: "fixan en hechos manifiestos de luxuria en la practica, y en las heregias pestilentes de Molinos, y otras iguales antiguas, y modernas, soltandose como ellos à todos los deseos de la Carne, cubriendo las mas torpes impurezas con el fingido pretexto de que eran violencias del Diablo" [obvious manifestations of lust are seen in the practice, and in the pestilent heresies of Molinos, and other similar ones, both ancient and modern, jumping as they do onto all the desires of the flesh, covering the worst impurities with the pretense and pretext that they were violations by the devil] (cap. 73).

Intimately connected with the long history of heretical cults, so that she became not an individual aberration, but part of an already proven heterodoxy, Echegaray loomed very large in the prosecutor's imagination, especially as an archetypal temptress. In his rhetorical framework, the exaggerated sexuality that inherently belonged to her as a woman was compounded with the lies that blamed the devil, also a female trait.

After a long description of sexual interaction among the devil, the confessor, and the accused, part of which he quoted directly from the confessor, the prosecutor compared their actions to those of "los Nosticos, Alumbrados, y Molinistas" (cap. 81). And, in one of many summary statements, toward the end of the *Acusación* he again asserted a connection between quietism and sexual sin when he again applied to Echegaray a common trope for women, the seductress (incarnated in Eve): "basta la simple relacion de esta vida, para conocer que esta Muger se ha hecho Renovadora de las pestilentes Sectas de los Molinistas, y Alumbrados, traguando, é inventando milagros, y fingiendo favores del cielo, para cubrir el torpe comercio à que con capa de direccion atrajo a su confesor" [the simple account of this life is enough to know that this woman has made herself the renovator of the pestilent sects of Molinists, and Illuminists, [], and inventing miracles, and faking heavenly favors, to cover up the sordid business with which, in the name of direction, she attracted her confessor] (cap. 95).

Here, the line of allegations of quietism and sexual immorality under the leadership of the devil culminated in the charge of too much power: the ability to deceive the confessor, which led him to engage in sexual intercourse.

But there is another story here. Echegaray and the confessor were locked in a power struggle that neither directly identified. Reading the *Acusación* from the perspective of late twentieth-century U.S. society, it is obvious that Echegaray's spiritual director engaged in what we would call "sexual harassment," while pretending to defend Echegaray from the devil's blandishments. The confessor portrayed himself as spiritually pure and strong enough to defeat dark forces. In a passage that the prosecutor's secretary transcribed from the spiritual director's narrative into the *Acusación*, the priest declared that he had been an eyewitness to Satan's seduction of Echegaray: the devil lifted up her skirts. After the confessor chased the demon away, he claimed that Echegaray "timida me dijo, que la mirase como esposa de Jesu Christo, y no la tocase el cuerpo" [timidly said to me, that I should look at her as the bride of Jesus Christ, and not touch her body] (cap. 76). Quoted from the confessor, more incidents of mutual sexual touching followed, episodes in which the spiritual director suggested that his confessant initiated the intercourse. But his own words demonstrate that he clearly played an active role, as when he asserted, "y con disimulo me aplicaba su mano à mi empeyne, para que se me quitasen algunos movimientos sensuales" [and dissembling she touched my penis with her hand, in order to stop for me some sensual movements] (cap. 81). According to his testimony, (1) he was aroused before she touched him, and (2) she touched him to calm him down. Unsurprisingly, the prosecutor responded to this statement by exclaiming, "se hace preciso preguntar à estos impudentes, ¿quien violentaba al Director à acercarse à esta infame tanto, que pudiera verificarse el conato diabolico al exercicio de mutuas torpezas?" [it is necessary to ask these impudent people, who forced the confessor to come so close to this infamous woman, so that one can verify the diabolical attempt to exercise mutual carnal sins] (cap. 81).

Ultimately, though, while the prosecutor appeared to blame both confessor and confessant for "comercio mas indigno, impuro, y criminal, y siempre con aparato de mysterio" (cap. 83) [the most low, impure, and criminal business, and always with the appearance of mystery], Bárbara de Echegaray stood trial alone, because of the deeply engrained social belief that women were inherently seductive, more associated with the world, the flesh, and the devil than men. A case in point: when two priests first attempted an exorcism on the accused woman, they managed only to quiet her and instill the desire for confession. The prosecutor attributed their lack of success to the *ilusa*'s gender: "pero el Demonio no hizo caso de sus Exorcismos; por que como no habia mas diablo, o a lo menos diablo mayor que esta muger" [but the devil ignored her exorcisms; because there was no more devil or at least no greater devil than this woman] (cap. 39). As a woman, she incarnated the devil and was therefore impervious to ecclesiastic attempts to bring about her conformity.

Still, only the Inquisition could save confessant and confessor from further sins, such as the sadomasochism that repeatedly preceded ecstatic experiences. Echegaray flagellated herself. The confessor whipped her. The devil tormented her with his tail. The theatrical violence led to false visions: "hasta que el Santo Oficio cortò el hilo de esta historia, no hay dia sin tormentos de Demonios, sugestiones, y hechos carnales, ò representados y executados en ella por los Diablos, y en que haya tenido despues de muchos azotes del Maestro, visiones, locuciones, y revelaciones, en que recibia fortaleza, y se aprobaba su falso espiritu" [until the Holy Office cut the thread of this story, there was no day without torment of demons, suggestions, and facts of carnality, or represented and executed on her by the demons, and in which she had, after many lashes by the Teacher, visions, speeches, and revelations, from which she gained strength, and which proved her false spirit] (cap. 88).

The prosecutor contended that the narrative of the sin, the telling of the story, was as dangerous as the violence. Perhaps because through the *Vida*, Echegaray was constituted as a subject worthy of being written about.

The brutal patterns detailed in the confessor's account are presaged in the account of Echegaray's early life, which the prosecutor reproduced, although he informed the readers (the inquisitors) that he doubted her veracity. The accused's childhood was fraught with tension, conflict, and violence. Her mother, she claimed, rejected her at birth, "exclamò furiosa, que no era su hija, y aunque los fuese, que se parecia a la mala Casta de su Padre, que se la quitaran" [she exclaimed furiously that she was not her daughter, and even if she was, that she looked like the bad caste of her father, and that they should take her away] (cap. 19). She asserted that her mother used to let pass three or more months without seeing her, and that she was therefore raised by an "india chichigua" until she was eleven or twelve years old. The story of her mother's violence strained the prosecutor's imagination. He disbelieved, but unwittingly gave evidence of severe child abuse: "quien podrá creer, que su Madre la golpease hasta desollarla los brazos, que la untase con chile todo el cuerpo, que se cerrase con ella en un quarto para zurrarla a su satisfaccion, tirandola de los cabellos, y arrastrandola por tierra [who could believe, that her mother would hit her until she stripped the skin of her arms off, that she would cover her whole body with chile, that she would lock herself in a room with her in order to flog to her satisfaction, pulling her by the hair, and dragging her along the ground] (cap. 21).

The descriptions, including the application of chile applied to her body, startle and dismay the contemporary reader. Yet social mores defined why the prosecutor automatically thought the tale untrue. The account of her mother's use of torture reflects the same baroque tendency toward exaggeration and drama as the description of the punishment used by confessor and devil, but to imagine that it is pure invention denies Echegaray the possibility of subjectivity.

One time, Echegaray averred, her mother was so angry that "la pegó una Zurra tan dura, que fue necesario tomar la providencia de llevarla à otra casa" [she whipped her so hard, that it was necessary to take the step of taking her to another house] (cap. 20). Her father, portrayed as loving her, then put her under care of a "Maestra" (teacher) who "la abofeteaba por qualquier pueril movimiento" (hit her for any childish movement) until he found out about the behavior and took his daughter away (cap. 22). When he fell ill, her mother continued her cruel and vicious treatment. Consequently, Echegaray, unprotected and unable to tolerate her mother's handling of her, declared, hoping to get relief, but revealing the unconscious racism of the time (and still prevalent today), that she would either "casarse con el primero que quisiese, aunque fuese un Indio mechudo, o darse a una mala Vida" [marry the first man she wanted, even if he were a hairy Indian, or become a prostitute] (cap. 26). To the prosecutor, with this pronouncement she had proved once again that she was a seductress, an evil woman.

The ninety-nine chapters of the *Acusación* end with a summary of charges, then the prosecutor's proposals for action. Convinced of Echegaray's guilt, he attempted to persuade his audience, the inquisitional judges, of her culpability as well. Because he did not consider her sufficiently repentant, in an unconscious echo of the narrative of the confessor's, devil's, and mother's behavior, he recommended that she be tortured, so as to discover the whole truth. As Elizabeth Mazzola has suggested about Anne Askew, when she kept silent, "her accusers turn to her body as a vehicle or location for these secrets . . . they employ torture . . . as an epistemological procedure which obtains the truth by 'unmaking' her body" (1995, 165). Perhaps Echegaray exhibited too direct a sexuality for the prosecutor to accept. In any case, his narrative displayed the misogynist assumptions characteristic of his time and place.

The bottom of the last folio of the *Acusación* contains the beginning of Bárbara de Echegaray's statement. In the first paragraph, she sounded desperate: denying all responsibility, she pleaded insanity. But, as was the case with Teresa Romero Zapata, further information about her has not been uncovered. Nevertheless, she most probably suffered the same fate.

Gayle Rubin asserts that: "Like gender, sexuality is political. It is organized into systems of power, which reward and encourage some individuals and activities, while punishing and suppressing others" (309). Nowhere is this more plainly visible than in colonial Mexican inquisitional proceedings that determined whether women's visionary experiences came from God or the devil.

Marginalized in their own society, Teresa Romero Zapata and Bárbara de Echegaray sought subjectivity in history through transcendence. The relationship with family and with confessors, and the visionary life they engendered under that tutelage, offered them the space to enact their subjectivity, denied in social interaction. The documents, even if they reproduce the accused's words in a distorted, inaccurate fashion and privilege the voice of the Father, illuminate the features not only of urban life, but also of dominant norms and values in colonial México. More, the self-righteous gendered rhetoric with which they are written displays absolutely rigid stereotypical notions about women, which were crucial ideological underpinnings of that society. The prosecutor's voice serves as the master's spokeperson's, embedded in the gendered, classed, and raced power structures that punished Teresa Romero and Bárbara de Echegaray (and many others) for a crime engendered at least as much by social as individual factors.

NOTES

1. The Inquisition called "Santo Oficio" was preceded by two others: one run by missionary fathers and the other by the bishop. Solange, Alberro, "Mujeres ante el Tribunalcle Santo Oficio de la Inquisición en la Nueva España," *Boletín Editorial, El Colegio de México* 15 (Sept-Oct): 16–22.

2. Examples of such crimes include: bigamy, solicitation in the confessional, sexual perversion, blasphemy, perjury, witchcraft, quackery, and astrology.

3. Perhaps he was thinking of information such as in Noemí Quezada, "The Inquisition's Repression of *Curandios*," in *Cultural Encounters*, Mary Elizabeth Perry, and Anne J. Cruz, eds. (Berkeley: University of California Press), table 3.1, pp. 42–45, where in a long list, one *curandera* was tortured and punished severely, but she was also accused of being an *alumbrada*. Her story is recounted on pp. 49–50.

4. The articles pertaining to New Spain recently published in Mary E. Giles', *Women in the Inquisition* (Baltimore and London: John Hopkins University Press), treat women of differing classes and races, faced with a range of charges, from blasphemy to heresy.

5. See Ruth Behar, "Sex and Sin, Witchcraft and the Devil in Late-Colonial Mexico," *American ethnologist* 14, 1: 34–54. There is an explanation of these practices and the official response to them.

6. In "Thin Lines, Bedeviled Words," Electa Arenal and I argued that women's "heterodox" spirituality in New Spain reflects a complex dynamic of race, gender, and class power struggles.

7. Jean Franco's term which she uses in *Plotting Women* (New York: Columbia University Press.)

8. The published extracts of the trial have been transcribed into modern Spanish.

9. The *Acusación* appears on pages 387–435 of the published version.

10. Because of lack of space, I omit the discussion of the relationship among the sisters.

11. A version of this statement appears on page 393.

12. Oral reading was still widely practiced in the seventeenth century.

13. When quoting from the manuscript, I use chapter numbers rather than folio numbers, for they are easier to find. (Chapters, each of which describes one instance of criminal behavior, are almost never more than two folio pages long.) Also, I transcribe accentuation, capitalization, punctuation, and spelling directly from the manuscript.

14. The doctrine proposed by Miguel de Molinos (1628–1691) laid the foundation for later quietist movements within the Catholic Church. His work was declared heretical by the church during his lifetime.

15. Prado uses the phrase "soberbia y arrogancia" repeatedly.

BIBLIOGRAPHY

Alberro, Solange. 1987. "Mujeres ante el Tribunal del Santo Oficio de la Inquisición en la Nueva España." *Boletín Editorial, El Colegio de México* 15 (Sept-Oct): 16–22.

Arenal, Electa, and Stacey Schlau. 1992. "Thin Lines, Bedeviled Words: Monastic and Inquisitional Texts by Colonial Mexican Women." *Estudios sobre escritoras hispánicas en honor de Georgina Sabat-Rivers.* Edited and introduced by Lou Charnon-Deutsch, 31–44. Madrid: Editorial Castalia.

Behar, Ruth. 1987. "Sex and Sin, Witchcraft and the Devil in Late-Colonial Mexico." *American Ethnologist* 14,1: 34–54.

Franco, Jean. 1989. *Plotting Women: Gender and Representation in Mexico.* New York: Columbia University Press.

Giles, Mary E. 1999. *Women in the Inquisition: Spain and the New World.* Baltimore and London: Johns Hopkins University Press.

Greenleaf, Richard E. 1991. "Historiography of the Mexican Inquisition: Evolution of Interpretations and Methodologies." In *Cultural Encounters: The Impact of the Inquisition in Spain and the New World.* Edited by Mary Elizabeth Perry, and Anne J. Cruz, 248–76. Berkeley: University of California Press.

J. J. R. 1946. "El proceso de una seudo iluminada. 1649." *Boletin del Archivo General de la Nación* 15, 1, 2, 3: 33–73, 216–45, 386–442.

Klor de Alva, J. Jorge. 1991. "Colonizing Souls: The Failure of the Indian Inquisition and the Rise of Penitential Discipline." In *Cultural Encounters.* Edited by Mary Elizabeth Perry and Anne J. Cruz, 3–22. Berkeley: University of California Press.

Lavrin, Asunción. 1989. "Sexuality in Colonial Mexico: A Church Dilemma." In *Sexuality and Marriage in Colonial Latin America.* Edited by Asunción Lavrin, 47–95. Lincoln and London: University of Nebraska Press.

Leonard, Irving A. 1993 [1959]. *Baroque Times in Old Mexico: Seventeenth Century Persons, Places, and Practices.* Ann Arbor: University of Michigan Press.

Mazzola, Elizabeth. 1995. "Expert Witnesses and Secret Subjects: Anne Askew's *Examinations* and Renaissance Self-Incrimination." In *Political Rhetoric, Power, and Renaissance Women.* Edited by Carole Levin, and Patricia A. Sullivan, 157–171. Albany: State University of New York Press.

Perry, Mary Elizabeth, and Anne J. Cruz, eds. 1991. *Cultural Encounters: The Impact of the Inquisition in Spain and the New World.* Berkeley, Los Angeles, Oxford: University of California Press.

Prado y Ovejero, Bernardo de. 1797. *Acusación del Fiscal Bernardo de Prado y Ovejero ante la Inquisición contra Bárbara de Echegaray.* Archivo General de la Nación, México. Inquisición, c. 125/ exp. s/n.

Quezada, Noemí. 1991. "The Inquisition's Repression of *Curanderos.*" In *Cultural Encounters.* Edited by Mary Elizabeth Perry, and Anne J. Cruz, 37–57. Berkeley: University of California Press.

Rubin, Gayle. 1984. "Thinking Sex: Notes for a Radical Theory of the Politics of Sexuality." In *Pleasure and Danger: Exploring Female Sexuality.* Edited by Carol S. Vance, 267–319. Boston: Routledge and Kegan Paul.

Stern, Steve J. 1995. *The Secret History of Gender: Women, Men, and Power in Late Colonial Mexico.* Chapel Hill and London: University of North Carolina Press.

Tambling, Jeremy. 1990. *Confession: Sexuality, Sin, the Subject.* New York: St. Martin's Press.

Whitney, Elspeth. 1995. "The Witch 'She'/The Historian 'He': Gender and the Historiography of the European Witch-Hunts." *Journal of Women's History* 7,3: 77–101.

Representing Gender, Deviance, and Heterogeneity in the Eighteenth-Century Peruvian Newspaper *Mercurio Peruano*

Mariselle Meléndez

In recent years, the heterogeneity and hybridity of Latin American people and their culture, have been an issue often debated and explored by critics. According to many of the critics, the above terms appear to be twentieth-century phenomena often debated in discussions involving nineteenth-century Spanish-American nationalistic discourses. However, an aspect conspicuously absent from these arguments is a close look into how Latin American hybridity and heterogeneity have been major concerns since colonial times.[1] As Serge Gruzinski has brilliantly stated in reference to the sixteenth and especially the eighteenth century, America became "a land of syncretism" and a "culture of hybridity" (1994, 15).

The problems of representation and containment of heterogeneous societies have been constant in Latin American history, as has been illustrated through legal, religious, historical and literary texts throughout the colonial period. Literary critics who study issues of heterogeneity in Spanish America seldom delve into the eighteenth century. This was a century in which texts as diverse as legal, and travel narratives, as well as medical treatises and newspapers, discussed the difficulties of containing a heterogeneous society that represented an enormous challenge to colonial authority. Women's roles in society, where the element of difference was a major concern, lend an interesting aspect to such discussions. The obsessive desire to control a multiracial population in which castes and women of all races and social classes became more mobile represented a major concern in texts of the time. In the case of women, dressing, eating habits, health, sexuality, and moral and social behavior became markers to categorize and criticize such mobility. As contemporary situations

I would like to thank Marcia Stephenson (Purdue University) for her comments and suggestions on this essay.

175

in Latin America as well as around the world have shown us, the above markers still function as avenues to define women's role in society.

This essay will analyze how a heterogeneous, visible, and mobile female population represented a major concern to some sectors of the male population. Heterogeneity, in this essay, implies the "diverse, multiple, and conflictive configuration" of a subject which produces signs of "contradiction, instability, and irregularity" in a discourse (Cornejo Polar 1994, 14–7). I will contend that mobility and social visibility become two distinctive components of such heterogeneity. My analysis will focus on one of the most important publications of that century: the Peruvian newspaper entitled *Mercurio peruano* (1964, 1791–94). Women's diverse nature and behavior as well as their social and racial backgrounds were so divergent that any attempts to confine them within a singular image during that period seemed troublesome. Race, class, sexuality, and cultural practices constituted many of the factors that separated one woman from another. This essay aims to demonstrate how women's social mobility and heterogeneity became a major threat to the ordering of colonial society; a society engaged in a radical process of reform which pursued stability through control of the colonial population. The difficulties in defining women and dealing with their differences in the context of society has pervaded history to the present time, when even today women's sexuality and cultural practices have been associated with disorder, deviance, and danger, yet still crucial to the service of public health and moral order. This article will allude to some twentieth-century cases that demonstrate how the role of women in Peruvian society after independence did not differ altogether from the colonial period. As has been demonstrated in this collection of essays, the social situations of past Latin American societies always help us to understand present social situations.[2]

SOCIAL PREOCCUPATION AND INCIPIENT NATIONALISM IN THE *MERCURIO PERUANO*

The study of eighteenth-century Peruvian newspapers confronts us with recurrent images of crisis, uncertainty, anxiety, and fear. In many of these images, women emerge as the center of discussion. Women's mobility in the public space had begun to generate anxiety within a masculine population who desperately wanted women circumscribed within the limits of domestic space or racial and social categories. For many men who assumed the role of keeping order and progress in colonial society, women symbolized an essential instrument in the stabilization and ordering of the nation.

Doreen Massey has described the identity of women in situations of subordination as closely connected with "the limitation on mobility in space, the attempted consignment/retreat to particular places on the one hand and the limitation on identity on the other" (1994, 179). For this reason, "the attempt to confine women to the domestic sphere was both a specifically spatial control and, through that, a social control on identity" (1994, 179). Circumscribing women to the domestic space or home was perceived as a "source of stability, reliability and authenticity" (1994, 180). These three aspects (stability, reliability, and authenticity) were not found in Peruvian society at the close of the colonial regime by the authors of the articles in the *Mercurio peruano*. Instead, these articles suggest that the visibility of woman in the public sphere constituted a constant uneasiness for the masculine sector of the period. In their writings, men expressed the need for control of women's bodies within the social space. Women's unconventional behavior was understood to be a disease with the potential to contaminate the health of the nation or, in order words, the moral order of society; a point to be illustrated in greater detail later.[3] For many who contributed to the newspapers, it was vital to eradicate such disease so that order could be reestablished. I will illustrate in the following pages how contributors to the *Mercurio peruano* articulated women's identity by focusing on woman's demeanor and behavior from within and outside the public space. In such definitions, the discourse of sexuality also functioned as a weapon to justify "the exclusion of behaviors potentially counterproductive to the execution of the national project" (Borim and Reis 1996, iv). In the Peruvian newspapers of the late-colonial period, writing was a useful tool for the ordering and legitimization of these projects which were strictly marked by masculine power. Still today, the government and the medical establishment, among other state organizations, have utilized writing as an apparatus to define and determine women's position in society within and outside the domestic space.

The *Mercurio peruano* was published for the first time in 1791 and was directed by the *Sociedad Académica de Amantes de Lima* (Academic Society of Lovers of Lima).[4] The purpose of the newspaper, according to its editors, was "hacer mas conocido el Pais que habitamos, este Pais contra el cual los autores extrangeros han publicado tantos paralogismos" [to make better known the country in which we live; a Country about which foreign authors have published many false ideas] (1964, 1: 1).[5] The newspaper intended to critique the chronicles and other writings related to the centuries of conquest and colonization which, according to the editors, were not capable of depicting an accurate image of Perú: "[e]l espíritu de sistema, sus preocupaciones nacionales, la ignorancia a veces, y el capricho han influido tanto en la mayor parte de estas obras, que el Perú que ellas nos trazan, parece un pais enteramente distinto del que nos demuestra el conocimiento practico" [the spirit of the system, the country's national preoccupations, occasional ignorance, and the caprice of some authors have influenced most of these works, to the point that the Peru depicted by them seems to be a country completely different from the one that practical knowledge shows us] (1964, 1: 1). Therefore, the newspaper attempted to offer more exact and accurate news concerning Perú and its people (1964, 1: 2). It would not be erroneous to suggest that the articles included in the *Mercurio peruano* constituted part of a politico-cultural project, the purpose of which was to correct, direct, and order society in such a way as to enable its progress in the social, economic, and intellectual realm. Its editors clearly displayed fervent love for their country and their commitment to "investigar noticias, depurarlas de la falsedad con que por lo comun se acompañan, y exponerlas a la publica luz" [investigate news, purge it of all the falseness that commonly accompanied it, and bring it to the public light] (1964, 2: 1).[6]

The evident interest in the country demonstrated by the editors (the editorials were always directed toward the patriots) drew them to study each element of society, since according to them, "the newspaper's variety" was their "best adornment" (1964, 2: 3). The image of women in the newspaper was seen as a vital component within the context of their national preoccupation. The "inconstancy" of woman, specially women from the upper classes, constituted one of the aspects that most caught the editors' attention (1964, 2: 4). These women were defined according to their interests, occupations, diversions, clothing, education, and health. They became the object of attacks and jokes, an attitude spawned from the threat that women's mobility or sexuality posed to men's masculine perception of the nation. Women's mobility was accompanied by the crossing of boundaries that separated the masculine space of power from the feminine one, while their sexuality carried cultural and social demands associated to the numeric reproduction of the nation. Much of the criticism toward women in the *Mercurio peruano* was directed toward the upper- and middle-class sector of the female population. These women constituted a sector which had the means to pay for different types of entertainment. They had the opportunity to attend meetings in salons, engaging in discussion about fashion and problems affecting women's lives, or simply to comment about current social events. They also constituted a sector which had the time, education, and economic means to engage in any desired intellectual pursuits. These social and personal enjoyments were seen by some contributors of the Peruvian newspaper as signs of deviance. Feminist groups in contemporary Peruvian society, such as "Acción para la liberación de la mujer peruana," "Promoción de la mujer" and "Grupo de Trabajo Flora Tristán" have also been seen, considered and defined in a similar manner by Peruvian authorities. Women belonging to these groups have also been middle-class and in some cases high-class educated women, who contrary to peasant women, posseses the means to pursue intellectual pursuits. However, *Mercurio peruano*'s contributors in their articles also addressed women belonging to the lower class of the population. These particular news items depicted the health of women and their moral behavior. In such cases, the physical constitution of black women or the social conduct of criminals, prostitutes, and concubines were also viewed by some authors of the articles as indications of deviance and danger.

MOBILITY AND SOCIAL VISIBILITY: THE CONFLICTIVE AND DIVERSE CHARACTER OF WOMAN

In one of the first issues of the *Mercurio peruano* appeared a column that pointed to male-centered preoccupation regarding women's pleasures. It was suggested that these female enjoyments led to the abandonment of women's domestic responsibilities. The article held the title "*Carta escrita* a la Sociedad sobre los gastos excesivos de una *tapada*" (Letter written to Society about the excessive expenses of a *tapada*). A husband complains of the excesses his wife incurs by spending, employing servants, and attending social gatherings, plays, bullfights, funerals, and other city events. He describes how her indulgences had become an instrument of his biggest trepidation. His wife had ruined him financially by accruing great debts to the silversmith, seamstress, dressmaker, and surgeon. Everything material that he possessed in the house had reached various states of arrears, including the dressers, couches, wallpaper, clocks, the chaise, and their bed. The husband also seemed to be troubled by his wife's constant desire to be outside the house, simply to attend and enjoy each event that occurred in the plaza. As soon as she has completed her bath, he claims, she would immediately begin plans to attend bullfights, plays, masses, and friars' and nuns' appointments: "Mas lo que me saca de tino es, que en medio de todas estas andanzas, no contentas con ellas, jamas pierde ningún [altercado]. Ella sabe por minutos quando ajustician a uno, quando azotan a otro; y aquella mañana madruga, almuerza temprano, y vamonos a la Plaza" [But what angers me is that not being satisfied with all her adventures, she never misses a quarrel. Within minutes she knows of every execution, or whipping, and on the morning of the event she awakens early, enjoys an early lunch, then proceeds to the *Plaza*] (1964, 1: 112–13). He adds that the minimal time his wife spent at home was always devoted to the entertainment of guests and showering them with gifts. Her supposed excesses exacerbated the situation by compromising her role as a mother since, as he points out, "[p]or fruto de nuestro tálamo tenemos tres hijitos, que se han criado ya ve al cuidado de la Ama y de cierta Querendona de mi Muger que es el oráculo de la casa" [as a result of our conjugal bed, we have three small children who have been raised and looked after by a wet nurse and a loving female friend of my Wife[7] who is the oracle of the house] (1964, 1: 113).

This article offers a glimpse into the mobility of women of high social ranks in the public space and the transformation of their domestic roles as elements which constituted two worrisome aspects for certain men of the eighteenth century. The consequences of this wife's behavior and her unwillingness to give up the pleasures she enjoyed at her parties and outings had serious economic repercussions. For this man, even the domestic space could not serve as an oasis of stability and trust. Instead, his wife had altered and modified it into a space of recreation and self-enjoyment rather than child rearing. She had transformed the home into an alternate space, a sort of microcosm where she was determined to reproduce the delectations that she enjoyed in the public space. In fact, the wife does not take on a traditional image of the mother, one expected to subscribe to the domestic space and to the authority of her husband. This image became part of several nationalistic projects from the eighteenth century forward. As Sallie Westwood and Sarah A. Radcliffe point out with regard to many Latin American countries, "nationalist imagery" has placed women as " 'mothers of the nation' symbolically and biologically" although "it is clear from the national stories that not all women are equally 'mothers' of the nation" (1993, 14–15). This wife, as portrayed by her husband, constitutes a mother who does not occupy the traditional mother role set forth by male authorities as representatives of the nation.

The husband's authority as head of the house is also diminished when a dear friend of his wife (*querendona*) becomes the authority (*el oráculo de la casa*) in charge of the household decision-making process. This loving friend, perhaps a female lover, as the Spanish meaning of the word implies (see note 7), has hindered total male control over his wife, his children, and his house. As a result, the transmission or reinforcement of his values to his children are being affected when his power and authority are threatened. Ultimately, this article underlines how difficult it was to control woman's spatiality and "the social control of their identity" as well as the husband's frustration in his attempts to confine his wife to the domestic sphere (Massey 1994, 179). In this case, the wife has blurred the distinctions between public and domestic space, melding them into a single suitable space for the fulfillment of her desires. Her behavior, therefore, was seen by her husband as a symbol of disorder and danger.[8]

Another article which reflected how some eighteenth-century women were moving away from traditional activities characterizing the space of domesticity was published on May 19, 1791 by Asignio Sartoc. In his essay, "Sobre la impertinente pretensión de algunas Mugeres, a que las llamen Señoras" [About the impertinent pretentiousness of some Women who insist on being called Ladies], Mr. Sartoc discussed an obsession he observed in certain women of Cuzco who called themselves *"señoras."* In the eighteenth century, the word *"señora"* (madam) implied noble status (those who controlled land or territories or were considered masters of a household). The word also implied a title of respect, and was often used to convey politeness. From a moral standpoint, it applied to a person who possessed control over her actions as well as the power to make her own decisions (*Diccionario de autoridades* 1963, 87–8).

These *Cuzqueña* women, Sartoc adds, provoked an "implacable war" *(guerra implacable)* against men by mobilizing other women into thinking likewise (1964, 2: 44). That women thought they could be called *"señoras,"* including those who didn't come from an illustrious lineage, disturbed Sartoc. Potential alteration of the lines that separated aristocratic classes from the middle class also irritated Sartoc, especially as he discovered such women organizing reunions with their compatriots to discuss their reasons for the right to be called *"señoras."* Sartoc considers this attitude as a rampant disease in need of immediate control. He describes what he perceived to be their malady as residing in the field of thought, stemming from "corrupt humor" *(humor viciado)* that made them demand ladyship of which they did not deserve (1964, 2: 45). The article ends with a plea from the author to eliminate "so much infection" so that "much depravity" could be avoided (1964, 2: 44). The metaphor of disease is utilized by Sartoc to highlight the possible contagion the original attitude of this woman could cause in the rest of the female *Cuzqueña* population. The reunions she carried out and her desire to mobilize her countrywomen were perceived by the author as dangerous distractions because they served as a knowledge exchange medium reserved exclusively for women. Their meetings *(tertulias)* focused on the discussion of historical bases which could serve as evidence with regard to the right to call themselves *"señoras"* despite their birthright.

Asignio Sartoc's article originated a polemic between a woman named Doña Lucinda and himself. In response to Sartoc's letter, Lucinda sent an article from Cuzco, entitled "Defensa del Señorío de las Mugeres" [Defense of the Ladyship of Women], which attempted to correct the position expressed by Sartoc.[9] According to Doña Lucinda, to be called *"señora"* was a privilege and right tacitly based on respect and power, while for Sartoc it was based solely on social status. Lucinda made her interest clear in the article not to criticize or contradict Sartoc's letter, but to invoke within him and other men empathy for women's right to call themselves *"señoras"*: "La antiquada posesión en que nos hallamos de disfrutar este honor" [The antiquated tradition in which we find ourselves enjoying this honor] (1964, 4: 63). Her letter clearly specified that the examples she offered would not refer to women from Castile or descendants of conquerors, but rather to *Cuzqueñas*. Her position questioned the belief held by some sectors of colonial society who still thought that titles of distinction should be granted based on Spanish lineage.

Doña Lucinda defended her ideas by offering an historical catalogue of religious, political, philosophical, and literary texts which referred to women as *"señoras."* Using biblical sources and authors such as Homer, Virgil, and Ovid, in addition to emperors such as Justinian, Caesar, and others, Lucinda cited specific passages in Latin that proved how erudite, distinguished men had themselves referred to women as *"señoras,"* doing so as a reflection of their respect for women. Many of the authors not only recognized women's dignity, but also regarded their intellectual capacity, calling them "eminent or illustrious" and "very keen" *(clarísimas)* (1964, 4: 66–7). Such a historical catalogue enabled Lucinda to demonstrate to Sartoc her knowledge of classic letters and philosophy, which at the time were considered a masculine domain. Thereafter, she clearly reminded him how a historic retelling and review of the authorities in the field of letters demonstrated that women should be recognized for their intellectual worth and knowledge, aspects that also proved their undeniable right to be treated with respect. Instead of attempts to disrespect women, Lucinda recommended he devote himself to issues contributing to the honor of the country. Lucinda ended the article with recognition of the animosity her letter might cause, and sarcastically pardoned herself by stating "Bien pudiera el amor propio lisonjarme con la satisfacción de siéndome accesible algun ramo de literatura no erraría por falta de razon instruida: ¿pero quien me asegura de una inadvertencia que me hiciese objeto del sentimiento, y acaso del odio?" [My self-esteem could very well flatter me with the satisfaction that, some branch of literature were accessible to me, I would avoid erring due to uneducated reason. However, who can assure me that because of my inadvertence I will not be the object of resentful feelings, or even hatred? (1964, 4: 67). Her anticipation came to fruition on April 19, 1792 as her article did not go unnoticed and a resentful Sartoc retaliated with a rebuttal publication entitled "Nuevo rasgo prosbólico contra el señorismo de las Mugeres de la Ciudad de Cuzco" [New outline against the ladyship of Women from the City of Cusco] (1964, 4: 267).

At the core of Sartoc's second article resounds a condescendingly sarcastic tone. Sartoc begins by praising Lucinda's knowledge of fine arts, philosophy, history, and theology, eventually asking himself "¿[Q]uien esperaba de la Sierra una Obra como la dicha, concebida tan felizmente por una Sabia del sexo?" [Who expected a Work such as this from the Sierra, so happily conceived by a Wise person of the female sex?] (1964, 4: 268). He follows this eulogy by questioning what he thought to be Lucinda's dubious command of Latin, who according to Sartoc, erred severely in her interpretation of Latin quotes. Sartoc continued by offering Lucinda a linguistic lesson, criticizing such details as her use of the phrase *"antiquada posesión,"* meant to refer to sources of illustration for her position which, he claimed, actually referred to something abolished, without use (1964, 4: 268). His article also wondered aloud why Lucinda needed so many examples to clearly state her position, and he accused her of employing this method of attack as a means to boast about her erudition: "¡Qué fecundidad de erudicion! Mas ¿para que la ha prodigado esta señora?"

[What fruitful erudition! However, why has this lady squandered it so lavishly? (1964, 4: 268–69).

With regard to Lucinda's directive that Sartoc should concern himself with issues of honoring the country, he retorted that this was his precise intention as he attacked women's claims to be called *"señoras."* He underlined that through eradication of the pernicious vices that characterized women as part of the social body, an exceptional means of honoring the country would be propagated (1964, 4: 273). Sartoc sustained that prevention of women's belief in the right to call themselves *"señoras,"* especially when such honor and title was not common to them all, was extremely patriotic. He ended the article emphasizing on the notion that his intention was never to generalize that all women of Cuzco were proclaiming themselves *"señoras"* without deserving such distinction. However, Sartoc did reiterate that "A su honor pertenece desterrar esos vicios perniciosos, que se hacen frequentes en las personas que componen su político cuerpo. Para desterrarlos, nada se halla mas eficaz que esas festivas invectivas, que paladeando el buen gusto de los entendidos, exponen al Publico el vicio, y le descubren toda su disonancia" [The honor is mine to banish those pernicious vices so common within the people who constitute the nation's political body. To eliminate those vices, there is no more efficient means than to offer those festive invectives which appeal to the taste of the experts, expose the vice to the Public and unveil all its dissonances] (1964, 2: 273).[10]

Sartoc's article reveals the anxiety and preoccupation felt within the masculine sector toward women's development in the intellectual sphere. He made this point clear when he stated "Las juiciosas deben renunciar la complacencia de instruirse por el riesgo de contaminarse. Y ¿porqué me permito yo, dirá alguno, excursiones á pais de tanta infeccion? Y le responderé, que hay cosas que es malo leerlas, y bueno haberlas leido" [The judicious women should renounce the satisfaction of learning because of the risk of becoming contaminated. Someone may also ask why I allow myself to enter such an infected territory, to which I would respond that while there are things bad to read, it is good to have read them] (1964, 2: 271). Lucinda's displacement within the field of letters was visualized by Sartoc as a threatening element, making it difficult to circumscribe women within the sphere of domesticity. Lucinda was defending women's right to unite, to demand their claim for respect and to be treated with distinction. Lucinda maintained that the *Cuzqueña* woman possessed the intelligence and capacity to discuss and debate her inclusion within the circle of knowledge. His perception of the situation as a disease stemmed from its substantial risk of transmission to the rest of female society who had the means to educate itself. *Cuzqueña* women attempted to create a space of power and recognition in opposition to the notion that women from outside Lima were ignorant. These female aspirations, together with their meetings and discussions within exclusive circles regarding their rights in society, intensified Sartoc's belief in an epidemic in need of containment and correction; a correction that would require removing the power gained by women from command of the language and discourse.

Not surprisingly, fear of women's interest in intellectual pursuits within the masculine sector has been a constant preoccupation since Perú's independence. We should remember Clorinda Matto de Turner's (1854–1909) constant reminder to male intellectuals and the female population of the time when she argued that "La instrucción ha traido el término propio para la mujer, conquistándonos el respeto de todos" [Education has brought the proper opportunity to women, conquering for us the respect of all] (1954, 252). As Lucinda, Clorinda also gained many enemies and attacks in her defense of women's rights to be educated, maintaining that education would bestow upon them a better position in society. Ironically, it was not until 1985, under Alan García's presidency, when women were granted ministerial positions in Peruvian government, although as Sarah A. Radcliffe reminds us, those posts "were limited to the fields of health [and] education" (208). In Perú, still today women who are able to mobilize other female sectors of the society in order to promote and defend their rights of equal access to the government and protection of their sexuality, health, and to economic progress, have been persecuted or attacked. Feminist organizations such as "Centro de la Mujer Peruana Flora Tristan" have denounced the disappearance of members of their groups, while the "Movimiento Amplio de las Mujeres" (MAM) has also criticized the constant threat that journalists and social investigators, dealing with female issues, have received by sectors of the society who fight female mobilization in society (Mogollón 1999, 1). Male sectors of Peruvian society still perceive these organizations as dangerous spaces of reflection, support, and protest.

The preoccupation with containing the mobilization of women in society is observed in two additional news articles which related to preventive measures for the guidance and protection of women from physical and moral disease. The first discusses "Las reglas que deben observar las Mugeres en tiempos de la preñez" [The rules that Women should observe when they are pregnant], and the second examines the necessity to create more houses of retreat *(Casas de recogimiento)*. Within the arena of pregnancy rules, the author of the article expressed that his interest lay in the facilitation and contribution to the existence of "sucesiones permanentes y Madres fecundas" [permanent heirs and fertile mothers] (1: 89). His preoccupation did well to reflect how male society since Antiquity perceived women's sexuality as the establishment of a "harmony between good social order and good sexual order" (Laqueur 1994, 59). Male authorities rationalized women's bodies and behavior by purporting that they should prescribe rules that would effectively guarantee the reproduction of inhabitants. The *Mercurio peruano* shared the vision of many European scientists in the eighteenth century for whom, as Thomas Laqueur points out: "Women's bodies in their corporeal, scientifically accessible concreteness, in the very nature of their bones, nerves, and, most important reproductive organs, came to bear an enormous new weight of meaning" (1994, 150).

Within the article governing women's rules during pregnancy, the author emphasized the vulnerability that distinguished female reproductive power which in turn justified her supposed necessity for protection and treatment. The author clearly stated the paramount need to guide those in charge of perpetuating human existence: "[aquellas que] custodia[ban] en su frente el sagrado fruto que [iba] a perpetuar la especie humana" [those women who guard the sacred fruit in their womb which is going to perpetuate the human species] (1: 88), adding that women inclined to moderate exercise were less apt to lose babies, while those with a greater predisposition were the hysterical ones (1964, 1: 90). The reference to hysterical women makes clear the masculine tendency of that era to the association and supposed inclination of women toward instability. Since the era of ancient medicine, hysteria was considered a female illness and the product of an unstable womb. Hysteria, in the preFreudian sense, alluded to "all the organic disorders of the uterus" and was characterized by a "disordered womb" (Dixon 1995, 15). According to the author of the newspaper article, women whose bodies were marked by instability (the hysterical ones) were those who most needed his council for proper function within the social order; that is, to successfully engage in the procreation of society.

The author continued with enumeration of a series of rules intended for women to ensure safe pregnancies. Each rule addressed the importance for women to refrain from satisfying their "depraved appetites" (1: 89), to remain under the supervision of a doctor to assure a state of health, and to have their diet monitored and modified in order to avoid overeating. Furthermore, tight-fitting suits were the target of reform and, consequently, forbidden. Women were to avoid "the great passions of the soul" such as rage and terror, but most crucial was their need to remain calm and avoid unnecessary movements (1964, 1: 93–4). The author presumed that "disordered movement" constituted a primary cause for abortion (1964, 1: 94).

These rules demonstrate the perceived importance that control of women's conduct and body represented for maintaining social order. As the author pointed out in the second part of the article, "era indispensable una instrucción a las preñadas sobre su conducta, por depender únicamente de estas la subsistencia [de las criaturas]" [it was essential to instruct pregnant women regarding their behavior, because the child's subsistence would depend exclusively on them] (1964, 1: 292). For male authorities at that time, including physicians and scholars, women were responsible for the future of the nation strictly from a reproductive standpoint. Her mobility and enjoyment of passions threatened the social order. The author advocated a position that became prevalent in the eighteenth century where according to many medical theorists, "the healthiest life" of a woman had to be "a rugged one of self-denial and hard work in which the tantalizing and readily available pleasures of rich food, soft beds, intellectual pursuits, and leisure time were purposefully forgone" (Dixon 1995, 133). One must bear in mind that still, even in twentieth-century Perú, the "social construction of the nation" as Westwood and Radcliffe remind us, has been centered "around questions of the body and the 'management of populations.' " As both critics add, "diverse women have all had to struggle against policies controlling their fertility, health and freedom of movement of the body." (Westwood and Radcliffe 1993, 14). Scrutiny and regulation of women's body and mobility have functioned historically as crucial elements to order the society and to maintain a better control of its citizens, especially female citizens and other ethnically and racially marginalized groups.

In January 1791, a peculiar news item was published in the *Mercurio peruano* which made reference to the horrifying consequences of a strange pregnancy involving a black woman in Lima. The article was preceded by a long essay describing the particularities in Perú. The article in question was entitled "Descripción anatómica de un monstruo" [Anatomic description of a monster] and described the case of a *negra bozal* who had given birth to a monster in 1788. Its aim was to highlight the enigma that such an event presented for Peruvian physicians and other curious people. According to the author, the child had no brain, which was instead supplanted by a type of membrane. The head was cut all the way to the eyebrows and the earlobes resembled a woman's breasts. However, the most unusual aspect of the child was the androgynous nature of the body. The male genitalia were located immediately below his umbilical cord while the female organ was in the correct place. According to the author, both genitalia seemed to meld into one, almost becoming confused with one another. After concluding the physical description of the body, the author demanded that scientists, philosophers, and physicians postulate possible explanations for the events that engendered such a monster. He believed that the primary focus should have been upon the African woman's locality of residence at the time the fetus was in development. Second, he demanded to know how it was possible that such a creature could survive and mature to a point which would allow a viable birth. Finally, the author suggested that the answer to this phenomenon may be discovered in the physical constitution of the African woman's body, who amazingly had given birth to another monster two years before, yet was able to deliver a normal child between the two monsters (1964, 1: 7).[11]

In this brief article, the pregnancy and the body of the black woman became objects of scrutiny, serving to underline the inferiority and natural difference of her reproductive capacity. Her questionable physical condition and life-style appeared to rationalize the birth of the creature. It is important to note that the case referred to a *negra bozal,* which according to prevalent stereotypes throughout the colonial period, was an epitome of barbarity or a person without reason.[12] The author seems to suggest this as a cause for the African woman's propensity to engender monsters; this propensity became his major concern, and an aspect which he declared in need of intense study by male authorities (physicians, scientists, and philosophers) due to the looming negative repercussions that could arise within a developing Peruvian population. The realization that a monster was able to survive and physically develop into an actual member of society presented an appalling and vexatious dilemma with the classification and inclusion of such a creature as a constituent of the nation. As a result, the body of the black female slave was perceived as diseased and malfunctioned and in need of proper observation, diagnosis, and correction in order to avoid the evolution of future monsters. The context of the article epitomized the black female body as abnormal; an abject element containment of which was paramount. Also illustrated in the newspaper article was the manner in which a female's reproductive capacity constituted "a key aspect of women's otherness" and how any change or variation in her body or reproductive capacity was construed "as disease states" (Jackson, Prince, and Young 1993, 363–4). Since the body of every pregnant woman demanded the scrutiny of the male gaze (physicians, scientists, and philosophers), as articles in the *Mercurio peruano* suggested, the body of the African woman prompted even greater evaluation and surveillance due to its ability to spawn such abject bodies of no use to the progress of the nation.

Nowadays, in Perú, institutions dominated by male authorities such as the government still try to impose control over women's bodies and sexuality, and especially women of lower classes who according to them, seem to represent an obstacle to their nationalist projects. In 1995, the government established the "Programa de Salud Reproductiva y Planificación Familiar" (Program of Reproductive Health and Family Planning); the program began submitting women who lived in rural and indigenous zones to practices of sterility against their will or without informed consent of the negative aspects of some of those practices. Feminist and other women's groups have considered this act a cruel and illegal attempt to meet "demographic objectives" (Sala 1998, 2). Some women were subjected to surgical operations, which due to complications, ended in death. They were forced into Fallopian tube ligation or other contraceptive methods which proved detrimental to their health. In many occasions, these women were threatened and subsequently agreed to surgical intervention under coercive measures. Testimony of a victim of the governmental practices related how a nurse came to her house and threatened her by saying "Si no vienes, cuando tengas otro hijo, ya ni lo vamos a inscribir. La próxima vez les haré traer con la policía." [If you do not come, when you have another baby, we will not register the child. Next time I will make you come [to have the operation] by bringing the police] (Mogollón 1999, 1). The woman said that her husband listening to that "se asustó y firmó." Después me hice operar por temor. Desde entonces estoy inválida" [became frightened and signed [the papers]. Subsequently, I underwent the surgical operation because of fear. As a consequence of the operation, I have remained disabled] (Mogollón 1999, 1). Female victims who came forward to denounce the practices employed by the Ministerio de Salud (Ministry of Health) have been the object of intimidation and harassment visits. This recent event brought to light by the "Comité para la Defensa de los derechos de la Mujer" (CLADEM) [Committee for the Defense of Women's Rights] demonstrates how women's bodies (especially the ones belonging to the lower strata of the society and with less means to defend themselves) were still subjected to intense scrutiny and to measurements which attempted to control their sexualities. Managing the female body has been an essential element of every nationalist project since colonial times due to its perception as a crucial aspect of the establishment of order within the nation.

On the other hand, the regulation of women's conduct as a crucial instrument in the establishment of social order became evident in an article published April 5, 1792, dedicated to the necessity of keeping in business the houses of retreat *(Casas de recogimiento)*. The article emphasized the progress and exigency for such institutions to oversee the behavior of women, especially prostitutes, criminals, and women of ill-repute. Their foundation harks back to the seventeenth century when Spanish ecclesiastical authorities believed that "many loose women in the city, lacking honest means of support and not wanting to be servants, had become *mujeres perdidas,* and lived on the fringes of social respectability" (Martín 1983, 163).[13] In the *Mercurio peruano,* the author pointed out that such houses prevented women from repeated trouble so that the government felt obligated to economically support the great work accomplished in such shelters. In these institutions, women were kept busy through education and adherence to rules of behavior, so that the establishments offered a vital service to the nation. According to the author, their work was successful, creating harmony among women under the vigilant power and scrutiny of their superiors: "Cuya armonía consist[ía] en la subordinación de los subditos a los superiores, y vigilancia de estos respecto a los subditos" [This harmony consisted of the subordination of the citizens to their superiors, and the vigilance of the citizens by their superiors] (1964, 4: 260).

The subjects to which the author referred were delinquent women (many of them belonging to lower classes or with no means of support) for whom the houses of retreat served as a type of vigilant justice *(justicia vigilante)*, invoking terror in the women due to "perpetuating themselves in such a narrow enclosure" (1964, 4: 261).[14] For male authorities, enclosure represented the most efficient way to reform women's customs. The article concluded with the assertion that no other institution rivaled the house of retreat as a site in which "se puedan reprimir el desenfreno, la disolucion, y los escandalos [y fomentar] miembros utiles para la sociedad" [licentiousness, decadence and scandal can be repressed in order to foster useful members for society] (1964, 4: 263). The productivity of women in society held its roots in obedience, vigilance, and subordination. Women's reclusion in the *Casas de recogimiento* served as an education in the orderliness with which they were to behave in society. The institution functioned as an implement to control the public disorder in which corrupt women participated. According to the author, the house of retreat guaranteed the security of public health, effectively alleviating the worries of masculine authorities. Women who altered the public space by allowing themselves to be overcome by passion constituted a type of diseased body. The cure to this affliction lay in surveillance and circumscription to a disciplinary space that would assure the health of the social body.

CONCLUSIONS: COLONIAL ORDER AND SOCIAL CURES. WOMEN AS SIGNS OF DEVIATION

It could be argued that many of the contributors and editors of the *Mercurio peruano* suffered a great preoccupation with the role of women in society. Their intent to protect the future of the nation facilitated their claims to be accountable for women and their behavior through suggestions of control mechanisms and means of modification. Women from the upper or middle class who remained outside the domestic space, instead delighting themselves in pleasure, were visualized as carriers of social disease which could infect the nation. In a similar manner, women who belonged to lower classes (blacks, criminals, prostitutes, and figures of ill-repute) were viewed as symbols of deviance, and as a result, a danger to the health of the country. The above articles focused their criticism on constant allusions to the threatening mobility of women in the terrain of the public space (plazas, social gatherings, theaters, *tertulias*) and intellectual realm (her incursion in the area of studies and knowledge), as well as in the social visibility of women whose lack of morality or racial constitution made them individuals in need of reformation and in certain cases, eradication.

Contributors to the *Mercurio peruano* offered a clear example of the heterogeneous nature that characterized women at that time; a heterogeneity marked by their "diverse, multiple and conflictive configuration" (Cornejo Polar 1994, 14–7). Women constituted subjects who generated instability and irregularity in the social order. Their deviance was viewed at different levels: from a socioeconomic standpoint (the wife who was referred to as the *tapada*), to an intellectual (Lucinda), health (women in general during times of pregnancy), physical constitution (*negra bozal*) and moral behavior (prostitutes, criminals, and figures of ill-repute) one. They all represented individuals who were difficult to enclose within a singular image, due to the diverse nature of their desires and means of life and survival in a society marked by masculine power.

At last, the *Mercurio peruano* directed criticism toward this diverse group of women reiterated the means by which social control of women's identity was accompanied by the "control of their spatiality" and behavior both inside and outside the domestic space and racial and social boundaries (Massey 1994, 179). The *Mercurio peruano* viewed spatiality as related to the social order of the nation, underscored by those inhabitants free from disease in a figurative and literal sense. The social control of women also depended on intense scrutiny of their sexuality; their reproductive capacity was to fulfill the task of multiplying the inhabitants of the nation. News included in the *Mercurio peruano* visualized the female body as a site for production and constitution of social, political, and cultural inscriptions, which as Elizabeth Grosz argues, accentuates the image of the "body as [a] cultural product" (1994, 24). In the newspaper, the body of woman was defined as one inclined to deviance, requiring study and correction to prevent contamination of the nation's public health. In short, the control of women's bodies and thus their visibility in the national public space reflected an uneasiness in the masculine society of that era, marked by their perceived need to control the threat of possible alterations within the established boundaries which separated masculine from feminine and public from private while attempting to maintain clear and intact racial and social demarcations. The allusions made in this essay to social and political situations involving women of eighteenth century Perú and thereafter, are able to establish a close relationship between the colonial situation depicted in the newspaper and current events. The control of women within the framework of the nation is still linked to issues of sexuality and social mobility. Their bodies even today are objects of intense scrutiny and are constantly seen as signs of deviance or disorder, in need of immediate correction or eradication. Presently however, women's rights in the political, legal, and economic realm are being demanded and defended more than ever, due in great part to the various feminist and female organizations which have strived to make women an integral part of society as well as individuals with the right to choose their own destiny and control their own bodies.

NOTES

1. An exception to this tendency is Antonio Cornejo Polar's study entitled *Escribir en el aire. Ensayo sobre la heterogeneidad socio-cultural en las literaturas andinas* (Perú: Horizonte, 1994). In the book, he explores the role of heterogeneity in the processes of literary production as reflected in Andean literature from colonial times to the twentieth century. According to Cornejo Polar, hybridity constitutes a "macro concept" which encompasses concepts such as heterogeneity, transculturation, "*literatura otra*" or "*literatura alternativa*" (1994, 12–3).

2. Virginia Vargas Valente, *Como cambiar el mundo sin perdernos* (Lima: Ediciones Flora Tristán), 29. Virginia Vargas Valente argues that in order to comprehend Peruvian women's social situation at the present time, we must understand how the process of conquest and civilization, as well as colonial institutions, affected the lives of heterogeneous women's groups such as the indigenous peasant, the African women, and the women from the middle class, among others.

3. The metaphors alluded up to this point (public health, infection, and disease) will be discussed later. These images are used by some of the writers in the *Mercurio peruano* in reference to women.

4. An important element often overlooked of the *Mercurio peruano* is the significant role it played in the diffusion of nationalistic sentiments that eventually would mature with the Wars of Independence. The editors proposed to rediscover the true character of the Peruvian nation; a rediscovery whose predominant factor consisted of arousing patriotic feelings in their readers. Its attraction towards national questions was related to the particular interests of its editors; young Creoles whose objective was to underline and present to the public the differences that existed between Perú and Spain (Requejo 1986, 15). Raúl Porras Barrenechea also makes a brief reference to this in his work *El periodismo en el Perú* (Lima: Miraflores, 1970), 11.

5. Its articles included meteorological observations, articles on hygiene, national education, historic examinations of the diversions of distinct racial groups, brief news related to other parts of the world, the state of the arts, mining issues, historical discourses about the Peruvian provinces, economic and religious news, poems, statistical tables, and news about the curiosities of Lima. The volume and page number according to the facsimile edition of the *Biblioteca Nacional del Perú* will be cited next throughout the text. English translations are mine.

6. The *Mercurio peruano* participated in the relationship between knowledge and incipient patriotism and nationalism which, as Karen Stolley argues, dominated the

eighteenth century (1996, 367). In January 1793, the editors summarized their political agenda as follows:

Nos parecia que la Patria miraría siempre con aprecio, ó á lo menos con tolerancia los esfuerzos literarios de unos Jóvenes, que hermanaban al deseo de servirla, el de evitar la ociosidad y el espiritu de bagatela. (1964, 7: 1)

[It seemed to us that our Homeland would look with regard, or at least with tolerance, the literary efforts of some young people who combined with their desire to serve her, the avoidance of idleness and a tendency to worthlessness]

Jóvenes todos, empleados algunos en el servicio del REY, otros graduados en los diversos exercisios de la Universidad, otros Ministros del Altar, hemos abrazado unánime y gustosamente la dificil empresa de abrirnos una nueva senda, que nos conduzca al termino feliz de ser útiles a la Patria. (1964, 7: 7)

[All young people, some of us employees to the service of the King, others graduated from diverse professions in the University, others Ministers of Altar, have embraced unanimously and with great pleasure the difficult task of opening a new path that will guide us to the blissful goal of becoming useful to the Homeland]

Este sentimiento precioso [preocupaciones a favor de la Patria] es característico de nuestra *Sociedad* [la Sociedad Académica de Amantes de Lima]. Todos sus Individuos piensan de un mismo modo quando se trata del servicio de la Patria y la Nación. (1964, 7: 11)

[This beautiful feeling (i.e. their preoccupation for their homeland) is characteristic of our Society (i.e. the Academic Society of Lovers of Lima). All their Members share the same ideas with regard to the service of the Homeland and the Nation].

7. "Querendona" can also mean "female lover." See María Moliner, *Diccionario del uso del español* (Madrid: Gredos), 907.

8. Thomas Laqueur, *Making Sex* (Cambridge, MA: Harvard University Press), 59. Since ancient times, authorities such as Plutarch have made philosophical and empirical remarks by stating that a man, to be able to control State, Forum, and Friends, needed "to have his 'household well harmonized.' "

9. Ironically, publication of Lucinda's letter was delayed for eleven months while the editors concerned themselves with the "multitude of issues" that were seen as necessary for publication (1964, 4: 68).

10. The controversy of women claiming the title *señoras* continued in a publication on February 12, 1792 entitled *"Conversacion sobre el señorismo de las mugeres"* [Conversation regarding the ladyship of women], in which a women's social gathering for the defense of Lucinda's position was described in a sarcastic manner. See *Mercurio Peruano* (1964, 4: 278–9).

11. In France and England during the late seventeenth century, monsters had become "clarifying counter-examples to normal embryological development" and a sign of "aberration in the natural order" (Park and Daston 1981, 53, 22). As a result, the medical disciplines of comparative anatomy and embryology began to scrutinize women's bodies in search of an explanation for how women's' behavior and physical constitution influenced the natural order.

12. Several articles included in the newspaper criticized and mocked the black population of the city, particularly *negros bozales*. One contributor described their public congregations *(congregaciones públicas)* in the following manner: "Se pintan las caras de colorado ó azul, segun el uso de sus paises, y acompañan á la procesion con unos alaridos y ademanes tan atroces, como efectivamente atacasen al enemigo. La seriedad y feroz entusiasmo con que representan todas estas escenas, nos dan una idea de la barbaridad con que hacen sus acometidas marciales" [They paint their faces red or blue, according to the custom of their country of origin, and march in procession, making screeches and gestures so appalling as if they were attacking their enemy. The seriousness and the ferocious enthusiasm with which they act out these scenes give us an idea of the barbarism that characterizes their martial attacks] (1: 117).

13. The first *Casa de recogimiento* in the Viceroyalty of Perú was established in 1670 with the aim of reforming repentant women, prostitutes and concubines, divorcees and criminals (Martín 1983, 163). According to Luis Martín, some "women of ill repute were detained against their will" (1983, 163).

14. Colonial authorities in the Viceroyalty of Perú encountered great obstacles in confining women to the *Casas de recogimiento,* because many of them were not willing to repent and apply for admission in such houses (Martín 1983, 165).

BIBLIOGRAPHY

Cornejo Polar, Antonio. 1994. *Escribir en el aire. Ensayo sobre la heterogeneidad sociocultural en las literaturas andinas.* Perú: Horizonte.

Dicccionario de Autoridades. 1963. Madrid: Gredos.

Dixon, Laurinda S. 1995. *Perilous Chastity. Women and Illness in Pre-Enlightenment Art and Medicine.* Ithaca, London: Cornell University Press.

Borim, Darío Jr., and Roberto Reis. 1996. "Introduction. The Age of Suspicion: Mapping Sexualities in Hispanic Literary and Cultural Texts." In *Bodies and Biases: Sexualities in Hispanic Cultures and Literatures.* Edited by David William Foster, and Roberto Reis, xiii–xxxii. Minneapolis: University of Minnesota Press.

González, Aníbal. 1993. *Journalism and the Development of Spanish American Narrative.* Cambridge: Cambridge University Press.

Grosz, Elizabeth. 1994. *Volatile Bodies: Toward a Corporeal Feminism.* Bloomington, IN: Indiana University Press.

Gruzinski, Serge. 1994. *La Guerra de las Imágenes. De Cristóbal Colón a "Blade Runner"* (1492–2019). México: Fondo de Cultura Económica.

Jackson, Stevi, Jane Prince, and Pauline Young. 1993. "Science, Medicine and Reproductive Technology. Introduction." In *Women's Studies: Essential Readings.* Edited by Stevi Jackson, 363–68. Washington Square: New York University Press.

Laqueur, Thomas. 1994. *Making Sex: Body and Gender from the Greeks to Freud.* Cambridge, MA: Harvard University Press.

Martín, Luis. 1983. *Daughters of the Conquistadores: Women of the Viceroyalty of Peru.* Dallas: Southern Methodist University Press.

Massey, Doreen. 1994. *Space, Place, and Gender.* Minneapolis: University of Minnesota Press.

Matto de Turner, Clorinda. 1954. *Tradiciones cuzqueñas.* Cuzco: n.p..

Mercurio peruano. 1964. Lima: Biblioteca Nacional del Perú.

Mogollón, María Esther. 1999. "La anticoncepción quirúrgica. La violación de los derechos humanos de las mujeres por parte del Estado." *Fempress* 213.

———. 1999. "El movimiento amplio de mujeres." *Fempress* 207.

Moliner, María. 1997. *Diccionario del uso del español.* Madrid: Gredos.

Otero, Gustavo Adolfo. 1953. *La cultura y el periodismo en América.* Quito: Liebman.

Park, Katherine, and Lorraine F. Daston. 1981. "Unnatural Conceptions: The Study of Monsters in Sixteenth and Seventeenth-Century France and England." *Past and Present* 92: 20–54.

Porras Barrenechea, Raúl. 1970. *El periodismo en el Perú.* Lima: Miraflores.

Radcliffe, Sarah A. 1993. " 'People Have to Rise Up-Like the Great Women Fighters': The State and Peasant Women in Peru." In *'Viva': Women and Popular Protest in Latin America.* Edited by Sarah Radcliffe, and Sallie Westwood, 197–218. London: Routledge and Kegan Paul.

Requejo, Juan Vicente. 1986. *El periodismo en el Perú.* Lima: Centro de Documentación e Información Andina.

Sala, Mariella. 1998. "Descubren campaña de esterilización forzada." *Fempress* 198.

Stolley, Karen. 1996. "The Eighteenth Century: Narrative Forms, Scholarship and Learning." In *The Cambridge History of Latin America.* Edited by Roberto González Echevarría, and Enrique Pupo-Walker, 336–74. Cambridge: Cambridge University Press.

Vargas Valente, Virginia. 1992. *Como cambiar el mundo sin perdernos: El movimiento de mujeres en el Perú y América Latina.* Lima: Ediciones Flora Tristán.

Westwood, Sallie, and Sarah A. Radcliffe. 1993. "Gender, Racism and the Politics of Identity in Latin America." In *'Viva': Women and Popular Protest in Latin America.* Edited by Sarah Radcliffe, and Sallie Westwood, 1–29. London: Routledge and Kegan Paul.

The Dragon and the Seashell

British Corsairs, Epic Poetry and Creole Nation in Viceregal Peru

José Antonio Mazzotti

The role of European, and specifically British interlopers in the development of a Creole Spanish-American identity as expressed in the sixteenth- to
eighteenth-centuries epic poetry has long been neglected by scholars. The
dragon in the title of this essay is obviously a reference to Sir Francis Drake,
but it also refers to some aspects of the imagery expressed by members of the
Spanish-American Creole elite in the formulation of their own discursive
identity vis-à-vis "heretical" groups of non-Iberian nationality.

What I want to explore here is the way in which some prominent members of that Creole elite used literary forms to enact their desire for social harmony during the sixteenth, seventeenth, and eighteenth centuries in Lima,
capital of the Viceroyalty of Perú. They expressed their perspectives by depicting ambiguous images of both the British enemy and the "colored" soldiers
who served in their own armies. In doing so, these Creole writers affirmed
their own "form of nationhood" (paraphrasing Richard Helgerson), setting up
the external Lutheran corsairs and the idolatrous internal enemy as their negative opposites. Those opposites would enable the Creoles to exalt the virtues and bravery of the descendants of Spaniards in the New World center
of Lima—the City of the Kings—as it was referred to by their own Creole
authors in numerous writings. By doing so, they established from the late-
sixteenth century some discursive patterns that would survive in the enlightened period and would model, if not the rhetoric of Independence, at least the
strategies of social control and organization of the early Republican era.

The participation of what we might now call "ethnic" soldiers was hardly recognized or even mentioned in most epic poems. The scenes of glory and heroism were reserved only for "white" soldiers, despite the fact that black, Indian,

mulatto, and *mestizo* troops were often the main component of the Spanish forces, or at least had some important degree of participation.[1] The entirety of the Peruvian epic poems deny any heroic presence to members of non-Iberian racial and social groups. In this sense, they are very different from their similar Cuban counterpart, *Espejo de paciencia,* by Silvestre de Balboa, written around 1608, a poem whose heroic protagonist is a black slave who saves the life of the Bishop of Santiago.

The texts I will mainly refer to are the *Primera Parte del Arauco Domado,* by Pedro de Oña, published in 1596, *Armas Antárticas,* by Juan de Miramontes, written around 1615 but only published in 1921, and *Lima Fundada o Conquesta del Perú* by Pedro de Peralta y Barnuevo, published in 1732. These three poems include passages about military actions in which "colored" soldiers are erased, despite their historically documented participation in the struggle against the corsairs. If epic poetry is, as Mikhail M. Bakhtin (1981, 15–18) states, a representation of paradigmatic actions within an "absolute past," then the use of this genre enforces the allegedly racial and cultural superiority of Creoles by denying the important role of their own troops. Thus, the Creoles used a prestigious literary register to express their own ideals of an ethnic national identity by whitening their military struggles. As David Quint says: "I distinguish between where the text responds to historical occasion and where it repeats a generic convention or commonplace, although it may do both simultaneously" (1993, 15). In this sense, it is important to note that the political and contextual functions of epic discourse have been neglected in the study of this part of viceregal cultural production. The traditional approach considers all such Europeanized forms of expression a simple imitation of Spanish and Italian models. However, placing these poets in dialogue with their context allows us to understand how this group of primary works helped model a dynamic agent who would assume different strategies to define its own identity vis-à-vis the Spaniards. John Mowitt (1988, xii) identifies the concept of agency "with the general preconditions that make the theoretical articulation of the critique of the subject possible." Although it may seem too simple to affirm, it is truly difficult to grasp the specificities of Creole culture and subjectivities without defining those "general preconditions" in which certain individuals and social groups interacted.[2] To remember the ambiguous position of many Creoles vis-à-vis Spanish officials is not only esential, but productive. The former were Spaniards, but not in a complete sense. They were Americans (in the original meaning of the term), but at the same time they consistently established their distances and discrepancies with Indians, blacks, and the numerous castes with whom they shared the same territory. Another important element of that historical context was the Creoles' desire to counter the *mestizo* neo-Incan nationalism which began to emerge during the seventeenth and eighteenth centuries (see Rowe 1976; Burga 1988). This challenging proto-hegemonic neo-Incan project was based in Cuzco, was led by its own elite, and had its own very distinct discourse (see García-Bedoya 1996).

When it comes to the poets I will refer to, we are dealing with two different moments of the viceregal period. Oña and Miramontes wrote during the first decades of bureaucratic consolidation; Peralta at the beginning of the Bourbon administration. At both moments, these three poets reveal important aspects of the local formation of a "creole nation," as Anthony Pagden (1987) calls this early form of communal projection of a separate identity.[3] We should note that in other discursive genres, Creole production is very explicit about its claims to the Spanish Crown. Bernard Lavallé, for example, has extensively studied manuscripts and printings related to the existing rivalry between Creoles and Spaniards within religious orders (see esp. Lavallé 1982, 1985 and 1993, 157–224). Part of this rivalry stemmed from the fact that, as Elizabeth Anne Kuznesof (1995) and Stuart Schwartz (1995) have shown, the first generations of Creoles had indigenous components. Both real and suspected blood "impurity" allow us to understand the Creoles' insistence on their whiteness before the scornful Spaniards.[4]

The characterization of Creoles as "impure" subjects of the Crown, led them to develop a continuous discourse of self-glorification about their native cities, including Lima, taking advantage of a common practice of praising cities in Spain itself. Creoles also defended their intellectual and biological superiority, without recognizing any possibility of mixed blood. Antonio de la Calancha (1638, f. 68), Buenaventura de Salinas y Córdiva (1957, 246), Francisco Fernández de Córdoba (8), Juan Espinosa Medrano (1982, 327), and other conspicuous Creole writers are good examples of this trend of symbolic ethnic self-cleansing. In this sense, the epic genre is not an exception, but at the same time, it is more than just a simple imitation of European models.

Before analyzing the aforementioned poems, it is important to say something about the impact of the British incursions into Peruvian waters. Here I don't mean to add more information to what has already been uncovered by historians like Kris E. Lane, David Beers Quinn, Peter J. Bradley, Leon G. Campbell, Guillermo Lohmann Villena, Bartolomé Escandell Bonet (1953), and others (see bibliography). I would just like to underscore a few key moments in which Creoles acknowledged the presence of British corsairs and experienced psychological and political repercusions.

For example, during the final year of Francis Drake's circumnavigation between 1577 and 1579, the Dragon of the Sea as Drake would later be called, touched upon the ports of Valparaíso, Arica (in current Chile), and Callao, among others.[5] Although he never disembarked at, or attacked the capital city of the Peruvian Viceroyalty or its port Callao, the general panic of the population of Lima was well-documented by contemporaries. According to one picturesque anecdote, the enslaved black population hid the brakes and saddles of their masters' horses so that the Spaniards and Creoles would be unable to defend the city and Drake could eventually liberate the slaves. Martín del Barco Centenera, the author of the long and heterogeneous poem *Argentina o Conquista del Río de la Plata* (1602), writes that the blacks acted this treacherously because they thought that as soon as "Francisco [Drake] alli viniera / en libertad a todos los pusiera" [Francis Drake would come / he would liberate every one]. Admiration for the British was common among the black, Indian, *mestizo*, and mulatto populations; it was a common element of many internal rebellions. During some of these, rebel leaders heralded the arrival of the British liberators, who, they claimed, would carry out the restitution of the Andean territories to their former owners, the Incas. Such an affinity for the British was also shared by some discontented members of the "república de los españoles," who saw in Drake the possibility of living without the Inquisition. Bartolomé Escandell Bonet registers the case of one such discontented Spaniard. His name was Juan de Santillana de Guevara, born in Avila. During his trial before the Inquisition, Santillana stated that "ynga . . . quiere dezir ynglés" [or Inga means English] and, therefore, that the Peruvian territories belonged by right to the English Crown, and that the Queen had the right to fight for and claim them.

This onomastic possession was again formulated by Sir Walter Raleigh in his *Account of the Discovery of Guyana*, published in 1596. Raleigh writes:

> And I farther remember that Berreo [the Governor of Isla Margarita] confessed to me and others (which I protest before the Majesty of God to be true), that there was found among Prophecies in *Peru*, (at such time as the Empire was reduced to the *Spanish* Obedience) in their chiefestie Temples, amongst divers others which foreshewed the Loss of the said Empire, that from *Inglatierra* those Ingas should be again in Time to come restored, and delivered from the Servitude of the said Conquerors. (Raleigh [1596] 1751, v. 1: 235)

Raleigh recommended that Queen Elizabeth conquer Perú through the Orinoco river and the Amazonian jungle, after establishing a permanent possession in northern South America. John Howland Rowe (1976, 25–32) actually refers to Raleigh's prediction in his article on eighteenth-century Incan nationalism. There Rowe directs us to the Prologue written by Spanish historian González de Barcia to his 1723 edition of the *Royal Commentaries of the Incas* by Inca Garcilaso de la Vega. González de Barcia, of course, refuted any theory of nominal correspondence between "Inga" and "Inglaterra," but he also failed to mention that the first refutation came from the Creole friar Antonio de la Calancha in 1638. Calancha writes:

> Es para reir lo que dice Gualtero Raleg [In descriptione Indiarum], i alega testigos Españoles, que se allò en el templo del Sol en el Cuzco, un pronostico, que decia que los Reyes de Ingalaterra avian de resti-

tuir en su Reyno a estos Indios, sacandoles de servidumbre i bolviendolos a su Imperio; debiò de soñarlo, ò pronosticò su deseo, debiò de usar de la figura Anagrama, que partiendo silabas i trocando razones, aze diferentes sentidos el vocablo; Ingalaterra dividida la palabra, dirà Inga, i luego dirà la tierra, i de aqui debiò de formar el pronostico, diciendo, la tierra del Inga serà de Ingalaterra, con esta irrision se haze burla de Gualtero. (ff. 115–16). [What Walter Raleigh says is comical, and he alleges to have Spanish witnesses, that in the Temple of the Sun in Cuzco a prediction was found which said that the Kings of England would give the Indians back their kingdom, taking them out of servitude and returning them to their Empire. He must have either dreamed it, or projected his own desire. He must have used the figure of Anagram, and by splitting syllables and switching reasons, makes different meanings for a word; Ingalaterra [England], divided, will say "Inga" [Inca] and then "la tierra" [the land], and from this he must have formed his prediction, saying that the land of the Inga will be of England; with this joke everybody makes fun of Sir Walter].

The threat of a British invasion and their alliance with the surviving Incas of El Dorado was a commonplace during the seventeenth century. Chroniclers like José Suardo and José de Mugaburu offer several entries about this theme in their respective Diaries of the city of Lima. Juan Antonio Suardo, for example, mentions that news about a "pichilingue" or Englishman reached Lima in March 1631. The British subject had been arrested in Cuzco "for having said that he was waiting for his relatives and friends, who would come very soon from Buenos Aires" (Suardo 1935, 124). Josephe de Mugaburu narrates details of an indigenous rebellion which occured in Chile in 1675, encouraged by the supposed presence "of the English enemy." Creole writers like Antonio de la Calancha accepted the idea of the existence of El Dorado, and believed that the surviving Incas could at any time become the collaborators in a British invasion. Calancha afirms that

Uno de los ijos de Guaynacapac ermano de Guascar i de Atagualpa (como dice Gualtero Raleg) se fue con millares de Indios Orejones, que eran los mas valientes, i poblò aquella parte de tierra, que està entre el rio grãde de las Amaçonas, i el Baracoã, que se llama Orenòque. (f.115)

[Fleeing from the war, one of the children of Guaynacapac, brother of Guascar and Atahualpa (as Walter Raleigh affirms in his Account), left with thousands of Indian Orejones (big ears, Inca nobles), who were the most courageous, and populated that part of the land, which lies between the great river of the Amazones and the Baracoan, which is also called Orinoco]

Therefore, the legend of El Dorado was alive among Spaniards and Creoles, and they feared that the richness of the lost city of the Incas would continually encourage English "liberators" to get in touch with the Indians.

With this context in mind, let's go straight to the epic poems in which the presence of British interlopers stimulated a local response. For example, in *Arauco Domado* by Pedro de Oña, the last two chants narrate the incursion of Richard Hawkins onto the Peruvian coasts in 1594. Now we know that Oña's poem was conceived as a response to Ercilla's *La Araucana,* and written in order to praise the actions of García Hurtado de Mendoza both in his Chilean campaign of 1557–59, and his administration as Viceroy of Perú in the 1590s. On the contrary, Ercilla had paid little attention to the "heroism" of García Hurtado de Mendoza, who was the eldest son of Viceroy Marqués de Cañete at the time of the Chilean expedition, and commander-in-chief of Ercilla himself. In *La Araucana* (first part published in 1569), Ercilla repeatedly criticized the cruelty and greed of the conquerors, and glorified the Araucanian warriors, relying upon Renaissance models that have been extensively studied.[6] But why would a young poet like Oña attempt to restore the fame and prestige of his Viceroy some thirty years later, aside from the usual purpose of seeking personal favors? The answer might be found in the two above-mentioned chants, which are devoted to exalting the heroism of the Spaniards and Creoles in their defense of Lima against Hawkins, and also in chant 3, in which Oña describes the efforts made by García Hurtado de Mendoza to reform—rather than abolish—the institution of the *encomienda.*

Let's start with Hawkins. Oña states that upon his arrival at the Peruvian coast, the English corsair was aware of the weakness of the Spanish military defenses. The Viceroy prepared the population and called all available men to reinforce the small number of troops stationed in the port of Callao. Oña described the new soldiers as *"caballeros"* or gentlemen, who formed two companies of sixty men each. The Viceroy also sent messengers to the interior cities asking for help in the defense of the Viceroyalty.

A few days later, the Viceroy prepared an expedition to chase away Hawkins. It was commanded by General Beltrán de la Cueva y Castro, and also included the aforementioned one hundred twenty men and several priests, according to the poem. Nothing is said about Indian, black, or mullatto troops, although we know that they would have existed. The expedition finally caught up to Hawkins and made him leave the Peruvian waters on May 17, 1594. This presentation of local heroism is the final step of Oña's strategy to validate the virtues and bravery of the white population of Lima.

But the problem dates from much earlier. It starts in the description of the aforementioned reforms of the *encomienda* system adopted by García Hurtado de Mendoza in the 1550s. As we know, the Crown abolished the old system of land division in 1542. As had been the case in Reconquest Spain, the *encomienda* was used in the first decades of New World colonization to reward subjects who had rendered notable military services. However, the New Laws of 1542, reflecting as they did the Crown's aspirations to directly control the Indian population and profits from the new lands, threatened the power acquired by the conquerors. The dispute between the Crown and the *encomenderos* provoked a general rebellion from 1544 to 1548, when Gonzalo Pizarro, one of Francisco Pizarro's brothers, challenged the power of Crown officials. He also insisted upon the validity of the *encomienda* system as just compensation from the King to the conquerors for their efforts during the conquest.

Oña was the son of one of those conquerors who had lost their *encomiendas* and who would leave nothing to their children except nostalgia and aspirations for social elevation. In his poem, Oña argues that the *encomienda* was not wrong in and of itself, but that the system just needed a few reforms to aleviate the exploitation of the Indians. He praises García Hurtado de Mendoza for having set tax controls and age limits for mining labor among the indians:

> Mandó que de los indios que tuviese
> el ávido vecino encomendero
> para labrar el cóncavo minero,
> el sesmo solamente se le diese;
> y que éste de varones sólo fuese,
> guardando al sexo tímido su fuero,
> los cuales a sesenta no llegasen,
> y que del sesto décimo pasasen.

> Ordena juntamente que del fruto
> de los veneros fértiles sacado,
> también al indio el sesmo fuese dado
> como en retribución de su tributo;
> y que cualquier vecino al estatuto
> fuese para los suyos obligado,
> partiéndoles el sábado postrero
> la dicha sesta parte del dinero.

> Y para la ejecución del mandamiento,
> por evitar escrúpulos y espinas,
> mandó que hubiese alcalde en las minas,
> hombres de sano, justo y buen intento;
> hizo que las comidas y sustento
> llevado por las fuerzas femeninas,
> a costa del vecino fuese en bestias,
> y así no fuesen tantas las molestias.
> (stanzas 27–29, chant 3)

[He commanded that from the Indians
that the avid encomendero had
for working in his mines
only a sixth would be given;
and that only men would work,
keeping the timid sex [women] privileges;
and the men should not be older than sixty
and not younger than sixteen.

He also commanded that from the fruit
of the fertile mines,
a sixth part should be given to the Indians
as retribution to their tribute;
and that any encomendero should be obliged
to his own people,
by dividing the following Saturday
the aforementioned sixth part of the money.

And for executing his command,
in order to avoid scruples and thorns,
he commanded that there should be sheriffs in the mines,
men of sane, just and good intentions;
he ordered that the food and sustenance
that women used to carry,
now would transported on the encomendero's mules
so the uncomfort would not be so much.]

Oña's position is consistent with his view of the Indians as potential peasant subjects under the direct control of *encomenderos* who avoided excesses.
Such a position, of course, favored the situation of the Creoles, who would
have inherited those *encomiendas* if García Hurtado de Mendoza's ideas had
been taken seriously and integrated into the general policy sponsored by the
Crown. It is, therefore, easy to understand how Oña's defense of the Creole
military heroism against the foreign corsairs not only whitened the Peruvian
participation, but also presented the Creole soldiers as members of a community that was not being recognized by the Crown, despite their contributions
and their potential capacity to hold *encomiendas* without excesses (see also
Quint 1993, 173).

Spanish authorities confiscated the first edition of Oña's poem, apparently because of the treatment he gives to the population of Quito during the
alcabala or tax rebellion of 1594.[7] In his narrative of the events, Oña emphasizes the cruelty of the punishment meted out against the rebels. Women in

Quito cry and their cry "reaches the stars," the poem says. The passages of chant 16, regarding the Quito rebellion, were suppressed by the authorities in the second edition of the poem in 1605. They reveal a de-centered viewpoint on Oña's part, one whose political inclination is toward the Crown, but whose emotional preference goes for those who, like him, suffered the consequences of the expansion of the absolutist monarchy and the decline of the *encomenderos*.

Some time later, in 1608, another author, Juan de Miramontes, finished a long poem in which he narrated Sir Francis Drake's incursion into the Peruvian coast and his lieutenant John Oxenham's raid on the Panama Isthmus, which at that time formed part of the Peruvian Viceroyalty. Oxenham was under orders to capture the city of Panama and thus facilitate the blockade of Lima by Drake. Miramontes was a Spanish soldier who only arrived in Perú in the 1580s, that is, after Drake's raid of 1579. Miramontes' obvious intention was to praise the Spanish and Creole troops who defended the coasts against Drake and Oxenham as well as to obtain favors from Viceroy Marqués de Montesclaros. At the time he finished his poem, entitled *Armas Antárticas,* Miramontes was serving as a soldier in the bataillon of spear and harquebus carriers who formed the personal guard of the Viceroy. Although not a Creole by birth, he was assimilated into the local Creole community, as was typically the case for those who lived for more than ten years in a kingdom not their own. This common practice had been legislated in the thirteenth century in the *Siete Partidas* of Alfonso X.

Here I would like to focus on the first part of the poem, on the first ten chants, which narrate both Drake's and Oxenham's actions. This part also includes numerous passages in which the maroons of Panama play a pivotal role in support of Oxenham's expedition. The rest of the poem presents a love story between two Incan nobles and a narrative of Pedro Sarmiento de Gamboa's expedition to the Strait of Magellan in order to establish a permanent Spanish colony there to prevent future incursions by British enemies.

The first two chants of the poem present a brief history of the conquest of Perú and the foundation of Lima by Pizarro. In chant 3, Drake proposes his ambitious attack in Perú to Queen Elizabeth, and chants 4 and 5 tell of Oxenham's landing on the eastern coast of Panama and his making contact with the maroons of the legendary kingdom of Ballano. The following two chants, 6 and 7, present the first defeat suffered by Oxenham and the maroons against the military forces sent from Lima. Chant 8 narrates Drake's deeds during his navigation on the coast of Perú, and, in chants 9 and 10, Oxenham is finally defeated and sent to Lima, where he would be judged by the Inquisition.

During this first part of the poem, Miramontes avoids any mention of "colored" soldiers within the Spanish forces. For example, he ignores the *mestizo* condition of Diego de Almagro the Younger in his presentation of the civil wars between the conquerors. Nor does he bother to point out that it was a black slave who beheaded Viceroy Núñez Vela after the battle of Iñaquito, in which the rebel Gonzalo Pizarro defeated the loyalist troops sent to defend the New Laws of 1542. Although these passages are not central to Miramontes' poem, they reflect the general trend of whitening any military action in which the conquerors and their descendants played a principal role.

Despite its historical simplifications, the poem develops a sympathetic image of the maroons in order to contrast them to the British privateers. While the Englishmen are robbing and raping, the maroons are more concerned about freeing other blacks from the hands of the Spanish slave owners of Panama.

On the other hand, the Urarave Indians of Panama help Oxenham to fight the Spaniards, finding in the British sailors the possibility of escape from Spanish servitude. However, the Indians' only collaboration with the Spanish comes at the end of the poem, in chant 20. There, the Indians of the southern port of Arica line up with long canes to simulate soldiers with spears in order to discourage Thomas Cavendish from disembarking in 1586.[8]

But in general, the poem barely mentions the participation of Indian and black soldiers within the Spanish troops. In this way, Miramontes stresses his concept of *armas antárticas* or Antartic arms, giving a completely white identity to the heroism of the southern hemisphere and therefore reinforcing the self-proclaimed image of intellectual and belic superiority that Creole and naturalized peninsulars expressed in numerous chronicles and diaries.

The last case of epic poetry I would like to touch upon comes from a much later period, when any hope of reviving the *encomienda* system was anachronistic. I refer to the 1732 long poem *Lima Fundada*, written by Pedro de Peralta y Barnuevo, one of the most prominent intellectuals of his time. In many ways, an equivalent of the late-seventeenth-century Mexican savant Carlos de Sigüenza y Góngora, Peralta was intensely active as a university professor, cosmographer of the kingdom, accountant of the royal finances, architect, historian and, of course, poet, among other occupations. His initial goal with *Lima Fundada* was to commemorate the bicentennial of the arrival of Pizarro in the land of the Incas. However, the poem, divided into ten chants, resembles the architecture of a space and a time of social harmony in the kingdom. In that context, Creoles have a dominant but still loyalist position vis-à-vis the majority of the Indian and black population. At the same time, the Creoles consider Pizarro the founder of their genealogy of local interests and prowesses.

The plot is relatively simple: from the outset, Pizarro is compared to Aeneas, the Trojan prince. He would cross immense oceans and hostile lands in order to found the greatest city of the New World, Lima or City of the Kings. Chants 1 and 2 narrate Pizarro's arrival at the coast of northern Perú and the defeat of Inca Atahualpa in Cajamarca. Chant 3 relates Pizarro's encounter with an Incan princess, doña Inés Yupanqui, a half-sister of Atahualpa and Huascar. The pair would fall for each other, thus creating the beginning of an ideal genealogy in which the Indians play the feminine role. Yet, history tells us that almost all the children of the two relationships that Pizarro had with Incan princesses would die at an early age.[9] So the genealogy that Peralta implies in his poem is more ideal and symbolic than simply genetic. As an archetype of military heroism and moral and intellectual superiority, Pizarro becomes a model for Creoles to imitate in their own lives.

Relying on a common place of epic poetry, Peralta's chant 3 includes the beginning of a conversation between Pizarro and an angel or genie of Lima sent by God to tell him in advance about the great responsibility that lies ahead of him—the founding of a new center of civilization—and the greatness of his future actions. Thus, the next four chants of the poem become a history of the conquest of Perú and of the first two hundred years of Spanish rule. Pizarro, like Aeneas, envisions the consequences of his actions and the development of a great kingdom, in which the descendants of the Spaniards will play a pivotal role. Chant 6, for example, is a long enumeration and description of Lima's most prominent Creoles (a list that reaches several hundreds) in the fields of the arts, sciences, religion, and the military. After the angel's long prediction, the poem concludes with the marriage of Pizarro to doña Inés and with the foundation of Lima in 1535.

What interests me now are those passages in which Peralta presents Drake's and other interlopers' raids on the coasts of Perú, and specifically how Peralta characterizes the local defense. These passages are included in chants 5 and 6, in which the angel is predicting the future events of the kingdom to an astonished Pizarro. Here again we find that Peralta repeats the discursive strategy of erasing any form of nonwhite heroism. For example, in the case of Drake and Oxenham, Peralta only credits the defense to the Martes de Lima, who fight Oxenham and the maroons. Obviously, those Mars of Lima are Creoles and Spaniards.

In the case of Thomas Cavendish, Peralta mentions in passing that the Viceroy Conde del Villardompardo armed "la nobleza y demás gente en el Callao," but gives no further details. With respect to John Hawkins, the only hero mentioned in the defense of Lima is General Don Beltrán de la Cueva y Castro. Furthermore, when Viceroy Marqués de Salinas sent three vessels to pursue the Dutch corsair Oliver Van Noort in the year 1600, Peralta mentions nothing about the social components of the navy. Finally, in describing L'Hermite's attack on Callao in 1624, Peralta would write "del fuerte Heremita a los furores / sin muros se opondrá muro inminente" [to the fury of L'Hermite / an imminent wall without walls will be opposed], that is, a human force so strong that it could prevent the Dutch corsair from disembarking. According to Peter J. Bradley (1989, 62), a substantial portion of the four thousand men enlisted by the Viceroy Marqués de Guadalcázar were blacks and free mullattos. However, Peralta again makes no mention of them at all.

These brief examples are but symptoms of a much deeper concern among Creoles. The relative discursive autonomy that Creoles achieved within their rivalry with the Spaniards allowed some room for self-definition within a highly prestigious genre like epic poetry. In other realms, Creoles gave explicit examples of their self-proclaimed superiority, like in that famous passage by Antonio de la Calancha, published in 1638, in which he states:

> si el Peru es la tierra en que mas igualdad tienen los dias, mas tenplança los tienpos, mas benignidad los ayres i las aguas, el suelo fertil, i el cielo amigable; luego criarà las cosas mas ermosas, i las gentes mas benignas i afables, que Asia i Europa [. . .]. Las causas universales se varian, i determinan segun la calidad de la materia, aziendo en diversos sugetos diferentes efetos, mas, ò menos, conforme la materia en que obra. El Sol derrite la cera, i endurece el barro; el fuego consume la leña seca i tambien la verde, mas no tan facilmente esta como aquella: Muy diferente es la complesion del negro i la del Indio a la del Español, por lo cual las causas generales q~ en este Reyno ocurren, no pueden producir iguales efetos en todos, sino en cada uno segun su temperamento, disposicion de celebro i organos corporales; i de esto procede la diversidad de ingenios, que se alla en las referidas naciones. (f. 68)

> [If Perú is the land in which the days are equal to each other, and the weather the most temperate, the air and water the most gentle, the soil fertile, and the sky friendly, then Perú will engender the most beautiful things and much kinder and more benevolent people than Europe or Asia [. . .]. Universal causes vary and act differently according to the quality of the matter, producing different effects in different subjects, depending on the quality of the material on which they operate. The sun, for example, melts the wax, but hardens the mud. The fire consumes dry firewood and green firewood, but the latter not as easily as the former. The complexion of blacks and Indians is very different from the Spaniards', thus the general causes of this kingdom cannot produce the same effects in everyone, but operate in each individual according to his brain's and organs disposition. This is why there is such a variety of people among the different nations of Perú.]

This kind of ethnocentrism was common during the seventeenth and eighteenth centuries, and is just the explicit manifestation of what Bernard Lavallé has called "militant creolism." However, in the case of epic poetry, Creoles managed to express a desire for warlike purification without directly or openly stating their opposition to peninsular groups.

One of the problems which remains concerns the kind of identity our Creole poets assigned to the majority of the population, that is, the so-called colored groups. In viceregal Peruvian epic poetry, blacks, and Indians are hardly recognized as Peruvians. Therefore, the limeño Creole elite assumed a name that would only become general during the Enlightenment. However, in a few texts, like Rodrigo de Valdés' poem *Fundación y grandezas de Lima,* published in 1687, and Bartolomé Arzáns' *Historia de la Villa Imperial de Potosí,* the vast indigenous population is assimilated into a corporate totality. Valdés represents Perú, for example, as a giant supported by one iron foot (the Spaniards and Creoles) and one foot of mud (the Indians). Valdés insists that peninsulars show a greater concern for the well-being of the Indians, for the depopulation of the Andean territory would cause the fall of the giant, that is, the definitive ruin of the whole kingdom. Similarly, Arzáns describes the Indians as the "feet and hands" of the kingdom, and decries the abuses and mistreatment given them by the Spaniards.

Both Valdés and Arzáns are still far from a democratic concept of what it means today to be Peruvian, a view that, at least rhetorically, would only appear at the beginning of the nineteenth century. But Arzáns and Valdés are also far removed from the views of Oña, Miramontes, and Peralta, who all defined a "Peruvian" identity based on a neo-European ethnic basis. After all, according to writers like Oña, Miramontes, and Peralta, it is the Creoles who save Catholicism and "civilization" from heretic Europeans and from indigenous and black idolaters.

The process of consolidating a Peruvian national identity has not ended, as anyone can see from examining the heterogeneity of social and racial subjects coexisting within the same territory and under the same inefficient central state. In this process, Creole epic poetry and its absence of "colored" heroes has been a traditionally neglected theme. Benedict Anderson's (1983) reference to printed periodical publications and their important role in the formation of an "imagined community" should be supplemented by the heavily ethnically charged ingredient of Creole epic poetry. In this sense, Anthony D. Smith's "ethnic origins of nations" as he refers to the pre-Enlightenment formation of "imagined communities," becomes a useful tool of analysis for this particular early modern Latin American case. Especially if we juxtapose the historical information about Indians and blacks who helped to defend the kingdom with the discursive models used and performed by conspicuous members of the "república de españoles."

Protecting the Peruvian "seashell" and its treasures from foreign privateers was not an easy task. However, it provided an excellent excuse for Creoles and naturalized peninsulars to express a self-consciousness about their vital importance to the Spanish Empire. Although much more could be said about Drake and other British interlopers in the development of a Creole strategy of self-glorification (as in the case of Juan de Castellanos' *Elegías de varones ilustres*, for example) my goal has been just to explore the intercontinental and international links that intervened in the formation of that early ethnic national identity. I hope these reflections will also suggest some of the interests and limitations of the early Creoles and their descendants who would take charge of the Peruvian "nation" (in the broad and modern sense of the word) during the early nineteenth century.

NOTES

1. There is ample evidence of this participation in diaries and documents of the epoch. See, for example, Juan Antonio Suardo, who testifies in his entry of October 28, 1630, the formation of an Indian battallion in homage to the birth of Prince Baltasar Carlos:

   > Su Excelencia [el Virrey] mandó que en el pueblo de la Magdalena, media legua desta ciudad, se hiziesse alarde y esquadron de Indios y assí, por la mañana, fue allí el Sargento Mayor Jil Negrete y otros Oficiales de la Milicia a prevenirlo y, a las dos de la tarde, estubo hecho *un esquadron de diez compañias y banderas con lanzas, chuzos y hondas en que habia cerca de quinientos indios* cuyos capitanes estaban muy galanamente vestidos y particularmente su Maestre de Campo, Gamarra, que sacó una camiseta muy curiosamente labrada, y pintada [. . .]. (Suardo 88, énfasis mío)

   > [The Viceroy commanded that a squadron of Indians form in the town of la Magdalena, half a league from this city [of Lima], and by the morning Sargeant Jil Negrete and other officers of the Militia went there to prepare the formation. At two in the afternoon, there was *a squadron of ten companies and banners with spears, pikes and slings with near five hundred indians*, whose captains were dressed very elegantly and particularly their Field Commander, Gamarra, who wore a curiously tilled and painted shirt. (Suardo 1935, 88, emphasis added)]

2. In this essay, I prefer to use the concept of "agency" rather than "subject" coinciding with Paul Smith, who writes: "[in some way] theoretical discourse limits the definition of the human agent in order to be able to call him/her the 'subject.'" And we can also agree when he argues "that the human agent exceeds the 'subject' as it is constructed in and by much poststructuralist theory as well as by those discourses against which poststructuralist theory claims to pose itself" (Smith 1988, xxx).

3. Anthony Pagden (1987, 91) affirms that "by the middle of the seventeenth century this [criollo] nation had established its own cultural and [. . .] political identity."

See also Luis Monguió, "Palabras e Ideas": *Iberoamericana* 174–75: 451–70, for a different interpretation of the concept of "nation" when applied to the Creole groups.

4. In addition to the dubious blood purity of Creoles, Gonzalo Aguirre Beltrán points out, in *El proceso de a culturación y el cambio socio-cultural en México* (México: Fondo de Cultura Económica).

> razón [. . .] tuvieron las autoridades peninsulares en desconfiar del español americano, desde el nacimiento infestado de los valores y significados indios por la criada que le servía de madre subrogada y, ya adulto, por su diario trato con la población vencida. El impacto inexorable de la comunicación con un mundo distinto hacía obligatoria la constante mudanza del cuadro dirigente para fortalecerlo con europeos fieles a la metrópoli. (Aguirre Beltrán 1992, 30)

> [The peninsular authorities were right in not trusting the Spanish Americans, who were infested by the values and Indian concepts of their native maternal nannies, and when they were adults, by their familiarity and daily contact with the vanquished population. The inevitable impact of the Creoles' communication with a different world than that of the Spaniards made mandatory for the Crown to fortify the highest administration with Europeans who were doubtlessly faithful to Spain.]

5. Sir Francis Drake's deeds deserved the attention of Lope de Vega in his long epic poem *La Dragontea* (1598), in which Lope recognized the bravery and notoriousness of the British interloper despite the fact that the poem is written in praise of the Spanish general Diego Suárez de Amaya.

6. See, for example, Juan María Corominas for the use of Castiglione's *Il Cortegiano* in Ercilla's poem and David Quint in *Epic and Empire* (Princeton: Princeton University Press) (157–85), for the paradigmes of Virgil's epic of the winner and Lucan's epic of the looser, both present in *La Araucana*.

7. See José Toribio Medina *Biblioteca hispano-chilena*, I: 42–79, who also documents the conflict between the Viceroy and the Archbishop of Lima, a conflict in which Oña would see himself involved. The wrath of the Archbishop against the young *protegé* of the Viceroy might have influenced other authorities in their censorship of the poem.

8. Captain Francisco Arias de Herrera, "con su plática experiencia / mandó a unos indios que al nacer del día / cañas por lanzas y a caballo puestos, / bajasen a la mar de unos recuestos" (Miramontes 1978, 349) ["with his practical experience commanded that / at dawn, some Indians go to the shore / riding horses and holding canes as if they were spears"]. The Indians, pretending to be soldiers on horses and spears showed up in great number and "viéndolos el inglés tuvo por cierto / que era gente española y que si intenta / saltar a saquear de Arica el puerto, / ha de volver con pérdida y afrenta" ["the British thought / they were Spaniards and that

if he tried / to sack the port of Arica / he would be defeated and humiliated"].
(*ibid.*)

9. See Rostworowski for a detailed biography of Doña Francisca, the most notorious of
Pizarro's children.

BIBLIOGRAPHY

Aguirre Beltrán, Gonzalo. [1957] 1992. *El proceso de aculturación y el cambio socio-cultural en México.* México: Fondo de Cultura Económica.

Anderson, Benedict. 1983. *Imagined Communities: Reflections on the Origin and Spread of Nationalism.* London: Verso.

Arzáns de Orsúa y Vela, Bartolomé. 1965. *Historia de la Villa Imperial de Potosí.* 3 Vols. Providence: Brown University Press.

Bakhtin, Mikhail M. 1981. "Epic and Novel." In *The Dialogic Imagination. Four Essays.* Edited by Michael Holquist; translated by Caryl Emerson and Michael Holquist. Austin: University of Texas Press.

Balboa, Silvestre de. [ca. 1608] 1962. *Espejo de paciencia. Edición facsímil y crítica a cargo de Cintio Vitier.* La Habana: Comisión Nacional Cubana de la Unesco.

Barco Centenera, Martín del. 1602. *Argentina y Conquista del Río de la Plata, con otros acaecimientos de los Reynos del Peru, Tucuman y el Estado del Brasil.* Lisboa: Por Pedro Crasbeek.

Bradley, Peter T. 1992. *Society, Economy and Defence in Seventeenth-Century Peru: The Administration of the Count of Alba de Liste (1655–61).* Liverpool: The Institute of Latin American Studies, University of Liverpool.

———. 1989. *The Lure of Peru. Maritime Intrusion into the South Sea, 1598–1701.* London: The MacMillan Press Ltd.

Burga, Manuel. 1988. *Nacimiento de una utopía. Muerte y resurrección de los incas.* Lima: Instituto de Apoyo Agrario.

Calancha, Antonio de la. 1638. *Chronica Moralizada del Orden de San Agustín en el Perú con sucesos exemplares vistos en esta Monarchia.* Barcelona: Por Pedro de Lacavalleria.

Campbell, Leon G. 1978. *The Military and Society in Colonial Peru, 1750–1810.* Philadelphia: The American Philosophical Society.

Corominas, Juan María. 1980. *Castiglione y La Araucana: Estudio de una influencia.* Madrid: Porrúa Turranzas.

Escandell Bonet, Bartolomé. 1953. "Repercusión de la piratería inglesa en el pensamiento peruano del siglo XVI." *Revista de Indias* 51: 81–87.

Espinosa Medrano, Juan de. 1982. "Prefacio al lector de la Lógica." En *Apologético.* Edición, prólogo y notas de Augusto Tamayo Vargas, 323–329. Caracas: Biblioteca Ayacucho.

Fernández de Córdoba, Francisco. 1621. "Prólogo." *Historia del Santuario de Nuestra Señora de Copacabana* by Fray Antonio Ramos Gavilán. Lima: Luis de Lyra. (Prologue has no page #s)

Flores Galindo, Alberto. 1986. *Buscando un inca: utopía e identidad en los Andes.* La Habana: Casa de las Américas.

García-Bedoya, Carlos. 1996. "El discurso andino en el Perú colonial: los textos del renacimiento inca." In *Asedios a la heterogeneidad cultural. Libro de homenaje a Antonio Cornejo Polar,* 197–216. Philadelphia: Asociación Internacional de Peruanistas.

Helgerson, Richard. 1992. *Forms of Nationhood: The Elizabethan Writing of England.* Chicago: University of Chicago Press.

Kuznesof, Elizabeth Anne. 1995. "Ethnic and Gender Influences on 'Spanish' Creole Society in Colonial Spanish America." *Colonial Latin American Review* 4, 1: 153–176.

Lane, Kris E., 1998. *Pillaging the Empire: Piracy in the Americas, 1500–1750.* Armonk, New York: M. E. Sharpe.

Lavallé, Bernard. 1993. *Las promesas ambiguas. Ensayos sobre el criollismo colonial en los Andes.* Lima: PUCP.

Lohmann Villena, Guillermo. 1973. *Historia Marítima del Perú. Siglos XVII y XVIII. Tomo IV.* Lima: Editorial Ausonia.

———. 1964. *Las defensas militares de Lima y Callao.* Sevilla: Escuela de Estudios Hispanoamericanos.

Medina, José Toribio. 1963. *Biblioteca hispano-chilena.* 3 vols. Santiago de Chile: Fondo Histórico y Bibliográfico José Toribio Medina, [1897–99].

Miramontes y Zuázola, Juan de. [ca. 1615] 1978. *Armas Antárticas.* Caracas: Biblioteca Ayacucho. Prólogo y Cronología de Rodrigo Miró.

Monguió, Luis. 1978. "Palabras e Ideas: 'Patria' y 'Nación' en el Virreinato del Perú." *Revista Iberoamericana* 174–75: 451–70.

Mowitt, John. 1988. "Foreword. The Resistance in Theory." In *Discerning the Subject.* By Paul Smith, ix–xxiii. Minneapolis: University of Minnesota Press.

Mugaburu, Josephe de, y Mugaburu (hijo), Francisco de. 1917. *Diario de Lima (1640–1694). Crónica de la Época Colonial. Colección de Libros y Documentos Referentes a la Historia del Perú,* Tomo VII. Horacio H. Urteaga y Carlos A. Romero, editores. Lima: Imprenta y Librería Sanmarti y Ca., 2 vols (1640–1670 and 1671–1694).

Oña, Pedro de. [1596] 1944. *Primera Parte del Arauco Domado.* Madrid: Ediciones Cultura Hispánica. Facsímil de la primera edición (Lima: Por Antonio Ricardo, 1596).

Pagden, Anthony. 1987. "Identity formation in Spanish America". In *Colonial Identity in the Atlantic World, 1500–1800.* Edited by Nicholas Canny and Anthony Pagden, 51–93. Princeton: Princeton University Press.

Peralta y Barnuevo, Pedro de. 1732. *Lima Fundada o Conquista del Perú.* 2 vols. Lima: Imprenta de Francisco Sobrino y Bados.

Quinn, David Beers. 1996. *Sir Francis Drake As Seen by His Contemporaries*. Providence: John Carter Brown Library.

Quint, David. 1993. *Epic and Empire: Politics and Generic Form from Virgil to Milton*. Princeton: Princeton University Press.

Raleigh, Sir Walter. [1596] 1751. "A voyage to the Discovery of Guiana." *The Works of Sir Walter Ralegh*, In *Political, Commercial and Philosophical, Together with His Letters and Poems*. 2 vols. London: Printed for R. Dodsley, at Tully's Head in Pall-Mall.

Rostworowski, María 1989. *Doña Francisca Pizarro, una ilustre mestiza*. Lima: IEP.

Rowe, John Howland. [1954]1976. "El movimiento nacional inca del siglo XVIII." In *Túpac Amaru II–1780*. Coordinated by Alberto Flores Galindo, 13–66. Lima: Retablo de Papel.

Salinas y Córdiva, Buenaventura de. [1630] 1957. *Memorial de las historias del Nuevo Mundo Piru*. Lima: Universidad Nacional Mayor de San Marcos.

Schwartz, Stuart. 1995. "Colonial Identities and *Sociedad de Castas*." *Colonial Latin American Review* 4, 1: 185–201.

Smith, Anthony D. 1986. *The Ethnic Origins of Nations*. Londres: Basil Blackwell.

Simth, Paul. 1988. *Discerning the Subject*. Minneapolis: University of Minnesota Press.

Suardo, Juan Antonio. 1935. *Diario de Lima* (1629–1634). Lima: Concejo Provincial de Lima. Publicado con Introducción y Notas de Rubén Vargas Ugarte S. J.

Valdés, Rodrigo de. 1687. *Fundacion y Grandezas de Lima*. Madrid: Imprenta de Antonio Román.

History and Plunder in *El carnero*

Writing, among Indians, a History of Spaniards and Euro-Americans in Colonial Spanish America

Alvaro Félix Bolaños

> . . . que como quier que estos indios se hayan mostrado a los descubridores e se muestran cada día muy simples e sin malicia, con todo, porque cada día vienen acá entre nosotros, non pareció que fuera buen consejo meter a riesgo e a ventura de perderse esta gente e los mantenimientos, lo que un indio con un tizón podría fazer poniendo fuego a las choças, porque de noche e de día siempre van e vienen, e a causa d'ellos tenemos guardas en el campo, mientras la población está avierta e sin defensión (Christopher Columbus).

> He querido decir todo esto para que se entienda que los indios no hay maldad que no intenten, y matan a los hombres por robarlos. En el pueblo de Pasca mataron a uno por robarle la hacienda, y después de muerto pusieron fuego al bohío donde dormía, y dijeron que se había quemado. Autos se han hecho sobre esto, que no se ha podido sustanciar; y sin esto otras muertes y casos que han hecho. Dígolo para que no se descuiden de ellos.
> —Juan Rodríguez Freile

In his edition of four official accounts (*relaciones*) on the conquest and colonization of the New Kingdom of Granada, written between 1538 and 1571 (that is, thirty-three years of the one hundred which occupy *El carnero*), the historian Hermes Tovar Pinzón reflects on the alleged invisibility of the Native American in the writing of history of colonial Colombia:

> . . . en tres regiones [Nuevo Reino, Popayán, y Cartagena] ex-
> istían hacia 1560, casi mil cacicazgos. ¿No estamos frente a una so-
> ciedad que nos hemos negado a reconocerla en su propio rostro y su
> propia piel? ¿Cuántos caciques habían desaparecido entonces? Con
> estas cifras debemos admitir que el territorio sojuzgado de la actual
> Colombia, hacia 1560, tenía al menos millón y medio de naturales,
> dispersos entre mil cacicazgos. (1988: 15)[1]

And with respect to the importance of this native population for the economic survival of the Spanish invaders, in the particular case of the Bogotá
plateau where the author of *El carnero* used to live, the historian Julián Vargas
Lesmes says:

> En muchos aspectos la ciudad del siglo XVI no podía funcionar ni
> crecer sin el aporte indígena. La puesta en operación de los servicios
> básicos o su mismo crecimiento dependía de su trabajo. Entre ellos, el
> abastecimiento de alimentos y leña, la conducción de agua, las obras
> públicas, la construcción de iglesias, de edificios y casas privadas.
> (1990a: 87–88)[2]

According to this, sixteenth- and seventeenth-century Native Americans
were more intimately and daily linked to the Spanish colonizers' lot than is
generally admitted in the historical treatises on the New Kingdom of Granada.
In the specific case of Santafé de Bogotá, the efforts of both Spanish and
Euro-Americans to find and utilize a native labor force propitiated, through
the so called *mita urbana* (rotation of forced labor in different areas as needed
by the colonizers), a constant influx of Indians to the city which by the end of
the seventeenth century made them the majority of the urban population.
"Durante los primeros años de la década del [15]90—Vargas adds—, el
número de indios en la ciudad fue bastante grande. Entre 800 y 1,100 tributar-
ios con sus familias y en ocasiones toda la comunidad venían a Santafé mesual-
mente. En 1602, según las cifras obtenidas para el mes de mayo, vinieron 1,082
indios" (1990a: 91).[3]

Despite all this, the Spanish authorities considered that number of Indians authorized by the local Royal Council, insufficient. Such insufficiency of
unpaid Indian labor showed not only Spanish and Euro-American excesses in
utilizing native servants (in order to maintain their everyday seigniorial life-
style), but also attests to the collapse of the Native American population at the
frontier during the period of colonization. The huge importance of the Muisca
groups in the project for a frontier society in the New Kingdom of Granada
would make us think that the native presence in yesterday's and today's historical, cultural, and literary treatises in this region would be prominent and nec-

essary. But that has not been the case. If something has unified the readings of *El carnero* made by literary critics, it has been the notion of the insignificance of the Native Americans as a theme in this work.

The conception of *El carnero* as a text dedicated only or mainly to the narration of Spanish and Euro-American deeds since the seventeenth century conforms to two ideas widely accepted by the majority of its readers: (1) the general attitude of the European and Euro-American of the colonial period in understanding the New World as a tabula rasa and its inhabitants as entities culturally dismissable (Freile's case as we will see). The general consequence of this attitude has been the marginal reference to, or total dismissal of, the native for the sake of a favorable representation of Spanish and Euro-American achievements. That same attitude is endorsed today by the majority of readings of this text; (2) the critic's urge for foundational origins, since the Independence from Spain, to fill in vacuums in the literary history of Colombia (or Latin America as a whole for that matter), by forcing texts written with no literary intention into the field of literature. Such an urge acquired huge proportions in Latin America during the sixties and seventies with the anxious effort to find a foundational literary tradition to explain the origins of the Latin American literary "Boom." The general strategy has been to find in texts of referential intention (like *El carnero*) instances of narrative imagination, collect them and then see them as proto-novelistic rudiments. From here to the identification of Juan Rodríquez Freile's "ambiguous" and "imaginative" text with the Spanish picaresque novels there is only one step, which the majority of critics have taken.

The bibliography demonstrating this tendency is extensive but some notable examples should be mentioned: Jean Franco, for whom *El carnero* is simply a collection of spicy anecdotes (by Spaniards and Euro-Americans, of course) with literary intention deliberately hidden inside a historical chronicle (1975, 19). Eduardo Camacho Guizado, for whom the *casos,* which comprise *El carnero,* are examples of a "situación desgraciada y consecuencias trágicas en la que se ven envueltos los hombres por dar rienda suelta a sus pasiones y vicios, o por caer en las tentaciones del demonio, el mundo o la carne" (1982: 147).[4] The term *"hombres"* does not include Indians. Roberto González Echevarría, for whom the majority of *casos* correspond to "a series of more or less impudent stories" (1990, 88), and the rest of the story corresponds to the development of the Viceroyalty. This tendency to consider *El carnero* as a protoliterary work has turned into an unquestionable truth as illustrated by Rafael H. Moreno Durán: "El lector que consulte *El carnero* lo hace llevado por su interés literario, más que por el puramente histórico (. . .). El interés de *El carnero,* reiteramos, es de estricta naturaleza literaria" (1994, 24–25).[5] The consultation of this text moved by literary interest is, of course, a personal decision of the critic, not an adequate definition of an *historia* or *relación* of a referential kind like *El carnero.*

Juan Rodríguez Freile writes in Santafé at a moment of great demand for native labor and huge concerns for its scarcity and his reference to the demographic collapse of the native population is a response to historical reality. According to the statistics on the *mita urbana* between 1615 and 1642 we find that precisely in the year 1638, when the writing of *El carnero* is concluded, the availability of native labor in Santafé falls to alarming levels for the inhabitants of this city. This might explain Freile's pessimistic tone when speaking about the absence of Indian labor to exploit. In that regard Vargas says:

> Con base en una serie que empieza en 1615, sabemos que la cuota anual estaba por encima de los 2,000 tributarios al año. A partir de 1627, el aporte empieza a bajar drásticamente. Llega a su punto más bajo en 1638–1639 en la cual tan sólo se cumple con un 40% de lo estipulado en 1615 (. . .). En términos generales, del comienzo al fin de la serie, el número de indígenas que servía dentro del trabajo forzoso disminuyó en un 50%, es decir, alrededor de 1,200 tributarios al año. Esta tendencia a la disminución debió pronunciarse durante la segunda parte del siglo XVII. (1990a: 92)[6]

Freile cites the drastic demographic collapse of the native population in the New Kingdom of Granada as one of the reasons for the deplorable state of affairs in this region. What is striking about Freile's reference to this demographic collapse, on the other hand, is his sudden interruption of it in a gesture of auto-censorship which, as far as I have seen, has not been addressed by the critics. Freile says: ". . . pues de todos ellos no han quedado más que los poquillos de esta jurisdicción y de la de Tunja, y aún éstos, *tenéos no digáis más*" (editor's emphasis, 1979, 189). The sensitive nature of this statement deserves an explanation. I have decided to interpret the sentence "*tenéos no digáis más*" in its literal sense, that is, as an equivalent to a call by the narrator to himself in order to avoid deliberations on the issue of the demographic collapse of the American Indians and the problem of moral guilt. It could be argued that this sentence simply stresses the uselessness of talking at length about despised Indian groups (for example, *tenéos no digáis más* or talking about that is not worth the effort), but this argument would not explain: (1) Freile's (and his contemporaries') frustration and anxiety due to his inability to get his hands on treasures which can only be supplied by Native Americans (either because only they know how to get to them, or because they form the only labor force available to do it); and (2) his explicit ulterior reference to his personal exploitation of an Indian elder (in the extraction of gold from a sacred lagoon) as a "sin" confessed before the reader (1979, 37). I will come back to this point later.

Such a statement is more striking if one takes into account that Santafé and Tunja were the jurisdictions with bigger concentrations of native dwellers at that time, and that for that very reason they were subject to greater abuses from the *encomienda* holders who put them in the deplorable demographic situation Freile complains about. On the general population of Santafé, the official Spanish historian for American themes, Juan López de Velasco, calculates that in 1572 there were about six hundred Spanish families and up to fifty thousand Indians; a century later there were more than three thousand Spaniards and about ten thousand Indians (1574, 637–639). In the case of Tunja, according to Aprile-Gniset, there were more than sixty *repartimientos de indios* [allotment of land and Indians to successful conquistadors], a staggering number if one considers that each *repartimiento,* or *encomienda,* as later it would be known, had one or several Indian communities. In the city itself, continues Jacques Aprile-Gniset, citing a sixteenth-century document, each Spanish family had at least ten household servants among Indians and blacks (1997: 16).

With such an abrupt "tenéos no digáis más" burst of silence over his discourse, the historian from Santafé chooses not to delve into the theme of the Native's sufferings during the one hundred years of history of Spanish colonization which occupy his attention. It is relevant to ask, why? What implication does this gesture of auto-censorship have on the composition of his treatise on the region? What connection can we establish between Freile's deliberate silence and the commentators' persistent reading of *El carnero*—from the seventeenth century up to now—as a work occupied only and mainly with the deeds of Spaniards and Euro-Americans in the New Kingdom of Granada? Why do both author and seventeenth century and modern day readers tend to favor the notion of the marginality or absence of the Native American from a history which cannot avoid making reference to their conflictive relations with Europeans and Euro-Americans in the region which would later become Colombia? With such questions I am hoping to propose a reading of this text which does not limit its interest to searching for interesting or exciting narrations of fictional and historical data from the past. I propose, instead, a reading that allows for the social, economic, political, racial, sexual, and cultural tensions of the past (all so vibrant in *El carnero*) to spill over into the present, especially as many of those tensions still linger unresolved today. After all, the process of plundering of indigenous communities, with its inherent physical, economical, and cultural hostility toward them, has not subsided in the Americas.[7]

The reading proposed here recognizes a deliberate association between the verbal articulation of the history of a Native American population and its European colonizers, and the actual situation of brutal subjugation suffered by their descendants at the time in which *El carnero* is composed and read. In other words, this proposed reading targets both the *El carnero* and the most common interpretations up to now. Texts of this kind dealing with what Walter Mignolo calls "colonial situations" (1989, 94) tend to apply a double standard in dealing with the pre-Columbian indigenous peoples (celebrated but extinct), and the author's contemporary descendants (reduced to poverty and denigration). José Rabasa, reflecting on similar issues in the case of México, refers to this double standard as follows: "Colonialist writing practices, then, do not just pertain to the (early) colonial period, but inform contemporary modernization programs that folklorize forms of life and deplore the loss of old—thereby confining Indian cultures to the museum and the curio shop" (1994, 246). An effect of such folklorization, as we will see in *El carnero,* is the vilification and concealment of contemporary Indians exercised both by Freile himself and by his critics.

A way for Freile to deal in his history with the inevitable reference to Indians is to drastically (and conveniently) make a separation between: (1) the pre-Columbian native who has an authentic, exotic, and occasionally admirable cultural idiosyncrasy, and who is—at the same time and fortunately— no longer hostile; and (2) the poor, miserably exploited, numerous and sordidly threatening Indian who lives at the time of composition of *El carnero.* Such differentiation corresponds to a conscious and urgent political act to nullify in these indigenous peoples, notions of legitimacy, justice, and merits that can be linked rightfully to social vindication for a century of exploitation. The first chapters of *El carnero,* completely dedicated to a pre-Columbian history of the Muisca, are clearly an effort by Freile to give a space in his text to the Indian subjectivity, but the result of this effort does not weaken Freile's celebration of the status quo nor of the existing abusive rule over the Native Americans. As a curious intellectual who receives the testimony of his native informant, Freile exercises a practice common even today among ethnographers: the salvation and redemption of evanescent traits of a culture dying because of its harsh contact with the West. Such an arrogant and pretentious attitude goes parallel with the notion that both a "good" intention and the exclusive nature of the testimony acquired have produced a veritable and objective history or description of the observed culture, and that such veracity and objectivity are irrefutable, specially if the culture in question lacks alphabetic writing.

Nevertheless, the problem with the ethnographic narrative about the Muiscas produced by Freile is not only its self-proclaimed objectivity and exclusivity, but also, and mainly, the very political act of differentiating the political interests of yesterday's Indians from those of contemporary ones. James Clifford, explaining the allegorical character of Western ethnographic narratives, expresses this problem in better terms: "Historical worlds will be salvaged [in the ethnographic text] as textual fabrications disconnected from ongoing lived milieu and suitable for moral, allegorical appropriation by individual readers" (1986, 114). To put the matter differently, in the view of Spaniards and Euro-Americans living in Freile's time, Muisca political vindications could be legitimate, but they are also obsolete precisely because of the obsolescence of the Muisca culture. As a result, the political vindication of the contemporary Muisca, descendants of the very objects of the ethnographic attention in the text, is illegitimate, because it has little to do with yesterday's "true" Muisca. It is a Catch-22.

While relating details of pre-Columbian civil wars in the Bogotá plains, Freile makes a subtle—albeit not innocent—association between these epic (or semi-epic) indigenous peoples of the past and the marginalized and criminal ones of his time:

> También envió el Guatavita sus mensajeros al Rimiriquí muy de buena gana por vengarse del Bogotá, con quien estaba atrasado por ciertas correrías que había hecho por sus tierras, con color que peleaba con panches y colimas y con otros caribes que estaban en los fuertes segundos [seguros?] y que confinaban con el río grande de la Magdalena, *que aunque hoy día duran algunas de estas naciones, como son vaqueríes y carares, que infestan y saltean los que navegan el dicho río, por la cual razón hay de ordinario presidio en él, puesto por la Real Audiencia para asegurar aquel paso.* (emphasis added, 29)[8]

The intention of this association is to create a difference between the idiosyncrasies of both native subjectivities. The Indians of today are simply criminals since any connection they might have with their ancestors can be reduced to the persistence of their negative traits. This is evident, for instance, in an association between the alleged drunken celebrations and sexual orgies of the Muiscas of the past and the characteristics of the Indians of the present. When talking about the truce agreed upon by the Bogotá and the Rimiriquí, so they could make their ritual offerings to their gods, Freile says: ". . . comiendo y bebiendo juntos en grandes borracheras que hicieron, que duraban de día y de noche, a donde el que más incestos y fornicios hacía, era más santo, *vicio que hasta hoy les dura* (emphasis added, 30).[9]

The effort to define and crystallize a notion of an American frontier culture, for the consumption of sixteenth-century Spaniards and Euro-Americans, involved in those who wrote about the *Indias Occidentales* a constant and careful textual process of segregation (racially, culturally, sexually, economically, and socially speaking) against the very subjugated ethnic group, who at the same time overwhelmed the colonizer with their numbers and strengthened their recently acquired seignorial status. Such an integral segregating effort was necessary and was frequently found in every textual and material articulation (from simple forensic *relaciones* and ostentatious epic poems to chivalric coat of arms and European architecture), which presented American social reality as a fortunate prolongation of Iberian culture and imperialism. Nevertheless the reality was one of conflictive and frequently brutal relations between a subjugated indigenous majority and an overpowering European and Euro-American minority. Under such circumstances Freile lived and wrote, that is to say, surrounded by Muiscas and *yanaconas* brought from different regions (those *encomienda* subjects, *ladinos,* servants, assimilated into urban work force, enslaved in frontier wars, Europeanized or not, etc.); surrounded also by their indispensable and numerous services, but at the same time by the fear and suspicion they inspired in him and his fellow Euro-Americans, who knew full well the dangers of a native people who are the majority of the population and who must be angry about their mistreatment.

The overwhelming presence of the native population in a city like Santafé from the end of the sixteenth century on, responded—according to Vargas—to a constant effort by the city dwellers to acquire Indian labor from the *encomienda* holders who monopolized that labor in the countryside. The fierce competition for that labor force resulted in the institutionalization of individual leasing of Indians, which forced them to the city where they served with no pay even though there was legislation calling for recompense for their work. The result was a permanent and increasing march of indigenous peoples into Santafé. "[H]ay que tener en cuenta que se movilizaban con la familia y probablemente la comunidad entera. La presencia mensual de 800 a 1,000 podía fácilmente multiplicarse por cuatro. Santafé no tenía medios para alojarlos y los indígenas se veían obligados a construir tambos en las afueras de la ciudad para conseguir alojamiento" (Vargas 1990a, 90–91).[10]

Moreover, the Muisca were visible not only in the public urban spaces, such as streets and market places, but also at the very core of the Spanish and Euro-American family which intimately and daily enjoyed their services, as is well illustrated by Vargas:

> La consecución del agua, el aseo y el mantenimiento de la casa, las labores de la cocina (o cocinas), la compra y adecuación de la leña y el carbón para mantener el fuego, el cuidado de los animales, las labores de la huerta, el aseo y reparación de la ropa, la crianza de los niños, la realización de los mandados, las compras en la plaza y en las tiendas, el traer y llevar de menajes, los depósitos de productos de las estancias y encomiendas, los encargos desde el campo, eran parte de las actividades cotidianas de la familia. Así mismo, por lo general, cada casa tenía horno para la fabricación de pan, bizcochos

u otro tipo de alimentos cocidos, jamón, por ejemplo. (1990b, 146–47)[11]

In spite of this kind of social environment, Freile defines, with no hesitation whatsoever, *El carnero* as a work uninterested in Native Americans, devoted primarily to soldiers, captains who conquered the territory, presidents and royal officials who founded and controlled the *Real Audiencia,* inspectors who visited, and bishops and ecclesiastics who celebrated and sanctioned the imposed Spanish culture: ". . . quise lo mejor que se pudiere, dar noticia de la conquista de este Nuevo Reino, y lo sucedido en el desde que sus pobladores y primeros conquistadores lo poblaron, hasta la hora presente, que esto se escribe" (1990b 9).[12]

According to this, the Sabana de Bogotá in which the Conquistadors settled was an open field ready to receive European civilization and evangelical proselytism, not a region legitimately and vastly populated by native cultures. The great numbers of indigenous people who were living there and resisted the Spanish penetration were simple exotic and dismissable beings who were obliged to give way to the benefits of the entering Western culture. Insisting on the presence of these native cultures would seem unnecessary unless we consider the violence exercised over them by their lingering and deliberate omission in the study of these texts, an omission—unfortunately—still considered "natural" today.

Understanding the story told in *El carnero* in Freile's terms implies celebrating a legitimate Spanish origin which, in turn, legitimizes the nature of the society in which this author lived and wrote. It has to depart, in other words, from the ratification of a status quo in which the Spanish presence in America implies the cultural and historical annihilation of the indigenous peoples. The resulting reading is one oblivious to the presence of the American Indian in *El carnero,* a presence which, despite the indifference of Freile and most of his readers of all times, becomes difficult to ignore. A current example of considering *El carnero* as a history only devoted to Spaniards and Euro-Americans is offered by Darío Achury Valenzuela for whom the Native American appears at the beginning as an object of conquest who is ready to be displaced by, and to step aside for, the new characters, the Spaniards.

> Por estas páginas han pasado, en confuso tropel, guazábaras de indios y fantasmas de aquellos capitanes, que al amanecer de un día, salieron en busca del fabuloso Dorado o del inasible reino de las amazonas y nunca jamás retornaron. Por entre estas líneas discurren ahora, lentas, las sombras de presidentes, oidores, visitadores, fiscales, arzobispos. (1979, xlviii)[13]

The tragedy of the invasion of the Sabana lands, the desperate resistance of the Natives, and the destructive disruption of the pre-Columbian social way of living are reduced by Achury Valenzuela to references of a "confusing throng," "scuffles of Indians," which luckily was dissipated with the legitimate arrival and placid settlement of all those venerable Spanish gentlemen. In spite of all this, and due precisely to the healthy complexity of this text, the problem of the treatment of the indigenous peoples as a theme in *El carnero* does not reside in their total obliteration but in the kind of presence that is given to them. In what follows, I will examine the presence of Native Americans given by Freile in his text in order to explain how, despite such presence and through the textual articulation of the cultural and material plundering of the Natives, a fragmented, controlled, and deplorable image of them is constructed. I will attempt to explain also how such an image manages to turn the indigenous peoples into an easily dismissable entity in the writing of the cultural history of the New Kingdom of Granada.

Beyond the frequent and brief references to the natives as servants for the Conquistadors and *encomienda* holders throughout the text, Freile treats the theme of Indians on five notable occasions: (1) He discusses pre-Columbian wars and customs, about the civil wars among the Muisca before the Spanish invasion, and the implantation of the Spanish rule (first four chapters of the text); (2) He recounts the Pijao Indians offensive and genocidal war against them led by Juan de Borja (chapter 19); On the theme of plundering and theft of gold he includes two major stories; (3) In the first one, the Indian, still culturally undiminished, is tricked and his treasure stolen (the case of the shaman as victim of a priest specialized in stealing gold idols, chapter 5); (4) In the second story, he shows the Indian already immersed in the Euro-American society as a contumacious and skillful thief of gold accumulated by his masters (case of the Peruvian Indian whose ears are cut off, chapter 16); (5) The final occasion deals with the Indian as a subversive threat. It tells about the false accusation of sedition against the Indian chief of Turmequé, Diego de Torres. Even though the accusation is false and is made in the context of conflicts among Spanish and Euro-American political powers, the white population takes it seriously and reacts in panic, demonstrating with such reaction not only the wide and constant presence of the indigenous population in this colonial society, but also the ever-present fear of an Indian rebellion (chapters 13 and 14). Vargas notices traces of paranoia among the Spaniards and Euro-Americans before the overwhelming majority of the indigenous peoples, especially when it comes to contemporary calculations of statistics:

> Para comienzos del siglo XVII, ya existe una población indígena mayoritaria en Santafé. Según el estimado del padre Pacheco, quien a su

vez se basaba en un informe del padre Medrano, para 1599 había
20.000 indios viviendo en Santafé, incluidos los sirvientes de los españoles. La exageración es evidente, pero puede ser indicativa de la
percepción de un aumento efectivo e inusitado del número de indígenas en la ciudad. (1990b, 57)[14]

In these five instances of military violence, cultural identities under siege,
and plundering of wealth, a systematic material and cultural despoliation of
the natives takes place, intended to deprive them of military, political, and economic authority, in order to reduce them to the state of a wretched colonial
with no possibility of possessing wealth much less of accumulating it. If we
take into account that these five instances take place between 1536 and 1605,
it is possible to consider them as a demonstration of a hostile attitude towards
the indigenous peoples which encompasses almost the entire century that occupies Freile's history.[15]

The location of the Native American in *El carnero* is always linked to
wealth ready to be plundered by means of violence or trickery. In the following quote from the Prologue, Freile laments the absence of rural Indian
labor which, unfortunately for him, was extinguished before it could make
the Spaniards and the Euro-Americans richer: "Es mucha la [riqueza] que el
[Nuevo Reino] tiene en sus venas ricos minerales, que de ellos se han llevado
y llevan a nuestra España grandes tesoros, y se llevaran muchos más y mayores si fueran ayudados como convenía y más el día de hoy por haberle fal-
tado los más de los naturales" (5).[16] The tragedy of the genocide to which
the natives have been subjected is not, of course, what concerns the author
(since for Freile they are naturally exploitable, dismissable and inferior beings), but the inconvenient consequences of this genocide for the economic
well being of Spaniards and Euro-Americans. Freile, instead, takes for
granted the servant role of the Indians who, in this case, did not fully com-
ply with their obligation to serve due to their inopportune demographic collapse.[17] In what follows, I will examine the treatment of the Muisca customs
and the case of the shaman deceived by the priest who tracks down Indian
treasures.

The presentation of the Muisca customs in this chapter of *El carnero* reveals moral prejudices and ideological assumptions rather than a faithful representation of their culture, as some critics think.[18] Basing himself on the
preconceived notion of their cultural inferiority, and therefore on his belief of
their inevitable subjugation to the culturally superior Spaniards, Freile tells of
the education of the Muisca: "En ser lujuriosos y tener muchas mujeres y
cometer tantos incestos, sin reservar hijas y madres, en conclusión bárbaros, sin
ley ni conocimiento de Dios, por que sólo adoraban al demonio y a éste tenían
por maestro" (17).[19] It should not come as a surprise, then, that in chapter 5,

which includes the story of the deceived and robbed shaman, Freile starts with the story of the biblical origin of the world and the Fall of Adam and Eve from Paradise due to the devil's manipulations. This long story is not a simple literary digression;[20] it corresponds, instead, to introductory censorship and recrimination of what Freile sees as despicable native rituals. For Freile it is imperative to begin with a moralistic preface which vindicates Catholic beliefs before delving into descriptions of indigenous ceremonies deemed scandalous and diabolic. Besides, the author of *El carnero* does not wish to meet, for instance, the same fate Fray Bernardino de Sahagún did in the previous century. Sahagún failed to explicitly and morally condemn the Indian customs before describing them in detail in his *Historia de las cosas de Nueva España* and was accused of writing things detrimental to the Christian faith.[21]

In the previous chapter, Freile had promised that he was going to explain the nature of the Muisca ritual known as *"correr la tierra"* [run across the land], a martial and religious ceremony in which the Muisca would run, on a kind of pilgrimage, between distant centers of worship located in sacred lagoons. It is precisely before initiating such an explanation that Freile offers the biblical story with the main purpose of pointing to a marginal position of the indigenous peoples in a cosmic order established by God and considered, of course, universal. According to the biblical creation of the world included by Freile in his text, God created man according to His own image and gave him an "alma racional, vistiéndola de la original justicia" [a rational soul endowed with natural justice], and among such attributes was his ability to recognize the magnificent power of God. This capacity, according to Freile, did not exist among the indigenous peoples, because they are not as rational and have a non-Christian religion.

The attention given to the Indians in this part of the text, far from being an acknowledgment of any value in the native culture, is a condemnation of it which in turn imposes on the Natives two options: the unilateral adoption of the "superior" European culture and the delivery of their mineral riches. That is why Freile, when talking about the New World, has to indicate how far behind it is in relation to the march of the divine order established for the universe and, additionally, how such position has to do with the dominance of the devil in the Indies: ". . . y estos naturales estaban y estuvieron en esta ceguedad hasta la conquista, por lo cual el demonio se hacía adorar de ellos, y le sirviesen con muchos ritos y ceremonias y entre ellas fue una el correr la tierra" (36).[22]

The notion of the inferiority and controllability of the native culture in *El carnero* is directly linked to the powerful, albeit implicit, disauthorization of the Indian to possess wealth. As a result, the reason for Freile to occupy himself with these rituals is not an ethnographic interest but the link between that customary ritual and the possibility of expropriating gold—since the lagoons involved in this native running ritual were also rich deposits of gold ready for plundering:

> En todas estas lagunas fue siempre fama que había mucho oro y que particularmente en la de Guatavita, donde había un gran tesoro; y a esta fama Antonio de Sepúlveda capituló con la Majestad de Felipe II desaguar la laguna, y poniéndole en efecto le dio el primer desaguadero como se ve en ella el día de hoy; y dijo que de sólo las orillas de lo que había desaguado, se había sacado más de dos mil pesos. (38)[23]

In the same fashion, when speaking in chapter 3 about the civil wars among the Muisca, Freile has carefully associated the contemptible nature of their political and military culture with the undeserved possession of gold treasures. The gold accumulated by the native king, Guatavita, appears linked to three circumstances: (1) the scandalous civil war among infidels of inferior culture; (2) the tyranny of Guatavita (who causes the rebellion of his own provinces and the beginning of the civil war), and the unjust mistreatment of his captain, Bogotá; (3) Guatavita's greed (he makes a cowardly escape, concerned only with hiding his treasure). This negative contextualization of the native monarch as a holder of wealth turns the subsequent expropriation exercised by the Spaniards into a legitimate act, and, in turn, provides moral authorization to the continued plundering of the indigenous people's wealth up to the time when Freile writes his text. It is in this context that Freile tells us: "No puedo pasar de aquí sin contar cómo un clérigo engañó al diablo, o a su jeque o mohán, en su nombre, y le cogió tres y cuatro mil pesos que le tenía ofrecidos en un santuario que estaba en la labranza del cacique viejo de Ubaque; y esto fue en mi tiempo" (38).[24]

In this story (based on historical facts), the greedy missionary Francisco Lorenzo, while pretending he was conducting a religious parade and by means of an elaborate scheme reminiscent of a *Decameron* story, imitated the voice of the devil—who supposedly was worshipped by the shaman—, and ordered him to change the place in which his idols made of gold were hidden.[25] The naïve character of this story obeys, thus exposing the hiding place of a generous treasure which the priest readily plunders. Robbing the Indian medicine man is, according to Freile's quick and emphatic clarification, robbing the devil through his own shaman (38); and since this theft amounts to deceiving the devil himself, such an act can be considered a kind of symbolic vindication against Lucifer for his trickery of Adam and Eve and the subsequent scorn of God for making them fall into temptation and out of Paradise. By extension, the theft of the indigenous people's wealth is necessary for the triumph of divine justice. When Freile suggests that the deceiving devil of Earthly Paradise is the same

one deceived in the story of the thieving Catholic priest, he is establishing a direct connection between the biblical story and the historical events of the
robbed shaman. Such a connection, in view of the fair deception of the devil,
not only justifies the expropriation of treasures owned by the idolatrous native,
but also makes it an absolute necessity. The bold deception and theft made by
the greedy missionary are thus sanctioned by the Holy Scriptures and by the
providentialist project of the Spanish Empire in the New World.

This story has particular effects in the logic of the universe created in *El
carnero:* (1) since the Native is abhorrent before divine law by reason of his paganism and worshipping the devil, he is unauthorized to possess wealth; (2)
the Native is stupid (or puerile at best) so it is easy to trick him. This in turn
justifies the need to take the wealth away from him since it does no good in his
hands; (3) robbing the Indian through trickery is a laudable and emulable act
even if a feigned Catholic ritual is needed (the Catholic priest makes a
painstaking scheme in which many churchgoers pretend to be in a religious
procession in the countryside to distract the indigenous locals). Above and beyond, this story is more than a rhetorical device with literary purposes.[26] It is
rather a powerful emblem of plunder and expropriation in the real story which
the author wants to transmit. What Freile does is not simply to tell a "true"
story that coincides with the facts and their chronology, but to establish three
undeniable "realities"—for him and his readers, including those of today: (1)
the superiority of the human generation developed according to the biblical
story and the Christian and Catholic tenets; (2) the inferiority of those human
beings developed at the margins of that story and their tenets, in this case, the
idolatrous Natives; and (3) the legitimacy of expropriating indigenous wealth,
because it is dedicated to the adoration of the devil.

The notion of the legitimacy of plundering Indian wealth allows Freile
to even suggest that the Native's attempt to protect his treasures threatened
by Spanish greed is in itself a diabolic effort. In other words, for Freile the
Indians are flatly "bad guys," because they do not allow the Spaniards and
the Euro-Americans to rob them. Let us see an example. Freile had mentioned before that the Spaniards were greedy. And he mentions it again in
the following passage: "Dijéronle a Guatavita cómo los españoles (. . .) eran
muy amigos del oro, que andaban por los pueblos buscándolo, y lo sacaban de
donde lo hallaban; con lo cual el Guatavita dio orden de guardar su tesoro"
(185).[27] These words by Freile had made many critics think that this author
denounces and condemns Spanish greed, but it is hardly the case. To begin
with, Freile places himself among those Spaniards and Euro-Americans
frustrated by the successful concealment of Guatavita's treasure: "Parece que
este fue consejo del diablo por (. . .) *quitarnos* el oro; que aunque algunas
personas han gastado tiempo y dinero en buscarlo, no lo han podido hallar"
(emphasis added, 185).[28]

According to this, the order to hide the treasure did not come from Guatavita but from his master, the devil. The concealment of the gold treasure is thus an action directed against Christ (the same as the concealment of the treasure owned by the shaman). The purposes for the devil's interference in this business are two, according to Freile's suggestion: (1) to gain the souls of the many natives assassinated by Guatavita so they would not tell of the place were the treasure was hidden (those are infidel souls going straight to hell); and (2) to take the gold away from the Spaniards, that is to say, keeping Christians from enjoying it. If keeping the gold from the hands of the Spaniards is a diabolic act, then, its possession by them is a sacred venture, a means for the Spaniards to fight the devil, paganism, and idolatry. This is another argument to justify the Spanish and Euro-American greed and brutality over the Indians, greed and brutality of which Freile himself has been a participant.

Why, then, is the story of the tricked shaman emblematic? Because it corresponds to a propitious and happy actualization, made after the fact, of the desired finding of treasures that for so long frustrated so many Spanish and Euro-American Conquistadors, pioneers—learned and/or religious ones— who sought a quick and easy way to get rich by taking advantage of the Native Americans; and because the admired success of this greedy missionary represents a vain victory of a parasitic society that, while living the paradox of their total economic dependency on the natives, fearing them and demographically decimating them, refuses to recognize the existence of the brutal misery to which it reduces them. These are the reasons for the veiled presence of the Indians in *El carnero,* their persistent marginalization, and the abrupt silence imposed over the theme of injustice against them. When he breaks the silence about the Native Americans, Freile makes an attempt to resolve the paradox and exorcise his guilt. For this he has to declare the human, cultural, and religious integrity of the Indian as contemptible. "He querido decir todo ésto para que se entienda que los indios no hay maldad que no intenten, y matan a los hombres por robarlos . . ." (303).[29]

Both Freile's writing and the majority of its readings from the seventeenth century on are predicated on the notion that the material and cultural plunder to which the Native Americans have been subjected for a whole century has more to do with "natural" and "inevitable" consequences of a Spanish and providentialist project than with the abusive, deplorable, and parasitic dependency of the Spanish and Euro-Americans on them. In the presence of this minimization of the meaning of the indigenous presence in *El carnero,* Freile compromises with the inescapable reality and concedes them a space on the stage of his historical discourse. But it is the case of a stage directed by an Euro-American who laments his meager success in plundering the indigenous people's wealth, attributing it precisely to their lack of collaboration. Freile admits, not without a lot of boldness, to his own attempts to take advantage of the Native's gold. While, again, talking about the sacred Muisca lagoons, he tells of the one in Teusacá:

> . . . yo confieso mi pecado, que entré en esta letanía con codicia de pescar uno de los caimanes [de oro], y sucedióme que habiéndole galanteado muy bien a un jeque, que lo había sido de este santuario, me llevó a él, y así que descubrimos la laguna y que vio el agua cayó de bruces en el suelo y nunca lo pude alzar de él, ni que me hablase más palabra. Allí lo dejé y me volví sin nada y con pérdida de lo gastado, que nunca más lo vi. (37)[30]

The shaman suddenly dies without having delivered the promised gold. The Indian's failure to keep his promise is a reason for Freile not to bother with burying him nor justifying such negligence. The sin confessed is not only his greed for gold but also his anti-Christian behavior with a defunct. For Freile, as is the case with the majority of Spaniards and Euro-Americans of his time, the Indian deserves considerations or *galanteos* [compliments] only when he has wealth to be expropriated.

As a result, their presence in the text cannot go beyond a portrayal in benign stereotypes supporting the social, cultural, and political integrity of the Spanish order, and for the ease of the Christian conscience of the reader. The indigenous peoples are thus present as reprehensible idolaters, as punishable criminals, as inept warriors and politicians, and mainly, as idle holders of riches which they do not need. Such a representation deserves a new critical reading that does not underestimate the meaning of the existence of indigenous peoples in *El carnero*, and much less the constant and uncomfortable admission on the part of the Spanish or Euro-American writer of his fear of this numerous and subjugated population.

Freile, the Euro-American colonizer, wants to write about the lot of the Spanish people in the New World, but these newcomers are surrounded by an American people they greatly depend on, very much despise, and who at the same time constantly alarm them. This kind of environment from which to write about the New World was shared by Freile and many other colonial historians writing about the *Indias Occidentales* since the first settlement was established in the land of *Española*. The colonizing writer has to have the Indians very close at hand and in large numbers to fulfill his dream of seignorial grandeur in the "new lands," but such closeness to them and their riches brings constant fear of their retaliation: hence, Columbus' early and clear way of defining his uncomfortable position as a European (or Euro-American, for that matter) writer in the first century of the Spanish colonization, as expressed in the first epigraph of this essay: ". . . although these Indians have shown themselves to the discoverers, and still do today, as very naïve and without guile, nevertheless, since they come every day to be among us, we thought it was advisable to be on the alert against losing our people or our supplies, since a single Indian with a single torch could do a lot of damage . . ."

NOTES

Special thanks to Josefa Salmón, Julio Schvartzman, and Stacey Schlau for their useful commentaries.

Translation: . . . although these Indians have shown themselves to the discoverers, and still do today, as very naïve and without guile, nevertheless, since they come every day to be among us, we thought it was advisable to be on the alert against losing our people or our supplies, since a single Indian with a single torch could do a lot of damage by setting on fire our grass-roofed huts, because these Indians go back and forth, day and night, and for such reason we have sentinels in the field while our entire population is exposed and defenseless. From "memorial que para los Reyes Católicos dio el Almirante Don Cristóbal" in the city of Isabela on January 30, 1494 (Colón, 149).

I have wanted to say all this so it is understood that the Indians are capable of any evil action and kill men to rob them. In the town of Pasca they killed a man in order to steal his wealth, and after killing him they set fire to the hut in which he used to sleep, and later they simply said that it caught fire by accident. Inquiry on the matter has been made but nothing has been proved; and, in addition, more similar deaths and cases have occurred. I say all this lest you drop your guard with them (Rodríguez Freile 1979, 303). This and the subsequent Spanish quotes of *El carnero* are from Achury Valenzuela's edition. All translations into English from *El carnero* and other Spanish texts are mine. There is an English translation of Rodríguez Freile's work by William Atkinson (1961) but its abridgment limits scholarly use.

1. . . . in three regions (Nuevo Reino, Popayán, and Cartagena) there used to be, around 1560, almost one thousand Indian chiefdoms. Are we not looking at a society whose true nature we have refused to accept? How many chiefdoms had already disappeared by then? With these figures we are compelled to admit that in the occupied territory of what is now Colombia there were, around 1560, at least one and a half million Natives scattered among a thousand chiefdoms.

2. In many respects the sixteenth-century city was not able to function or grow without the Natives' contribution. The functioning of its basic services as well as its own development was dependent on the Natives' labor, including the supply of food and firewood, the carrying of water, the city's maintenance, the construction of churches, buildings, and private houses.

3. During the early 1590s, the number of Indians in the city was considerable.

Between 800 and 1,100 tributary Indians, all with their families, and on some occasions the whole community, came to Santafé de Bogotá every month. In 1620, according to the figures obtained for the month of May, 1,082 Indians came. These figures are significant if we consider that the native population amounted to almost 80 percent of the total population of Santafé in the seventeenth century: ". . . para 1688, Piedrahíta calcula 3,000 españoles y 10,000 indios, la mayoría asentados en las lomas de la ciudad (Pueblo Viejo) y algunos viviendo en el norte (Pueblo Nuevo)" . . . by the year 1688, according to Piedrahíta's calculation, there were 3,000 Spaniards and 10,000 Indians, mostly located on the outskirts of the city (Pueblo Viejo) and some living in the North (Pueblo Nuevo). (Julián Vargas, 1990a, "La mita urbana," in *La Sociedad de Santa Fé Colonial,* 91 (Bogotá: CINEP, centro de Investigación y Educación popular.

4. [Unhappy situations with tragic consequences in which men are involved on account of either their unleashed passions and vices, or their fall into the temptations of the devil, the world, and the flesh.]

5. The reader consulting *El carnero* does so moved by its literary nature more than by a purely historical concern (. . .) Any interest in *El carnero,* I insist, is of a strictly literary nature.

6. With respect to records that start in 1615, we know that the annual quota reached over two thousand tributaries per year. From 1627 on, this figure starts falling drastically. It reaches its lowest level in 1638–39 when only 40 percent of the figure established in 1615 was met (. . .) In general terms, from the beginning of the series, the number of Indians who served as forced labor diminished by 50 percent, that is, about 1,200 tributaries per year. This situation worsened during the second half of the seventeenth century.

7. In the Colombian case there was the occupation of the Episcopal Conference (between July 5 and August 5 of 1996) in Bogotá by indigenous peoples who protested the government indifference to the wave of killings of indigenous peoples on the part of drug-sponsored paramilitary mafias. The reason for this conflict centers on the question of land tenure. "Since April of this year [1996], 10 indigenous leaders from various Indian nations have been assassinated, bringing the total to 200 since 1990" ("Colombia" 1996, 32). But this is only one example among many. Violent neo-liberal policies on the part of the Colombian Government has caused serious problems for the indigenous people lately. The Embera Katio people, in the Department of Córdoba, continues to be threatened by the construction by the Urrá Company of a hydroelectric plant which will alter the flow of waters in the river Sinú from which this community derives their livelihood; a most compelling case is the one of the U'wa people, located in the departments of Boyacá, Santander, and Norte de Santander, whose physical and cultural integrity is threatened by a national government license given to Occidental Petroleum Company to extract oil in the Native's territory. For many more similar cases in the Americas see IWGIA (International Work Group for Indigenous Affairs), *The Indigenious World* 1998–99 (Copenhagen: IWGIA, 1999.

8. . . . the Guatavita also sent, with great pleasure, his emissaries to the Rimiriquí in an effort to take revenge on the Bogotá with whom he had old differences due to Bogotá's penetration into his territory with the pretext of pursuing Panches, Colimas, and other cannibals who were entrenched in forts nearby the Magdalena river; *and even today some of these nations still linger, such as Vaqueríes and Carares who infest the area and assault anyone traveling down the mentioned river, for which reason there is usually a fort on it built by the Royal Council to secure the passage.*

9. . . . they were feasting and drinking all together in a big orgy which lasted all day and all night long, and in which the most sacred Indian was the one who would commit the most incest and fornication acts, *a vice which still lingers among them today.*

10. We have to take into account that they would come with the entire family and probably the entire community. The monthly presence of eight hundred or one thousand could easily be multiplied by four. Santafé did not have the means to house them so the Natives were forced to settle in the city's outskirts.

11. The daily chores in a Spanish and Euro-American household included carrying water, cleaning and maintaining the entire house, cooking in the kitchen (or kitchens), buying and carrying firewood or charcoal for the oven, taking care of animals, working in the vegetable garden, doing the laundry, mending clothing, raising the master's children, doing errands, shopping in stores and markets, carrying supplies, storing produce from *encomiendas* and farms, and running errands between the countryside and the city. In the same fashion, every house in general had an oven to bake bread, pastries, and several other types of cooked foods like ham, for instance.

12. I wanted, as best I could, to inform about the conquest of this New Kingdom, and what happened in it from when its first settlers and first Conquistadors settled it, until the present time of writing.

13. Through these pages have passed, in a confusing throng, scuffles of Indians as well as ghosts of those captains who, at the dawn of a given day, went forth to seek the *Dorado,* or the unreachable world of the Amazons, to never return. Between these lines advance now, slowly, the shadows of presidents, town officials, overseers, archbishops.

14. Around the first years of the seventeenth century there already exists a majority of Indians in the population of Santafé. According to calculations of Father Pacheco, who in turn takes the information from Father Medrano, around 1599 there were twenty thousand Indians living in Santafé, including the ones serving the Spaniards. The exaggeration is evident, but it is indicative of the kind of perception the Spaniards and Euro-Americans had of an actual and extreme increase in the number of Indians in the city.

15. The Muisca Civil Wars took place between 1536 and 1537 more or less; The Pijao offensive according to Freile took place between 1570 and 1577; Borja initiated the war against the Pijao in 1604–5; the story of the shaman tricked and

robbed by the priest thief took place in 1552, according to Fray Pedro Simón, or between 1573 and 1590, according to Freile; the story of the Peruvian Indian who got his ears cut off took place in 1584. The story about Diego de Torres took place around 1581.

16. The New Kingdom of Granada has a great deal of wealth in its veins, precious minerals, huge treasures, which have been, and still are, taken to our Spain, and much more and bigger ones could have been taken had they (the Spaniards and Euro-Americans) been helped, as was appropriate, and especially today, since they lacked most of the native labor needed.

17. Achury Valenzuela offers a different reading: Freile's remarks on the demographic collapse of the Natives are "una tremenda acusación de genocidio, lanzada a la cara de su gente española" [a tremendous accusation delivered right to his Spanish people's face] ("Prólogo" to *El carnero* 1979: lxxxii). This opinion is shared by Moreno Durán: "al denunciar [Freile] la oprobiosa expoliación de los indios en las minas" [when Freile denounces the opprobrious exploitation of the natives in the mines] (31). But such "denunciation," as we shall see, overlooks a connection between this genocide and the vibrant and daily economy of Spaniards and Euro-Americans like Freile himself.

18. For Achury Valenzuela, Freile is a faithful historian who transcribes very well the pre-Columbian cultural reality, as a result he attributes any possible problem with this indigenous history to his native informant: "(la historia) comunicada por ese indio al autor, *quien la reproduce en el libro con una fidelidad de versión taquigráfica,"* [The story communicated by that Indian to the author *who reproduces it in his book with word-for-word fidelity* (1979: lxxxii).

19. They were lustful and had many women and committed many incestuous acts, without sparing daughters or mothers; in conclusion, they were barbarians with no laws or knowledge of God because they only adored the devil whom they regarded as their master.

20. Achury Valenzuela regards it as such, whereas Susan Herman sees it as simple allegory showing how Euro-American characters fall into the devil's temptation.

21. On Sahagún's problems in this regard see Adorno, Rolena "Literary Production and Suppression," *Dispositio* 11, 28–29: 1–25.

22. . . . and these Natives were in this blindness up until the conquest, for which the devil made them worship him, and they served him with many rituals and ceremonies, and one among those ceremonies was to run across the land.

23. It was widely known that these lagoons contained much gold, specially the Guatavita lagoon where there was a great treasure; and based on this knowledge Antonio de Sepúlveda agreed with King Philip II to drain the lagoon, and, in coming through with this agreement, he gave the lagoon its first drainage as can be seen today; and he said that only from the edges of what had been drained more than two thousand *pesos* were taken.

24. I cannot continue without first telling the story of how a priest tricked the devil, or his medicine man in his place, and got from him three or four thousand *pesos* which

he had made as offerings to the devil in a shrine which was located on the farm of the old chief of Ubaque; and this took place in my time.

25. The connection between the *Decameron* and *El carnero* had been made before by Jean Franco and Roberto González Echevarría, among others. González Echevarría in particular says: "Indeed, I suspect this kind of manual [*Decameron*] may be the model used by Rodríguez Freyle in planning *El carnero*, which contains precisely such an array of cases" (1990: 67). The problem with this assertion lies in its premise that the "array of cases" of *Decameron* are of the same kind as those in *El carnero*, the fictional narrative kind predominantly relating to urban, European (or Euro-American) impudent acts. González Echevarría's purpose with this limiting connection is to link *El carnero* to a seventeenth-century Spanish literary genre known also to deal with trickery and effrontery of mainly urban characters: the picaresque. That is not the premise of the present essay.

26. Darío Achury Valenzuela calls it an "actualización fantástica" [a coming into fiction] and Enrique Pupo-Walker a "ficción que resume y ordena imaginativamente el espacio historiable" [A fiction which imaginatively summarizes and gives order to a space susceptible of historical writing] (1982: 154).

27. They told Guatavita how the Spaniards (. . .) were very fond of gold, which they were looking for in every town, and how they would dig it up from every place they would spot it; for which Guatavita ordered to hide his treasure away.

28. It seems that this was the devil's advice so he could *take the gold away from us;* and although some people have spent time and money looking for it, they have not been able to find it (emphasis added, 185).

29. I have wanted to say all this so it is understood the Indians are capable of any evil doing and kill men to rob them (. . .).

30. . . . I confess my sin, that I entered in this parade with the desire to secure one of the alligators (made of gold), and it happened that, after paying many compliments to someone who used to be a shaman in that shrine of that lagoon, he took me to it, and once we reached the lagoon and he saw the water, he just fell on his face, and I was never able to pick him up nor get another word from him. I left him there and came back empty-handed and with the loss of my investment which I never saw again.

BIBLIOGRAPHY

Adorno, Rolena. 1986. "Literary Production and Suppression: Reading and Writing about Amerindians in Colonial Spanish America." *Dispositio* 11, 28–29: 1–25.

Achury Valenzuela, Darío. 1979. "Prólogo." *El carnero* by Juan Rodríguez Freile, ix–lxxxvii Caracas: Biblioteca Ayacucho.

Aprile-Gniset, Jacques. 1997. *La ciudad colombiana.* Cali: Editorial Universidad del Valle.

Camacho Guizado, Eduardo. 1982. "Juan Rodríguez Freile." In *Historia de la literatura hispanoamericana. Epoca colonial.* Coordinated by Luis Iñigo Madrigal, 145–150. Madrid: Ediciones Cátedra.

Clifford, James. 1986. "On Ethnographic Allegory." In *Writing Culture. The Poetics and Politics of Ethnography.* Edited by James Clifford, and George Marcus, 98–121. Berkeley: University of California Press.

Colón, Cristóbal. 1984. *Textos y documentos completos, relaciones de viajes, cartas y memoriales.* Edited by Consuelo Varela. Madrid: Alianza Editorial.

González Echevarría, Roberto. 1990. *Myth and Archive. A Theory of Latin American Narrative.* Cambridge: Cambridge University Press.

"Colombia: Indigenous Peoples Mobilize to End Violence, Land Invasions." 1996. *Abya Yala News* 10, 2: 32–33. Journal of the South and Meso-American Indian Rights Center.

Franco, Jean. 1975. "Introducción: la imaginación colonizada." In *Historia de la literatura hispanoamericana,* 15–36. Barcelona: Editorial Ariel.

IWGIA (International Work Group for Indigenous Affairs). 1999. *The Indigenous World 1998–99.* Copenhagen: IWGIA.

Herman, Susan. 1993. "Conquest and Discovery: Subversion of the Fall in *El carnero*." *Modern Language Notes* 108: 283–301.

López de Velasco, Juan. [1574] 1894. *Geografía y descripción universal de las Indias.* Vol. 15, 177: 637–639. Madrid: Bibioteca de Autores Españoles.

Mignolo, Walter. 1989. "Colonial Situations, Geographical Discourses and Territorial Representations: Toward a Diatopical Understanding of Colonial Semiosis." *Dispositio.* 14: 36–38.

Moreno Durán, Rafael H. 1994. "Introducción." In *El carnero. Conquista y descubrimiento de el Nuevo Reino de Granada,* 15–67. Madrid: Testimonio Compañía Editorial. El navegante editores.

Pupo-Walker, Enrique. 1982. *La vocación literaria del pensamiento histórico en América: desarollo de la prosa de ficción, siglos XVI, XVII, XVIII y XIX.* Madrid: Gredos.

Rabasa, José.1994. "Pre-Columbian Pasts and Indian Presents in Mexican History." *Dispositio/n* 19, 46: 245–270.

Rodríguez Freile, Juan. 1979. *El carnero.* Edited by Darío Achury Valenzuela. Caracas: Biblioteca Ayacucho.

———. 1961. *The Conquest of New Granada.* Translated by William Atkinson. London: Folio Society.

Tovar Pinzón, Hermes. 1988. "Introducción." In *No hay caciques ni señores,* 11–19. Barcelona: Sendai Ediciones.

Vargas Lesmes, Julián. 1990a. "La mita urbana. Trabajos y oficios en Santafé." In *La sociedad de Santa Fé colonial,* 85–118. Bogotá: CINEP, Centro de Investigación y Educación Popular.

————. 1990. "Economía doméstica y vida cotidiana. Santafé a comienzos del siglo XVII. El caso de la familia Estrada-Arias." In *La sociedad de Santa Fé colonial*, 119–211. Bogotá: CINEP, Centro de Investigación y Educación Popular.

Vargas Lesmes, Julián y Marta Zambrano. 1990. "La población indígena de Santafé." In *La sociedad de Santa Fé colonial*, 47–84. Bogotá: CINEP, Centro de Investigación y Educación Popular.

The Literary Appropriation of the American Landscape

The Historical Novels of Abel Posse and Juan José Saer and Their Critics

Gustavo Verdesio

Latin American historical novels produced from the 1970s on purport to be, undoubtedly, a rewriting of history.[1] Their purpose is, then, somehow revision-ist. Yet, another thing they (especially those that focus on colonial times) do is to present a view of the Latin American territory. This is so because, having chosen historical personages—that were part of the "Discovery" and "Conquest" of the New World—as the protagonists of their stories, the authors face the challenge of giving a new version of the first images of the Americas produced by those early European observers.

I believe the different perspectives and viewpoints of these turn of the century authors call for an analysis that allow us to see whether their views on the Colonial Encounter are a novelty or not. It would also be interesting to see how they relate to the legacy of the Conquistadors' views. The study of the novels *Los perros del Paraíso*, *Daimón* and *El largo atardecer del caminante*, by the Argentinean writer Abel Posse, could serve as a sampler of some of the different views held by Latin American writers of our time. A brief comparison with *El entenado*, by another Argentinean, Juan José Saer, will help us to provide a more complete picture of the range of the aforementioned views.

The first of the above-mentioned novels proposes a revision of the exploration and commercial enterprise led by Christophoro Columbus. Posse chooses to present such endeavors in a way that dramatically differs from the previous Latin American fictionalizations of the "Discovery" (notably that of Carpentier's): he presents us with a mystical Columbus, whose plan was to sail to the unknown in order to find the Garden of Eden. From the outset, the text informs the reader that Columbus, at a very early age—prompted by the persuasive preaching of a certain friar—embraced the belief that that place actually existed (1994, 26). Throughout the narration, the topic develops until the crucial event, the "Discovery," takes place; from that moment on, a tremendous struggle begins between Columbus and the rest of the crew.

The main idea behind the novel is that European civilization was (and probably still is) based on a profound belief in "doing," whereas the American lands were the place where mere "being" predominated.[2] In this light, the arrival of the European expedition in the Caribbean is "a profound offensive against Nature on behalf of "doing" and against the mere "being" (127).[3] Having arrived to this point, it is necessary to remember that these ideas about "doing" and "being" are not Posse's creation: he takes them from the Argentinean philosopher Rodolfo Kusch, who coined them in some of his books (see 1976 and, especially, 1977).[4] According to this author, the American world view differs from the European one in that the latter is much more obsessed with "doing," with activity, with the world of objects (1976, 21, 28), whereas the former dispenses with that kind of external stimuli in order to concentrate on more spiritual, inner matters. Although this brief overview of Kusch's ideas is, no doubt, a simplification, it is fair to say that it pales as such in comparison to the degradation to which Posse subjects them.

In the novel under study, as we have already seen, Columbus' search is presented as an attempt to accomplish a rare deed: the return to Paradise (109). At this point, it seems opportune to point out that the views attributed to Columbus seem to be (at least partially) shared by the authorial voice that relishes portraying the American lands as follows:

> Aire dulcísimo, sol alto, mar fresco y salino. Sus olas corren suaves, se escurren y quiébranse en una playa de arena blanquidorada. De una palmera cayó un coco que se abrió, invitante, con su leche sabrosa que conserva la temperatura del rocío, como es sabido. En lo alto, un mico juguetón hace dos piruetas, saluda y desaparece en la fresca espesura. (1994, 200)

> [Extremely sweet air, high sun, cool and saline sea. Its waves run softly, they slip away and break at the shores of a goldenwhite sand beach. A coconut fell from a palm tree and opened in an inviting way with its flavory milk kept at dew's temperature, as everybody knows. Up there, at the top of the tree, a playful monkey performs a couple of stunts, salutes the public, and disappears in the cool thicket.]

Against the background of that landscape, the Admiral moves completely naked, in full contact with Nature. This description of edenic nature is uttered by the narrator. It may not be an adventurous assumption to attribute to the authorial voice an attitude similar to Columbus': the former, also, seems to aver the paradisiac nature of the new lands.

This exoticism, this Europeanized representation of the American lands is somehow related to the theories of Magical Realism, of which García Márquez's Nobel Prize acceptance speech is a good example. In that speech, the Colombian narrator stated that he envisioned his role as a writer as similar to the one played by the chroniclers like Pigafetta (who wrote a diary of Magellan's circumnavegation voyage): to account for the wonder inherent in American Nature. This statement begs, at least, for a question: since when does the native of any land marvel at the natural landscape that sourrounds him/her since his/her birth? What I am trying to say is that, in spite of García Márquez's opinion, it is very difficult to imagine somebody admiring a physical environment that, after all, is the only one she/he knows. The wonder and the surprise that the novelty of the American landscape caused among the first European explorers does not seem likely to be felt by a native observer.

Nevertheless, Posse's novel seems to subscribe to García Márquez's ideas when he deals with the topic of the exceptional nature of the landscape "discovered" by Columbus. Moreover, he focuses on another referent that helps this very European way of viewing the New World come full circle: I am referring to his representation of the Amerindian as a noble savage. Throughout the text, Amerindians are presented either as angels or as primitive beings:

> Formas admirables, pelos lacios, piel tostada. Muertos porque caídos de la templanza paradisíaca—seguramente por alguna travesura amatoria—en la neblina pegajosa donde merodean los pálidos irlandeses. El almirante se apersonóa la playa y pudo admirar aquellos cuerpos desnudos rodeados de perros vagabundos y curas pecosos que les arrojaban agua bendita. Inmediatamente comprendió: no eran ángeles. Eran seres primigenios, no degradados por la falta original. (1994, 131)

> [Admirable forms, straight hair, tanned skin. Dead because they fell from the Paradisiac temperance—because of a love related mischief—in the sticky fog where the pale Irish lurk. The Admiral approached the beach and was able to admire those beautiful naked bodies surrounded by stray dogs and freckled priests throwing holy water to them. He immediately understood: they were not angels. They were primitive beings, free from the degradation that comes from original sin.]

In this fashion, the text adds a primitive, almost angelic dweller to the exotic and paradisiac nature where "being" rules; a dweller whose purity is soon going not only to be corrupted by European civilization, but also contaminated by progress: "Los ángeles, azotados, enflaquecidos, repartidos en encomiendas. Raleados por los suicidios o desaparecidos en lo hondo de las minas. Víctimas del progreso. Definitivamente cortados del alma del mundo donde habían crecido hermanados con los pumas y las papayas" [The angels, whipped, thinned, distributed to the *encomiendas*. Their numbers thinned by suicide or by their falling at the bottom of the mines. Victims of progress. Definitively severed from the soul of that world where they had grown up in harmony with pumas and papayas] (1994, 251).

Posse's views about the American lands and its dwellers are complemented by the reiteration of a number of old myths that only reinforce the European representation of the continent. For example, the novel echoes Columbus' narrative as regards the existence of cannibals in the Caribbean, thus perpetuating the dichotomy the Admiral established in his Diaries: on the one hand, the tame and complacent *Tainos*, on the other, the scary cannibals or Caribs, village plunderers and human flesh eaters: "la excesiva pasión religiosa . . . de los caníbales caribes: creían, teófagos, que se puede comer al dios, su belleza, su coraje. Comiendo a los bellos taínos pensaban que perderían la fealdad y ferocidad características de su raza" [The excessive religious passion . . . of the cannibalistic Caribs: they believed—theophagi—that it was possible to eat god, its beauty, its courage. They thought that by eating the beautiful *Tainos* they would loose the ugliness and ferocity characteristic of their race] (1994, 82); "En cuanto a los caníbales que castran, engordan y devoran a los taínos, que son la belleza, aspiran a reencarnarse con sus formas perfectas y atractivas. Prefieren los testículos, es verdad, y los asan y los comen como manjar, porque presienten en ellos el origen de la simiente de perfección" [As regards the cannibals that castrate, fatten and devour the *Tainos*, who are beauty itself, they aspire to reincarnate with the victims' perfect and attractive shapes. They prefer the testicles, it is true, and they barbecue and eat them as a treat because they suspect they are the origin of the seed of perfection] (1994, 186).

As we can see, Posse does not seem to be content with reproducing the dichotomy between good *tainos* and bad Caribs created by Columbus: he also dares to contribute an apocryphal explanation for the latter's cannibalism. In spite of his pseudoethnographic effort, we can assert, as Peter Hulme has already suggested, that it is not clear whether these cannibals have ever existed outside Columbus' imagination: neither the Admiral nor the other members of the expedition ever saw them. In sum, there is no ethnographic proof whatsoever regarding the existence of the Caribs as either a cannibalistic breed or as an Arawak group different from the *Tainos* (Hulme 1986, 45, and passim).

There is still another myth that the novel reinforces: the stereotypical representation of the tropics. The description of the feasts of the Natives, the *areitos*, is a pretext that allows Posse to postulate an anachronistic view of the culture of the tropics: in his portrait, the region shows a strong presence of African culture and an abundance of drums; the Amerindians swing at the beat of present-day musical rhythms that are the trademark of the music from that geographical area (83). The picture gets completed by the description of a Native princess that the narrator conceives as a "protomulata," due to the way in which she dances to the drum beat[5]: "Anacaona, de maravilla. Piel canela y cobriza. Giraba con las piernas abiertas siguiendo el *areito*. Por momentos el son se aceleraba, cumbanchero, y ella movía las grupas con una rapidez que no le costaba gracia. Una verdadera protomulata de fuego" (1994, 205). [Anacaona: wonderful. Cinnamon and copper skin. She spun around with her legs open, following the *areito*. At times the *son* speeded up, *cumbanchero*, and she moved her rump with a speed that did not detract from her grace] (1994, 205). Among the many problems that can be found in this passage, the sexist representation of the American woman as an object of desire deserves mention. In relation to this topic, I would like to point out that it also perpetuates the myth (created by Columbus himself) that represents indigenous women as immodest and lecherous beings.[6] Yet, there are still other problems I am particularly concerned with: for instance, the procedure that consists in the extrapolation of our present back to the times of the Colonial Encounter (that attributes the image of a mulatto Latin American present to a past in which, in actuality, the African cultural influence simply did not exist), that instead of having a demystifying effect seems to reinforce many Western stereotypes about the region—seen as a good time, cheerfully silly resort populated by lustful *mulattas* and lazy men. The outcome of the use of this creative device is a confusing, mystifying, ahistorical and ethnocentric representation of alterity. In Posse's hands the freedom of the artist, the use of poetic license, seem to be only able to produce a historically irresponsible discourse.

Posse indulges still in another poetic manipulation of fact (and he may even think it is a funny one) when he postulates a communication between the Inca and Aztec Empires prior to the arrival of the Spaniards, which is in fact impossible to support through the evidence available to us, so far. At the beginning of the novel we are presented with an encounter between the leaders of both Amerindian states in Tenochtitlán. In that occasion, the indigenous leaders discuss the possibility of an invasion of European lands by the joint forces of the Incas and Aztecs (31–35). In the pages that refer to the fictional summit it is possible to find all kinds of nonsense, for example, the description of the Inca Empire as a socialist regime—another popular myth—(58) or the assertion of the existence of balloon exploration among the Incas, one of which would have landed in the city of Dusseldorf (!). At this point, given the fact that it is obvious that Posse knows he is simply inventing things, one may ask oneself what kind of purpose this distortion of history may have. Although this is a question that only Posse can answer, there is still something that one can state: that kind of distortion contributes to the continued reproduction of a mystifying representation of the Amerindians and their past. Following this line of thought, it can also be said that if these fictions are a re-writing of history, it is not a revisionist one as regards the mystification of indigenous subjects and cultures.

Anoher objectionable moment in the narration is the one that describes Columbus as the first *mestizo*, because rational consciousness had abandoned him (243).[7] Undoubtedly, this presupposes the following assumption: (1) the inhabitants of the New World and their descendants were not capable of rational consciousness; and (2) by lacking that human trait they were, somehow, beings essentially different from the European Conquistadors. In this case, different may even mean inferior. Yet, even without interpreting the novel in this way, it is possible to see the definition of *mestizo* as an attempt to deprive the Amerindian (and the *mestizo*, of course) of one of the most inherently human faculties: reason.

Last but not least, another myth this novel reiterates is that the Indians believed in the divine nature of the Spaniards (204). As is well known, Columbus was the creator of that myth, stating in his *Diary* that the Amerindians thought the Spaniards came from heaven—actually, the Spanish word he uses is *cielo*, which means both "sky" and "heaven" (33). Posse, by repeating this scene (that has very little factual and ethnohistorical grounding), manages to become an accomplice of the Admiral.

In *Daimón* (1991), a novel written a few years earlier than *Los perros del paraíso*, we can already find some of the characteristics we found in the latter. The historical character Lope de Aguirre comes back to life and decides to continue his American pilgrimage with the intention of succesfully accomplishing his failed rebellion. This literary device allows Posse to make Lope travel through different geographical locations as well as through several historical moments. In this postmortem spiritual voyage Aguirre, little by little, manages to liberate himself of a series of ideological constraints that come from his European upbringing—a liberation that contributes to present the story of Aguirre's pilgrimage as a search for the roots of American identity.

According to Fernando Reati, one of the things in the novel that distinguish American identity from its European counterpart is the former's conception of sexuality: "al hacer confluir en el Diablo a los dioses del amor y la guerra, o Eros y Thanatos, la narración sugiere que el cristianismo niega el cuerpo humano al exorcisar al demonio, a diferencia de otras cosmogonías que aceptan el principio del placer sexual" [The narration suggests, by making the Devil encompass the gods of love and war, or Eros and Thanatos, that when Christianity exorcises the demon, it denies (at the same time) the human body, while other cosmogonies accept the sexual pleasure principle] (1995a, 96). The way in which not only the Amerindians, but also other living beings (that may represent American Nature in general) understand and practice sex is exemplified in the novel by two copulating *tatúes* (armadillos), who perform: "con la brevedad y la simpleza de un deseo sin perversidad" [with the brevity and simplicity of a desire that lacks any perverseness] (*Daimón*, 1991, 38). Europeans, instead, practice sex with a violence that does not lead to satisfaction—an attitude, that is, as Reati points out (1995a, 96), clearly illustrated by the scene where Aguirre rapes Ursua's companion, Doña Inés (*Daimón,* 41). In this way, Posse gives currency and afterlife to certain mythical ways of representing both the American and the European worlds: the former is presented as informed by a vitalism very much in touch with Nature, whereas the latter takes the shape of a rationalism that operates as America's opposite. The consequence of his attitude, as we saw during the analysis of *Los perros del paraíso,* is the representation of Americanness (and the *mestizo* subject, symbolized by that fictional Columbus abandoned to sloth amongst the delights of the paradisiac nature of the tropics) as totally deprived of any rationality.

According to the novel, there is still another issue about which the American and the European worlds differ: how to achieve happiness. The idea that happiness cannot be found in the outside world, as European culture has it, is one of the themes of the novel about Aguirre. These are, in actuality, echoes of Rodolfo Kusch's ideas, which inform Posse's narrative project and determine, to some extent, the plot—which is presented, as we have already seen, as a pilgrimage, a learning process, a process of conversion from one cosmogony to another.

When Aguirre leaves the rainforest through which he wandered for one hundred and fifty years, he heads toward the Spanish imperial cities in order to give his last battle. The surprise of the pilgrim is tremendous when he finds an unrecognizable America: totally Europeanized and dominated by a mercantilist spirit. The way Aguirre assesses the situation he has to confront can be illustrated by the following dialogue: "Diego Tirado, capitán de a caballo (cuando lo tuvo) observó: 'Se adueñaron de los bordes y de los mares . . . ' Y Lope: 'Dices bien. Tienen los bordes pero yo tengo el corazón. Ellos aun no han tocado América.' " [Diego Tirado, Cavalry Captain (when he had a horse) observed: 'They took possession of the margins and the seas . . . ' And Lope: 'You are right. They have the margins but I have the heart. They have not even touched America yet' "] (*Daimón* 1991, 98). Later in the narration, the pilgrim decides to return to his old group of *marañones* (as he used to call his soldiers) who are as resucitated and as anachronistic as he is. He undertakes his return to the heart of America (to those territories that civilized Europe calls "barbaric," because of their location outside the lettered city) accompanied by a wise man of Quechua descent, the Indio Huamán, who from this moment on will play the role of a spiritual guide for Aguirre. Reati avers that this return, provoked by Aguirre's rejection of mercantilism and Western reason, reveals that the pilgrim, by choosing Huamán as his companion "no sólo opta por el pueblo americano en su lucha contra el sistema mercantilista, sino además por el pensamiento nativo contra el racionalismo europeo" [not only opts for the

American people in this fight against mercantilism but also for indigenous ways of thinking that oppose European rationalism] (1995a, 99).

Later in the novel, while Aguirre descends from Machu Picchu to the coast "comprende que no basta la transformación exterior de la sociedad sin un cambio interior profundo" and "en un gesto que simboliza su nuevo aprendizaje, al final del capítulo abandona una tertulia de criollos por la puerta de la servidumbre, cambia sus botas por ojotas de indio, y retorna a Machu Pichu (*sic*) para recibir su última y más profunda lección" [He understands that to transform the exterior of the city is not enough; that what is required is an inner, profound change and in a gesture that symbolizes his new learning process, by the end of the chapter he abandons a *criollo* social gathering through the servants' door, he changes his boots for Indian sandals—*ojotas*—and returns to Machu Picchu with the purpose of receiving his last and most profound lesson] (Reati 1995a, 101).

The picture of Aguirre offered by Reati (a Latin-Americanized one, immersed in a non-European way of thinking) is inspired by the structure of the novel, that organizes its structure under the semantic aegis of the Tarot (each chapter's title is the name of a Tarot card). Reati reads the novel, then, as Posse's attempt to appeal to ways of thought, to cosmogonies that do not have European Reason as their foundation. This critic's article states that the use of the semantic world of the Tarot as an organizational principle shows that Posse's project consists in recovering cosmogonies of non-European origin. In other words, Reati believes that by using the Tarot's mystic world and by vindicating Huamán's spiritual wisdom (an emblem of indigenous thought), Posse is trying to call attention to, and recover, non-Western world views.

I think Reati's assertion is arguable and needs to be discussed. Let us begin by acknowledging that the text is, indeed, organized by a succession of the different Tarot cards that open each and every chapter. Having said that, it is important to distinguish between non- or antirational discourses (like the Tarot) and non-Western ones. I have no problem to concede the Tarot may qualify among the nonrational discourses or world views, but I have trouble accepting that it constitutes a non-Western way of thinking. Besides, Posse's alleged solidarity with indigenous cosmogonies does not show consistently throughout the novel, as Reati himself seems to acknowledge when he says that the text presents the notion of "sudamericanidad" as something that is outside the field of "doing;" that is, as something that lies outside human history and develops in the "mythical eternity of 'being' " [*la eternidad mítica del 'ser'*] (1995a, 102).[8] Reati is here, perhaps unwittingly, acknowledging the ahistorical nature of the notion of "sudamericanidad" proposed by the novel. That is to say, he is accepting that history, understood as the course of human events in time, is something totally alien (in the text) to American cosmogonies. These views about Latin American thought are dangerous in that they relate to some Hegelian ideas about the continent, which, in the view of the German philosopher, Georg Wilhelm Hegel, lacked any history whatsoever and, therefore, was in a realm outside the world of the Spirit (or the world of Being, in the sense that Enrique Dussel gives to the term).[9] America has a history only because Europe has come to give it to her, and only in this fashion does her development in time acquire meaning. Posse seems to propose that Americans should renounce their right to make history. As an alternative to "doing" (i.e.: making history), he is more prone to recommend a return to a Garden of Eden (like the one discovered by Columbus in *Los perros del paraíso*) that consists in refraining from any action, in order to allow for an immersion in a contemplative and tropical torpor. We are here, again, before a trivialization of Kusch's ideas about the identity of Amerindian thought.

Besides, it should be taken into account that Kusch's ideas, even in their original form, have some problems, too. For example, he talks in his books about American or indigenous thought in general, as though all the ethnic groups that inhabited the continent had the same world view (this critique can be found in: Verdesio, 2000). Although his investigation was limited to a few ethnic groups of Andean origin, he felt he could extend his findings about their thought and world view to (and make broad generalizations about) the rest of the Amerindians of the continent. This careless, indiscriminate attribution of cosmogonies is something Posse inherits and repeats without even bothering to question his source of inspiration: for him, as for Kusch, there is such a thing as an American, indigenous (regardless of ethnic differences) thought. The major difference between these authors, though, is that Kusch clearly considers the Amerindians as the true representatives of Americanness, whereas Posse's novels seem to define the latter in a rather inconsistent way: sometimes the indigenous roots are a part of Americannes, but sometimes they are not. He forgets, above all, the emblematic character of the indigenous element when his novels appeal (very frequently) to *criollo* icons as the ultimate representatives of Americanness: the weight he gives to some historical figures like Juan Domingo Perón, Che Guevara, and many others, as well as the historical events in which they were key players, seems to suggest they are the ones who truly represent the identity of the region. The reader should take into account that none of the historical situations in which Aguirre gets involved in his pilgrimage have Amerindians as protagonists.

Latin American history, then, appears represented in *Daimón* as a history viewed from the vantage point of the present of contemporary independent Nations where the role of the Amerindians is a very sad one: it consists in legitimizing the situation of enunciation of the *criollo* subject that emits his/her discourse from a modern Nation-state built by *criollo* elites. Although Reati claims that Posse's version of history is as cyclical as some of the indigenous conceptions of time (1995a, 104)—notably the Inca and Mexica ones—it is my impression that the eternal return of Aguirre seems closer to Western philosophical or anthropological elaborations (such as Nietzsche's, an author that Posse admires, and Mircea Eliade's) than to the Andean Pachacutis or to the Meso-American succession of Katunes. Viewed from this angle, the opposition to Cartesian Reason Reati sees in Posse's novels seems to be less a form of vindication of Amerindian cosmogonies than a preference for irrational Western philosophies. Otherwise, the Amerindians (and their cultures) would have a much less degrading representation in *Los perros* and *Daimón*, where they appear as mere symbols of a certain irrationalism—a reified vitalism only perceivable from the perspective of a European observer that yearns, nostalgically, for a return to previous stages of the Western civilizational process.

In this respect, Posse's attitude is related to Juan Jose Saer's in *El entenado*. In this novel, the author narrates the story of a cabin boy who is forced to live among some unidentified Amerindians of the River Plate region.[10] The novel appears to the reader as an attempt to reconstruct a historical episode about which very little is known due to the absence of firsthand documentation: the "discovery" of the River Plate.[11] More specifically, the event recreated is the landing of Juan Díaz de Solís and some of his men (seven, ten, or forty, according to the different documentary sources) on the northern shores of the River Plate, somewhere in the territory of what today is Uruguay. After the killing of the rest of his companions, the only survivor (the cabin boy) is forced to adapt to a way of life among the Amerindians that bears no resemblance at all to the one he was used to in his native Spain. The Amerindians (the Colastiné) have a useful role reserved for the youngster: they will make him a witness of their culture (and *The Witness* is, indeed, the title of the novel in its English version).

Although Saer makes a great effort to invent a Colastiné world view, the result (like in the novels by Posse) is the reaffirmation of some Western stereotypes about Amerindian cultures. He is not very interested in giving exact data about the territory where the action takes place, nor is he interested in describing the physiognomic traits of the aborigines, or their clothing, and so forth, as Rita Gnutzman points out (1994, 634). Therefore, the novel does not offer a reproduction of an indigenous landscape but reveals, instead, a total lack of interest in historical and ethnographic verisimilitude (Gnutzman 1994, 635). One of the consequences of this attitude is an acritical acceptance of the official version of the history of the "discovery" of the River Plate, that affirms the cannibalism of the Amerindians who ambushed Solís and his crew. When I studied the series of texts that built, throughout the years, the aforementioned official history of the first colonial encounter in the River Plate (which presents it as cannibalistic feast), I reached the conclusion that the portrait of the Indians who attacked Solís (whose ethnic identity is still unknown and it may remain so unless new documents are uncovered) produced by the official narrative is not based on any serious and rigorous ethnohistoric investigation (Verdesio 1996, 63–78). Saer, far from proposing an alternative story, contents himself with reproducing the accepted (but not proved) version that attributes cannibalistic habits to the indigenous group that the ill-fated Solís encountered.

This acceptance of the most popular tradition, together with the most absolute contempt for ethnohistoric reconstruction, are the preconditions that allow him to depict the Colastiné culture in a way that presents them as deficient and fragile in some fundamental respects. For example, by proposing that the memory of this imaginary culture is only able to survive thanks to the written narrative of a European subject, he is indirectly endorsing the superiority of certain European forms of preservation and communication of knowledge: the alphabet, historiography and even ethnography seem to be the only means capable to perform the rescue of that aboriginal culture (whose semiotic and intellectual competences are inferior to the narrator's) from the most ignominious oblivion. Amaryll Chanady sees in this presentation of the relationship between Indians and Europeans a reproduction of Tzvetan Todorov's ideas as developed in *The Conquest of America*, where he proposes the hypothesis that the victory of Western culture was due to its superiority in the art of mastering signs and messages (Chanady 1992, 685). That superiority, of course, was based on the existence of alphabetic writing and in the training and practice of interpretive techniques applied to semiotic systems.

In the novel, then, the Colastiné world (where the verb "to be" does not exist, where objects exist only if they are perceived by human beings of an alien culture, and where reality can be apprehended only through a brutal cannibalistic ritual) lacks the minimum consistence needed for the perduration of its memory. It is the discourse of the European Other that operates, in turn, as a discourse *on* the indigenous Other, that makes the preservation of Colastiné culture's memory possible. It is from this Western perspective, from a register that resembles ethnography's (which has hitherto been the register preferred by the West when it had the need to speak about—when it had to invent—the Other), that *El entenado* presents indigenous history. At first glance, as we saw in the case of *Daimón*, a perspective that seems to be alien to European culture reveals itself, in the end, as a subtle turn of the screw that allows the European subject of discourse to continue the propagation of myths such as the superiority of his/her culture over the rest; a superiority that is based, at a gnoseological level, on the superiority of Western forms of storage and communication of knowledge. As Chanady indicates, the Other is presented in Saer's novel as a more primitive part of the Western self, as a being that lives in a previous stage of civilization and intellectual development (1992, 697–97). In sum, what Chanady sees in the text is a repetition of what Johannes Fabian has termed the *denial of coevalness:* the assignation to the Other, by the European observer, of a moment in time that can only be conceived as a past moment in the history of the development of Western culture. The geographic, physical distance between the Other and the European subject is transformed into a distance in time, allocating the former to a more backwards moment in the evolution of the human species—of which European culture is the privileged historical agent. It is in this way that, according to de Certeau (1986, 68), historiographical and/or ethnographic texts make room for the creation of their own situation of enunciation. We are talking about a conception of universal history and the evolution of the human species—understood as a teleological narrative that inexorably leads to world progress through European leadership—that leaves the Amerindians outside the narrative it creates. In Saer's novel, as Chanady avers, Europeans represent—again—development and progress, whereas the aborigines—with their reiterative rituals, with their repetition of the same—are the incarnation of stasis, of what does not advance (1992, 703).

In all fairness, it should be pointed out that there is a moment in the novel where a Europeanized world view of the American territory is questioned, as Arcadio Díaz Quiñones rightly points out: the passage where the narrator presents the European explorers expecting to encounter a territory that takes the shape of a blank page where they could freely make their inscriptions (1992, 12). Much to their surprise, the voyagers did not find an empty land but a territory inhabited by complex, unintelligible by Western standards, human beings.

In El largo atardecer del caminante (1996), by Abel Posse, also, a somewhat less European perspective seems to be at play. In this novel, the main character (Cabeza de Vaca) is presented as a kind of cultural mestizo but for reasons very different from the ones that defined the mestizo character of Columbus in Los Perros del paraíso: his pilgrimage through American lands, his knowledge of the territory, his interaction with its inhabitants, seem to have transformed him into a cultural subject essentially different from his fellow Spanish Conquistadors. In other words, all those experiences seem to have made him an Other to European culture.

With the help of the Amerindians, he learns to communicate with Nature, to interpret the Earth. This is clear in the episode where he goes through a rite of passage and praises a certain kind of baqueanos: those knowers of the land, those holders of chorographic knowledge—as opposed the geographic one (1996, 130). In order to explain the distinction between these two ways of conceiving the knowledge of the land (one of European origin—geography—the other, generally associated with Amerindian groups—although any other group with a close contact with its own territory can have this kind of knowledge), let us resort to the words of the Renaissance cosmographer Alonso de Santa Cruz:

> Geografía es una demostración o figura de toda la Tierra conocida con las partes más principales que de ella depende; y difiere de la corografía porque ésta, describiendo todos los lugares particular-

mente, manifiesta cada uno por sí y lo que en ellos se contiene, descri-
biendo hasta las más pequeñas partes que en ellos se hallan, como son
puertos, aldeas, vueltas de ríos y cosas de esta cualidad; . . . el fin de la
corografía consiste en representar sucesivamente una parte del todo,
como queriendo pintar o remedar un ojo o una oreja, pero la geografía
tiene atención al todo conforme a su proporción, como si quisiese
pintar toda la cabeza. (1983, 203)

[Geography is a demonstration or picture of the known Earth with
the most important parts it has; and it differs from chorography because the latter, describing all the sites in particular, manifests each
one of them and what they contain, describing even the smallest parts
that can be found in them, such as ports, villages, rivers and the
like; . . . the end of chorography consists in representing, successively,
parts of the whole, like when you paint an eye or an ear, but geography
pays attention to the whole, as if it wished to paint the whole head.]

This knowledge of the particulars of a certain terrain, this chorographic
wisdom, is not the only peculiarity that presents Cabeza de Vaca as different
from his connationals. For instance, his acknowledgement that America was
not a New World but an entirely different, Other World (1983, 72, 83); his
gratefulness to the Indians for having helped him to survive, for being "better
animals of the earth" (*mejores animales de la tierra*, 74) than him, make it difficult for the protagonist to have a Western view as strong as the one presented
by the characters of the other novels we have seen (*Los Perros del paraíso*,
Daimón, El entenado). In *El largo atardecer del caminante*, Posse attributes even
some ecological concerns to the Amerindians—concerns we do not know
whether the actual inhabitants of that region really had—; they are presented
as people who believed that human beings did not need to exert their domin-
ion over Nature (1996, 89). In other words, the text presents a European subject (Cabeza de Vaca) who seems more willing to interact with an alien nature
than most of his compatriots. However, in spite of the novel's less mystifying,
less ethnocentric tendency, Posse lets a couple of Western myths slip into the
narrative; myths that we have already seen at work in the other novels analyzed
here. I am referring, for instance, to the myths about the indigenous belief on
the divine nature of the Spaniards (77, 131) and the one that presents the corruption of the Garden of Eden at the hands of the Spanish Conquistadors and
Western civilization: "En cierto sentido se puede decir que estábamos
cruzando el paraíso Primordial. La serpiente corruptora no era otra que esa
larga hilera de soldados acorazados, maldiciendo su suerte mientras luchaban
contra ramas de espino y miles de mosquitos y tábanos" [In a certain sense it
can be said that we were crossing the Primordial paradise. The corrupting ser-
pent was no other than the long line of armoured soldiers cursing their luck

while they struggled with hawthorn branches and with thousands of mosqui-toes and horseflies] (1996, 224).

The myth that states that the Amerindians believed the Spaniards were gods has its correlate in the image of a perfect, virginal Nature that was not prepared at all for the arrival of the Western, "civilized" visitors that set out to destroy it, because it did not look like their native landscape. Other passages suggest that the aforementioned communication between the different aborig-inal groups existed (1996, 131). Yet, what shows the Western provenance of Posse's views in this novel is Cabeza de Vaca's reaction when he finds out that the lands he explored are being put on the map: he gets really anxious about it and he wants to know and "see how that coast would be" ["ver cómo sería aquella costa"] (1996, 20). This suggests that for Cabeza de Vaca the land is, or looks, the way cartography describes it, for maps give a more adequate descrip-tion of the land he explored than his own testimony and recollections of it. Much to his surprise, the cartographic representation does not include the Malhado island (a place where he spent several years of oppression and suffer-ing). This makes him feel that he has been literally erased from the map (20). Once again, Western cartographic representations are given preeminence over chorographic knowledge—a knowledge that, as we have previously seen, is usually identified with those cultures that ignore the basics of geographical conceptions. The Amerindians' practical knowledge of the land is irrelevant to both geography and Western culture.

In sum, the four novels we have seen in this paper are, despite their alleged revisionist intentions, still subject to very European ways of representing the American territory that owe a lot to cognitive structures that arose from the Colonial Encounter. The European gaze, the noble savage myth and the priv-ilege of geography over chorography still dominate the narration and perpetu-ate mystifying ways of representing the continent. However, the most curious reproduction of the myths created by the Conquistadors does not come from these novels but from supposedly less likely sources. I am referring to some re-search papers about the historical novels that deal with the Colonial En-counter. This should be a source for concern if we believe that our perceptions of the present and the future depend, to some extent, on our reconstruction of the past, on our recreation of tradition. From this perspective, the foundation offered by the historical novels under study is a source for distortion and mys-tification, to say the least.

The first striking thing about the academic articles that analyze these novels is that a high percentage of them seems to lean towards an attitude that could be qualified as celebratory. Save some exceptions, the general attitude can be synthesized as follows: this type of historical fiction is something posi-tive that helps us rethink our continental history and destroy old myths. For example, Elzbieta Sklodowska asserts that this Latin American narrative trend has a subversive character because it opposes official history (1990, 345); it is also ideologically revisionist because it questions itself, because it puts into question its own legitimacy (1990, 350). Leaving aside that, as Donald Shaw points out, Sklodowska fails to tell us why she thinks these novels (especially *Los perros*) put into question the principle and foundation of their own writing,[12] another issue she leaves unexplained is Posse's ideological intention (1993, 185). This is not an insignificant issue because, as the present investigation suggests, the celebration of *Los perros* as a progressive text inevitably implies a failure to notice its ideological bias—that is, it implies a blindness vis-à-vis its faithful reproduction of old myths and legends about the colonial encounter.

Sklodowska seems to be dazzled by Posse's use of anachronism as a distancing device (1990, 349) as well as by the parodic repetition of history (351). Although I believe the celebration of parody (which is only a rhetorical device, with no relation whatsoever to axiological value) and of the rewriting of history (which is just a stylistic option without any concrete ideological orientation) necessitates a better, more solid justification, the most serious problem I see with them is their total lack of critical spirit. Yet, because Sklodowska is not the only critic who approaches the historical novels in this way, I propose to briefly examine other critics' insights on Posse's and Saer's works.

Amalia Pulgarín believes that the importance of recent Latin American historical novels lies in their reinterpretation of our past (1994, 625). In this critic's opinion, the rewriting proposed by those novels could contribute to an unveiling of history (625). She also calls attention to their demystifying and parodic character (625) as well as their subversive intentions (627). She, like Sklodowska, celebrates the use of anachronisms and praises another esthetic procedure: the carnavalization of history (1994, 627). In the case of *Los perros*, she calls attention to the novel's deconstructive reading of Columbus' texts that opens the door for a challenge to the image of the new lands produced by the Admiral (628).

Another critic, Raymond Souza, talks about the parody and scorn to which the historical sources are subject in the novel (1992, 46), while Jorge Campos celebrates the desacralization of Columbus's image (1983, 19). María Rosa Lojo, for her part, argues that Abel Posse reinvents the image of the past propagated by the official tradition (1995, 155). The rewriting of history represents, in Lojo's opinion, a semantic revolution (156), while the desacralization of things divine (157) finds its opposite in the exaltation of the female Amerindians' naked bodies (who are, in actuality, presented by the text as *"protomulatas,"* as we have already seen earlier) as vehicles for approaching the sacred (158). However, the critic does not bother to tell the reader why she sees a connection between aboriginal nudity and the sacred. Seymour Menton says that the subversion of historicity originates in Posse's distrust of historical sources (1992, 937), and he closes his article by stating that the novel is an argument against power in all its possible forms (938). Shaw believes that Posse puts into question the very idea of historical progress (1993, 185).

Rita de Grandis, who studies *El entenado,* makes remarks that are similar to the ones we saw in the texts of the critics of Posse's novels. For instance, she calls attention to the novel's critical stand as regards the fictional character of history and to its parodic reading that questions history's objectivity (1993, 30). She even says, in a somewhat enigmatic fashion (I confess I had trouble understanding the meaning of the phrase), that the novel "evaluates and critically challenges cannibalism" [evalúa y desafía críticamente el canibalismo] (1993, 32). Maybe she is trying to attribute to Saer a revisionist attitude vis-à-vis cannibalistic rituals: the Colastiné ritual described in the text has very few points of contact with the one described by the classical texts by Hans Staden, Jean de Léry, and Roger Barlow about anthropophagic practices among the Tupi-guarani of neighboring regions. Yet, if what she wants to affirm is that Saer is questioning, in any way, European prejudices about cannibalism, her argument finds no support in the text: as I explained earlier, the Argentinean writer does not modify at all the official version of the "discovery" of the River Plate. On the contrary, he reproduces the unsupported allegations of native cannibalism and builds his entire novel on that myth. Rita Gnutzman reads Saer's novel as a response to colonial chronicles (1992), and so does (although her main interest is to study the novel as a reflection on memory) María Luisa Bastos (1990), while Gabriel Riera thinks *El entenado* is not just a parodic reading of history but also an approximation to what exceeds representation: the invention of the Other (1996, 390). However, he does not tell us what kind of value that reflection on the invention of the Other has or what its motive is. Another critic, María Cristina Pons, views the text as a critical discussion of the textual production of Otherness—in dialogue with canonical historiographic texts and their "rhetoric of distance" (1997, 417–418)—in the framework of Western culture. Although this may be the case, she goes as far as to read the novel as a reflection on the legitimacy of those representations of the past that intend to recover the history of a forgotten or silenced collectivity; as an attempt to produce a rewriting of history that incorporates alternative voices (1997, 422). I think the absence of other voices in the novel outside the narrator's (remember that the European witness represents, in the sense of "to speak for," the whole ethnic group) contradicts Pons' optimistic interpretation.

All these critics seem to relish Posse's and Saer's use of certain narrative and rhetorical procedures (such as anachronism, carnivalization, parody, and irony) that are common to many of the contemporary Latin American fictional narratives. All of them seem to celebrate and welcome, to different degrees, the rewriting of history that those novels perform. However, one of the things they do not seem to perceive is that rhetorical procedures and literary fashion are not good or bad, progressive or backwards per se. In other words, they do not acknowledge that procedures of any kind take their value from the uses to which the authors put them: the rewriting of history that both Posse and Saer perform is not subversive by itself. On the contrary, as I have tried to suggest throughout this article, it is very far from being subversive, because it subscribes to many of the myths, prejudices, and distortions propagated by the official versions of history.

A striking example of the critics' attitude towards the relation between literary fashion and ideological content is Blanca de Arancibia's study on Posse's novels. She starts by admitting that those texts propose a mythical reading of America (1994, 74) and that they do not produce "an image of America, but a phenomenon structured like America [*a imagen de América*] (1994, 82). Posse's Baroque style contributes, in her opinion "toward the creation of the clichés suggested by 'Spanish America' and 'Spanish American Literature.' " . . . The 'excessive language' does not reproduce 'the real,' but a stereotyped idea of America as the 'continent of excess' " (82). Until now, Arancibia seems to be in agreement with my analysis of some of the problems in the novel: Posse's rejection of history, his mystification of the continent, and his stereotypical description of America. But when she summarizes her observations, she offers a surprising conclusion: "in their relationship with history, his novels are intended not so much to rewrite it or to recognize an Otherness . . . than to become substitutes for historical discourse itself. This is because their resistance is more radical: it is a rebellion against History" (83). After having acknowledged most of Posse's ideological problems, she forgets about them, or better yet, she dismisses them and ends up concluding that the novels are radical because they oppose history. That seems to be the magical procedure that makes one a radical: if one rewrites, opposes or derides history, one is resisting. The question is: what is one resisting? And: with what is one going to replace history, after one is done with it? With novels like Posse's, that reinforce the myths and legends created by the Conquistadors? I hope not.

I am convinced that the celebratory attitude of some of the scholars quoted in this paper has its roots in a very specific Latin American critical tradition: the one that praised and promoted the novels of the "Boom" of the 1960s. According to this tradition—whose most vocal spokesperson was Carlos Fuentes—the bourgeois realist novel is dead and the only possible saviors of the genre are those writers who put the emphasis on language and structure instead of on observation and description (Fuentes 1980, 17). The idea behind Fuentes' project was the vindication of an esthetic tradition with roots in what the English-speaking world calls "Modernism" and Latin Americans call "Vanguardia." The list of artists and writers regarded as models includes: James Joyce, Franz Kafka, Pablo Picasso, Antonin Artaud, Luigi Pirandello, and Sergei Eisenstein (Fuentes 1980, 18). What causes Fuentes' admiration for modernist writers is their emphasis on language and structure; an emphasis that allowed them to create parallel and totalizing realities (Fuentes 1980, 18–19). But Fuentes (less a scholar than a writer) was not alone: many Latin American critics and writers from the 1960s praised formal experimentation, because it allowed them to root the Boom novels in a prestigious European literary tradition. The praise of form for form's sake led those writers and critics to propose an axiology that privileged, regardless of ideological content, the works that were inspired by a very specific European esthetic tradition. In that axiology, the only works that deserved some attention were those that experimented with language and form.

Nowadays, the same standards are applied, *mutatis mutandis,* to the novels by Posse and Saer. The critics that continue that critical tradition do not contribute to the rigorous, responsible revision of the writing of history about the New World. On the contrary, they contribute (perhaps unwittingly), like the novelists studied in this paper, to the long chain of biased Western interpretations of Latin American history. Their gaze, that values form and experimentation over ideological content, ends up repeating and celebrating those myths and historical distortions. That is, it ends up looking as colonized, and as colonizing of the American territory, as the chronicles that served as sources for the novels they admire. It is my contention that only by reading Latin American discursive production from a less Europeanized—that is, less oblivious of indigenous cultures—perspective will we be able to start, some day, that eternally postponed process of decolonization Latin American intellectuals have always yearned for.

NOTES

1. We will see later that this is the most commonly held opinion among the critics that have written about these novels.

2. The opposition between "doing" and "being" (as we will see later) is expressed in Spanish as between "hacer" and "estar." Because the latter verb does not exist in English, I am going to translate it as "being." In Spanish, there are two verbs ("ser" and "estar") that cover more or less the same semantic range as the English "to be." "Estar" has a more passive component than "ser," although this trait does not fully explain the difference between both terms. More about this in the following endnotes.

3. From now on, all translations are mine.

4. Actually, in the above-mentioned passage, the terms used in Spanish are "ser" and "estar." I will explain the reason for the variations used by Abel Posse later.

5. This is one of the stereotypes about the region: the mulattoes are supposed to be great dancers. Posse seems to subscribe to this popular belief, too.

6. I am referring to the passage where Columbus describes a young female Amerindian who, by his European and Catholic standards, behaved like a whore (*puta*) when she approached the Spanish crew (1994, 199).

7. Columbus' loss of rational consciousness illustrates, as we will see later, the division Posse sees between European and American cosmogonies. In Viviana Plotnick's opinion, those two world views are characterized in the novel as follows: the indigenous one privileges openness, intensity, and the dyonisiac whereas the Western one is best represented by closure, rationality, and hierarchies (1993, 179–80).

8. This opposition between "doing" and "being" should not confuse the reader: both in *Los Perros* and in Rodofo Kusch's works "being" (*ser*) appears as synonymous with "doing" and both terms represent the European world view, whereas "estar" represents the Latin American cosmogony. In *Daimón*, the situation is different because Posse substitutes "doing" for "being" (*ser*) while he uses "being" (*ser*) instead of Kusch's "estar." In *Daimón*, then, the opposition is between "doing" and "being" (*ser*, that in this occasion means "estar").

9. According to Enrique Dussel, Being, as a Greek philosophical creation, is an ontology of totality. What lies outside of Being does not, for all practical purposes, exist at all: it is a non-Being. This is the way in which Dussel interprets the famous Parmenides aphorism (what is, is; what is not, is not) and Socrates' method (designed to extract a knowledge already possessed by his disciples—and already prefigured in the *topos uranos*): as reproducers of the ideology of Being, of the same; as intellectual artifacts that deny the Other, who is Nothing because it is located outside the totality—which is tantamount to saying outside of the realm of Being (Dussel 1975, 15–17). In the same fashion, classical Greek culture conceived the political and cultural arena as a Being that comprised the borders of the Hellenic world: beyond that frontier was the periphery, the barbarians, the non-Being (Dussel 1980, 15–16).

10. They are called "Colastiné" in the text, a name of a real ethnic group that inhabited a territory that is not the one where the narrative takes place.

11. The literary critics that have studied this novel seem to know even less than the historians about that historical event. Some of them have asserted, erroneously, that Francisco del Puerto (the name of the real life cabin boy) was rescued by the expedition of Sebastian Cabot, ten years later. In actuality, according to the available documentation, the ex-cabin boy stayed with the Amerindians that inhabited the area that surrounds the mouth of the Paraguay River (Medina 1908, 1: 169). Sebastian Cabot even goes so far as to accuse del Puerto as the intellectual author of a massacre performed by some unidentified Indians on the Spaniards on April 10, 1528 (Medina 1908, 2: 160; Harrisse 1896, 422–423). See, as examples of modern critics' misinformation, the comments by Evelia Romano Thuesen, "*El entenado*," *Latin American Literary Review* 23, 45 (1995) 43–63; Rita De Grandis, "*El entenado* de Juan José Saer y la idea de historia," *Revista Canadiense de Estudios Hispánicos* 18, 3 (1994) 417–426; 419) on del Puerto's alleged return to Spain.

12. Viviana Plotnick and Blanca de Arancibia think, like Elzbieta Slodowska, that the novel undermines its own authority, but unlike the latter, they support their claims. Plotnick says that parodic elements, fake citations, the distortion of history, are all devices that promote the reader's distrust for the narrator (1993, 146). The text

questions, in this way, its own credibility. Blanca de Arancibia states that the narrator, by proclaiming his/her presence, denounces authorship as authority and contributes to cancel the narrative contract (1994, 72).

BIBLIOGRAPHY

Bastos, María Luisa. 1990. "Eficacias del verosímil no realista: dos novelas recientes de Juan José Saer." *La Torre (NE)* 4, 13: 1–20.

Campos, Jorge. 1983. "Nueva relación entre la novela y la historia: Abel Posse y Denzil Romero." *Insula* 440–441: 19.

Chanady, Amaryll. 1992. "Saer's Fictional Representation of the Amerindian in the Context of Modern Historiography." In *Amerindian Images and the Legacy of Columbus.* Edited by Rene Jara and Nicholas Spadaccini, 678–708. Minneapolis: University of Minnesota Press.

Colón, Cristóbal. 1982. *Los cuatro viajes del Almirante y su testamento.* Madrid: Espasa Calpe.

De Arancibia, Blanca. 1994. "Identity and Narrative Fiction in Argentina: The Novels of Abel Posse." In *Latin American Identity and Constructions of Difference.* Edited by Amaryll Chanady, 67–85. Minneapolis: University of Minnesota Press.

De Certeau. 1986. "Montaigne's 'Of Cannibals': The Savage 'I.' " In *Heterologies. Discourse on the Other. By Michel de Certeau.* Translated by Brian Massumi, 67–79. Minneapolis: University of Minnesota Press.

De Grandis, Rita. 1994. "*El entenado* de Juan José Saer y la idea de historia." *Revista Canadiense de Estudios Hispánicos* 18, 3: 417–426.

———. 1993. "The First Colonial Enconunter in *El entenado* by Juan José Saer: Paratextuality and History in Postmodern Fiction." *Latin American Literary Review* 21, 41: 30–38.

Díaz-Quiñones, Arcadio. 1992. "*El entenado:* Las palabras de la tribu." *Hispamérica* 21, 63: 3–14.

Dussel, Enrique. 1980. *Filosofía de la liberación.* Bogotá: Universidad Santo Tomás.

———. 1975. "Palabras preliminares." In *Liberación latinoamericana y Emmanuel Levinas.* Edited by Dussel, Enrique y Daniel Guillot. Buenos Aires: Editorial Bonum.

Fabian, Johannes. 1983. *Time and the Other: How Anthropology Makes Its Object.* New York: Columbia University Press.

Fuentes, Carlos. 1980 [1969]. *La nueva novela hispanoamericana.* México: Joaquín Mortiz.

García Márquez, Gabriel. 1983. "La soledad de América Latina." *La Prensa* 2, 22: 6.

Gnutzman, Rita. 1994. "*El entenado* de Saer o el cuestionamiento de las crónicas." In *Conquista y contraconquista. La escritura del Nuevo Mundo.* Edited by Julio Ortega and José Amor y Vázquez, 633–639. México: El Colegio de México; Brown University.

———. 1992. "*El entenado* o la respuesta de Saer a las crónicas." *Iris:* 23–36.

González, Eduardo. 2000. "Caliban; or, Flesh-Eating and Ghost Text in Saer's *El entenado.*" *Dispositio/n* 50. 1–18.

Harrisse, Henry. 1896. *John Cabot the Discoverer of North America and Sebastian His Son.* London: Benjamin Franklin Stevens.

Hulme, Peter. 1986. *Colonial Encounters: Europe and the Native Caribbean, 1492–1797.* London and New York: Methuen.

Kusch, Rodolfo. 1977 [1970]. *El pensamiento indígena y popular en América.* Buenos Aires: Hachette

———. 1976. *Geocultura del hombre americano.* Buenos Aires: Fernando García Cambeiro.

Lojo, María Rosa. 1995. "La invención de la historia en *Los perros del Paraíso,* de Abel Posse." *Estudios Filológicos* 30: 155–160.

Medina, José Toribio. 1908. *El veneciano Sebastián Caboto al servicio de España.* 2 Vols. Santiago de Chile: Imprenta y Encuadernación Universitaria.

Menton, Seymour. 1992. "Christopher Columbus and the New Historical Novel." *Hispania* 75, 4: 930–940.

Plotnick, Viviana. 1993. "La reescritura del descubrimiento de América en cuatro novelas hispanoamericanas contemporáneas: Intertextualidad, carnaval y espectáculo." Ph.D. diss. New York University.

Pons, María Cristina. 1997. "La historia como 'caníbal' en *El entenado* de J. J. Saer." *Memorias de JALLA. Tucumán 1995.* Tucumán: Proyecto "Tucumán en los Andes."

Posse, Abel. 1996 [1992]. *El largo atardecer del caminante.* Buenos Aires: Emecé.

———. 1994 [1983]. *Los perros del Paraíso.* Buenos Aires: Emecé.

———. 1991 [1978]. *Daimón.* Buenos Aires: Emecé.

Pulgarín, Amalia. 1994. "Historiografía y metaficción: *Los perros del Paraíso,* de Abel Posse." In *Conquista y contraconquista. La escritura del Nuevo Mundo.* Julio Ortega, and José Amor y Vázquez, 625–631. México: El Colegio de México; Brown University.

Reati Fernando. 1995a. "Los signos del tarot y el fin de la razón occidental en América: *Daimón,* de Abel Posse." *Dispositio/n* 20, 47: 93–108.

———. 1995b. "Posse, Saer, Di Benedetto y Brailovsky: deseo y paraíso en la novela argentina sobre la Conquista." *Revista de Estudios Hispánicos* 29, 1: 121–136.

Riera, Gabriel. 1996. "La ficción de Saer: ¿una 'antropología especulativa'? (Una lectura de *El entenado*)." *MLN* 111: 368–390.

Romano Thuesen, Evelia. 1995. "*El entenado:* relación contemporánea de las memorias de Francisco del Puerto." *Latin American Literary Review* 23, 45: 43–63.

Saer, Juan José. 1994 [1983]. *El entenado.* Buenos Aires: Alianza editorial.

Santa Cruz, Alonso de. 1983. *Alonso de Santa Cruz y su obra cosmográfica.* Edited by Mariano Cuesta Domingo. Madrid: Consejo Superior de Investigaciones Científicas.

Shaw, Donald. 1993. "Columbus and the Discovery in Carpentier and Posse." *Romance Quarterly* 40, 3.

Sklodowska, Elzbieta. 1990. "El (re) descubrimiento de América: la parodia en la novela histórica." *Romance Quarterly* 37, 3: 345–352.

Souza, Raymond. 1992. "Columbus in the Novel of the Americas: Alejo Carpentier, Abel Posse, and Stephen Marlowe." In *The Novel in the Americas.* Edited by Ramond Leslie Williams. Niwot: University Press of Colorado.

Todorov, Tzvetan. 1982. *La Conquête de l' Amérique: La question de l' autre.* Paris: du Seuil.

Verdesio, Gustavo. 1996. *La invención del Uruguay. La entrada del territorio y sus habitantes a la cultura occidental.* Montevideo: Graffiti; Trazas.

———. 2000. "En busca de la materialidad perdida: un aporte crítico a los proyectos de recuperación de las tradiciones aborígenes propuestos por Kusch, Dussel y Mignolo. *Revista iberoamericana* 66. 192: 625–638.

"Writing with his thumb in the air"

Coloniality, Past and Present

Sara Castro-Klarén

In *España aparta de mi este cáliz*, as the savage Spanish civil war drew to an end, César Vallejo wrote on the death and resurrection of the soldier Pedro Rojas. A short version of the first line of the poem: "Solía escribir con su dedo gordo en el aire" appears as the title of one of the last books written by Antonio Cornejo Polar, *Escribir en el aire: ensayo sobre la heterogeneidad socio-cultural en las literaturas andinas* (1994). I return to Vallejo's idea of writing in the air with a pen made of flesh (*pluma de carne*), with the thumb, in the absence of pen and paper, because the image of "escribir en el aire" bears an emblematic relevance to the cultural and ethical conundrum affecting the study or rather the writing of colonial situations, past and present.

Vallejo's poem is not a farewell to arms. If anything it establishes an inescapable and concrete link between past and present. The image of Pedro Rojas, writing in the air, memorializes the undying will to perdue in solidarity, for his finger, spelling "viban" as if it were living speech, writes over and over again: "¡Viban los compañeros!"

Pedro Rojas passes on, but the passage that configures his death is fraught with ambiguity, for the poem doubly inscribes the meaning of "¡Pasa!" In the couplet: "Papel de viento, lo han matado: ¡Pasa! / Pluma de carne, lo han matado: ¡Pasa!"; "¡Pasa!" could be understood as either an exclamation shouting the death of Pedro Rojas or as a coded dialogue between the sentinel and the voice of the man reciting the secret word in his search for safe passage. The poem seeks to stand as a living memory to the struggle. It refuses the esstrangement of the past; it writes the past as a living present for Pedro Rojas, "después

---

I write this essay in memory of Antonio Cornejo Polar, unexcelled colleague, brilliant critical intelligence, and compatriot.

de muerto, / se levantó, besó su catafalco ensangrentado, / lloró por España / y volvió a escribir con el dedo en el aire: / '¡Viban los compañeros! Pedro Rojas'."

This volume of essays, in a way flows from Vallejo, for the intent of many of the essays included is to problematize the question of the past for us, the living. Can or should students of colonial Latin America afford to think of the past as a foreign country? What does it mean to employ textual strategies for reading the artifacts of the past as if the conditions of textual production imbedded in or side-stepped by the texts themselves were over and done with and thus the texts free-float in time and space until they reach our desks for "literary" interpretation? What similarities exist between colonial texts, or modern texts, for that matter, and Vallejo's two scenes of writing? Is our task as intellectuals concluded after the appreciation (added value) and celebration of the semiliterate Pedro Rojas, the man who writes the memory of his engagement in the Spanish Civil War with his own flesh? Or do we enlarge the scope of our gaze to consider the second scene of writing, the moment when Pedro Rojas, already dead, writes again, lest his life be forgotten, the same verse that took him to his death?[1] To a very large extent both Gustavo Verdesio and Alvaro Félix Bolaños, in questioning the relationship of past to present in the existing approaches to colonial studies, are, in fact, raising the problem of solidarity, that is, the political position of academic intellectuals in the world today as a system of forces constituted by the past.

THE PAST AS A PRESENT PROBLEM

Gustavo Verdesio's question: "What is the use of our work?" is indeed far-reaching. It raises the fundamental and increasingly vexed question of use value in literary and cultural studies. As such it is not a question that emerges specifically or attains exclusively to colonial studies. It spans over the entire scope of academic work in the humanities, and it links with several of the theses developed by Bill Readings in *The University in Ruins* (1996). According to Readings, literary culture has been disengaged from its connection to the national subject. It has lost its raison d'être as constituted in the nineteenth century (1996, 75). Literature is no longer the language of national culture in the United States. Readings argues that the "general notion of culture . . . as the organic synthesis that acts as both the totality and the essence of particular knowledges," (75, 81) without which there can be no essence and no center, which appeared fully articulated in Bishop Newman's *Idea of a University* (1878?),[2] is no longer in place. In this framework for liberal education and more specifically, for the study of literature, the humanities were situated in opposition to practical knowledge and the principle of utility. The study of literature became an end in itself. The unity of knowledge sought by the liberal education was the imminent principle of intellectual culture; academic knowl-

edge was produced by an assemblage of learned men in the pursuit of intellectual culture. Intellectual culture applied both to the production of knowledge
(truth) by means of the various disciplines and to the teaching of individuals.
This inherited understanding of the place of literature in the production of intellectual knowledge and the production of the national subject has now dissipated (Readings, 77). However, its force wanes unevenly. It grinds with
intensely jarring sounds in the context of *colonial* studies where the clashing
and brimstone of cultural struggles, contesting subjects, and general conditions
of yet unexamined heterogeneity twirl and swirl in fascinating and frustrating
movements.

To a large extent Verdesio's question is prompted by the pervasive and unacknowledged reading practices of New Criticism present in most of the scholarship dedicated to Latin American colonial texts and its connection to the
institution of literature built in this century by the idea of liberal education in
conjunction with the production of the national subject. Anchored on the idea
that the (autonomous) text itself suffices as the terrain of intellectual operations to be engaged by the (autonomous) liberal subject, New Criticism, in its
many transformations, continues to authorize the separation of the "aesthetic"
object from its conditions of historical production. In this regard, Readings observes that, in the United States, the idea of literary culture, was structured on
the notion of the canon rather than on the idea of an ethnic tradition. This
shift allowed for the minimization of the weight of ethnicity and elitism of the
English model in both Newman and F. R. Leavis (83–84).[3] However, as Wendell Harris reminds us, "canons are made up of readings, not of disembodied
texts" (1991, 110). And reading practices return us to questions of generalized
cultural understandings, to the power negotiations implicit in the constitution
of academic knowledges and the construction of normative criteria.[4]

Part of the work of New Criticism was to construct the criteria for the
Master Pieces series. But the paradox that New Criticism conceals in its move
to establish a canon of master pieces is that, despite its divorce from historical
context and historical scholarship in establishing a canon, it, in fact, calls for
continuity and rupture criteria and thus introduces history through the back
door. The historical criteria that inhabits the pleats of New Criticism performs
its work silently. It organizes the canon within a historical perspective which,
in fact, goes unexamined. The ensuing tension between reading strategies designed to address the purely "aesthetic" (autonomous) nature of the "literary"
text but which, in fact, conceals the historical grounding of the texts together
with the problem of periodization, leaves relatively superficial marks when it
deals with highly modernistic, linguistically self-reflexive texts. However, colonial intertextualities, frontally engaged, as they always are, with the knowl-
edge/power question, unavoidably point to the gaping impasses implicit in the
"aesthetic" approach to literature and culture. This can be readily seen in
Bolaños's article on *El carnero* as well as the very mixed critical reception of

testimonio texts. In these colonial textualities, the national subject is either cleansed, absent, contested, or mistaken[5] but seldom, if ever, reaffirmed.

The crisis of the literary model is compounded when the "national" subjects implicit in the reading protocols of the critic and the critic, as a historical individual, do not coincide in the same sociohistorical location. This awkward and unacknowledged lack of fit between reading practices and national subjects appears not only marked by the dynamics of the teaching machine, but also inscribed by a special relation of distance, by affects interdicted by *lejanía*. Such is the case of many Latin American intellectuals working in the North American academy[6] and of Euro-American subjects studying Latin American texts.

Yet another type of distance which affects the interpretation of Latin American culture, also occurs in the North American academy. The cultural battles over the canon, the demonstration that the canon is "an ethnocentric and nonrepresentative basis on which to ground the kinds of claims that have been historically made for literature" (Readings 1996, 85), has left the study of literature in a position that is "neither practical nor ethically defensible" (Readings, 85). This paradoxical situation arises from the changing "status of knowledge inherent in the disciplinary problematic in the contemporary university"(86). In a world in which all choices are good, the ethical relation of the academic intellectual to the production and reproduction of knowledge is indeed blurred and ethically fragile.

Because the link between literary studies and the formation of the citizen has been broken, literature has lost its once privileged position. It is now a field among others. The canon has lost its sacredness, and it has come to function as one of several other forms of delimiting the field. Literature is now an archive that stores all kinds of texts occupying roughly similar niches. It is not the (selective) museum that once housed the treasures of the nation. This archive no longer amounts to an organic vision of national literatures or cultures, "nor does anything within the system of knowledge require that it should" (Readings, 86). This battle over the canon may be new in the United States, but I venture to say that it is the very stuff of which the history of Latin American letters is made, for the *criollo* national subject and its coincidence with the rise of literature has been a phenomenon of very short and precarious duration. Disputes which questioned the limits and criteria that organized divisions between a potential versus an official canon, a personal as opposed to a pedagogical canon, an accessible as opposed to a critical canon have fueled the pages of Latin American Literature since the Lunarejo's (Juan de Espinosa y Medrano) defense of the Baroque aesthetic, onto Andrés Bello and Domingo Faustino Sarmiento, and, of course, José Carlos Mariátegui and Jorge Luis Borges and more recently feminism.

To some extent a parallel story could be told in relation to the study of Latin American Literature in the departments of Spanish, romance, and foreign languages in the United States. Without glossing over the history of the peripheral and conflicted position that the study of Spanish (with its own inner breaks and contradictions) occupies in the United States academy, it can nevertheless be observed that the decoupling of the national subject from the study of literature in the English departments, made visible at the annual meetings of the Modern Language Association, and the emergence of the archive as multiple and inorganic, has had a direct impact on the question of use, that is to say the (ethical) justification of the discipline for all scholars in the field of literature. The conservative detractors of the postmodern shift vociferously brought it up year in and year out with their ridicule of the titles of the MLA panels. Finally the ferocity of their attack found in the reception of Rigoberta Menchú the sublime object of their discontent. In this debate, history entered, once again, mutilated and disguised, but in full force, through the back door of the cultural wars over postmodern (hybrid) subjects, narratological appreciations, academic locations, archival orders, and authentic subjects. But it failed to address fully and ethically the fact that the Menchú text, like Vallejo's poem, is a narrative about war. As such the hermeneutics deployed on testimonial texts which deal with the trauma of war, a war that has never stopped since its Spanish colonial inception, demand an approach that far exceeds the confines of the literary and which return us to history, to the fullness of experience. Spanish departments, as the authors of the introduction suggest, need to take a long look at the literary practices that adorn the walls of their treasured (prison) houses.[7]

Before the moment when the authority of the literary canon began to unravel, the assumption in place held that Latin American Literature was the museum where the monuments of high culture and spirituality of each nation were put on exhibit. It was the equivalent of an international centennial exposition. The use value hinged on the manifest proof of literary achievement and the "expression" of a culture-language constituted in its difference. Once the museum doors were opened and one passed the front exhibit halls and into the *fondos* or archival records—residues, shards, sedimentation, protoformations, fragments of wholes, fragments of series—the whole question of canonicity and representation (use) gave way.[8] Stimulated by the changing desires and seductive agendas of cultural studies, a whole other corpus of hidden, forgotten, and even concealed jewels appeared strewn in the many layers of the *fondos*. But for many, the use value of these texts was still governed by both evolutionist, aesthetic, and modernist criteria—the chronicles seen as proto-novels or proto-ethnography, the nun's diaries as proto-feminist textualities.

However, I do not want to leave the impression that the doors that opened vistas beyond the canonical front exhibit halls were opened by either cultural studies in the United States or simply the loss of centrality suffered by literature. One could configure other narratives on the voyage to the *fondos,* a word which in Spanish means archival storage, financial solvency, as well as the depths. The most important point to note here is that the gaze into the long past and into indigenous and provincial cultural realms neglected by the modernist canon was never allowed rest or self-complacency. It was always disrupted by writers who, like José María Arguedas or Augusto Roa Bastos, kept in the forefront of consciousness alternative stories, narrative modalities, and ethics of knowledge. Their work demanded reading strategies that reached deep into the colonial and pre-Columbian past and rhetorical *fondos*. In their unflinching historical gaze they dwelled into the production of subjects other than the national subject as constituted by a narrative of ever modernizing (Eurocentric) Latin American literature. The appearance of testimony and the force of ethno-history as well as issues in self-reflexive anthropology all contributed to the de-centering of the purely literary modes of interpretation of Latin American culture and literature.

The idea of colonial literature is clearly no longer viable. A nominalist switch to colonial discourse only compounds the problem, for as Neil Larsen has argued, this switch conceals a misconception regarding the category of the aesthetic, conceived narrowly as a kind of formalism that excludes the social and the material as "extrinsic" content.[9] There is no text that is not aesthetic, for the aesthetic is always part and parcel of all communication. To separate the aesthetic from colonial texts is to grant exclusive rights over the domain of the aesthetic to eurocentric categories—gender modalities, certain kinds of troping, conceits, and language games. It is to deny the aesthetic dimension in the communications dynamics of the colonial archive and pre-Columbian textualities. The real problem, as Larsen points out, is not historicism but rather "a perplexity over how to interpret the uniquely and profoundly tragic historical outcome of the epoch of conquest and colonization" (1995, 107).

In this regard, and if I may be permitted a personal note, I must say that it was Julio Cortázar's epistemological challenge to the aesthetic of the "realistic" novel and to the modernist subject—*cronopios, Ubu Roi* and pataphysics—that opened the way for me to become a reader of Guamán Poma and other "dishevelled" colonial texts. The key to a decolonizing enterprise neither resides in any particular literary approach, nor is it sufficient to call for a non-eurocentric mind set for, as José Rabasa has pointed out, "Eurocentricism is a pervasive condition of thought" and not simply an uncritically held cultural ideal (Rabasa 1993, 18). Decolonizing knowledge and subjectivity assume rather a relentless attention to the writing of history, that is to say the mounting of a critical approach to historiography, in the broadest sense of the term. And in order not to fall into the trap of self-transparency, self-vigilance goes hand in hand with an open and critical commitment to the question of ethics.

When colonial discourse, that "system of statements that can be made about colonial peoples, about colonizing powers and about the relationship between these two; that system of knowledge and beliefs about the world within which acts of colonization take place . . . [that system of statements that] works to constitute reality . . . for the subjects who form the community on which it depends,[10]" is mistakenly taken for an amplification of colonial literature, the field of colonial studies begins to suffer strong distortions, tensions, and contradictions. Many of them seem to be the prompters for the concerns discussed in the essays of the editors of the volume. However, it seems that the differences in approach and results between the old study of colonial literature and colonial discourse, or for that matter postcolonial theory, cannot be sufficiently stressed.

In *Inventing America: Spanish Historiography and the Formation of Eurocentricism* (1993), José Rabasa succeeds in getting beyond the problems imbedded in "colonial literature." Rabasa's critique of "colonial discourse" takes up and pushes beyond Edmundo O'Gorman's study of the chronicles as epistemological and rhetorical presuppositions. Departing from Michel Foucault's concept of discursive formation and Edward Said's *Orientalism* (1979), Rabasa shows, for instance, that the "generic differences between histories, chronicles, and *relaciones* (accounts) corresponds to rules that not merely reflect aesthetic formulas but define who has the authority to speak and what is legitimate knowledge"(1993, 5). Not unlike Said, Rabasa is less concerned with correcting the factual mistakes incurred in the making of "colonial discourses" than in detecting and analyzing the tropes and epistemological operations by which America is produced as a "new" and subordinate world in relation to a Europe that from the moment of discovery was able to conceive of itself as the center. It is in this vein of inquiry that Rabasa's critique of colonial discourse shows that the "production of America is coterminous with the formation of Europe and its Others' "(6) as well as with the colonization of subjectivities otherwise known as a globally extended eurocentric epistemology. For Rabasa, deestabilizing the ground of factuality entails, as it did for Edward Said, a critique of representation, a permanent awareness of the rhetorical moves that produced and continue to produce them now, effect the real. Thus, any sense of referential plenitude underscores the colonial writing of the world which subjugates Indian and other subaltern knowledges (9–10).

From the following, it is clear that the term "colonial discourse," as it has been pressed into accelerated and multiple general uses, needs to undergo critical examination if it is to maintain the edge once given to it by Edward Said. Understood as a form of discourse and not as a form of description of a "reality" out there, "colonial discourse" pointed to the operations of knowledge and power—military, scientific, political, artistic, documentary—by which Europe produced the non-European world as difference. As Rabasa points out "colonial discourse" managed to graft "colonial situations and cultural artefacts into the analysis of discourse" (10), a move which did not exclude the colonized from breaking through the gaps of the hegemonic thrust of colonial discourse. It follows then, that for critics interested in the decolonization of knowledges, it is necessary to go beyond a description of the colonizing forces put in place by colonial discourse and the resistances it encountered as it fanned its forces around the globe. It is necessary to join those Latin American subjects who have written alternative histories and alternative subjectivities as they went about deconstructing the modes of subjectivation they encountered in different lived colonialities. In this regard, Rabasa asserts that "the history of Latin America can be read as the constant construction of alternative histories and subjectivities"(14). I think that his emphasis on the positive side of the construction rather than on the negative side of the resistance needs now further exploration in the field.

Indeed, I see Bolaños and Verdesio calling for such a critical reappraisal in the current situation in colonial studies. Their move is not to be confused with a desire to restore literary studies to their former place in the academy. The questions they ask address the problem of the production of knowledge in a deeply historical sense. Although the term "power" is rather hard to spot in the essays included in the volume, I think that the problematic they address cannot fully be discussed without paying close attention to Foucault's entanglement of the knowledge/power question. I address this question in the last part of this essay.

PARADIGM SHIFT

The omnivorous category "Latin American Literature" is no longer, if ever it was, a stable construct. One of the destabilizing factors has been the irruptive introduction of the colonial archive which has forced a reconsideration of questions of origin, constructions of teleological canons, and, of course, the national, public intellectual as the subject of the production of knowledge in the various regions and time zones of Latin America. The "aesthetic" core, as constructed by formalist and modernist theories of canon formation, has been unable to resist the pressure exerted by all the disheveled texts (colonial and modern) which exhibit alternative knowledges, (aesthetic) configurations and demand reading strategies of their own.

In conjunction with other forces, the study of literature gravitated towards the study of "culture." Culture appeared as a more encompassing concept. Endowed with the legacy of modern anthropology, culture was conceived as the complex whole of life patterns and practices of belief and feeling. Beyond Levi-Straussian myth reading and all its attendant problems, there lay the promising notion that the study of culture was "only apparently the study of custom, beliefs, or institutions [and that in fact it was] fundamentally the study of thought" (Geertz 1973, 352).

Insufficient attention was paid, however, to the fact that the anthropological definition of culture, as James Clifford points out, emerged as the liberal alternative to racist classification of peoples and human diversity. "It was a sensitive means for understanding different and dispersed 'whole ways of life' in light of colonial contexts of unprecedented global interconnection" (1988, 234–35). Cultures in the plural pointed beyond the original eurocentric evolutionary value as originally drawn by José de Acosta in his *Historia natural y moral de las Indias* (1590). Culture in this sense was not too distant from Matthew Arnold's own concept of "high" culture, for cultures now were conceived as stable, enduring, syncretic, and ahistorical. Clifford notes that culture thus appears as "a process of ordering and not of disruption. It changes and develops as a living organism" (235). Valentine Daniel has clarified the normalizing assumptions embedded in the idea of culture as a total system. It leaves no outside that can resist it. The work of culture thus conceived, Daniel points out, is to "colonize, convert and conquer," to normalize "fugitive elements that may drift within their expanding semeiosic field," leaving no space for counterpoints that cannot be subsumed or tamed by the power of culture (1998, 68–69).

As a whole, the field of colonial studies remained distant from the postmodern critique of anthropology. Only a handful of scholars in the field began testing the concept of culture as a semiotics in which human behavior is understood as symbolic action. Clifford Geertz's view of culture as an "interworked system of construable signs, [as] a context, something within which there can be intelligibility" (1973, 14) that is thickly described, began to open the horizon of colonial studies beyond a narrowly conceived textuality and put in place the idea that "colonial" studies were not circumscribed to the "chronicles."[11]

Cultural semiosis offered the possibility for a clear reference to the totality of signs, for an approach to the ceaseless exchange and negotiation of symbolic systems and subjects in tension. Cultural semiosis seemed particularly attuned to the problems of colonial struggles. It proposed, for instance, a way of thinking about the engagement between alphabetic cultures and pictographic and knotting modes of recoding the past and producing knowledge. Keenly aware of the conceptual and locational inadequacy of "literature" as a discipline, and coming from an intellectual tradition which owed more to anthropology and the philosophy of history than to "literary" studies in the United States, Walter Mignolo called for a fundamental shift,[12] often referred to as a "paradigm shift."

If what is meant by paradigm shift is something like Thomas Kuhn's thesis in *The Structure of Scientific Revolution* (1962), a revolution that overthrows the older paradigm and replaces it with an incompatible framework,[13] such an event has not yet taken place in the study of colonialities. And Verdesio, who seems to be calling for such a shift, does well to remind us of this fact. Such a shift seems not only ambitious but daunting. It implies a complete re-hauling of the field of Latin American studies and the humanities in general and not just literature. What is more, as José Rabasa reminded me recently, a paradigm shift in Kuhn's sense, takes place behind the backs of the subjects working in a given period.[14]

As I understand it, the shift that Walter Mignolo has in mind entails massive new learning, mastering of a multidisciplinary bibliography that spans both sides of the Atlantic and a thorough, critical theoretical reorientation. The project far exceeds the confines of the work possible inside the monolingual confines of Spanish departments, loaded as they still are with the remnants of New Criticism and philology. Due to the fact that Spanish failed to develop into a modern intellectual language in Europe, its monolingualism severely curtails the possibilities of stepping out of the ideologies and epistemologies already inscribed in Spanish configurations of knowledge—some of which we see decried in Verdesio's analysis of the reception of the new historical novel—which fly contrary to the work of Latin American intellectual history. Spanish monolingualism runs counter to the long standing Latin American project of decolonization, which began with recognizing the insufficiency of the monolingual Spanish intellectual tradition and sought, from its earlier manifestations—Garcilaso de la Vega, Inca, onto the Modernistas, Mariátegui, Borges, Mansilla, Arguedas, and Cortázar—to furnish its arsenal with learning available in any language whatever. A fundamental shift entails breaking out of the confines not only of literature and its correlation with national subjects, but it also means breaking out of, or reconfiguring the intellectual and linguistic confines of Spanish departments in the United States.[15]

A fundamental shift implies critical and systematic delearning of the paradigms that sustain the inertia of the field. It should not prove surprising that *The Darker Side of the Renaissance* (1995) comes immediately to mind as one of the best examples of the fundamental change that Walter Mignolo has called for. In their effort to map new routes for colonial studies, several of the scholars writing in this volume cite the work of José Rabasa, Antonio Cornejo Polar, and Mabel Moraña. Despite key theoretical differences, the work of these critics is highlighted here for their keen interest in historicizing the study of the past, relocating the locus of enunciation of the scholar, and redirecting the gaze of the critic towards the self-deployment of subaltern subjects pleated in the narrative of the *criollo*-national subject. Seen under this light, Cornejo Polar's emphasis on the cultural heterogeneity of Andean literary legacies is not too far away from Rabasa's inquiry into the colonial ordering and subordination of the Tlacuilos's ways of knowing. Such a family resemblance or shared adjacency points to the urgent need for comparative studies between the history of Meso-American and Andean colonialities.[16] It also holds the promise for opening up new ground and furthering a shift that in time may be recognized as paradigmatic.

It is perhaps not too risky to say, that despite the perception of differ-ences in research agendas which have to do more with the originary place of some scholars working in the field rather than with the stated desired desti-nation, a fundamental shift is indeed at work. The problematic outline by the Latin American Subaltern Studies Group is a call for radical change which in many ways dovetails with Mignolo's earlier essay. Reading against the grain has indeed cleared out the underbrush in the forest. But a fundamental shift will not be in place until a genealogical look into history cuts through vast swaths of growth in the forest of standing "truths." In order to disman-tle the assumptions which allow the invisible continuity of colonialist knowl-edge practices such as the uncritical approach to the canonizing formulas that end up performing the "cleansing operation" that Bolaños so forcefully demonstrates in his consideration of Arciniegas, Colombian historiography and *El carnero* read as a colonial picaresque, the field needs to track down the way in which discourse constitutes objects and makes them available for study.[17]

A shift to a genealogical approach requires scholars to sustain ambitious and long-term projects in order to become historians (see Rabasa in this col-lection) or philosophers of entire systems of thought. One of the major obsta-cles, it seems to me, stems not from the differences among those calling for a shift, but rather from the trendiness in the field. The demand that legitimates research with the value of novelty runs counter to the huge investment in learning that needs to be made in order to break out of the old paradigm. Slow, consistent, and solid accretion may turn out to be a good method for produc-ing changes in epistemological assumptions. Instead of books on trendy sub-jects read by the very few, we may have to rely on far-reaching articles capable of making a material difference; that is to say articles whose publication does not allow for things to remain the same.

In this regard, the recent article by Lindsay Walters, the executive editor for the humanities at the Harvard University Press, is most relevant. In a way the title says it all: "A Modest Proposal for Preventing the Books of the Members of the MLA from Being a Burden to Their Authors, Publishers, or Audiences." Walters basically argues that scholarship in the humanities would be better served if we returned to the publication of substantial and path-breaking articles of interest to audiences beyond the disciplinary tenure committees who require a book, no matter how slim, marginal, or repetitious or self-centered.[18] Scholars of Latin American letters seldom consider in which ways does their work modify the existing knowledge in other disci-plines. If we are concerned with the decolonization of knowledge and with breaking out of the restrictions built around us by colonial discourse one of our major objective should be to establish dialogue with other disciplines—anthropology, historiography, English, political theory—as well as other area studies.

GLOBALIZATION, THE NATIONAL SUBJECT AND LATIN AMERICANISM

On a previous occasion, I have written on the disarray, the plethora of approaches with no center or direction that passes for a field of study. In "Interrupting the Text of Latin American Literature: Problems of (Missed) recognition,"[19] I argued that part of the problem of disarray in the field, and especially the situation of the locus of enunciation of the critic, has to do with the unsettling problematic of identity in a globalized world. What each of us thinks and does is inevitably bound up with who we think we are. This not to say that the personal is the political. But it is to acknowledge that the dynamics of self-recognition imply a consciousness of the bounds of identity which in turn tie up the questions of ethical responsibility that the editors of this volume consider paramount in the exercise of critical practices.

Although we have come to realize that identities, even when hegemonic, are never solid, organic or stable, this is neither saying that they do not exist nor that they have ceased to be constructed. The question then devolves not on whether we respond to single and hegemonic identities or to multiple (heterogenic) subject positions, but how we go about constructing identities and how we negotiate different subject positions, for the construction of identities bears heavily on practices of interpretation, from the everyday to the philosophical. The problem of identity orients the authorization of protocols of entanglement and makes possible the assemblage of observation and enunciatory positions.

Globalization has only exacerbated questions of identity for it has at once clarified and complicated the problem of positionality. The new mode of production of wealth has displaced the territorial states. It has redefined the role that they once played in the world's imperial division of (intellectual)labor. This has brought about the awareness that "[se] exige un cambio radical de las representaciones culturales que América Latina ha generado sobre sí misma [A radical change is needed in the cultural representations of itself that Latin America has generated]."[20] This radical change affects three chief categories: the territorial nation, the identity of the national (*criollo*) intellectual, and historiography. As the postnation condition gains ground over the international order, there appears the diasporic intellectual (Martiniquean, Indian, Nicaraguan, Jamaican, Argentine, Peruvian, Australian, Cuban, Vietnamese, Algerian) as an actor in the metropole. He/she navigates alongside, but not in place of, the ship of the national intellectual, who is no longer always at home either. The dynamics of de-territorialization and re-territorialization in the knowledge/power production animate the complex, vexed, and indeed fruitful debate over a Latin Americanism from and about Latin America.

Questions of identity overflow into questions of solidarity. Can the national intellectual transport his originary "*punto de mira*" [perspective] without suffering the impact of the forces of deterritorialization? Are these national agendas any more liberating, emancipatory, ethical than the agendas generated in the diaspora? As Alvaro Félix Bolaños and Luis Fernando Restrepo show in their essays, writing the nation, in the case of Colombia, has meant a monumental job of erasure of subjects and concealment of violences which could easily compete with any other "outside" colonizing force now. Or are the forces of globalization such that all enunciatory positions have become diasporic, bound ineluctably for the borderland?

Perhaps it is too early to tell. Perhaps the nation-state, already missed by some,[21] will manage to make a comeback as the best point of articulation for meeting the demands for (economic, and cultural) justice the world over. For the interests that produce globalization as universal democratization and equal access to markets are, in fact, local and not at all neutral. As Santiago Castro-Gómez and Eduardo Mendieta put it: "Todos hoy viven en una situación de riesgo, por lo tanto es necesario un protagonismo (agency) sobre la vida propia al nivel cognitivo, hermenéutico y estético" [Today everybody is at risk, and as a result it is necessary for everybody to exercise agency over his/her life at the cognitive, hermeneutic, and aesthetic levels.](11). However, as things stand now, theoretically, with the big fear of essentialisms and representation, "la respuesta no puede venir marcada por representaciones de tipo esencialista que establecen diferencias orgánicas entre pueblos y territorialidades" [The answer must eschew essentialist representations that establish categorical differences between peoples and territorialities](12). The problem is not Latin Americanism, as some would have it, for Latin American studies has built a field of knowledge which, despite its northener gaze and interests, has provided us with a treasure of knowledge about Latin America and with positions and positionalities in the world's academies. The question for the decolonizing agenda is how to marshall that knowledge to the service of a fundamental shift. How to muster agency and how to establish solidarities[22] without reestablishing forms of domination based on false identitarian politics. How to provide, from an ethical position, a critique of colonialism-globalization?

On a previous occasion,[23] reflecting on the challenge of cultural studies to "literature" and on the irritation with which some of the better known propositions of cultural studies have been received in Latin America,[24] I proposed that the pursuit of a critical pluralism capable of leading to emancipatory movements needed to find a way of escaping the endless decentering relativism rampant today. An ethical inquiry would have to come to grips, as I said above, with the question of identity and modes of subjectivation.

As we now understand the question, there is no identity that is natural or extra-political. Judith Butler (1990) argues that the radical strategy for feminism is not so much to improve the condition of women, for that goes without saying, within networks of power that subject, but to subvert the constitution of women's identity within the patriarchal paradigm. Within this logic it follows the advocacy for a coalition politics in which women, constituted as resisting subjects, would *maintain* rather than overcome their differences in the form of a series rather than an amalgamation, as Ernesto Laclau and Chantal Mouffe (1985) also propose. The contradiction implicit in the idea of a coalition of resisting subjects, is lessened, if we posit, as William Connolly (1993) proposes, not natural, "unified and coherent subjects, but rather *agonal subjects* for whom power is both constraining and enabling,[25] a notion not too distant from the practices on colonial subjects such as Garcilaso de la Vega, Guamán Poma, Sor Juana Ines de la Cruz, and others.

For the agonal subject, as distinct from the Augustinian subject,[26] respect for others, that is for difference, is based on one's own resistance to attempts to govern their conduct.[27] Liberty is itself the practice of, rather than the absence of power. Because identity is constituted in difference, it is then the irreducibility of the other (Guamán Poma's project) to one's own strategy that teaches one to respect others as free subjects, precisely because they are different.[28]

In a globalized world, in which power is distributed asymmetrically and neo-colonization processes are still very much under way, the agonistic subject, the subject attendant to *respeto,* would seem to represent a good place for both resistance as well as coalitions in plurality. *Respeto* in Chillihuasi means indomitable pride in one's culture. Respect and politeness towards all living things—nature, people—is exercised in utter self-confidence and in memory of the ancestors (Bolin 1998, 5). *Respeto* also means solidarity, itself imbued with the Andean ideals of reciprocity and love for the *pachamama* on which all living things depend (Bolin, 8–10).

Here in the metropolis William Connelly has developed intensely and extensively the political consequences of Michel Foucault's agonistic subject as well as those flowing from "the care of the self (as other)" for the constitution of a radical liberal democracy.[29] If identity is conceived as a set of limits of density that enables selves to choose, think and act; and if identities can only be maintained in the face of that from which they differ, then the formation of particular identities becomes inevitable. This means that no matter how aggressively national and regional identities come under fire by globalizing or neo-globalizing projects, identities such as Argentina, or Latin America, or the diasporic intellectual situated in the metropole, are always in the making. The question is, then, not how to contain or foster the formation of identities, but rather how to keep them from becoming congealed, naturalized, and potentially violent to the (evil) other. Only *respeto* or agonistic identities can keep one from uttering again: "Quisiera tener entendimiento raso y estilo curioso para dar a entender la pena que siento de daño tan irremediable, si el cielo no viene al remedio . . . que quisera quemarlo por dogmatizar a él y a su hermano, que tiene el ídolo de su padre escondido" (137). [I wish I had the plain reasoning and careful style necessary to communicate the grief I feel at the prospect of such sure harm. If heaven does not intervene . . . I would want to burn him for teaching him and his brother false beliefs, and for having his father's idol hidden away] (Alvarez 1558, 143)

In the face of galloping globalization a reworking of pluralism by positing an agonistic subject, *respeto*, capable of *reciprocal recognition*, offers a way out of the particularisms that Beatriz Sarlo (1994) decries, as well as the breached communication circle postulated by some readers of *testimonio*. Within an epistemology of reciprocal recognition, the subaltern[30] does not only speak but is in fact also heard. He/she is not burned for keeping in hiding his/her father's (idols) knowledge. His knowledge is acknowledged, not as the voice of the marginal, but in dialogic situation, for pluralism; as Connolly points out, it is not sufficient to stem the reemergence of congealed subjects. Tolerance, as predicated by multiculturalsim in the United States is an "undeveloped form of critical responsiveness" for it relies on mis-recognition. In contrast, the critical responsiveness engaged by agonal subjects does not appropriate or assimilate, for it departs from the idea that identities are both differential and collective (Connolly 1995; xv).

Critical responsiveness thus "opens up a cultural space through which the other might consolidate itself into *something*, that is not afflicted by negative cultural markings"(1993, 29) as the subaltern has been when he/she is posited in the Hegelian master/slave dynamic. For Connolly, the subaltern does not need to be thought of as negativity, for difference is not reduced to a preexisting code (as in "can the subaltern speak?"). In this new political space strangeness in oneself and others can be engaged without ressentiment or panic, for "freedom resides in the spaces produced by such dissonant junctures"(Connolly 1993; xx)

In this vision of agonist democracy, in this culture of *respeto*, the self is not robbed by difference, the self is instead difference. Thus, the ethics of agonistic engagement call for studied indifference, the ceremonial politeness and distance of Chillihuasi, rather than the fake familiarity of the television multicultural village. In a world of contending identities, collaboration can only be selective (Connolly 1995; xviii). The point within the contest of Latin American studies and the past and present colonialities is that there is neither need to establish a north/south gnoseological opposition nor a literature/cultural or colonial studies/postcolonial theories studies one. What is necessary is to transform the way in which we experience difference and the many ways in which the several imperial legacies have produced differences that divide and impede the work of their dismantling.

CONCLUSIONS

Instead of summarizing the arguments presented above I would like to conclude by taking up two moves which, placed side by side, begin to yield an agenda for specific directions into a/the new paradigm. In the essays included in this volume, José Rabasa speaks of producing an inventory for a decolonizing colonial studies. For his part, Walter Mignolo in "Posoccidentalismo:el argumento desde América Latina" (1998)[31] argues for a fundamental break with "el relato histórico de América debido a la cuestión étnica y por lo tanto al sujeto de la historia (1998, 40).[32]

I think that there is general agreement on the need to break with evolutionist historiography which, of course, includes the history of literature; to move beyond the ideological constraints and assumptions of the reading practices and criteria for canon formation authorized by New Criticism; to break with the existing eurocentric periodization which produces terrible distortions in the constitution of objects of study. A good example of such a challenge is Antony Higgin's study, "(Post-) Colonial Sublime," which moves alongside the colonial Baroque and the colonial sublime, thus complicating our understanding of the production of poetry before the independence movements and illuminating a little more than the determining role played by Jesuit intellectuals throughout the colonial period. *The Shape of Inca History* by Susan A. Niles (1999) offers an excellent example of how to read culture beyond the alphabetic sources and how to produce views into the past which are shaped by the epistemologies of the conquered.

A break with existing periodization, an example of the annexation of Latin American history to the European production of the world, will require much learning across many fields of inquiry. It is a task beyond the capacity of a single scholar and that is why it perhaps remains enveloped in the inertia that organizes the field. It goes without saying that collaborative work is an urgent need and in that regard the new *Literary History* that Mario Valdés, Linda Hutcheon, and Djelal Kadir are organizing promises to be a keystone in the construction of a new paradigm.

Whether the term is used or not, there seems to be agreement on the need to adopt a genealogical approach to time and space. A genealogical approach could also provide the ground for the multiplicity of time and cultural formations to come up to the surface of Latin American history. Rabasa is indeed very firm on the need to deconstruct antiquarian historiography in order to reveal the ways in which the pre-Columbian past has been and continues to be organized and appropriated by past and present colonial enterprises.

Essential, it seems to me, is the long postponed development of a lexicon of terms that lifts away the eurocentric loads of concepts such as "Indians," "Indies," "America," and even Latin America. Perhaps adopting Guamán

Poma's false (true) etymology could be one way of beginning to signal the force of another perspective. Instead of continuing to write "Indians" after Columbus, why not write, "In-dia," after Guamán Poma. Such a gesture would begin to signal an assumed critical perspective onto the object of discourse. A remapping of critical consciousness should entail developing a toponymy that makes semantical the relations that articulate the spaces mapped.

Most, if not all of these moves dovetail with Mignolo's proposal for an overarching post-occidentalist approach, in as much as under occidentalism Europe has assigned to itself the exclusive capacity to know different times and cultures. In a sweeping reperiodization of his own, Mignolo proposes to enter into the realm of three key moments of occidentalism in Latin America in order to lay them bare and produce new ground for understanding the epistemological work of imperial legacies. He considers the first moment to be the annexation and conversion of the "Indians," the second would be the birth and expansion of anthropology and the production and annexation of the "primitives," and the third would be the Humboltian moment when science annexes once again the territories and peoples of America to a Eurocentric scientific grid of knowledge.

To gain an understanding of each of these moments and the repercussions of such annexations in our day, a great deal of new research is needed. We are only beginning to understand the problematic of evangelization with the work of Luis Millones and others on the Taqui Oncoy and the Huarochri narratives in Perú, the work of López Austin and Serge Gruzinski in México. Less is known, from a genealogical optic, of similar processes of colonization in Paraguay and Brazil, for instance. Even if all this genealogical work were at hand, to begin to have any sense of completeness demands comparative work. Its absence really hampers colonial and modern studies.

In his forthcoming "Rethinking the Colonial Model," Walter Mignolo writes a genealogy of vast scope on the constitution of the "colonial difference" first, and the constitution of the "imperial difference" afterward. There he emphasizes the "irreducible difference between talking "about" the colonial difference and talking "from it" (forthcoming, 9). For Mignolo, this distinction is all important for without it, "knowledge would remain in the des-incorporated world of universal categories. The irreducible category shall be maintained" (forthcoming, 9). Otherwise one risks, once again, the very absorption of which eurocentrism was made. The article is monumental and it elaborates on the making and transformation of the colonial difference from the sixteenth century on (60). It will no doubt refuel the debates on the colonial difference as well as literary history/the history of literature. It especially opens up new perspectives on how to distinguish spatio-temporal moments which can take the place of the present Western periodization.

Finally, in our consideration of the agonal subject and the possibility of solidarity coalitions we must take into account the conditions of the Latin American diaspora. The current United States census estimates that there are now approximately forty million Hispanics living north of the Rio Grande. The border land conditions of de-territorialization and re-territorialization dovetail only too neatly with the problematic of conquest and coloniality to be ignored here. Gloria Alzandua's *Borderland/La frontera*, proposes the "generation of a border epistemology." Both Walter Mignolo and José Saldivar[33] see in the concept of the borderland the ground that might propitiate recognition and alliances between Chicanos and Latin Americans. The diaspora could be regarded as a productive space in which to overcome oppositional thinking. However, in order for the borderland not to become yet another bloody trench, we need to posit the agonistic subject or better yet the Andean cultural category of *respeto,* for had it been left in place by the waves of occidentalization, "otro sería nuestro cantar" [we would be singing a very different song].

In conclusion, to say that other (colonial, subaltern, feminine, In-dian) rationalities have much to contribute to our understanding of the present as a legacy of the past is not to write out of nostalgia. It is to dig into the *fondos* of the archive as Inge Bolin did in *Rituals of Respect* or Susan A. Niles does in *The Shape of Inca History,* and find "new" solutions stemming from that which has been forgotten (de Certeau) by the imperial gaze but kept still in the pleats of the complex and never ending colonial situation. It is then, in the wake of César Vallejo, a refusal accepted either to the strangement of the past or its annexation to single, colonialist reason.

NOTES

This part of the title corresponds to my translation of the lead line in César Vallejo's poem "Pedro Rojas," also known as poem III in *España aparta de mí este cáliz* [1939]. See Julio Vélez, ed. *César Vallejo, Poemas en prosa. Poemas humanos. España, aparta de mí este cáliz*. (Madrid: Catedra, 1988), 261–263.

1. It is important to remember that the story of Pedro Rojas is based on real life stories of executions of railroad workers who had been incarcerated and on the words written on a crumpled piece of paper: "Abisa todos compañeros y marchar pronto / nos dan de palos brutalmente y nos matan / como lo ben perdío no quieren sino / la barbaridá" [warn all the comrades and leave soon / they beat us brutally and kill us / since they see that all is lost they only want / atrocity]. [found in the pocket of a poor *campesino* buried in a cemetery in Burgos]. For further connections of Vallejo's poems with the lives of combatants in the Spanish Civil War see Antonio Cornejo Polar's last chapter in *Escribir en el aire* (1994, 228–239), as well as Antonio Ruiz

Vilapana, *Doy fe. . . . un año de actuación en la España nacionalista* (Paris: Imprimérie Coopérative Etoile, 1937?), 38–39.

2. See Frank Turner, ed., *John Henry Newman's Idea of a University* (New Haven: Yale University Press, 1996). In that volume also see, Sara Castro-Klarén, "The Paradox of Self, in *The idea of a University*," 318–339.

3. See F. R. Leavis, *English Literature in Our Time and The University* (1979). Cambridge: Cambridge University Press.

4. In "Canonicity," PMLA, 1991, 110–121, Wendell V. Harris notes that the operation of canonicity entails license for infinite exegesis of certain texts. He affirms the play of criteria which Alastair Fowler noted when he distinguished at least six kinds of canons in simultaneous general use in the institution of literature. According to Harris the six kinds of canons (potential, accessible, official, personal, cortical, and pedagogical) could indeed be expanded if we recognize that the ultimate function of canon formation is to compete (1998, 118) in a constant process of texts selection informed by criteria which are themselves subject to change.

5. For a discussion on the problems of constituting a Latin American postmodern canon avant la lettre see Neil Larsen's "Latin America and Postmodernism: A Brief Theoretical Discussion," in *Reading North by South: On Latin American Literature, Culture and Politics* (Minneapolis, MN: University of Minnesota Press, 1995, 155–163.

6. In his critique of the work that deconstruction and cultural studies have performed on the study of Latin America, Roman de la Campa takes up the question of distance (*lejanía*). He proposes the introduction of a "cartography of comparative frames" for the study of Latin America. "Me refiero a una configuración que reconozca la condición transnacional de lo latinoamericano y sus practicantes—latinoamericanistas de diversos estilos, ideologías y modos de subsidio—que permita también re-significar una nueva relación entre las disciplinas de lo social dirigidas hacia la investigación empírica y las nuevas humanidades orientadas hacia descalces discursivos" [I am referring to a configuration that recognizes the transnational condition of Latin Americanness and of its practitioners—Latin Americanists of different styles, ideologies and types of subventions—, that will also permit us to redefine a new relation among social disciplines oriented toward empiric research and the new humanities oriented toward discursive inquiries.] (78). See Roman de la Campa, "De la deconstrucción al nuevo texto social: pasos perdidos o por hacer en los estudios culturales latino americanos," in Mabel Moraña, ed. *Nuevas Perspectivas desde/sobre américa latina: El desafío de los estudios culturales* (forthcoming).

7. I make here reference to Fredric Jameson, *The Prison-house of Language: A Critical Account of Structuralism and Russian Formalism* (Princeton: Princeton University Press, 1972).

8. I am aware of and I agree with Neil Larsen's argument that explains the rise of *testimonio,* and other less canonical texts as an exhaustion of the critical approaches

put into place by the boom of the Latin American novel in the United States and other international markets. See Larsen *Reading North by South*, 1–24.

9. In "Aesthetics and the Question of Colonial 'Discourse'," Neil Larsen shows that the idea of counterposing literature as the domain of the "aesthetic" to the historico-material creates a false dualism. Larsen argues for "the necessity of taking up aesthetic categories precisely so as to be able to break with colonizing frameworks"(1995, 104). The uncritical rejection of aesthetic criticism in the case of colonial texts ratifies, rather than challenges the traditional colonizing perspective, "in effect granting to 'Eurocentricism' the exclusive right to make aesthetic judgements"(105).

10. See Bill Ashcroft, Gareth Griffiths, and Helen Tiffin, eds., *Key concepts in Postcolonial Studies* (London: Routeledge and Kegan Paul 1998), 42.

11. E. Valentine Daniel takes issue with Clifford Geertz's sense of culture as a system capable of offering meanings for all levels of human activity. He prefers to think of culture as a "dense cluster of semeiotic habits" (1998, 67). For Daniel the hermeneutic power of culture is due to the protean nature, to the "absolute dynamism" of the term (68). Human life is shot through with that dense cluster of signs. Daniel goes on to argue that human beings themselves are but dense clusters of signs. Thus, "to be is to be significantly"(80). Individuation is then brought about by a dense clustering of signs just as much as culture is the result of dense clustering which gives the appearance of essence (80). Daniel concludes that "it is the semeiotic concordance brought about by habit "that gives human beings a sense of coherence and integrity from which the ability to act is born" (81). See E. Valentine Daniel, "The Limits of Culture," in Nicholas B.Dirk, *In near Ruins: Cultural Theory at the End of the Century* (Minnesota: University Press of Minnesota, 1998), 67–91.

12. See Walter Mignolo's "Afterword: On Modernity, Colonization and the Rise of Occidentalism," in his *The Darker Side of the Renaissance* (Ann Arbor: University of Michigan Press, 1995). He notes there that the purpose of his book is to undo the Renaissance's foundational Eurocentrism (1995, 315). He reviews his intellectual formation in Córdoba, Argentina. Mignolo states his differences with Jacques Derrida on the question of writing and literacy and notes that Jack Goody and Ian Watt's article "The Consequences of Literacy," published a few years before *On Grammatology*, were, in fact, more influential on his thinking concerning the relation of the spread of literacy and the West's systems of colonial domination. (321) Antonio Gramsci, Frantz Fanon, Edward Said, Edward Glissant, Edmundo O'-Gorman, Giambattista Vico figure prominently in Mignolo's formation in the philosophy of history as an intellectual quest at best distant from the program of studies in Spanish departments.

13. For a brief characterization of Thomas Kuhn's thesis on change in scientific knowledge see the entry for paradigm in *The Cambridge Dictionary of Philosophy* (1999): 641–42.

14. José Rabasa, interviewed by author on October 1, 2000.

15. English departments are open to the whole of european intellectual traditions as well as to Third World texts provided they are in English, because, due to their hegemony, they do not bother to read in other languages. Roughly the same can be said for French. But that is indeed not the case with the Spanish language and yet the departmental configuration is predicated on a notion of equivalence that is just not there.

16. Paul Bové, *Mastering Discourse: The Politics of Intellectual Culture* (Durham: Duke University Press, 1992), writes of the influence of the history of science by George Canguilhem on the work of Michel Foucault. Canguielhem traced the ways in which some sciences extended—like vectors—throughout culture. He showed how they thus open new spaces for new forms of knowledge production. Sciences thus *co-hered*, they *shared adjacency* (7).

17. It is important to remember here, especially after having cited Neil Larsen's critique of the idea of replacing literature with discourse, that "discourse," as analyzed by Michel Foucault gets shortchanged in these two communications. Paul Bové, *Mastering Discourse; The Politics of Intellectual Culture,* reminds us that to give a definition of "discourse" would by itself amount to yet another essentialist move. Nevertheless we understand that language is discourse, an enduring flow made visible by "tracing the genealogy of discipline as a series of events existing as transformations of one another"(1992, 6). Discourse is "the organized and regulating, as well as the regulating and constituting functions of language that it studies." "Discourse produces knowledge about humans and their societies but the truths of these discourses are relative to the disciplinary structures, the logical framework which they are institutionalized, they can have no claim on us, except that derived from the authority and legitimacy, the power granted to or acquired by the institutionalized discourse in question" (1992, 9).

18. See Lindsay Walters, "A Modest Proposal for Preventing the Books by Members of the MLA from Being a Burden to Their Authors, Publishers, or Audiences," PMLA 115, 3 (May, 2000): 315–17.

19. A Spanish version of this essay can be found in Mabel Moraña, ed., *Nuevas perspectivas desde/sobre América Latina: El desafío de los estudios culturales* (Santiago de Chile: Editorial Cuarto Propio/Instituto Internacional de Literatura Iberoamericana, 2000), 387–405.

20. See the "Introduction" to Santiago Castro-Gómez, and Eduardo Mendieta, eds., *Teorías sin disciplina: Latinoamericanismo, postcolonialismo y globalización en debate* (México: University of San Francisco/Miguel Angel Porrúa, 1998), 8.

21. See Beatriz Sarlo, *Escenas de la vida posmoderna* (Buenos Aires: Ariel, 1994).

22. Solidarity, as Ernesto Laclau, and Chantal Mouffe point out, needs to be rearticulated away from the homogeneous nation of class and into the concept of a series of equal and cooperative struggles trying to overcome domination and achieve liberty. See, *Hegemony and Socialist Strategy: Towards a Radical democratic Politics* (New York: Verso, 1985), 182. It is important to keep in mind that "equivalence is always hegemonic in so far as it does not simply establish an alliance between given

interests, but modifies the very identity of the forces engaging in that alliance"(1985, 183–84).

23. In the foregoing arguments concerning the agonal subject I am rephrasing parts of my unpublished paper "Interrupting the Flow of Latin American Literature Problems of (Missed) Recognition," which I read at the Conference on Cultural Studies at the University of Pittsburgh in the Fall of 1998.

24. See John Beverley, *Against Literature* (Minneapolis: University of Minnesota Press, 1993), Beatriz Sarlo, *Escenas de la vida posmoderna* (1994); and George Yúdice, "Postmodernity and Transnational Capitalism in Latin America," in *On Edge the Crisis of Contemporary Latin American Culture* Edited by George Yúdice, Jean Franco and Juan Flores (Minneapolis: University of Minnesota Press, 1992); and "Cultural Studies and Civil Society," in *Reading the Shape of the World: Towards an International Cultural Studies* (Edited by Henry Scharz, Richard Diens et. al. Boulder, Colorado Westview Press, 1996).

25. See William Connolly, *The Ethos of Pluralization* (Minneapolis: University of Minnesota Press, 1995).

26. In the *Augustinian Imperative: A Reflection on the Politics of Morality* (Newberry Park, CA: Sage, 1993), William Connolly shows that to this day Euro-American political theory and practices remain under what he calls the "Augustinian Imperative," that is "the insistence that there is an intrinsic moral order susceptible to authoritative representations"(1993, xvii). This imperative makes its pursuit obligatory and thus opens the quest to "move closer to one's truest self by exploring its inner geography"(xvii) through confession and submission to the higher authority of God, himself produced by confession (44), and the need to ward off the anxiety of death (81). As he examines the birth of difference in Saint Augustine, an analysis reminiscent of Borges on the hierarchs, Connolly posits that for Augustine to consolidate the Christian self there had to be heresies to denounce and demote. Connolly asks: "What price have those constituted as pagans, infidels, heretics and nihilists through out the centuries paid for this demand to confess an intrinsic moral order?"(81). Many histories rush to detail the answer to this question, but none is better known to students of Latin America than the Spanish and Portuguese evangelization of Mexicas, Andeans, Mayas, Tupinambas and so forth.

27. It is ironic and very fitting, as we speak of colonization past and present, to verify how much in common the Andean ethic of "respect" has with the ethics of the Agonal subject proposed by Connolly at the opening of the second millennium of European imperialism. For a close study of the ethics of respect—*respeto*—see Inge Bolin, *Rituals of Respect: The Secret Survival in the High Peruvian Andes* (Austin: University of Texas Press, 1998). It is interesting to note that Marisol de la Cadena, in her postmodern and very worthy approach to the history of indigenismo in Cuzco, rediscovers *respeto* as the key cultural formation elaborated by the market women in their search for empowerment in a neocolonial and still racist historical environment. De la Cadena, however, fails to see the Andean, precontact roots of this cultural formation. See Marisol de la Cadena, *Indigenous Mestizos: The Politics*

of Race and Culture in Cuzco, Peru, 1919–1991 (Durham: Duke University Press, 2000).

28. Bartolomé Alvarez's "memorial" to Philip II, *De las costumbres y conversión de los indios del Perú* [1588], complains and registers the impossibility of the colonial-evangelizing logic for understanding the Andeans' reason and desire for holding onto the two religions on parallel tracks of respect under colonial domination. He writes that in "la dureza de sus corazones y la torpeza de sus entendimientos" [The hardness of their hearts and the dullness of their reasoning] (142) and "entre otras razones que dicen o hallan para acreditar su intento[los malos evangelistas], es darles a entender que nosotros somos unas gentes diferentes de ellos y ellos son otras diferentes de nosotoros; y así para ellos[los indios] dicen ser la doctrina de sus padres y pasados, y para nosotros la nuestra; y que los sacerdotes los engañamos, y que a ellos no les conviene lo que les enseñamos" [Among other reasons [the bad missionaries] adduce or find to justify their efforts, is that of telling them that we are people different from them and they from us; and, as a result, they say that what suits them [the Indians] is their ancestral religion, and what suits us is ours; and that we, the priests, deceive them, and that what we teach them is not good for them.] (134). See, Bartolomé Alvarez, *De las costumbres y conversion de los indios del Peru, Memorial a Felipe II*, [1588], María Carmen Martín Rubio, et al., eds. (Madrid: Ediciones Polifemo, 1998).

29. For a discussion of the radicalization of Michel Foucault by William Connolly see Jon Simons, *Foucault and the Political* (London: Routledge and Kegan Paul, 1995), 95–126.

30. Ileana Rodriguez has shown that the subaltern is a category which designates subjects located in the interstices of power. They live in constant negotiation, "agenciándose" (making it) within the networks of knowledge/power. See Ileana Rodriguez, "Hegemonía y dominio: Subalteridad, un significado flotante," in *Teorías sin disciplina: Latinomaericanismo, postcoloneidad y globalización en debate*, eds., Santiago Castro-Gómez, and Eduardo Mendieta (México: University of San Francisco/Porrúa, 1998), 31–58.

31. See Walter Mignolo, "Posoccidentalismo: el argumento desde América Latina," in *Teorías sin disciplina*, 31–58.

32. The meaning of "posoccidentalismo" in Mignolo's article goes hand in hand with Fernando Coronil's development of the term. In his call for a move beyond occidentalismo, conceived as the mirror image of Edward Said's orientalismo, Coronil writes: "lo que caracteriza al occidentalismo, tal como lo defino aquí, no es que moviliza a las representaciones estereotipadas de sociedades no occidentales, ya que la jerarquización etnocéntrica de diferencias culturales no es privilegio exclusivo del mundo occidental, sino que dicho privilegio está íntimamente conectado con el despliegue del poder global de occidente. . . . Como sistema de clasificaciones que da expresión a formas de diferenciación económica y cultural en el mundo moderno, el occidentalismo está inseparablemente ligado a la constitución de asimetrías internacionales suscritas por el capitalismo global . . . retar al orientalismo requiere que el Occidentalismo sea desestabilizado como un estilo representacional que pro-

duce concepciones polarizadas y jerárquicas del Occidente y sus Otros y las convierte en figuras centrales de la narrativa de la historia global y local" [What distinguishes Occidentalism, according to my own definition, is not its capacity to activate stereotypical representations of non-Western societies, because that ethnocentric hierarchization of cultural differences is not an exclusive privilege of the Western world; it is instead, a privilege intimately linked to the display of Western global power . . . as a system of classifying, which expresses forms of economic and cultural differentiation in the modern world, Occidentalism is inseparably linked to the construction of international asymmetries endorsed by global Capitalism . . . a challenge to Orientalism requires a destabilization of Occidentalism as a representational style that produces polarized conceptualizations and hierarchies of the West and its Others, which are turned into central figures of narratives of global and local history.] (131). In *Teorías sin disciplina,* 121–142. For an English version of this article see "Beyond Occidentalism: Toward Nonimperial Geohistorical Categories," *Cultural Anthropology* 11, (1) (1996): 51–87.

33. See José Saldivar, "Las fronteras de Nuestra América; Para volver a trazar el mapa de los estudios culturales norteamericanos," in *Casa de las Americas,* 204. 1996.

BIBLIOGRAPHY

Acosta, José de. *Historia Natural y Moral de las Indias.* 1590. New Edition. Introduction by Edmundo O'Gorman. Mexico: F. C. E., 1940.

Alvarez, Bartolomé. *De las costumbres y conversión de los indios del Perú. Memorial a Felipe II. (1588).* Edited by María Carmen Martín Rubio, Juan J. R. Villarías Robles and Fernín Del Pino Díaz. et al. Madrid: Ediciones Polifemo, 1998.

Ashcroft, Bill, and Gareth Griffiths, and Helen Tiffin. 1998. In *Key Concepts in Post-Colonial Studies.* London: Routledge and Kegan Paul.

Audi, Robert. Gen. Ed. 1999. *The Cambridge Dictionary of Philosophy.* Cambridge: Cambridge University Press.

Beverley, John. 1993. *Against Literature.* Minneapolis: University Minnesota Press.

Bolin, Inge. 1998. *Rituals of Respect: The Secret of Survival in the High Andes.* Austin: University of Texas Press.

Boone, Elizabeth Hill and Walter D. Mignolo, Eds. 1994. *Writing Without Words: Alternative Literacies in Mesoamerica and the Andes.* Durham: Duke University Press.

Bové, Paul A. 1992. *Mastering Discourse; The Politics of Intellectual Culture.* Durham: Duke University Press.

Butler, Judith. 1990. *Gender Trouble: Feminism and the Subversion of Identity.* London: Routledge and Kegan Paul.

Castro-Gómez, Santiago, and Eduardo Mendieta, eds., 1998. *Teorías sin disciplina: Latinoamericanismo, postcolonialismo y globalización en debate,* México: University of San Francisco/Miguel Angel Porrúa.

Castro-Klarén, Sara. 1996. "The Paradox of Self in *The Idea of a University*. In *The Idea of a University, John Henry Newman*. Edited by Frank Turner, 318–338. New Heaven: Yale University Press.

———. "Interrupting the Text of Latin American Literature: Problems of (Missed) Recognition."

———. "Interrumpiendo el texto de la literatura latinoamericana: problemas de (falso) reconocimiento." In *Nuevas perspectivas desde/sobre América Latina: El desafío de los estudiios culturales*. Edited by Mabel Moraña, 387–405. Santiago de Chile: Editorial Cuarto Propio/Instituto International de Literatura Iberoamericana, 2000.

Clifford, James. 1988. *The Predicament of Culture: Twentieth-Century Ethnography, Literature, and Art*. Cambridge: Harvard University Press.

Connolly, William. 1993. *The Augustinian Imperative: A Reflection on the Politics of Morality*. Newberry Park, CA: Sage.

———. *The Ethos of Pluralization*. 1995. Minneapolis: University of Minnesota Press.

Cornejo Polar, Antonio. 1994. *Escribir en el aire: Ensayo sobre la heterogeneidad sociocultural en las literaturas andinas*. Lima: Editorial Horizonte.

Coronil, Fernando. "Mas allá del occidentalismo: hacia categorías geohistóricas no imperialistas." In *Teorías sin disciplina. Latinoamericanismo, poscolonialidad y globalización en debate*. Edited by Santiago Castro-Gómez and Eduardo Mendieta, 121–142. México: University of San Francisco/Porrúa, 1998.

Daniel, E. Valentine. 1998. "The Limits of Culture." *In Near Ruins: Cultural Theory at the End of the Century*. Edited by Nicholas B. Dirks. Minneapolis. University of Minnesota Press.

de la Cadena, Marisol. 2000. *Indigenous Mestizos: The Politics of Race and Culture in Cuzco, Perú, 1919–1991*. Durham: Duke University Press.

de la Campa, Román. "De la desconstrucción al nuevo texto social: pasos perdidos o por hacer en los estudios culturales latinoamericanos." *Nuevas perspectivas desde/sobre América Latina: El desafío de los estudios culturales*. Edited by Mabel Moraña, 77–95. Santiago de Chile: Editorial Cuarto Propio/Instituto International de Literatura Iberoamericana, 2000.

Geertz, Clifford. 1973. *The Interpretation of Cultures*. New York: Basic Books.

Harris, Wendell V. "Canonicity." PMLA, 106 (1991) 110–121.

Jameson, Fredric. 1972. *The Prison-house of Language; A Critical Account of Structuralism and Russian Formalism*. Princeton: Princeton University Press.

Kuhn, Thomas. [1962]. 1996. *The Structure of Scientific Revolutions*. Chicago, Ill: University of Chicago Press.

Laclau, Ernesto and Chantal Mouffe. 1985. *Hegemony and Socialist Strategy: Toward a Radical Democratic Politics*. New York: Verso.

Larsen, Neil. 1995. "Latin America and Post modernism: A Brief Theoretical

Discussion." In *Reading North by South: On Latin American Literature, Culture and Politics*. Minneapolis: University Minnesota Press.

———. 1995. "Aesthetics and the Question of Colonial 'Discourse.'" In *Reading North by South: On Latin American Literature, Culture and Politics*. Minneapolis: University Minnesota Press.

Leavis, F. R. 1979. *English Literature in our Time and the University*. Cambridge: Cambridge University Press.

Menchú, Rigoberta. 1992 [1983]. *Me Llamo Rigoberta Menchú y así me Nació La Conciencia*. Edited by Elizabeth Burgos. Sevilla, España: Padilla Libros.

Mignolo, Walter, D. 1995. *The Darker Side of the Renaissance*. Ann Arbor: University of Michigan Press.

———. 1998. "Posoccidentalismo: el argumento desde América Latina." In *Teorías sin disciplina. Latinoamericanismo, poscolonialidad y globalización en debate*. Edited by Santiago Castro-Gómez, and Eduardo Mendieta, 31–58. México: University of San Francisco/Porrúa.

Moraña, Mabel, ed. 2000. *Nuevas perspectivas desde/sobre América Latina: El desafío de los estudios culturales*, 387–400. Santiago de Chile: Editorial Cuarto Propio/Instituto International de Literatura Ibero americana.

Niles, Susan A. 1999. *The Shape of Inca History: Narrative and Architecture in an Andean Empire*. Iowa City: University Iowa Press.

Nugent, David. 1997. *Modernity at the Edge of Empire: State, Individual, and Nation in the Northern Peruvian Andes, 1885–1935*. Stanford: University Stanford Press.

Rabasa, José. 1993. *Inventing America: Spanish Historiography and the Formation of Eurocentrism*. Norman: The University of Oklahoma Press.

Readings, Bill. 1996. *The University in Ruins*. Harvard University Press.

Rodríguez, Ileana. 1998. "Hegemonía y dominio: Subalteridad, un significado flotante." In *Teorías sin disciplina. Latinoamericanismo, postcolonialidad y globalización en debate*. Edited by Santiago Castro-Gómez and Eduardo Mendieta, 101–120. México: University of San Francisco/ Porrúa.

Ruiz Vilapanda, Antonio. 1937 *Doy fe . . . . un año de actuacción en la españa nacionalista*. Paris: Imprimerie Coopérative Etoile.

Said, Edward. 1979. *Orientalism*. New York: Vintage Books.

Sarlo, Beatriz. 1994. *Escenas de la vida posmoderna*. Buenos Aires: Ariel.

Simons, Jon. 1995. *Foucault and the Political*. London: Routledge and Kegan Paul.

Vallejo, César. 1988. *España, aparta de mi este cáliz*. In *César Vallejo, Obra Poética*. Edición Crítica. Coordinador, Américo Ferrari. Paris: Archivos.

Walters, Lindsay. "A Modest Proposal for Preventing the Books by Members of the MLA from Being a Burden to Their Authors, Publishers, or Audiences." PMLA: 115, 3 (May 2000): 315–17.

Yúdice, George. 1992. "Postmodernity and Transnational Capitalism in Latin America." In *On Edge the Crisis of Contemporary Latin American Culture.* Edited by George Yúdice, Jean Franco and Juan Flores. Minneapolis: University of Minnesota.

———. 1996. "Cultural Studies and Civil Society." In *Reading the Shape of the World: Towards an International Cultural Studies.* Edited by Henry Schwarz, Richard Diens et al. Boulder, Colorado: Westview Press.

Index